WHAT THE HEALTH

WHAT THE HEALTH

Eunice Wong

with

Kip Andersen & Keegan Kuhn

Library of Congress Control Number:		2017900454
ISBN:	Hardcover	978-1-5245-7575-5
	Softcover	978-1-5245-7574-8
	eBook	978-1-5245-7573-1

The information in this book is presented for educational purposes only. This book is not in any way a substitute for the advice of a physician or other medical professionals based on the reader's specific conditions. The authors and publisher specifically disclaim all responsibility for injury, damage, liability, loss, or risk, personal or otherwise, that may incur as a direct or indirect result of following any directions or suggestions given in the book.

Print information available on the last page.

Rev. date: 03/23/2017

To order additional copies of this book, contact:
Xlibris
1-888-795-4274
www.Xlibris.com
Orders@Xlibris.com
755309

Contents

Part One: YOU

Part Two: THE WORLD

For my darling Chris, the love of my life,
the clear natural light,
and for Konrad and Marina:

"If we lay a strong enough foundation/
We'll pass it on to you/ we'll give the world to you/
And you'll blow us all away/ someday, someday."

—E.W.

Dedicated to those who speak up for truth and justice
for the planet, for the animals, and for all of humanity
working together toward a thriving future.

—K.A. & K.K.

All truth passes through three stages.
First, it is ridiculed.
Second, it is violently opposed.
Third, it is accepted as being self-evident.

—Arthur Schopenhauer

WHAT THE HEALTH

Part One

YOU

Prologue

My name is Kip Andersen. I'm a documentary filmmaker in San Francisco.

When I was in high school, my dad suffered third degree heart block, a life-threatening condition. "Third degree" is the most serious kind. He was only 49.

It happened in the middle of the night. We lived in the suburbs, and the ambulance didn't put on its siren. The paramedics quietly came in and got my dad.

I slept through it all. My parents didn't want to scare me.

But when I woke up, I was very scared. My dad was in the hospital. None of us ever imagined that he would have a dangerous heart condition. He had high cholesterol, sure, but he was on medication for that. He was a lifelong military man, fit and proud—in fact, when he was hospitalized, he was about to be promoted to Captain. But in the military, once there's something wrong with your heart, you're essentially forced to retire.

My father came back from the hospital with a pacemaker in his chest and an honorable discharge from the career that had defined him for decades. He had to start over.

My image of him—my dad, the embodiment of strength— shifted. I knew now there was a frightening vulnerability hidden inside his body. I was afraid for him, and I was afraid for myself. All my life I had heard about the inescapable link between genetics and disease. I didn't know what was going on beneath my own skin.

My mom's father died of a diabetes-related heart attack when he was around 60. I was maybe 6 at the time. I loved him very much. Then my dad's father died of prostate cancer, and my grandmother died of stomach cancer. My mom's sister has had diabetes for 25 years and is losing her eyesight. My mom's brother also has diabetes.

"You'll get diabetes, too," they tell me with concern.

My family's health history hangs over me. Diabetes, heart disease, cancer. I'm meticulous about my check-ups. When I was 18, I used to take Metamucil and an aspirin every day. I run, I bike, I do yoga. I don't smoke or drink soda; I get enough sleep. I eat organic.

There must, I thought, be a tiny window of influence on the diseases that run in my family, that I can affect through my lifestyle.

Then one morning, I was brushing my teeth when I heard something on TV.

"...World Health Organization this morning has classified processed meat, such as bacon and sausage, as carcinogenic, directly involved in causing cancer in humans..."

I rushed in, my mouth full of toothpaste, but the segment was over. They had moved on to *The 1-second trick to rocking an off-the-shoulder top!"*

I turned the TV off.

I rinsed my mouth and went straight to my computer. I quickly found a report from the cancer agency of the World Health Organization. "After thoroughly reviewing the accumulated scientific literature," experts from ten countries had classified processed meat as a Group 1 carcinogen (the same group as cigarettes, asbestos, and plutonium[1]), and red meat as a Group 2 carcinogen.[2]

I was shocked. Everyone knew hot dogs weren't health food, but *carcinogens*?

My first thought was that this was new information. It wasn't.

On September 24, 1907, the *New York Times* had run a front-page headline: "CANCER INCREASING AMONG MEAT EATERS...On the Other Hand, Italians and Chinese, Practically Vegetarians, Show the Lowest Mortality of All." The results of a two-year, "exhaustive study of cancer" "proved conclusively that diet is a most important factor in the increase of the disease and its death rate."[3]

This was information from over a century ago. I had been living in low-grade dread for years, believing that my genetics sentenced me to crippling, chronic, and maybe fatal diseases in the years to come. Diet seemed like too easy an answer.

I'd eaten meat since I was a baby, starting with Chicken and Rice baby food. My parents believed meat was an essential part of a healthy diet. That's what they'd been taught all their lives.

But was this like I'd been smoking my entire childhood? My brain was flooded with questions. Was there a cancer connection with chicken and pork? What about dairy and eggs? Fish? Other diseases? If there's been a scientific connection between meat and cancer for over 100 years, why weren't there warning labels on meat by now, like tobacco? Why wasn't this public knowledge?

I discovered that every 50 grams of processed meat eaten daily raises your risk for colorectal cancer by 18 percent.[4] Fifty grams is less than two pieces of bacon, or two slices of ham.[5] I also found that eating meat only 4 times a week increases your cancer risk by 42 percent, according to an Oxford study.[6]

This was crazy. Almost everyone I know eats meat at least four times a week.

I checked out the American Cancer Society website. In several spots they recommend limiting red meat. In their "Ingredients for a

Healthy Kitchen," however, they counsel stocking up on extra-lean hamburger, ground turkey breast, chicken breast, fish, eggs, cheese, milk, and yogurt.[7] They provide recipes for dishes like quick-easy-chili with extra-lean ground beef,[8] and advise people to "choose lean meats—look for the words 'loin' or 'round' in the name."[9]

This would be like the American Lung Association telling you what kind of tobacco to smoke and how to roll cigarettes.

I got on the phone.

"Thank you for calling your American Cancer Society," the friendly young man said. "My name is Sam. I'm a cancer information specialist. How may I help you today?"

"Yeah, hi," I said. "I was wondering why your website encourages people to eat processed meat, which is a Group 1 carcinogen, the same group as tobacco and asbestos, as well as red meat, which is a Group 2 carcinogen."

There was a short silence.

"Let me just place you on a brief hold," Sam said.

It was a brief hold. We got disconnected.

I dialed a different number.

"Keegan?" I said, when my friend and fellow filmmaker picked up. "We have to make another film."

CHAPTER 1
GENETICS: THE WRITING ON THE CELL

When I visited my dad in the hospital, the room was mostly dark. The only light came from the fluorescent bar on the wall. My father was asleep, his skin gray. His hands lay palm up on the hospital blanket. A monitor beeped and I heard laughter from the nurses' station in the hall.

A wave of helplessness and deep anxiety for my dad washed over me.

I remember thinking, *how many years before it's me lying in that bed?*

I feel the same helplessness when I see my aunt or uncle. They both have diabetes. My mom's dad died of diabetic complications. My aunt is becoming blind.

I've always been careful to keep my weight down and not eat too much sugar. But it's in my genes.

7

I wondered, though, after the little bit I'd learned about meat and cancer, if there was a larger picture to genetics and disease. I was particularly preoccupied with the diabetes in my family. *You'll get it too...*

It was worth looking into.

What I found was remarkable. I turned up study after study showing that eating animal products—meat, dairy, or eggs—significantly increases your risk for developing Type 2 Diabetes.[1]

But when I went on the website of the American Diabetes Association (ADA), their "Diabetes Meal Plans" recommended lean meats, poultry, fish, and non-fat dairy products.[2] Their recipes included Moroccan Lamb Stew, oven-barbecued chicken, Asian pork chops, barbecued meatballs, and blackened tuna with tangy mustard sauce.[3]

Maybe I was missing something. The scientific reports linking animal products and diabetes are filled with numbers and language I don't understand.

Perhaps an expert at the ADA could clarify things for me.

***

"With Type 2 Diabetes, there's an enormous genetic component," Dr. Robert Ratner, Chief Scientific and Medical Officer of the American Diabetes Association, told Keegan and I.

His words hit me in the pit of my stomach.

"There's no question that we're in the midst of a diabetes epidemic," Dr. Ratner said. "The Centers for Disease Control and Prevention do population-based surveys in which they ask people about diseases, and then follow up with blood tests to confirm it. Their most recent report, in 2014, estimated that 29 million people in the United States have diabetes. Of those, approximately 8 million people *do not know* they have the disease. It only showed up on the blood test.

"We're seeing an increase in new diagnoses of both Type 1 and Type 2 diabetes in the US and around the world. Worldwide, we're looking at approximately 350 million people with the disease."

"Why are there so many more people with diabetes now?" I asked.

"It's unclear why the incidence of Type 1 diabetes is going up," Dr. Ratner answered. "With Type 2 diabetes, as I said, genetics plays a huge role. That risk is brought out by the interaction of diet, exercise, environment, genetic propensity—you need all of that together for the disease to occur."

I made a mental note. If the disease requires all those factors, then—maybe?—genetics wasn't playing such a "huge" role.

"There are two populations of Pima Indians who are virtually genetically identical," Dr. Ratner said, going on. "The ones in central Mexico are subsistence farmers: thin, with virtually no diabetes. The other group lives on an Arizona Indian reservation. They're obese, with a 50 percent prevalence of diabetes.

"Another example," he said, "is the case of first, second, and third generation Japanese, starting in Japan, who move to Hawaii, and then to Seattle. You see a progressive increase in the development of Type 2 diabetes the farther they get from Japan, and as more generations pass."

"What's happening in Japan that's different from Seattle?" Keegan asked from behind the camera.

"There's no question that lifestyles are different," Dr. Ratner replied. "They're walking more. Their diet is clearly very different. There's no question that the Western-type diet seems to correlate with an increased risk of diabetes."

Huh.

"Which part of the Western diet is the culprit?" I asked.

"There are so many potential confounders. There is no such thing as a diabetes diet."

I thought of the recommendations on the ADA website, but said nothing.

"More recently," Dr. Ratner said, "new devices have been developed for the delivery of insulin, and the ability to monitor glucose in patients without having to go to the doctor's office. The convenience of treating diabetes has been revolutionary in the last thirty years."

I looked down at my notes. "What's the best way to prevent diabetes?"

"It's unclear."

"I've come across a lot of studies," I said, "saying diet is a huge contributor, and you could potentially cure or reverse diabetes with a purely plant-based diet."

Dr. Ratner seemed to stiffen just a tiny bit.

"I don't believe there is sufficient evidence to demonstrate that," he said.

"How does a low-fat plant-based diet compare to the ADA diet you recommend?"

"We don't recommend a specific diet. We recommend healthy eating."

"The one on the website."

"We recommend *healthy eating.*"

I tried again. "You have a meal plan, and recommended foods on your website—"

"They are selections of foods to consider."

"If you compare those selections, then, to a plant-based—"

"No one's done that study."

I rifled through my papers and pulled one out. "There was one in *American Journal of Clinical Nutrition* in 2009," I said, reading from it. "A 74 week study[4] comparing a low-fat plant-based diet to the ADA plan in Type 2—"

Dr. Ratner grabbed his coffee mug and swiveled away in his chair. "I think we're done here. I'm not getting into an argument about—"

I looked up, startled. "No, no. I just want to know if this is true—"

"Any diet works," he said, turning to face me. He leaned in with his eyebrows raised. "Any diet works. If. People. Follow it."

I was a little thrown. "But—if it's not the proper diet—"

"I'm not going to get into that." He shook his head.

"Into diet?"

"No. If that's where you want to go with this, I'm sorry, I'm not the person you should be talking to."

"Then—who do we talk to about diet?" I was completely confused. He had just told me there was no question the Western diet was associated with an increased risk of diabetes.

He looked at me. "You can talk to anybody you *want*." It sounded like a big FU. "We do not advocate a specific diet."

"Why not?"

"Because the data doesn't exist to support it."

"We have data here—"

Dr. Ratner stood up abruptly. "We're done."

I looked up at him. "I'm sorry?"

"We're done. I'm not going to get into that argument with you." He plucked the microphone off his tie.

"Why is it an argument? I just have this study here—"

"There are lots of studies," he interrupted, standing over me. "Lots of studies in the literature. Many of which have never been replicated, or, frankly, are *wrong*. That's why we do peer review, okay?"

"The *American Journal of Clinical Nutrition* isn't peer-reviewed?"[5]

"I don't know what study you're referring to," he said, pocketing his phone. "In the absence of being able to see that study, I'm not going to comment."

"I could show it to you," I said hopefully. "I just want to know whether—"

"I'm sorry, I don't have time for that." He turned his back and walked out of the room.

I looked over at Keegan behind the camera. He was as dumbfounded as I was. My heart was thumping.

"That was bizarre," said Keegan.

After a moment, we packed up our gear in silence. I noticed my hands were shaking.

***

The ancient Greeks believed in three goddesses, more powerful than any others. Sometimes they were depicted as a maiden, a matron, and an old crone.

Three days after a child was born, they would arrive at the cradle to determine the course of the baby's time on earth. The first goddess spun the thread of life. The second determined the length of the thread. And the third—the most feared, known as "the inevitable"—cut the life-thread. The baby's path was fixed from that moment on.

The Greeks called them *Moirai*. We know them as The Fates.

In 21st century America, not many of us still believe in the three goddesses with their spindle and shears. But we have replaced them with a modern substitute: genetics.

There are diseases and disorders that are 100 percent genetically determined. No matter how or where you live, if you have the genetic combination for these conditions, they will manifest. These include Down Syndrome, sickle-cell anemia, cystic fibrosis, hemophilia, and Huntington's Disease, a degenerative brain disorder. Every single person with the gene for Huntington's will eventually develop it.[6] It may indeed feel, for those with such disorders, that the Fates had woven them into the cloth of life.

But I want to unpack the genetic component of the top causes of death in our country, like heart disease, cancer, stroke, Alzheimer's, and diabetes,[7] along with contributing factors like obesity. People often believe their genetic lot is the most powerful influence over whether they'll fall victim.

I've believed that since I was a teenager. I did everything I thought I could to stave off my family's diabetes, cancer, and heart failure. But deep down, it felt like running away when a monster is chasing you. You have a choice: you can run or stand still. If you stand still, the monster will get you far sooner. If you run, you'll buy some time, but ultimately—come on, we're talking about a monster here. It's going to get you in the end.

I kept going over the interview with Dr. Ratner. He was very emphatic about genetics playing a major part in the development of Type 2 diabetes, but almost everything else he said—before he refused to talk to me—actually contradicted that statement.

He was the one who brought up the Pima Indians, who did or did not develop the disease depending on how they lived. He brought up the Japanese, whose Type 2 diabetes soared when they moved away from Japan and its traditional lifestyle and diet.[8]

Diet, exercise, environment, genetic propensity—you need all of that together for the disease to occur.

There's no question that the Western-type diet seems to correlate with the increased risk of diabetes.

Those were his statements, not mine. But when I asked him to hone in on how diet might prevent or reverse the disease, I flicked a switch I didn't even know was there. It shut everything down, and I was left in the dark.

Time to grope around for some lights.

***

When I first heard the news snippet on meat and cancer, I had no idea there was a health revolution brewing all around me. Throughout the country, there's a growing movement of doctors challenging the conservative teachings that I—and everyone I know—had grown up with.

Keegan and I packed our cameras and hit the road.

Dr. Neal Barnard, a trim man with light brown hair, is president of the Physicians Committee for Responsible Medicine (PCRM), a non-profit organization of 12,000 doctors.[9] He's also on the medical faculty at George Washington University. Keegan and I visited him at the PCRM offices in D.C.

"I think of genes in two ways," Dr. Barnard told us. "There are dictator genes. Those genes give orders—blue eyes or brown hair—and you don't have any choice. The genes for diabetes, heart disease, or certain forms of cancer, they're more like committees giving suggestions. But you've got a lot of control over whether those genes ever express themselves.

"The vista on diet-related disease is spreading out in a bigger way than we ever imagined. We thought maybe diet affected heart disease and a few cancers. Then there was diabetes. Now it's also brain disease—not only stroke but also Alzheimer's. We thought that was entirely due to genes and age. Now we know it's due, to a very substantial degree, to diet. We've got control. Not perfect control, but certainly control we never had before."

Our journey had begun.

Keegan had heard about a bariatric surgeon in Texas named Dr. Garth Davis. In addition to running the Davis Clinic, one of the busiest surgical weight loss clinics in the country, he's also Head of Bariatric Surgery at one of Houston's biggest hospitals.

Dr. Davis starred in the TLC show "Big Medicine," and wrote a bestselling book in 2008 called *The Expert's Guide to Weight-Loss Surgery.* In that book, he recommended eating a high-animal-protein diet. But while following his own advice, he felt sicker and sicker, and got fatter and fatter. He began poring through the scientific literature on nutrition and diet, examining epidemiological, experimental, and prospective cohort studies, analyzing research designs and conclusions, and even went back to 19th century accounts of African eating patterns. He ended up overhauling his previous, very publicly stated beliefs on nutrition.[10]

On the flight to Houston to visit Dr. Davis, I looked through my plastic oval window. I could see the plane's wing, and the bright blanket of clouds beneath us. Next to me, Keegan was reading Dr. Davis' new book, *Proteinaholic*, a strong rebuttal to his previous book.

I thought back on our interview with Dr. Barnard. His words made me feel like a prisoner watching the heavy cell door open just a tiny sliver. Was this for real, or was that door going to slam shut again?

We talked with Dr. Davis in an examining room at his clinic. I'd watched Youtube clips of him from *Big Medicine*, and was surprised to see he looked far more youthful and powerful in person, despite his salt and pepper hair and starched doctor's coat. In the *Big Medicine* clips, he looked puffy and tired. He's now a prize-winning Ironman triathlete.[11]

"In order to get many diseases, two things have to happen," Dr. Davis said. "First, you have a genetic predisposition. Second, something sets that gene in motion. Let's take Okinawans, from one of the Japanese islands. They're skinny, they don't have a lot of cancer, and they're one of the most long-lived cultures in the world.[12] But if you move an Okinawan to America, they gain weight rapidly. They get heart disease, they get diabetes. In China, they used to think they didn't have diabetes. Now suddenly they have a huge increase in the disease, and they're blaming it on Western food, specifically the large amounts of meat."

I found it fascinating that Dr. Davis had essentially given us the same migration-disease model that Dr. Ratner from the ADA had used. But Dr. Davis was following the example through to its conclusion.

We heard something similar from Dr. Caldwell Esselstyn, a celebrated cardiologist who has been practicing medicine for over 40 years. He works at the Cleveland Clinic, rated the best cardiac care center in the country by *US News and World Report*.[13] He's also a former Olympic rowing gold-medalist.

"Let's suppose you were to look at the genetics of the Papua Highlanders, the Tarahumara in Northern Mexico, or the rural Chinese," Dr. Esselstyn said to Keegan and I in his library. "They have different genetics, but there's no heart disease in these populations. . The field of epigenetics is breaking through in spades right now, in which you can actually alter genetic expression. You can turn genes on and off, and by what? By the environment, and perhaps nothing is as powerful as food.

"And it's not just heart disease," Dr. Esselstyn continued. "When you look globally, there are certain cultures where breast cancer is much less frequently identified than in the US. Kenya. Rural Japan in the 1950s. Yet, what happened to the Japanese women, when they migrated to the US for the second and third generation, still pure Japanese American? They had the same rates of breast cancer as their Caucasian counterparts."

The World Health Organization (WHO) pinpoints four factors as the main causes of death before the age of 86:

1) poor diet
2) high blood pressure
3) obesity
4) tobacco use.[14]

Three of the four are diet-related.

The National Research Council and Institute of Medicine came to the same conclusions, finding that diet and activity patterns— far ahead of tobacco, alcohol, drug abuse, gun violence, and car accidents—are the primary factors behind premature deaths in this country.[15]

No more than 10-20 percent of risk for the primary causes of death come from our genes.[16] Only about 5-10 percent of cancer cases are attributable to genetic defects, with the other 90 to 95 percent rooted in lifestyle and environment.[17] Colon cancer, the second most lethal cancer in the country,[18] is the cancer most directly affected by what you eat.[19] According to WHO, 80 percent of all heart disease, stroke, and Type 2 diabetes can be prevented.[20]

"We have known now for decades that the 'actual' causes of premature death in the United States are not the diseases on death certificates, but the factors that cause those diseases," Dr. David Katz, director of Yale's Prevention Research Center, said in *Time* magazine.[21]

Scientific literature from the mid-1980s shows that *eating saturated fat, which is mainly found in animal products like meat, dairy, and eggs, is more strongly associated with death than smoking cigarettes.*[22]

Think about that!!! I'm not normally a multiple-exclamation-mark kind of guy, but seriously, *think about that.* If you took your family to a neighborhood cookout, and the dad next door offered you—and your child—a cigarette and a light, how would you react? And yet we accept, with thanks, the glistening beef burgers from that same dad.

What's the difference between taking the cigarette and the burger? The smell and the taste. The social assumptions. The habits. The lack of knowledge.

People think heart disease, cancer, and diabetes are inherited, not realizing that what they've actually inherited are the eating habits of their parents and grandparents.

"People are exposed as children to a certain way of eating that they carry into their adulthood. They pass it on to their children. That's why they develop the same diseases their parents and grandparents may have had before them, but it is not inevitable," Susan Levin, director of nutrition education at PCRM, and a registered dietitian with a specialty in sports nutrition, told us. She's also an avid runner, and when we interviewed her, she was 39 weeks pregnant. It was poignant to hear Levin talk about how parents influence their children, knowing how close she was to giving birth.

"We have much more control over our lives than sometimes we even want," she said. "That's why a lot of people take the medications. They really want to believe, 'I don't have control over this. This happened to my parents, so just give me the drugs. I don't need to change because it's inevitable.'"

I thought of the Greek Fates and particularly the third goddess, "the inevitable," standing with her shears over every cradle. Levin is right. The thought of predestination can bring a peculiar comfort to many. It takes away responsibility.

"The majority of conditions that kill people in this country," said Levin, "are completely preventable for most of us. It's up to us to take that responsibility and change—change the culture and the epidemics. I think we could do that within a generation."

Dr. Michael Greger is a physician and *New York Times* bestselling author—an intense, hilarious, and excitable guy with encyclopedic knowledge—who runs the non-profit website NutritionFacts.org. NutritionFacts provides daily nutrition updates collected from the most current medical literature. Dr. Greger and his team "read through every issue of every English language nutrition journal in the world—so you don't have to." Like Dr. Garth Davis, Dr. Greger is a research junkie.

"The reason we know cancers like colon cancer are so preventable is because rates differ dramatically around the globe," Dr. Greger tells us. "There can be a 10, 50, 100 fold difference in colon cancer rates, from some of the highest measured in Connecticut, down to the lowest rates in Kampala, Uganda, for example.[23] There are places where colon cancer, our number two cancer killer, is practically non-existent.[24] It's not some genetic predisposition that makes people in Connecticut die from colon cancer while people from Uganda don't. When you move to a high-risk country, you adopt the risk of the country. It's not our genes; it's our environment.

"We can change the expression of our genes—tumor suppressing genes, tumor activating genes—by what we put into our bodies. Even if you've been dealt a bad genetic deck, you can reshuffle it with diet.

"Tell him about your family history," Keegan prompted me. I did.

"Wow, you're perfect," Dr. Greger said. "People with a family history of disease often throw up their hands: 'I've got bad genes.' No, these are the people who have to eat exquisitely healthy. Bad diets often run in families. You eat how you were taught to eat. For most Americans, that's not good news.

"But we can regain our health—by eating the plant-based diets of populations that don't suffer from these diseases. Much of what we know about diet comes from studies going back to rural Africa and rural China in the 1920s, where Westerners set up missionary hospitals. They saw millions of people, and to their surprise, they weren't suffering from Western diseases.

"There were populations where high blood pressure rates were zero. Heart disease rates were zero. Thousands of autopsies found no heart attacks. It's not like these Western-trained doctors couldn't recognize heart attacks. The diseases weren't present. If you want to avoid them, you have to change your diet."

I love Dr. Greger. Ask him a question and it's like pressing the ON button for information. He was still talking.

"Nathan Pritikin and other lifestyle medicine pioneers started asking, 'What if we put people with advanced chronic disease on the diet followed by these populations that don't get the diseases in the first place? Maybe we could slow it down.'

"Instead, something miraculous happened. The diseases started to *reverse*."

Prevention, I now believe, is possible. But halting a disease in motion and turning it around? Miracle drugs, maybe, could manage that. Diet, I don't know. Maybe Dr. Greger was talking about something atypical.

When Keegan and I got back to the West Coast, we visited Dr. Michael Klaper, a tall, lean man with a white beard and bright brown eyes. We first met him when we made our film, *Cowspiracy*. He's on staff at the TrueNorth Health Center in Santa Rosa, California, and has been practicing acute care medicine for forty years. For the last thirty, he has focused on diet and lifestyle medicine, trying to keep people out of hospitals and off the operating table.

He greeted us warmly.

"What are some of the leading causes of the country's major diseases?" Keegan asked him.

"Oh my," Dr. Klaper sighed expressively. "If I could get all my medical colleagues in a room, I would say, 'Please, I don't care if you are an internist, a family physician, a rheumatologist, dermatologist, gastroenterologist—pick a medical specialty—Square One is to realize that the vast majority of patients in your waiting room are there because of what they eat.

"The current American diet is based on animal flesh and processed food: saturated fat, denatured animal protein, cholesterol, oils, refined sugars. This food is incredibly toxic to the blood vessels and the immune system, and it flows through our bloodstreams, and our children's, every four or five hours. The results are predictable. We're becoming grossly obese, arteries are clogging up. High blood pressure, diabetes, cancers. Autoimmune diseases have direct correlations with the meat and salt in animal products. The vast majority of diseases are created today by what people are eating in the West.

"Until that is recognized," Dr. Klaper said, "we're just going to be treating symptoms. We're not getting to the root cause of disease, and that is the great transgression that the medical profession inadvertently perpetrates on the public."

Dr. Klaper had pinpointed the question circling in my head, growing more compelling with every interview. With this landslide of evidence connecting chronic diseases with eating animal products, why did my doctor, who knows my family's health history, never once tell me to lay off the meat, dairy, and eggs?

I started off asking, "What don't I know?" Now, I began to wonder if I should be asking, "What doesn't my doctor know?"

CHAPTER 2

MEDICAL SCHOOL: THE DOCTOR OF THE FUTURE

Thomas Edison, inventor of the light bulb and motion picture camera, said over one hundred years ago, "The doctor of the future will give no medicine, but will instruct his patient in the care of the human frame, in diet, and in the cause and prevention of disease."[1]

Fast forward to the early years of the 21st century. We live in a brave new world of billion-dollar pharmaceuticals and space age medical procedures. It's no big deal for surgeons to inflate miniscule balloons inside congested blood vessels, leaving behind a stent (a permanent wire mesh to prop an artery open), or harvest an artery from a patient's leg, cut through their breastbone, and splice the leg artery around the heart. (We can also suck fat out of your butt and put it in your lips. Now there's medical progress.)

And yet our rates of chronic disease are smashing through the roof. In 2012, half the US adult population had at least one chronic health condition. One out of four adults had at least two.[2] Eighty-six percent of health care spending in 2010 covered people with one or more chronic conditions.[3] $315.4 billion were allocated to heart disease and stroke.[4] Cancer, that same year, cost $157 billion.[5] $245 billion for diabetes.[6] In 2008, obesity-related causes racked up $147 billion in medical costs.[7]

Drugs, hospitals, and surgeries. Edison's prediction has not come true. Because doctors cannot teach what they do not know.

Dr. Alan Goldhamer is the founder and head of the TrueNorth Health Center. Unlike many doctors, he attended schools that prioritized nutrition and lifestyle as critical to sustaining and promoting health. This philosophy underpins his whole practice. Since 1984, he has been running TrueNorth, which has helped over 15,000 people recover from chronic conditions, with the help of plant-based nutrition, lifestyle changes, and sometimes medically supervised water or juice fasts.[8]

"Learning about diet and lifestyle is an extremely minor part of medical training today," Dr. Goldhamer said to Keegan and I. "Medicine now is about the use of drugs and surgeries to suppress symptoms associated with the disease, and they do a brilliant job. It just doesn't have anything to do with health."

Dr. Neal Barnard put us in touch with Dr. Milton Mills, Associate Director of PCRM. Keegan and I went to meet Dr. Mills, a critical care physician at Fairfax Hospital in Virginia. We talked with him outside on a bright sunny day. His hospital declined to let us film him there.

Dr. Mills, who is African-American, is a robust guy with a shaved head and a big voice. He treats patients in ICUs suffering from heart attacks, end stage kidney disease, and many other urgent illnesses. He frequently donates his time to free medical clinics.

He told us a story about applying to medical schools.

"One of my interviewers asked me, 'What are you interested in?'" he recalled. "I said I wanted to focus on preventive medicine and help people understand they don't have to live a life of illness. He looked at me and said, 'Well, you don't want to end up like the dentist. They fluoridated the water and now they have no patients.' I must have looked horrified, because he tried to explain, 'We operate from the disease model. We're in the business of treating sick people. We are not in the business of trying to prevent people from becoming sick.'"

We talked with Dr. Michelle McMacken in Brooklyn, New York. Dr. McMacken teaches at New York University's School of Medicine, and has been practicing primary care for over a decade.[9]

"My experience at medical school is probably very similar to that of many other physicians," she told us. "You get your training under a paradigm that promotes screening tests, pills, and procedures, when in reality, behavior choices, particularly food, probably have the most power of all. Most medical schools, when teaching nutrition, teach about deficiencies. But the issues of today are not issues of deficiencies, they're primarily issues of excess.

"Even though the information is out there, it's not taught, and of course doctors themselves have to be comfortable sharing that information. If a doctor is eating an unhealthy diet, it's harder to advise a healthy diet to your patients. But it's a systemic issue. It's not the doctor's fault if he or she hasn't been taught about nutrition.

"And with the way medical care is reimbursed through third party payers, who want to keep costs down," she continued, "even a doctor who understands the power of diet and lifestyle is very, very pressed for time to talk to patients about it.

"My experience from teaching nutrition to doctors is that many doctors are eager to hear this information. We're in a crisis. Patients need to hear it. Doctors need to hear it. We need to start teaching it in medical school."

The situation is the same for dietitians. "We have to follow a very centralized federal standard to become dietitians," Susan Levin said. "Even more alternative schools have to follow the same guidelines because there's only one board exam. Unfortunately it's on us, as healthcare professionals, to read medical journals and learn the research."

During Dr. Greger's very first interview applying to med school, the interviewer said to him, "Nutrition is superfluous to human health."

I wondered if medical education was different in the 1950s, when Dr. Esselstyn went to school.

"How many classes of nutrition did you have?" I asked him.

"None."

"None?!"

"There has to be a seismic revolution in medicine," Dr. Esselstyn said. "Many of us are concerned that the medical schools are run by the pharmaceutical industry. You get all this marvelous training for illness. You become brilliant about diagnosing, and once something's diagnosed, you decide what drugs or procedures are required. Nobody asks, '*Why* do you have this hypertension?' You don't suddenly wake up when you're 30 with hypertension. For the last thirty years, every time you consumed certain foods, your body took a hit. And it catches up to you."

Any increase from none is an improvement, I suppose, but it didn't seem that way talking to Dr. Klaper.

"I had four one-hour lessons in nutrition during medical school," he recalled. "Nutrition for burn patients, renal failure patients, pediatric patients with failure-to-grow syndrome, and... I can't even remember what the last one was. In all the years of medical school, that's the formal nutrition training I've had."

"Wow," said Keegan. "Is that standard?"

"Unfortunately, yes," Dr. Klaper answered. "I went to lecture at Harvard a few years ago, and one of the med students picked me up at the airport. I asked her, 'How many hours in nutrition do you get?' She said, 'I think we get four lessons in nutrition: nutrition for burn patients, renal failure patients, and children.' She wasn't sure what the last one was either. I was appalled but not surprised. Nutrition is the poor sister of medical education."

"Why?" I asked.

"First, nutrition is viewed with disdain. Physicians feel, 'We're practicing *real* medicine, suturing wounds and fixing fractures. Nutrition? Boring. Send them to the dietitian.' Second, physicians don't want to open that discussion because they don't know much about it. And finally, we have to look at the physician's own diet—the filet mignon they had last night, and the Lobster Thermidor they're looking forward to tonight. That's what really keeps nutrition from being recognized as a keystone of disease treatment.

"Between these three fortresses—the disdain, the ignorance, and the doctors' own unwillingness to change—nutrition doesn't enter the examination room.

"Wake up, my fellow doctors," Dr. Klaper urged. "Nutrition is the bedrock of true health. It's time to become true physicians by treating the cause of disease."

Most people consider their doctors a reliable source of nutrition advice. But the truth is often like drawing the curtain back on the Wizard of Oz.

Only 25 percent of accredited medical schools in the US required their students to take a single dedicated course in nutrition in 2009.[10] The National Academy of Medicine recommended, back in the 1980s, that medical schools provide a minimum of 25 hours of nutrition instruction.[11] Thirty years later, the few schools offering courses on diet and disease provided less than 24 hours of nutritional instruction on average,[12] with most students getting only 11 to 20 hours, out of the thousands of hours spent in medical school.[13]

And once students graduate, they don't even get that. The Accreditation Council for Graduate Medical Education (ACGME), the primary organization responsible for continuing medical education for doctors, has a 37-page booklet outlining the continuing education requirements for cardiologists. The requirements include interpreting a minimum of 3,500 electrocardiograms, and interpreting "a minimum of 100 radionuclide studies to include SPECT myocardial perfusion imaging and ventriculograms."[14] Nutrition education is not mentioned once. ACGME asserts in its 36 pages of requirements for doctors of internal medicine, that "internal medicine is a discipline encompassing the study and practice of health promotion, disease prevention..."[15] And yet again, there is not a single nutrition-related requirement included.

"I give lectures to doctors," Dr. Davis told us. "I ask them, 'What do you think of the EPIC study?' This is the biggest study ever done on nutrition and disease, and I get blank faces all around. 'What about the Adventist Health Study 2? The Nurses' Health Study?' Blank. Not only are they not reading the nutrition journals, there's ignorance that the literature is even out there.

"We're compartmentalized as physicians. The heart doctor treats the heart. The GI doctor treats the stomach. The diabetic doctor is treating diabetes as a dysfunction of the pancreas. No one's looking at the whole person. They don't ask what the patient is eating. Sometimes the patient isn't even in the picture. In a hospital, the doctors don't say, 'Mrs. Smith in room 201.' They say, 'The colon cancer in 201.' The laser focus is on the disease. No one's looking at *how* the disease got there.

"Doctors also don't believe patients are going to change," Dr. Davis said. "They don't even give them a chance. 'I'm not wasting my time bringing diet up because they're not going to do it. I'm giving them meds.'"

In an intrepid attempt to remedy the situation, Dr. John McDougall, a pioneer in preventing chronic disease with nutrition, drafted California Senate Bill 380, which was introduced in February 2011. SB 380 "would require physicians and surgeons to complete, by December 31, 2016 [more than five years away when the bill was introduced] a mandatory continuing education course in the subject of nutrition and life style behavior for the treatment of chronic disease." All doctors licensed after January 1, 2012, would have four years in which to complete this course.[16]

"My son graduated from medical school two years ago, and he can't remember a course on nutrition," Dr. McDougall testified before the California State Senate. "The majority of diseases in this country are dietary-related... And yet physicians who have been trained for seven-plus years know virtually nothing about human nutrition... Not only is this a travesty for the patient, it's insulting to the doctor. Not to be able to deliver this kind of a powerful tool for their patients, to teach them about the causes of dietary diseases... This should have been fixed forty years ago when I was a medical student; it should have been fixed two years ago when my son graduated from medical school, and it's not going to be fixed unless somebody does something about it, and that is to mandate basic education on human nutrition."[17]

Dr. McDougall's bill originally stipulated 12 continuing education credit hours, every four years, towards nutrition education.[18]

That number was quickly dropped to seven hours of up-to-date nutrition instruction, every four years.[19] But...

"Seven hours, that's a lot. Even if it's over one four-year period, seven hours is a lot for one subject." That was the representative for the California Orthopedic Association at the hearings.[20]

To put this in context, the California Medical Board currently requires physicians to complete 100 hours of continuing education credits every four years.[21] Seven hours is less than 10 percent of the requirements. Yet chronic diseases are responsible for 70 percent of deaths, and 86 percent of health care costs are spent treating patients with chronic disease.[22]

Seven percent of continuing education hours, dedicated to a subject that affects 70 to 80 percent of conditions that send people to their doctors, into hospitals, and to their graves, is not "a lot."

The California Orthopedic Association voted against the bill. Those seven hours of nutrition education, apparently, were too much for doctors to handle and would take them away from the things that really mattered.

Even more astoundingly, the California Medical Association (CMA) opposed the bill. Teresa Stark, a lobbyist for CMA and now Director of State Government Relations at Kaiser Permanente,[23] spoke at the hearing.

"We oppose any CMA mandates on physicians," Stark stated. "This should be left up to the individual physician. It's a very slippery slope."

Stark talked about the progress underway in nutrition education. "The soda companies are now putting [the total number of] calories on the front of the beverages. That's a positive thing... They're going to solve this problem."

Okay.

And here's the California Academy of Family Physicians: "[Doctors] have to make an intelligent decision about how to educate themselves... I urge you to vote no [on SB 380]."[24]

The state's mainstream medical groups all actively opposed a minimum amount of basic nutrition education for practicing physicians.

I could not believe this.

In the end, despite the fact that Senator Mark Wyland, one of the members of the committee, had, as one of his top campaign contributors, the California Medical Association,[25] SB 380 passed.

The bill passed, but not without a small change.

The required number of hours for nutrition education was dropped from 12, to 7, to 0. This is what SB 380 looked like after the various ~~eviscerations~~ amendments:

> This bill would ~~require specified physicians and surgeons to complete, by December 31, 2016, or as otherwise specified, a mandatory continuing education course in the subject of nutrition and lifestyle behavior for the prevention and treatment of chronic diseases~~ authorize the board to also set content standards for an educational activity concerning chronic disease, as specified.

SEC. 2 (a) All practicing primary care physicians and all other physicians and surgeons who provide care or consultation for chronic diseases shall complete a mandatory continuing education course in the subject of nutrition and lifestyle behavior for the prevention and treatment of chronic diseases. For the purposes of this section, this course shall be a one-time requirement of seven credit hours within the required minimum established by regulation, to be completed by December 31, 2016. *SEC. 2. The [Medical] board [of California] may also set content standards for any educational activity concerning a chronic disease that includes appropriate information on the impact, prevention, and cure of the chronic disease by the application of changes in nutrition and lifestyle behavior.*[26]

The "progress" made here lies in the word "may": "The [Medical] board [of California] *may* also set content standards... on the impact, prevention, and cure of the chronic disease by the application of changes in nutrition and lifestyle behavior."

In other words: "If they want to." The bill was rendered utterly toothless.

So if nutrition is an optional subject, what are the *required* continuing medical education topics?

There are a couple of sobering state-specific requirements, from "Prevention of transmission of infectious agents through safe injection practices" in Nevada, to "Instruction on HIV/AIDS" in D.C., "Domestic Abuse" in Kentucky, and 6 hours of something called "Cultural Competence" in New Jersey.

But the medical theme linking the whole country together— from Oregon, Rhode Island, New Mexico, Iowa, Ohio, West Virginia, Vermont, Texas, Tennessee, Massachusetts, and Iowa to California— was end-of-life care and pain management.[27]

California, the state that rejected 7 hours of nutrition education every four years for its doctors, requires 12 hours of end-of-life care and pain management for its licensed physicians.[28]

Is the focus in the medical profession today on helping people live?

Or is the focus on helping people die?

CHAPTER 3

DIABETES: DEADLY SWEET

Seventh-Day Adventists are the fastest-growing religious denomination in North America,[1] and the most diverse.[2]

Adventists also provide an extraordinary research window into diet and disease.

"God calls us to care for our bodies," Adventists believe, "treating them with the respect a divine creation deserves." They exercise regularly and do not smoke, drink alcohol, or take illicit drugs. They advocate "a well-balanced vegetarian diet that avoids the consumption of meat coupled with intake of legumes, whole grains, nuts, fruits and vegetables, along with a source of vitamin B_{12}."[3]

Loma Linda, a town in Southern California, is home to about 9,000 Adventists and is one of the world's five longevity "Blue Zones"—the only one in the United States—where people live notably longer, healthier lives, often past 100.[4] (I know you're wondering: the other four are Okinawa, Japan, which Dr. Davis mentioned; Nicoya, Costa Rica; Sardinia, Italy; and Ikaria, Greece. Residents of all five Blue Zones eat plant-based diets, accented infrequently, if at all, with animal protein.[5])

About 50 percent of Adventists are vegetarians, who eat no meat but do eat dairy and eggs.[6] But there are also large numbers of Adventist vegans, who don't eat any animal protein at all, as well as those who eat small amounts of fish and/or meat. Because they live close together in the same environment, and share the same healthy lifestyle, the dietary distinctions among them take on a special value for researchers.

Scientists from Loma Linda University have done several large studies, called the Adventist Health Studies, following first 24,000, then 34,000 Adventists over the last four decades, and now 96,000 Adventists in the current study, Adventist Health Study-2,[7] which received a $5.5 million grant from the National Institutes of Health in 2011.[8]

All the Adventist Health Studies show that as more animal protein is eaten, the risk of developing diabetes climbs higher, as surely as a flight of stairs:[9]

Diet	Prevalence of Diabetes
Vegans (no meat, dairy, or eggs)	2.9%
Vegetarians (adding dairy and eggs)	3.2%
Pescatarians (adding fish)	4.8%
Meat-Fish-Dairy-Egg eaters	7.6%

Compared to the rest of the country, 7.6 percent for the meat eaters doesn't seem like much, but keep in mind that Adventist meat eaters actually eat very little meat.

And that little bit makes a difference over the long term.

The scientists took their findings and discovered that if a person ate meat only once a week, over the span of 17 years, that person would have a *74 percent higher risk* of developing diabetes than a vegetarian.[10]

That number is shocking enough, but it amazed the scientists that this was true for meat eaters who were not overweight. The 74 percent increased risk was calculated by comparing vegans and vegetarians to meat eaters of a similar weight. Conventional wisdom holds that obesity is almost a prerequisite for diabetes.

But something else was going on inside the bodies of the slim meat eaters.

"Diabetes, of all the diseases, may be the most affected by meat." Dr. Davis folded his arms and leaned back on the examining table. "The European Prospective Investigation into Cancer and Nutrition (EPIC) study, the largest study of diet and disease ever undertaken,[11] monitored over half a million people for almost fifteen years.[12] EPIC showed that meat, particularly processed meat like bacon, sausages and hot dogs, is powerfully correlated with the development of Type 2 diabetes. But eating fruits and vegetables was shown to decrease diabetes development.[13] Not only that, but they also discovered that eating glucose and fructose—both sugars—is associated with *less* diabetes.[14] These are studies done with human beings. The rat studies show something different."

The Nurses' Health Studies and Health Professionals Follow-Up Study, two of the largest epidemiological analyses in the country, came to the same conclusions as the Adventist Health Studies and the EPIC study. The two Nurses' Health studies followed 122,000 nurses since 1976, and 116,000 nurses since 1989. Fifty-one thousand male healthcare professionals were monitored since 1986 in the Health Professionals Follow-Up Study. They were all conducted by Harvard. The researchers found that the risk of developing diabetes jumped to 48 percent by eating an extra half serving of meat a day.[15]

The impact of genetics on diabetes seemed to be receding further and further into the distance.

"A great example with genetics and diabetes is the Pima Indians," Dr. Davis said. *The same group mentioned by Dr. Ratner from the American Diabetes Association...*

"The Pima Indians in Arizona originally ate lots of squash, beans, and corn, with very little meat," said Dr. Davis. "Around 1890, white settlers dammed the Gila and Salt rivers, and the Pima could no longer grow food. The government gave them meat, flour and sugar subsidies. So the Arizona Pima Indians had to switch to a diet with tons of protein and fat.

"They now have the highest rate of diabetes and obesity of any culture ever.[16] Understand this: the Pima were originally eating carbs in the form of plants. They had no diabetes. When the subsidies of meat, fat, and processed carbs began, their diabetes rates soared to about 40 percent.[17]

"The Tarahumara Indians who live in the Copper Canyon in Mexico are a genetically identical population," he went on. "They eat predominantly squash, beans, and corn. They have almost no diabetes. So a gene has to set you off, but you can eat a diet that prevents the gene from expressing itself."

I looked over at Keegan. He shook his head in disbelief. I knew what he was thinking. Dr. Davis had used the very same example as Dr. Ratner, about diabetes, genetics, and diet. Yet Dr. Ratner had veered away from his own words, saying there was insufficient evidence on the relationship between a plant-based diet and the disease—despite having just handed us a big chunk of the evidence himself.

I told Dr. Davis about our meeting with Dr. Ratner.

"It seemed suspicious," I said.

Dr. Davis frowned. "I always hear this conspiracy: 'Doctors want to keep you sick.' That's not true. Doctors do what doctors have always been taught to do: treat disease."

I accepted Dr. Davis' reprimand. I certainly believe the vast majority of healthcare professionals care deeply about helping their patients.

But the interview at ADA still gnawed at me. It rankled even more when I looked up guidelines for preventing Type 2 diabetes from different mainstream organizations.

The American Association of Clinical Endocrinologists states, "Medical nutrition therapy is recommended for all people with prediabetes or DM [diabetes mellitus, the full name of the disease]."[18] "Unhealthy dietary habits and a sedentary lifestyle are of major importance in the development of T2DM [Type 2 Diabetes Mellitus]," writes the European Society of Cardiology in conjunction with the European Association for the Study of Diabetes.[19]

And finally, I looked up the American Diabetes Association's own official Standards of Medical Care in Diabetes, 2016: "Evidence supports the importance of maintaining a healthy diet in order to prevent diabetes onset… data suggest that consumption of a diet enriched in whole grains is helpful in preventing type 2 diabetes. Finally, increased consumption of nuts and berries in the context of a diet high in vegetables and whole fruits has been correlated with reduced diabetes risk."[20]

Earlier, the ADA Standards of Care stated, "[I]ntensive lifestyle modification programs [diet, exercise, etc.] …have been shown to be very effective (58% reduction after 3 years)."[21]

Ways to prevent Type 2 diabetes were not so "unclear" after all.

I realized, while looking through this literature, that I had a very fuzzy idea of what diabetes actually is, despite my aunt, uncle, and grandpa all suffering from it. Something to do with sugar, right? But why then would meat be so powerfully associated with it?

"Before 1990 or so," Dr. Barnard told Keegan and I, "people thought diabetes might be caused by genetics, bad luck, or eating too much. Then, through special scanning techniques, we were able to look into the muscle cells of the human body, and see a build-up of tiny particles of fat. That fat build-up is causing insulin resistance."

"I honestly don't even know what insulin is," I confessed.

Dr. Barnard nodded. "Diabetes means there's too much sugar in the blood. Normally, your pancreas makes a hormone called insulin, which enters the blood stream. The tiny molecules of insulin in the blood are like keys. They attach to the surface of a muscle cell, or a liver cell, and just like a key, they open up that cell to allow sugar inside. That's normal and good—sugar is the body's fuel.

"But if you have Type 2 diabetes, particles of fat accumulate inside the cell. The fat is like chewing gum jamming the lock of your front door. That is insulin resistance. There's nothing wrong with your key. The lock is gummed up. So the sugar builds up in your blood."

A light bulb came on.

When we talked to Dr. McMacken, she clarified the issue further.

"I always thought eating sugar was the problem," I said.

"A lot of people think that," she said. "There is probably more confusion around what causes Type 2 diabetes than around any other disease, among doctors, patients, and the media. People don't understand that high blood sugar is a *symptom* of diabetes. It is not the *cause* of diabetes. The foods most clearly linked to the development of Type 2 diabetes are processed meat, like bacon, hot dogs, cold cuts, salami, pepperoni, ham, sausage. There's a number of studies showing that the more processed meat there is in your diet, the more likely you are to get Type 2 diabetes.[22] And of all the foods, whole grains are the most protective against the disease.[23] The root cause of diabetes has to do with our insulin not working properly, which is very directly related to extra body fat. Until that message gets out, we're never going to break the cycle."

The fat in meat, dairy, and eggs behaves differently in the human body from the fat found in plant sources, like nuts, avocados, and olives.[24] The saturated fats found mostly in animal tissue can lead to lipotoxicity (literally: "fat" + "poisoning"[25]) causing problems like inflammation, free radicals, mitochondrial dysfunction (mitochondria are tiny energy-generators inside our cells[26]), and the build-up of toxic breakdown products.[27] The monounsaturated fats found mostly in plant sources, on the other hand, can not only be more easily detoxified, but can also help protect against the harmful effects of saturated fat.[28]

In a study done at the Imperial College School of Medicine in London, scientists matched 21 vegans and 25 omnivores for gender, age, weight, percentage of body fat, activity levels, and waist circumference. These people were basically the same except for what they ate. For seven days, the researchers had their 46 subjects eat the same number of calories and perform the same amount of daily exercise.

Muscle biopsies revealed that there was significantly more fat caught in the muscle cells of the omnivores after seven days, even though they were specifically selected to be the same weight as the vegans.[29] It is the accumulation of *saturated* fat—the kind found in animal tissue—inside the muscle cell that is connected to insulin resistance.[30] The plant-based group was also found to have better blood sugar levels, better insulin levels and sensitivity, and substantially better function in the pancreatic cells that produce insulin.[31]

Michael Abdalla, 69, is from Atlanta, Georgia. About ten years ago he was diagnosed with Type 2 diabetes, and eight years ago he had two stents—tiny wire mesh tubes used to prop open blocked arteries—inserted permanently.

Abdalla, a heavy-set Lebanese-American man with a tidy white beard, showed us the medications he is required to take every day for his diabetes and other conditions. Ziploc bags full of pills lay on his bathroom counter.

"Most people use pill boxes," he said. "I can't; I have so many pills they won't fit in the boxes, so I have to use these bags. I'm taking about 16 drugs, not counting the insulin in the morning and the insulin at night—32 to 34 units of insulin. I have to punch a needle in my finger to check my blood three or four times a day."

He held up some of the bags. "Some of these meds are for diabetes. This one is for peeing. I have to use this for my prostate and this is for my heart. This is for blood pressure. It goes on and on and on. It's frustrating and very stressful. I don't know how long my liver is going to last taking all this stuff."

"Your doctors say that's the only option?" I ask.

"That's what they say. 'You've got to take them until you die.' If I get off *this*, my sugar goes up. If I get off *that*, my heart will be in trouble. Both my father and mother had diabetes. The doctors tell me, 'Hey, they had it. You have it.' My life is a never-ending trip to the pharmacy. I've got an endocrinologist, cardiologist, urologist, every kind of –ologist you can think of."

He plopped the bags back on the counter with a sigh.

"I'm 69. I'd like to live longer. I've got five grandchildren. They're my life, these five grandchildren, and I want to live for them."

***

Diabetes is the top cause of new cases of adult blindness, kidney disease, and non-accident-related limb amputations.[32] Seventy-three thousand amputations (not related to accidents) were performed in 2010 on adults with diabetes.[33] The disease also heightens your risk for heart disease (like my grandpa), stroke, Alzheimer's, skin conditions, and hearing problems. The excess blood sugar in a person with diabetes can damage the walls of their capillaries,[34] blood vessels so tiny that red blood cells can only travel through them one at a time.[35] The capillaries, when healthy, nourish the nerves in the body's extremities, particularly in the legs and feet. If not taken care of, the tingling, numbness, or pain felt in the tips of the toes and fingers can spread upward, triggering a loss of feeling in the entire limb.[36]

The US has the highest diabetes rate among 38 developed nations, according to the International Diabetes Federation.[37] One out of 4 people with the disease don't know they have it.[38] Over the last ten years, the rate of diabetes in this country has doubled.[39]

Some ethnic groups are hit harder. African-Americans are nearly twice as likely to be diagnosed than Caucasians. And once African-Americans have diabetes, they're over 4 times more likely than Caucasians to have kidney failure, they're more likely to suffer blindness and other vision damage,[40] they're up to five times more likely to require a lower limb amputation,[41] and twice as likely to die from the disease.[42] Latinos and Latinas, Native Americans, and Asians and Pacific Islanders all have a higher prevalence of diabetes as well.[43]

The CDC projects that, if things continue as they are, 1 out of 3 adults will be diabetic by 2050.[44]

Another 86 million adults, right now, have pre-diabetes, a condition in which blood sugar is higher than normal but not yet at the threshold for diabetes.[45]

"There are so many pre-diabetics now that if they gain a little more weight or become a little less active, there will be 100 million diabetics in this country," cardiologist Dr. Joel Kahn told Keegan and I at his home in Detroit. He has been practicing medicine for over 25 years, and is the director of the Kahn Center for Cardiac Longevity in Michigan.

"Nothing will change with a new drug or a new injection," Dr. Kahn said. "What will change things is teaching the public that this is a preventable disease. Diabetes in adults is about 90 percent preventable with simple lifestyle habits. They happen to be the same lifestyle habits that work for heart attack prevention. Some of the best data shows that the amount of fruits, vegetables, and whole grains you eat is the best marker of your risk for diabetes. The more you eat of those foods, the lower your risk. You add 30 or 40 minutes of walking and standing during the day, sleeping 7 hours a night— these factors have come on the map as predictors of heart attack and diabetes."

"Is it true that diabetes is reversible?" Keegan asked.

"If you take ten days out of your life," Dr. Kahn said, "at home under medical management, or at a center like the McDougall Center or the TrueNorth Center, the odds are that after ten days on a plant-based (no added oil) diet, with moderate exercise and stress reduction plan, you will be off medication, or off the majority of medications."

Ten *days*? To reverse one of the health epidemics of our country?

The reversal of diabetes, which I thought was some kind of isolated occurrence, turned out to be almost commonplace among the healthcare professionals we talked to.

I asked Susan Levin at PCRM about it.

"When people come to us with diabetes, we want them to get off the animal products, and just from that, we see tremendous success," she said. "Their blood sugar gets under control. Their diabetic symptoms like vision and nerve damage start to improve. That's without focusing on sugar. You can certainly take high glycemic foods—foods that quickly turn to sugar in your body—out of your diet as well. But the primary thing we focus on is getting the animal products out."

"Can you talk about the effect of pharmaceuticals on diabetes, versus controlling it with diet?" Keegan asked.

"We've seen that adopting a low-fat, plant-based diet can be about as powerful as most drugs for Type 2 diabetes," Levin said. "And that is purely a diet change. We don't ask people to exercise, meditate, or anything else. Just stop eating animal products and focus on low-fat foods. We found that their Type 2 diabetes would suddenly go into remission, and they were able to get off some of their drugs. That's in the short term. Over the long term, the effects get better."

Changing your diet still might seem like a big inconvenience. Easier to take a pill, many think. Metformin is a widely prescribed medication for Type 2 diabetes. Its most frequent side effects include diarrhea, nausea, vomiting, and abdominal pain.[46] It can also lead to other complications, like fatal lactic acidosis.[47] And in contrast with

PCRM's plant-based program in which the results improve over time with no ill consequences, the effectiveness of metformin drops within a few years; over time, it can lead to inflammation of the pancreas and pancreatic cancer, according to a study from the University of California, Los Angeles.[48]

As I was standing in line at the supermarket the other day, I was flipping through a magazine and noticed an ad for a new Type 2 diabetes drug. I'll call it X:

What is the most important information I should know about X?

X may cause serious side effects including possible thyroid tumors, including cancer.[49]

Gah.

The *New England Journal of Medicine* published a study in which scientists tried to intensively lower the blood sugar of 5,000 people with diabetes, using up to five different kinds of drugs, with or without injections of insulin.

The results were appalling.

The people on the intensive drug treatments began *dying at a higher rate*. The study had to be terminated. It was "concluded that the harm associated with the increased rate of death…outweighed any potential benefits and recommended that the intensive regimen be discontinued for safety reasons."[50]

Death from medication shines a whole different light on diet-based treatments.

"About 80 percent of people with Type 2 diabetes that we see are able to achieve normal glycemic levels without the use of medications," Dr. Goldhamer said to us. "When people benefit from diet and exercise, you can absolutely reverse this condition in a significant percentage of patients. To the degree that people are willing to sustain the diet and lifestyle changes, they can sustain the results."

To the degree that people are willing to sustain the diet and lifestyle changes, they can sustain the results. That sounded like hard work. I love eating. I would never be able to sustain a starvation diet over any period of time.

Most of the time, people with diabetes or pre-diabetes are told to lose weight, and the best way to lose weight is to eat less. Isn't it?

Scientists and legions of frustrated Americans will tell you otherwise. Cutting calories, portion restriction, and other deprivation plans do not work. The weight comes back with a vengeance.[51]

Now for something totally different: the All-you-can-eat plan.

Remember the study I tried to ask Dr. Ratner about, from the *American Journal of Clinical Nutrition* (the world's most widely-recognized, peer-reviewed nutrition journal[52])? The one that triggered his shutdown?

That study, supported by grants from the National Institute of Diabetes and Digestive and Kidney Diseases, and by the Diabetes Action Research and Education Foundation,[53] took 100 overweight people with diabetes, and randomly assigned them to either a plant-based diet or a calorie-cutting, low-fat diet following the guidelines of the American Diabetes Association. (Apparently such a diet exists.) The ADA diet was very reduced in calories. But the plant-based group was allowed to eat as much as they wanted—no portion control or carbohydrate restriction—of grains, legumes, vegetables, and fruits, although oils and nuts were limited.

Every person in the study was given thorough guidance over 74 weeks, which is about a year and a half. At the end of that time, the scientists found that the plant-based group had significantly better blood sugar control. They also had substantially lower cholesterol, and lost more weight than those on the reduced-calorie ADA diet.[54] Many other studies have come to similar conclusions.[55] Whole grains, beans and other legumes in particular appear to have the strongest health benefits for diabetics and pre-diabetics, helping to decrease insulin resistance.[56]

"When you get the animal fat out of your diet," Dr. Barnard said, "it changes the body chemistry in such a fundamental way that your natural insulin can start working again. People who have had diabetes can improve it so much through diet that they don't need medication, or can even get rid of it."

This information isn't new. Almost 40 years ago there was another study, also published in the *American Journal of Clinical Nutrition*, showing that a plant-based diet slashed the insulin requirements of men with Type 2 diabetes by more than half. Some of the men had been living with diabetes for twenty years, injecting 20 or more units of insulin every day. They were not allowed to lose weight—if the numbers on the scale dropped, they had to eat more (grains, legumes, fruits and vegetables). And not only did they dramatically reduce their insulin requirement, half of the subjects were able to get off insulin completely. Did I mention how long this took? About sixteen days.[57]

You don't need to go to any musty library to find this information. The 74-week study comparing a plant-based diet with the American Diabetes Association diet, for example, though originally published in the *American Journal of Clinical Nutrition*, is now featured on the ADA's very own Diabetes Care page.[58]

I felt a huge burden lifted from my shoulders. It's funny how long it takes human beings to accept the truth. It often has to be presented to us over and over before we believe it. The realization that my genetics do not condemn me to a life of chronic illness was finally taking full root in my mind.

I leaned back in my chair and stretched my arms overhead. It felt good to surface from the piles of printouts and cascading tabs on my computer screen. In front of me was legitimate, well-respected, and widely recognized scientific research, spanning decades and multiple countries, conducted with thousands and thousands of subjects. But it was news to me.

I thought of Dr. Barnard's insulin analogy, the lock and the key. The key has to work in order for health to occur.

And something was gumming up the lock of public awareness.

Chapter 4
Chicken: What the Cluck?

I have loved eating chicken since I was a kid. Chicken nuggets, chicken noodle soup, chicken potpie, and when I got older, Chicken Parmesan, Chicken Tikka Marsala, and good old Buffalo wings.

Chicken is the most popular meat in the United States. Even people who "don't eat much meat," eat chicken. The average American in 2015 ate over 90 pounds of chicken.[1] That's a huge increase from 1909, when each person ate less than 20 pounds.[2]

Chicken is supposed to be a lean, white meat, lower in cholesterol, sodium, and saturated fat than red meat. People eat chicken because it's the healthier choice.

Isn't it?

As Dr. Esselstyn put it, it's a question of whether you want to be shot or hung.

"Heterocyclic amines (HCAs) are clear-cut carcinogens," Dr. Barnard told Keegan and I. "They can form in any meat as it's cooked,[3] but by far, the biggest source is chicken. We sent researchers into the top chains of fast food and family restaurants, and took 100 food samples. We found carcinogens in every single chicken sample.[4] These were independent laboratory tests."

The WHO report had only targeted processed meat and red meat as cancer-causing. Now chicken also contains carcinogens?

"Is that all chicken?" I asked, not quite believing it.

"It's typical factory-farmed chickens," Dr. Barnard said.

Aha! I thought. *Not true for organic!*

"It's also true for organic," Dr. Barnard continued. "It's true for chicken that was not fried, chicken with the skin removed, and skinless chicken breast. The carcinogens are still there. And remember, this is true for other meats as well."

The presence of carcinogenic HCAs may explain why well-cooked meat is linked to higher risks of cancers of the breast, colon, esophagus, lung, pancreas, prostate, and stomach.[5]

Nor are these slightly increased risks. The Long Island Breast Cancer Study Project found that women who consume more grilled, smoked, or barbecued meat over the course of their lives could have a 47 percent greater risk for breast cancer.[6]

I asked Dr. Milton Mills about chicken.

"I tell people this all the time," he said, "and I mean every last word: if I still ate meat, I would not eat chicken. We have genetically altered chickens to go from hatchlings to market weight in 6 to 9 weeks. That is the equivalent of a human child growing 300 pounds in ten years.[7] Growth stimulants in the tissues of these animals make them grow at these phenomenal rates. When you ingest that tissue, you are also ingesting those growth stimulants, which may cause your cells to start growing at an unnatural rate that can cause you to develop a tumor. I think that is one of the reasons we are seeing more and more poultry linked to a variety of different cancers."

A 2010 Harvard report showed that high chicken consumption in men with aggressive prostate cancer could increase the progression or recurrence of the cancer by 300 percent. The same study found that by eating less than a single serving of chicken or turkey a day, you can increase your risk for prostate cancer by four times. The HCA carcinogens mentioned by Dr. Barnard seem to accumulate more in poultry muscle fibers than in other types of meat.[8]

A similar result was shown with colon cancer. Thirty thousand people were studied over six years, and researchers found that those eating red meat at least once a week roughly doubled their risk for colon cancer. But those who ate chicken or fish at least once a week *tripled* their colon cancer risk.[9]

And then there is pancreatic cancer, one of the most deadly forms of cancer. Only 6 percent of those with the disease will survive five years after the diagnosis.[10]

Every 50 grams of chicken eaten daily (about a ¼ of a chicken breast) will increase your risk of pancreatic cancer by 72 percent,[11] as discovered by the EPIC study.[12]

Smoking is the most thoroughly analyzed risk factor for pancreatic cancer. Smoking for 50 years doubles your risk for the disease. People working in chicken processing plants, however, have about 9 times the risk for both pancreatic and liver cancer, according to a study following 30,000 poultry workers.[13] They also have higher rates of cancers of the nasal cavities, mouth, throat, esophagus, and rectum. There are fears that the poultry viruses causing these cancers can be spread to the public when chicken or turkey is prepared or poorly cooked.[14]

EPIC researchers also found that eating chicken is related to greatly increased risk of various blood cancers, including non-Hodgkin's lymphoma, B-cell lymphomas, and every grade of follicular lymphoma. The risk grew between 56 percent and 280 percent for every 50 grams of poultry eaten daily.[15]

A cooked, boneless chicken breast can weigh over 380 grams.[16] Fifty grams of chicken is nothing when it comes to lunch, but it can mean increasing your risk for prostate cancer by four times, an 18 percent higher risk of colorectal cancer, a 56 to 280 percent higher risk of blood cancers, and 72 percent higher risk of pancreatic cancer.

Over the last thirty years, esophageal cancer in this country has risen by 500 percent.[17] The esophagus is the tube connecting the throat and the stomach. Meat and high-fat meals appear to be closely related to this dramatic increase.[18]

Red meat has been strongly connected with cancer within the esophagus, while chicken is linked to cancer where the esophagus and stomach meet.[19] The fat in both types of meat triggers acid reflux, which is believed to be one of the drivers of this disease.[20]

But wait—isn't chicken a low-fat food? That's one of the reasons we eat chicken.

Not so much.

The EPIC study gave poultry the dubious distinction of being potentially the most fattening meat of all.[21]

"A brilliant advertising campaign has convinced us, 'It's white meat. It's healthier,'" Dr. Klaper told us. "The truth is, those birds are raised to be as fat as possible at slaughter. The fatter they are, the more money the chicken producer makes. Most of them are given growth-promoting substances. These birds get so fat they can't stand up. People who think chicken flesh is lean should see the layer of fat that floats to the top of chicken soup. These birds are fatty, sick animals. To think that chicken is healthier is simply wrong. Poultry flesh is one of the worst things people can eat."

Choosing chicken over other meats, as Dr. Pamela Popper puts it in her book, *Food Over Medicine*, is like "rearranging the deck chairs on the Titanic."[22]

A single serving of chicken today can have over 200 calories from fat alone. One hundred years ago, that same single serving of chicken might have only had about 16 fat calories.[23]

Contrary to what most of us believe, a skinless chicken thigh can contain more fat—including saturated fat—than over two dozen different cuts of lean beef.[24]

"Everybody thinks chicken is the greatest health food," Dr. Davis told us, "but the EPIC study showed that the number one food causing weight gain was chicken—the food that my obese patients are eating tons of because they think it's good for them. In any serving of chicken, there are more calories from fat than there are from protein."

People also choose chicken over red meat believing it has less cholesterol and sodium. The American Heart Association, after all, tells us to "Eat More Chicken, Fish and Beans," because "red meats (beef, pork and lamb) have more cholesterol and saturated (bad) fat than chicken."[25]

But...

"The number one dietary source of cholesterol in America is chicken," Dr. Joel Kahn told Keegan and I. "Chicken is the top dietary source of cholesterol because of the sheer volume of chicken that is eaten. And it has nearly as much cholesterol per gram as red beef."

People think trimming the fat will help reduce cholesterol, but cholesterol is mainly found in lean sections of meat, including poultry.[26]

We asked Dr. Kim Williams about cholesterol in chicken. Dr. Williams is the Immediate-Past President of the American College of Cardiology, a 47,000-member organization, as well as the Chief of Cardiology at Rush University Medical Center in Chicago.

"The amount of cholesterol in a chicken breast is more than you would find in a pork chop the same size," Dr. Williams, an African-American gentleman with crinkly eyes and a trim beard, told us in his office. "Even if it's no skin, not fried."

According to the University of Wisconsin-Madison, 100 grams of lean, boneless pork contains 62 mg of cholesterol. The same amount of lean boneless, skinless chicken contains 84 mg of cholesterol.[27]

The story is the same with beef. A 3.5-ounce serving of chicken leg contains 134 mg of cholesterol, while the same serving size of sirloin steak has 89 mg, and beef ribs have 94 mg. Three and a half ounces of chicken breast contain 85 mg of cholesterol, slightly lower than the steak and ribs, but still carrying more cholesterol than beef brisket, at 63 mg.[28]

And as Dr. Kahn emphasized, the marginally lower amount of cholesterol in chicken is irrelevant when you factor in the enormous amounts of chicken we eat.

How about the low-sodium reputation of poultry then, another major reason people choose it over other meats?

It's an excellent idea to reduce your salt intake. Extra salt in your bloodstream is directly related to high blood pressure, which is a major factor in heart disease, stroke, kidney disease, osteoporosis, stomach cancer, and other diseases.[29] Eating too much salt kills four million people every year. In fact, it is the second greatest dietary risk for death and disability around the world. (The number one dietary risk, interestingly, is not eating enough fruit, which seems to kill almost five million people yearly.[30])

Salt is formed from sodium and chloride. And the number one source of sodium in the American diet, for adults between ages 20 and 50 is...

Chicken.[31]

More than beef, sausage, bacon, cheese, and pizza.

"The poultry industry injects chicken carcasses with salt water," Dr. Greger told Keegan and I.

Uh, why?

"Because it adds water weight. It can increase the weight as much as 20 percent. You buy meat by the pound, so the meat industry can make 20 percent more profit for almost nothing. Salt is one of the cheapest ingredients available. And it can still be labeled, '100% natural.'"

Some chickens sold in supermarkets are so swollen with salt water they contain 840 mg of sodium per serving.[32]

A McDonald's Cheeseburger, by comparison, contains 680 mg of sodium.[33]

Chicken is also linked to urinary tract infections (chicken is the original source of *E. coli* bacteria associated with UTIs[34]); suicide and depression (chicken is the biggest source of dietary arachidonic acid,[35] associated with substantial increased risks of suicide and clinical depression[36]); and accelerated aging symptoms like tissue stiffness, inflammation, cataract formation, macular degeneration, and bone, heart, kidney, and liver damage[37] (chicken is the number one source of aging toxins,[38] formed chiefly when foods rich in protein and fat are subjected to high heat[39]).

And then there is the simple fact that chicken is a filthy food.

About *90 percent* of the nation's retail chicken is contaminated with fecal matter. Yes, that includes the kind you buy at your clean, local supermarket. This is according to a 2011 FDA report, which monitored bacteria such as *E. faecalis* and *E. faecium*, on meat, concluding that 90 percent of chicken parts, 91 percent of ground turkey, 88 percent of ground beef, and 80 percent of pork chops have fecal contamination.[40] We'll find out later how feces gets on the meat.

Eating that fecal contamination leads to dangerous, sometimes life-threatening infections like *Salmonella* poisoning,[41] the leading cause of death from a food-borne illness.[42] And chickens, rather than their eggs, are the number one source of *Salmonella* poisoning.[43] There were 278 *Salmonella* outbreaks stemming from chicken and turkey in at least 41 states, between 1998 and 2012.[44]

This is the very reason, conventional wisdom wags its finger, why chicken needs to be properly handled and properly cooked. But what constitutes "proper" handling of chicken?

A team of researchers worked with 60 different families, asking each to cook a raw chicken. The researchers examined the homes afterwards, and discovered the kitchens were swarming with bacteria from chicken feces—on counters, refrigerator and oven handles, silverware, sink faucets, and door knobs.

The researchers repeated the experiment, instructing the families to wash the contaminated surfaces with soap and hot water afterwards. It made no difference.

At last, the families were told to use bleach. The research team still found, admittedly to a far lesser degree, *Salmonella* and *Campylobacter* from fecal contamination on kitchen surfaces like the counter, cupboards, and utensils.[45]

As Dr. Greger writes in *How Not to Die*, "The reason most people have more fecal bacteria in their kitchen sinks than their toilet seats[46] is likely because they prepare their chickens in the kitchen, not the bathroom."[47]

How could such a trick of colossal proportions, crossing generational, racial and economic lines, be played on the American public for so long?

I kept revisiting the facts.

Chicken has higher concentrations of carcinogens, and triples the risk of colon cancer, while red meat "only" doubles it. It is the first meat doctors would eliminate for health reasons. As potentially the most fattening meat, it contains more fat than 24 different cuts of beef. Chicken has more cholesterol than a pork chop and often more than beef, including steak and ribs. It has more sodium than beef, bacon, or a Mickey D's cheeseburger. Ninety percent of commercial chicken is contaminated with feces, which is transferred during preparation to the rest of your kitchen. And *Salmonella* bacteria in chicken kills more people than *E. Coli* in beef.[48]

I do not feel like chicken tonight.

CHAPTER 5
FLESH FOOD

The truth about poultry almost makes red meat—that WHO-classified carcinogen—look good.

However.

"We've got to stop imagining that there's some animal out there that's really healthy to consume," writes Dr. Pamela Popper.[1]

The largest, most wide-ranging examination of the link between meat and death was the NIH-AARP (National Institutes of Health-American Association of Retired Persons) Diet and Health Study, which observed over 560,000 people, ages 50-71, over ten years.[2] The researchers found, after factoring in elements like smoking, alcohol, exercise, weight, age, and fruit/veggie intake, that eating meat is connected with a higher risk of death from cancer, death from heart disease, and, well, death in general.[3]

The Nurses' Health Study and the Health Professionals Follow-Up Study reached the same verdicts: consuming red meat—unprocessed and processed—was linked to dying from cancer, heart disease, and early death.[4]

What is so lethal about meat and other animal products?

"Animal proteins are very rich," Dr. Goldhamer said. "Excess amounts of fats and proteins lead to the diseases of dietary excess: heart disease, stroke, diabetes, cancer. They used to be known as the Diseases of Kings, because only the wealthy royalty got them. Now, of course, these diseases are equal-opportunity killers. Two-thirds of adults are now overweight or obese.[5] We have an epidemic cascade of debilitating disease that's overcoming the country, an epidemic we're creating with our diet and lifestyle choices."

"There's a large amount of carnitine in animal muscle," Dr. Klaper said, giving Keegan and I a chemistry tutorial. "Gut bacteria turns carnitine into a molecule called Trimethylamine. Your liver turns that into Trimethylamine oxide (TMAO).

"That is a molecule from *hell*," he continued emphatically. "It drives cholesterol into the artery walls. Pack your colon full of meat three times a day, for twenty years, and watch what you set off in there."

"Within minutes of eating animal products," said Dr. Greger, "your system receives a burst of inflammation that paralyzes your arteries. Their normal ability to relax is cut in half. This stiffened, inflammatory state continues for five or six hours before finally coming back to baseline. Then along comes lunch, and we hit our arteries with another load of meat, eggs, or dairy. Many of us live in a danger zone of chronic low-grade inflammation, which can increase our risk for inflammatory diseases like diabetes, heart disease, and certain forms of cancer."

Inflammation is one of the most explosive and illuminating fields of medical research today. Inflammation is a primary cause behind fat accumulation in muscle cells, leading to insulin resistance and diabetes.[6] Cancer scientists are examining the mutually enforcing relationship between cell mutation and inflammation. And inflammation has been shown to be a major factor behind the rupturing of arterial plaque, which can cause blood clots leading to heart attacks and strokes.[7]

"Initially, scientists thought it was animal fat causing the inflammation,"[8] Dr. Greger continued. "But it turns out the inflammation may be caused by endotoxins, which form part of the cell walls of bacteria.

"Animal products are packed with bacteria that can trigger inflammation. But even when cooking kills these bacteria, the endotoxins released from the bacterial cell walls are not destroyed.

"When we eat these toxins, they're absorbed into our system. In fact, the saturated fat in animal products may ferry them across the gut wall into our blood.[9] When these bacterial endotoxins get into our bloodstream, our body goes crazy.

"I want to reiterate: this inflammation happens within *minutes* of eating animal foods. It's not that there will be some damage decades down the road. There's immediate damage."

"Animal products are the main source of saturated fats, trans fats, and the only source of cholesterol in the diet," Susan Levin said. "These fatty foods make your blood thicker. Animal foods are also completely devoid of fiber, which most Americans lack. Fruits and vegetables contain antioxidants that help boost your immune system. High-fat foods like meat and dairy suppress your immunity."

"So how much meat, dairy, or eggs would you recommend I eat?" I asked her.

"I would recommend you eat no meat, dairy, or eggs."

Wow. I was hearing this from a pregnant dietitian.

"If I could deliver one message to researchers looking for the cause of diabetes, clogged arteries, high blood pressure, and obesity," said Dr. Klaper, "I would tell them: *it's the food*!"

"You can see with every sequential reduction in animal products, people live longer," said Dr. McMacken. "They have less heart disease, less cancer, less diabetes."

"There's a take-off on the slogan, 'Beef: It's What's for Dinner,'—'Beef: It's What's Rotting In Your Colon,'" said Dr. Greger. "I saw that at a party once, and had to be the one to say, 'Meat is actually digested in the small intestine, never makes it down to the colon. Sorry to be a party pooper, no pun intended.' No fun to hang around biology geeks. But I was wrong—about 12 grams of protein does make it down into the colon and goes through a 'putrefaction process.' It produces by-products that can be toxic, and can contribute to inflammatory bowel disease and perhaps colon cancer."[10]

Still, rotting-flesh-in-your-gut aside, there has to be some kind of benefit to meat, after all these years of being told it's an essential part of our diet. Muscle building? Protein? Iron?

"What can't you get in a plant-based diet that you can get in meat?" I asked Dr. Barnard.

He stared at me. "Cholesterol," he said. "Heterocyclic amines. *Salmonella, E. Coli.*"

I tried again. "Are there any *healthy* things found only in animal products?"

"Every nutrient from meat, dairy, and eggs can be found, in a form that is as healthy or healthier, in plants," he replied. "Meat has proteins, some iron, some zinc, but it's very low in vitamins. Not a speck of vitamin C. No complex carbohydrate. Zero fiber.

"When we transition people from a meaty diet to plant-based," he went on, "we always track what they're eating. Their vitamin intake goes up. Their nutrition overall improves dramatically. These same people might worry, 'Will I get the nutrition I need on a plant-based diet?' The fact is, you're not getting the nutrition you need on a *meat*-based diet. You're going to get dramatically better nutrition on a plant-based diet."

Let's look at iron.

Iron deficiency is the most common nutritional deficiency in both the United States[11] and the world. Two billion people—over 30 percent of the global population—are anemic, many due to iron deficiency.[12] People on a plant-based diet are no more likely to be iron deficient than meat eaters.[13]

There are two types of dietary iron: heme-iron (found in animal tissue like meat) and non-heme iron (found in plants). "Heme" comes from "hemoglobin," the molecule in red blood cells. An easy way to remember: animals bleed (heme); plants do not (non-heme).

Heme-iron is more easily absorbed than non-heme iron. Sounds like a good thing, right? The higher bioavailability of iron from muscle tissue and blood, though, is a serious drawback disguised—and often trumpeted—as a benefit.

The body will keep absorbing iron from animals, even when no more is needed.

Non-heme iron, however, allows the body to control the amount absorbed. If the body has enough iron, the intestines can dial down the absorption of plant iron. If the body needs more, it can turn up the absorption.[14] Our digestive systems block the intake of plant iron—if we already have a sufficient supply in our bodies—about five times more efficiently than animal iron.[15]

Getting our iron from plants protects us from excess iron, which is a dangerous thing. Once it's absorbed, there are very limited ways to get rid of it.[16] It's trapped in the body.

Iron is a pro-oxidant. Pro-oxidants promote oxidation.[17] What happens when iron is oxidized? The Tin Man rusts. As a pro-oxidant, iron can damage DNA. Iron from meat has been associated with higher risks of heart disease,[18] stroke,[19] Type 2 diabetes,[20] and even cancer.[21]

Scientists can tell, by examining tumors, how much meat the cancer patient has eaten.[22]

(*Anti*oxidants, which are protective to the body and the immune system, can be found mainly in fruits and vegetables—food from plants contain, on average, 64 times more antioxidants than food from animals.[23])

You can avoid heme-iron by getting your iron from sources like lentils, tofu, chickpeas, peas, cashews, soybeans, blackstrap molasses, quinoa, barley, other whole grains, tempeh, sunflower seeds, dark leafy vegetables, fortified cereals, broccoli, and watermelon.[24]

You can also boost your iron-absorption by up to five times if you eat iron-rich foods along with Vitamin C.[25] (And if you don't need the non-heme iron, your body won't absorb it!) Delicious iron/Vitamin C combos include lentil soup with cabbage and green peppers; rice and beans with salsa; stir-fried broccoli and tofu; kiwi and orange sections sprinkled with toasted sunflower seeds; bran cereal topped with strawberries; and hummus with lemon juice. A lot of vegetables, like broccoli and bok choy, are sources of both iron and Vitamin C.[26]

Cooking with a cast-iron skillet (the heavy black kind that makes you feel like an Iron Chef) will also up your iron intake. Avoid coffee, even de-caf, and tea while you're eating iron-rich meals. The tannins in them inhibit iron absorption.[27] Dairy and eggs also obstruct iron absorption in a big way.[28]

***

There's been a new focus lately on bowel bacteria. Stay with me. It's really interesting.

"Bowel bacteria is fascinating," Dr. Davis enthuses. "It might be the source of everything. We're finding it related to heart disease, cancer, obesity. The bowel bacteria in a meat eater is very different than that found in a plant-eater. A great study[29] showed that a person's bowel bacteria are completely changed after just five days of eating meat. And five days after eating a plant-based diet, you get a completely new bacterial floor.

"There's something called Trimethylamine oxide (TMAO)," Dr. Davis went on. (Dr. Klaper's Molecule From Hell.) "The liver converts the carnitine and choline in meat to TMAO, which is associated with heart disease and prostate cancer. Interestingly, someone on a plant-based diet can eat carnitine and choline and *not* produce TMAO. If you give antibiotics to a meat eater and kill some of their bowel bacteria, they also do not produce TMAO. Something about the meat eater's bowel bacteria causes the processing of these nutrients to go awry.

"What we eat controls the microbes in our intestines, and this may be the center of controlling the diseases in our body."

"What about eating meat once or twice a week?" I asked.

"Great question. A subgroup of the large EPIC study was in Oxford, where they looked at meat eaters who didn't eat much meat, as well as vegetarians and vegans.

"The minimal meat eaters did much better than those who ate a lot of meat, but neither meat-eating group did as well as the vegetarians and vegans when it came to life expectancy, heart disease, and certain cancers. And the vegetarians/vegans in the study were only getting about 20 grams of fiber a day—not a lot—and they had low vitamin B_{12} levels. So the study was comparing a healthy group of minimal meat eaters to an unhealthy plant-based group, and still the plant-based group did better.[30]

"What we see in a lot of these studies is a rapid increase in the rate of death and disease with just small amounts of meat—there's not a big difference between someone eating a lot of meat compared to someone eating a moderate amount. If you compare a diet of moderate meat to *no* meat, however, you see a big difference.

"In the Adventist Health Study, which is one of the best," Dr. Davis continued, "scientists looked at the vegans in the community; the lacto-ovo vegetarians who do eat dairy and eggs; pescatarians (fish eaters); light meat eaters, and regular meat eaters.

"The researchers found that from vegan to vegetarian, you get sicker. From vegetarian to pesco-vegetarian, in some cases people got sicker and in some cases they stayed the same. But then you move on to meat, and you definitely get a jump in heart disease, cancer, and early death."[31]

Dr. Barnard was more blunt. "You don't smoke moderately, you don't inject a moderate amount of heroin, you don't snort a moderate amount of cocaine if you want to be healthy. You shouldn't be eating a moderate amount of something that's going to kill you, and that's what meat-based diets do."

Grass-fed beef is healthier than factory-farmed meat though, isn't it?

"Meat products by their very nature are risky," Levin said. "It doesn't matter how the animal was raised. The risk is in the meat. With red meat, you have high amounts of iron, fat, cholesterol, no fiber. It doesn't matter where that cow came from."

I liked how Dr. Greger put it: "Twinkies are better than lard, okay, but wouldn't you want to eat a health-promoting food?"

But then there is The Question.

"What about the whole protein thing?" I asked Dr. Milton Mills.

He rolled his eyes and dropped his head back with a loud sigh. "Oh my god. You want me to jump off this building, don't you?" He chuckled and gently punched me on the shoulder. "All protein is made by plants. I'll state that again for the record: *all protein is made by plants*. What distinguishes protein from carbs and fats is the presence of nitrogen. Only plants have the ability to take nitrogen from the air, break those molecules apart, incorporate that nitrogen into amino acids and make protein.

"Animals eat plants and reprocess those amino acids into their own tissues. All animal protein is simply recycled plant protein. And you really want to get your protein directly from plants, because plant proteins have a much more beneficial effect on our physiology.

"It is not necessary to eat animal tissue in order to get protein," he said emphatically. "If anything, we need *less* protein."

That's nutritional blasphemy. Our nation is obsessed with protein.

Protein has what researchers call a "health halo effect," an idolization of the nutrient that doesn't have much to do with science.

"[Protein is] one of those rare things that has a lot of different meanings to a lot of different people and they are all positive," Barry Calpino, a VP at Kraft Foods, said in the *Wall Street Journal*.[32]

People eat protein to lose weight. People eat it to gain weight. People eat it for energy. People feed copious amounts to their children, believing it will make them strong and healthy. Most of us believe we should eat as much protein as possible.

Just 10-35 percent of your total calories, however, should come from protein. That's the recommendation from organizations like the American College of Sports Medicine, the USDA, and the Food and Nutrition Board, Institute of Medicine, National Academies.[33]

You can calculate your recommended daily protein intake this way:

(Pounds of body weight) × (0.35 grams of protein)[34]

By that calculation:

Body Weight (pounds)	× 0.35 =	Recommended Daily Protein Intake (grams, rounded up)
100	× 0.35 =	35
125	× 0.35 =	44
155	× 0.35 =	55
180	× 0.35 =	63

But this is how much protein people are actually eating:

American males over the age of 20 eat an average of 98.9 grams of protein a day. American females over the age of 20 eat an average of 68 grams of protein per day.[35]

This means that men, on average, are eating enough protein to sustain a 282-pound man. Women are eating enough protein for a 194-pound woman.

I know America has issues with obesity, but still—that's a bit much.

Susan Levin told us, "Most Americans—meat eaters, vegetarians, and vegans—get about twice the amount of protein they need."

"Guess what nutrient 97 percent of Americans are deficient in, not even reaching the bare minimum recommended requirement?" said Dr. Greger. "Fiber. There's zero fiber in animal products. People don't even know how much fiber they're supposed to get. So the question is not, 'Where do you get your protein?' It's, 'Where do you get your fiber?'"

I certainly had no idea how much fiber I was supposed to get. I thought the only people who had to think seriously about fiber were those who spent too long in the bathroom.

It turns out a person should eat 25-30 grams of fiber a day. But the average adult in the US currently consumes only 15 grams. It's also important to get your fiber from food, not supplements.[36] (A note to my 18-year-old self with his daily Metamucil sludge.)

"Fiber does everything," Levin said. "Insoluble fiber acts like a scrub brush through your system, and soluble fiber picks up the toxins, excess hormones, and cholesterol generated by your body, and pulls it all out. It helps with your heart health. It helps your energy level because it keeps your blood sugar stable. It helps control your weight because it fills you up without a lot of calories. It helps prevent cancer and diabetes. Most Americans get less than half the fiber they need, but the conversation is always about protein. Protein has taken on this magical marketing campaign over the decades."

Ask anyone why we need meat.

"Protein," says the Wall Street banker.

"Protein?" says the Valley Girl.

"Protein!" says the Fitness Buff.

"We need to get our protein," says the Young Mom.

In 2015, Maple Leaf Foods Inc., the largest producer of processed meat in Canada, came out with an ad campaign called, "Protein Builds."[37]

In the mind of the public, protein = meat. Meat = protein. But...

"Grains are loaded with protein," Dr. Esselstyn said to us, counting the items off on his fingers. "Beans are loaded with protein. Vegetables are loaded with protein."

"If you eat a diet that is calorically adequate," said Dr. Goldhamer, "even just brown rice and broccoli, you will get enough—both quantity and quality—of protein. Two thousand calories of brown rice and broccoli is about 80 grams of protein a day, including the essential amino acids that you need in order to maintain optimum health."

½ cup of firm tofu = 20 grams of protein.

½ cup of lentils = 9 grams.

½ cup of brown rice = 2 grams.

¼ cup of dried shiitake mushrooms = 10 grams.

¼ cup of pumpkin seeds = 10 grams.

2 tablespoons of peanut butter = 8 grams.

A slice of whole wheat bread = 4 grams.[38]

This little list contains 63 grams of protein. That's enough for a 180-pound person.

"I never count protein, I just eat," Dr. Davis said. "For an average-sized guy like myself, I need about 56 grams of protein a day. I train for triathlons. I lift weights. Fifty-six grams is optimum; probably I really need 30 to 40 grams. There's no way you're not going to get that if you're eating enough calories."

"Is there such a thing as protein deficiency?" I asked.

"I've never in my professional career seen a protein deficiency," Dr. Davis replied. "You could get protein deficient if you're not eating enough calories, like starving kids in Africa, or a really sick hospital patient. But becoming protein deficient on three meals a day? It's not going to happen."

"Soy is a popular plant-based protein," I said. "But I've heard it can mimic female hormones, make guys grow breasts, and give you cancer."

Dr. Davis sighed. "If that were true, I'd have double D's, because I eat a lot of soy. Soymilk really took a bite out of dairy sales, and now you're seeing all kinds of anti-soy stuff out there. The truth is the opposite of what you're hearing.[39] Girls who eat more soy are less likely to menstruate at an early age, which is incredibly beneficial in reducing long-term breast cancer risk. Girls who eat soy when they're young, as well as women who have had breast cancer and then consume soy, have *less* recurrence, not more recurrence, of breast cancer. There are cancer doctors telling their patients, 'Don't eat soy.' That's not what the science shows. In Asia they eat tons of soy. They don't get breast cancer. But when Asian people move to America and stop eating soy, their cancer rates go up."

"I feel very confident saying that soy is good for you," Dr. McMacken told us. "People who eat more soy tend to have much lower rates of breast cancer, and soy has been shown to reduce the risk of breast cancer recurrence in women that have had the disease. There's a lot of confusion and misinformation about soy."

A 2012 analysis, combining the results of several studies, examined the eating habits and other lifestyle factors of over 9,000 breast cancer survivors. The results indicated, as Dr. Davis and Dr. McMacken said, that eating soy lowers the risk of recurrent breast cancer by about 25 percent.[40] Another study, published in the *Journal of the American Medical Association,* surveyed, for four years, 5,042 breast cancer survivors. Again, the results indicated that women who regularly ate or drank soy products had 32 percent less risk of recurring cancer, and a 29 percent lower risk of death, compared with women who consumed little or no soy.[41]

Soy can help prevent breast cancer as well. A University of Southern California study found that women who drink a daily average of one cup of soymilk or eat half a cup of tofu have about 30 percent lower risk of developing breast cancer, compared to women who had little or no soy in their diet.[42]

The big scare about soy and breast cancer is that soy contains isoflavones, a kind of phytoestrogen (plant-estrogen), which is chemically comparable to estrogen, the primary female sex hormone. Estrogen is linked to cancers that are sensitive to hormones, like breast or endometrial cancer.[43]

Isoflavones and other phytoestrogens, however, are not the same as estrogen.

"While isoflavones may act like estrogen," writes Marji McCullough, a nutritional epidemiologist,[44] "they also have *anti-estrogen* properties. That is, they can block the more potent natural estrogens from binding to the estrogen receptor...They also have anti-oxidant and anti-inflammatory properties and work in other ways to reduce cancer growth."[45]

Dr. Barnard has a great analogy, comparing estrogen and phytoestrogens to airplanes. Estrogen is a massive jumbo jet. Phytoestrogen is a little Cessna. There's a huge difference in size, but if the little Phyto-Cessna is occupying the docking area (the estrogen receptor), the Estrogen-747 can't land and unload its damaging hordes of passengers into the terminal.

As for man-boobs, a meta-analysis (which combines data from multiple studies) with a foundation of more than 50 treatment groups, published in the journal *Fertility and Sterility*, showed that soy products did not affect testosterone levels in men.[46] Not only that, but an analysis of 14 studies, published in the *American Journal of Clinical Nutrition,* demonstrated that men eating more soy had a 26 percent lower risk for prostate cancer. The men had 30 percent lower risk if they ate non-fermented products like soymilk and tofu.[47]

As far as the safety of soy is concerned, you could have a tofu scramble for breakfast, miso soup for lunch, edamame for a snack, and marinated tempeh at dinner. Research shows that 3-5 daily servings of soy are safe and beneficial.[48]

"Soy is definitely good for you," Dr. Davis said. "It's loaded with every amino acid your body needs. It comes from a natural bean source. It does not create inflammation. It has been shown to prevent cancer. It drops cholesterol like crazy. You want to drop cholesterol, forget the meds. Eat soy."

Soy is so rich in protein, however, that you might overload on the nutrient if your every meal and snack contained soy, every single day. Remember, just half a cup of firm tofu gives you 20 grams of protein.

And too much protein is not a good thing.

"I got to a plant-based diet because I was overweight and sick," Dr. Davis said. I thought back to the YouTube clips I had seen of him—puffy and tired. "Whenever I saw patients who were sick or gaining weight, I told them, 'You need to eat more protein.' That's what I heard in medical school and the media. I followed my own advice and got sicker and sicker. I was 35, with high cholesterol, a high liver function test, I was overweight, sick, and eating more protein than you could imagine. I was taking more and more medications, just like my patients. I said to myself, 'This can't be right.' Lo and behold, I found that the problem may in fact be the protein. When I was 40, I was vegetarian but still obsessed with protein—veggie burgers out the wazoo, lots of processed stuff, lots of whey (dairy) protein shakes because I thought that's what athletes do. I ran my first marathon that year in 3:56. Now I'm 45 and plant-based, and I'm running a marathon at 3:35. Every time I drop my protein intake I feel stronger, better, and faster."

Pound for pound, the strongest, biggest animals on this planet are herbivores.[49] Elephants. Gorillas. Bison. Rhinos. Hippos. Giraffes. Would you like to ask a silverback gorilla—who can lift over ten times his body weight and pull down large trees with the strength of over ten adult human males[50]—where he gets his protein? Me neither.

"This idea that you need meat to be strong is just foolish," Dr. Mills exclaimed. "'I need chicken, I need fish to build muscle tissue.' Utter nonsense. You want to be strong? Do what an elephant does.

"People say, 'Chimps eat animal protein. Why shouldn't we?' Sure, they eat termites, because chimps don't eat high protein foods like grains, legumes and nuts like we can; they're mostly fruit-based. Larger primates like humans, gorillas, or orangutans are strict herbivores. Chimps also scratch their butts in public and throw feces at people. I don't think we should do that."

"Some people are scared to go plant-based because they've heard you have to carefully combine proteins," said Keegan. "They'd rather eat chicken and not worry about complete proteins."

"Okay, quick tutorial," Dr. Mills said. "All proteins are made up of 20 amino acids in different combinations. Our bodies can manufacture all of them except 9. Those are the 'essential amino acids' we need to get from food. A 'complete protein' means a protein that contains all 9 essential amino acids. For years it was thought that in order to be healthy, you had to eat complete proteins at each meal.

"That myth has been debunked,"[51] he said flatly. "First, if you eat from a variety of different plant foods (without calculating what kind of protein you get from each), you will get your complete proteins. Second, you do not have to eat all 9 essential amino acids at a given meal. And third, getting your amino acids from animal tissue is unhealthy. I cannot stress this enough.

"Nutritionists also used to say that a chicken egg was the perfect protein for human consumption, because it most closely resembled human tissue. If you follow that line of reasoning, we should be eating each other. Human tissue has exactly the amino acid composition that our bodies utilize."

He paused.

"It's not necessary for us to be cannibals, and it's not necessary to eat animal tissue or animal protein."

CHAPTER 6
CANCER: FEEDING THE GROWTH

Cancer terrifies me. There's something freakish about our own cells inexplicably massing into mutant growths. With cancer, our bodies seem to take on an alien malevolence that we can't control. There are over 37 trillion cells in the human body.[1] My inner hypochondriac starts to panic at the thought of all those cells. Thirty-seven trillion opportunities for cancer.

After all that I'd learned, I went back on the American Cancer Society website. The last time I was there, I hadn't noticed that recommendations and recipes for chicken and turkey were all over the site. Six of their 10 "Healthy Recipes—Main Dishes" are chicken entrées. Dr. Barnard's voice echoed in my head: "We found carcinogens in every single chicken sample that we took." And Dr. Mills: "We are seeing more and more poultry linked to a variety of different cancers."

I knew now that chicken, red meat, and processed meat are substances capable of causing cancer in living tissue. But how exactly does cancer happen?

Dr. T. Colin Campbell, in his landmark book, *The China Study*, lays out the three stages of cancer:

1) Initiation
2) Promotion
3) Progression

Dr. Campbell compares the mechanism of cancer development to planting a lawn. Initiation: the seeds embed in the soil. Promotion: the grass begins growing. Finally, progression: the grass runs rampant, swallowing the sidewalk, the driveway, and everything around it.

Carcinogens—such as the heterocyclic amines found in cooked chicken and meat—can plant the seeds of cancer. Initiation can happen in an incredibly short time. Minutes, sometimes. All it takes is for the carcinogen to be absorbed into the body and bonded to DNA. When the next generation of cells are formed, they, "and all their progeny will forever be genetically damaged, giving rise to the potential for cancer," writes Dr. Campbell.

Cancer initiation, except for very rare instances, is irreversible.[2]

All of us, I discovered, carry cancerous cells within us.

"We're all producing tumors all the time, and the question is, how many?" said Dr. Kim Williams.

Oh my god, I thought. *There are tumors inside of me, right now?* All the fear stemming from my family's health history coursed through me like ice water.

"Many of us don't even know we have cancer," Dr. Greger told Keegan and I. "DNA mutation can cause the first cancer cell, but one cancer cell never killed anyone. Two cancer cells never killed anyone. But a billion cancer cells? Now we're running into problems.

A tumor can be as small as the tip of a ballpoint pen. In fact, many of us live with microscopic tumors in our breast and colon."

Up to 20 percent of women ages 20 to 54 who died from non-cancer-related causes were shown in their autopsies to have undetected breast cancer. And autopsies show that up to 39 percent of women in their 40s had growing breast cancers too small to be detected.[3]

What bridges the gap between an unnoticed pinhead tumor, and a malignant, grapefruit-sized lump that will destroy the body?

Just like grass seeds lodged in the dirt, those first few cancer cells will not sprout and proliferate unless certain conditions for growth are provided. This is the *promotion* phase. Grass seeds require lots of water, sunlight, air, rich soil, and other nutrients. Without these things, the seeds will simply not grow, as many a frustrated suburban dad can attest. If they've already begun to sprout, and water and sunlight are taken away, the growth will be suspended.

This means that the promotion phase of cancer is reversible. It all depends on whether or not the disease is given the right conditions to grow.[4]

I found this incredibly exciting. It was a tiny bit of control in the face of a disease that many regard as a death sentence.

If grass seeds require water and sun to grow, what did cancer—the cancers we produce all the time in our healthy bodies—require to multiply and spread?

"When people develop cancer," Dr. Popper writes, "what really is going on, on a certain level, is that cancer promoters have outnumbered the anticancer agents in the diet."[5]

But what about breathing polluted air, or absorbing chemicals through our skin?

"Your skin covers about twenty square feet," Dr. Greger wrote in *How Not to Die*. "Your lungs, if you were to flatten out all the tiny air pockets, could cover hundreds of square feet. And your intestines? Counting all the little folds, some scientists estimate that your gut would blanket thousands of square feet, vastly more expansive than

71

your skin and lungs combined. What you eat may very well be your primary interface with the outside world. That means that regardless of the carcinogens that could be lurking in the environment, your greatest exposure may be through your diet."[6]

I already knew that chicken and other meats can cause cancer. But what foods protect us from cancer?

The answer is stunningly simple.

Plants.

The American Institute for Cancer Research (AICR) is a non-profit organization dedicated to advancing the knowledge that cancer can be prevented, and educating the public on the link between diet and cancer.[7] In its ten Recommendations for Cancer Preventions, AICR states: "Eat more of a variety of vegetables, fruits, whole grains and legumes such as beans."[8]

The WHO declares, "Diets high in fruits and vegetables may have a protective effect against many cancers."[9] And Cancer Research UK says, "Some foods, such as red and processed meats and salt, increase the risk of developing cancer. While others, such as fruits, vegetables and high fibre foods, can help prevent the disease."

"When most Americans are not eating a plant-based diet, and understanding that this diet is healthy and cancer-protective, that is cause for concern," said Alice Bender, MS, RDN, and AICR Head of Nutrition Programs.[10]

Study after study after study[11] has confirmed what your mother told you. Fruits and vegetables are packed with disease-preventing nutrients and compounds like fiber, carotenoids (the bright red, orange and yellow pigments in some vegetables), Vitamin C, Vitamin E, folate (a B Vitamin), selenium (an essential mineral for the body), flavonoids (powerful anti-inflammatory antioxidants), and other potent antioxidants and phytochemicals.

Phytates, another natural compound found in plant seeds (and therefore in all seeds, nuts, beans, and whole grains), has been shown through in vitro studies to suppress the development of practically all human cancer cells tested, including breast, cervix, colon, liver, pancreas, prostate, and skin cancers.[12] Healthy cells were not affected.[13] Phytates also increase the activity of your body's natural killer cells that track down and clear out cancer cells.[14]

The AICR tells us that the benefits of eating a plant-based diet is "likely to be due not only to the exclusion of meat, but also to the inclusion of a larger number and of wider range of plant foods, containing an extensive variety of potential cancer-preventive substances."[15]

Fiber is a big one. Susan Levin already told us about that. In addition to acting as a scrub brush inside our intestines, it also binds to toxins[16] such as carcinogens, excess cholesterol and estrogen, carrying them quickly through the thousands of pleated square feet in our digestive tracts, and out of our bodies. And again, fiber is found only in plant foods.

It's been shown by Yale scientists and others that breast cancer risk is lowered by 62 percent for premenopausal women who eat six grams or more of soluble fiber daily (that's about one cup of black beans), over women who eat less than four grams a day. And the risk for estrogen-receptor-negative breast tumors, which are more difficult to treat, was lowered by 85 percent for premenopausal women on a high fiber diet.[17]

Eating a lot of fiber can also help lower the risk for esophageal cancer by as much as a third,[18] and high fiber intake has been associated for years with decreased risk for colorectal cancers.[19]

Then there are whole grains and legumes. The AICR in 2007 published the most comprehensive analysis of cancer and diet ever performed, using half a million studies and nine independent scientific teams from around the world. The report that resulted was then reviewed by 21 of the leading global cancer specialists. And one of the AICR's summary recommendations to help prevent cancer is to eat whole grains and/or legumes, like beans, lentils, soybeans, split peas, and chickpeas with every single meal, every single day.[20]

A 2009 report in the journal *Food Chemistry* was "a first step towards the identification of foods endowed with the most potent chemopreventive [ability to prevent or reduce the risk of cancer] activities."

The scientists took 34 everyday vegetables like cauliflower, eggplant, carrot, radicchio, potato, romaine lettuce, garlic, and Brussels sprouts, and tested their compounds on eight different kinds of human cancer cells in petri dishes: breast, kidney, lung, pancreas, prostate, and stomach cancers, as well as brain tumors and childhood brain tumors.

The results were amazing. To take just a few examples, radishes did nothing to halt pancreatic cancer cells. But they were 100 percent successful at terminating the spread of stomach cancer cells. Likewise, orange bell peppers were helpless against stomach cancer, but were powerhouses in stopping prostate cancer cells, inhibiting that cancer by over 75 percent. Breast cancer growth was almost cut in half by beetroot, orange bell pepper, English cucumber, jalapeno, potato, and radicchio. Brussels sprouts, cauliflower, garlic, green onion, and leek went further: they totally "abolished" breast tumor cell development.[21]

Two vegetable families were particularly effective at halting cancer: cruciferous vegetables, like broccoli, Brussels sprouts, cauliflower, kale, and bok choy; and allium vegetables, like garlic, onions, scallions, leeks, and chives. "The inclusion of cruciferous and Allium vegetables in the diet," wrote the scientists, "is essential for effective dietary-based chemopreventive strategies."[22]

Garlic was the gold-medal winner of all the vegetables tested. It was the most effective fighter against breast, lung, pancreatic, prostate, stomach, and child and adult brain cancer, and second-most effective against kidney cancer, right after leeks (another Allium family member).[23]

Nor are these benefits only achieved in a petri dish.

People who ate 68 grams (about a cup) of broccoli sprouts significantly inhibited the bloodstream levels of an enzyme linked to cancerous tumor development,[24] only three hours after eating the sprouts. The broccoli sprout snack was just as effective, or even more so, than the chemotherapy agent specifically concocted to lower that enzyme.[25] Broccoli sprouts or chemo? Hard decision.

Researchers at Johns Hopkins University asked women booked for breast reduction procedures to consume broccoli-sprout juice one hour before their operations. After the surgeries, the scientists examined the breast tissue, and discovered they contained substantial accumulation of sulforaphane, the compound in cruciferous vegetables shown to have anti-cancer properties. So the vegetable juice that the women drank found its way—quickly—to areas of the body not directly in contact with the digestive system.[26]

Chlorophyll, the green pigment found in vegetables and leaves, is, like fiber, a substance that can bind to carcinogens and keep them from infiltrating our DNA.[27] In a nerve-wracking experiment, human volunteers drank a low-dose carcinogenic beverage of radioactive aflatoxin, either with or without spinach chlorophyll added. The scientists found that the spinach chlorophyll seemed to block roughly 40 percent of the carcinogenic substance.[28]

Australian researchers in 2011 zeroed in on colorectal cancer, and found that cabbage, cauliflower, broccoli, and Brussels sprouts are linked to a decreased risk for colon cancer in the middle and right side of the body, while carrots, pumpkins and apples seem to lower the risk farther down on the left side![29]

But you don't need a complicated flowchart of disease-fighting vegetables. Just eat a wide variety. Choose vegetables of different colors. As the scientists in the *Food Chemistry* study put it, eating "a diversified diet, containing several distinct classes of vegetables (and hence of phytochemicals) is essential for effective prevention of cancer."[30]

But what if the cancer seeds have already started growing? Could the protective properties of fruits and vegetables also potentially turn the deadly ship around?

In 2005, Dr. Dean Ornish, famous for demonstrating that heart disease can be reversed without drugs (more on this later), took 93 prostate cancer patients in the early stages of the disease, who had had no conventional treatment such as surgery or radiation, and divided them at random into either a low-fat plant-based diet group who also did moderate exercise such as walking and yoga, or a standard diet group. There were no other treatments involved—no radiation, surgery, or chemotherapy. Dr. Ornish and his colleagues monitored the patients for a year.

The standard measure of prostate cancer progression is elevated levels of PSA (a protein produced by the prostate gland). After a year, the PSA levels of the plant-based group had dropped—meaning their cancer was not spreading—while the standard diet group's PSA levels had risen.

The really astonishing part of the experiment happened when the scientists took blood serum from both groups and mixed them, separately, with prostate cancer cells in petri dishes.

The blood from the plant-based group inhibited the cancer growth by 70 percent. Blood from the standard diet group inhibited the growth by only 9 percent.[31] The bloodstream of the plant-based group was almost eight times more hostile to cancer growth.

"A research team at UCLA wanted to try this for women and breast cancer," Dr. Greger said, "but they didn't want to wait a whole year. They said, 'Let's see what a plant-based diet can do after two weeks, along with moderate exercise.' Before putting them on the diet, the researchers drew the blood of the women and dripped it on breast cancer cells. It killed off just a few of them.

"Two weeks later on a plant-based diet, they dripped their blood on the same kind of carpet of cancer cells, and the plant-based blood cleared off the whole plate. There was a dramatic rise in what's called apoptosis, or programmed [cancer] cell death.[32] Their bodies were somehow able to reprogram cancer cells to kill themselves."

Dr. Greger paused. "This was after just two weeks of eating a plant-based diet. What kind of blood do we want in our bodies? Do we want blood that's going to roll over when new cancer cells pop up? Or do we want blood circulating through every nook and cranny in our body with the power to slow down and stop it?"

"We already have the cure for cancer," Dr. Goldhamer said simply. "The cure for cancer is prevention."

***

I have several friends who are cancer survivors. They know, better than anyone, that cancer is not foreign to the body. The body's own mechanisms have turned against itself. And yet, in describing the disease, many of these friends used the metaphor of an alien growing inside them.

Imagine if an alien hijacked your body.

Imagine that it wants to turn you into a host for its own incubation, until it grows to maturity and becomes so malignant that it destroys you.

Do you feed the alien what it needs to become unstoppable?

Or—while strengthening yourself—do you starve it?

CHAPTER 7
WHAT IS MILK?

Milk comes from cows. We buy it in glass, plastic, or cardboard. We pour it into cups and give it to our children. It turns into ice cream, butter, yogurt, and cheese. We get our calcium from milk. Our parents, teachers, doctors, and even our government tell us it's a vital part of our diet.

But after all that, very few people have considered what milk actually is.

It is the breast milk of a cow who just had a baby.

Like humans and all other mammals, female cows produce milk only when they are pregnant or have given birth.

The milk we buy at the supermarket is a bovine bodily fluid, the sole natural purpose of which is to jumpstart the transformation of a newborn, 65-pound calf[1] into a 1,500-pound cow. That's heavier than a polar bear, the largest bear on earth.[2]

By its very nature, even the most pristine, organic, local milk from the happiest of grass-fed cows, is teeming with growth hormones, fats, IGF-1 (insulin-like growth factor 1), and female sex hormones like estrogen and progesterone.

In today's modern dairy industry, with its emphasis on industrialized profit, cows are regularly restrained on a metal device often called a "rape rack," and impregnated with a sperm gun. When the baby calf is born, the farmers separate the newborn from the mother,[3] so the calf does not drink the lucrative breast milk.

Male calves are sold for veal meat,[4] or beef.[5] Female calves are raised to replace their mothers as dairy cows. All calves kept alive are fed milk replacer—business dictates that the replacer "must be cheaper than milk otherwise you might as well feed the calf with mother's milk."[6]

Once the calf is taken away, the mother cow is hooked up to a milking machine, often alongside hundreds or even thousands of other cows.[7]

When her milk production begins to drop, a cow is brought to the rape rack to start the cycle over again.[8] Cows on modern dairy farms are milked about 300 days every year, and they are pregnant for a large portion of that time.[9]

"Modern milk is sucked off of large pregnant bovines, and the estrogen [the primary female sex hormone] content of that is very high," said Dr. Klaper. "When humans drink cow's milk, our urine flows with these estrogens. These are active mammalian estrogens, unlike the phytoestrogens in soy. This is a major factor in why little girls are going through puberty at ages 7, 8, 9, from this river of milk, ice cream, and butter that we are feeding them.[10]

"Why are American women getting so many breast lumps?" he asked. "Could it be the cheese, yogurt, and milk, filled with cow estrogens, pouring through their breast tissue?[11] The uterus is a hormone-responsive muscle, and women sprout uterine tumors.[12] The male breast is responsive to estrogens, and guys on the couch with their cheese nachos and deep-dish pizzas look down and say, 'Gee, man boobs.'[13] Gentlemen, you're eating cow estrogens on huge levels.

"There is no human on earth who needs the milk of a cow, anymore than they need the milk of a giraffe or a mouse. If I could eliminate one food substance—*any* food substance—from the American diet immediately, it would be the products made from the milk of an animal."

Dr. Popper concurs: "[I]f you're going to make an important first step that would improve your health, get the dairy out of the diet."[14]

The closer a cow is to giving birth, the more natural sex hormones are found in her milk—up to 33 times more than a non-pregnant cow. Dairy cows are pregnant for the majority of time that they are milked. Sixty to 80 percent of estrogens that we eat come from dairy products.[15]

This leads to much graver problems than man-boobs.

"People choose organic dairy because they don't want chemicals and hormones," said Dr. Barnard. "You know what? The biggest chemical factory is inside the cow. The hormones in milk affect our own hormones and can contribute to any kind of hormone related cancer: breast,[16] uterine,[17] prostate,[18] testicular,[19] ovarian.[20]"

Eating dairy has also been shown to be connected to bladder[21] and colorectal cancer.[22]

"Milk, because of what it is, makes things grow faster, and that includes cancer cells," said Susan Levin. "This is not a product even in its purest state that you want to consume."

"How much is too much?" I asked.

"A bit of anything linked with cancer, to me, is too much. We're exposed to so many carcinogens already. If you don't have to drink cow's milk—and you do not—then *don't*. Take control where you can."

"Cows' milk protein may be the single most significant chemical carcinogen to which humans are exposed," Dr. T. Colin

Campbell said in *The Guardian*.[23] Dr. Campbell was one of the lead scientists of the famous China-Cornell-Oxford Study, a massive 20-year study that found 8,000 statistically significant correlations between eating animal protein and risk of disease in 65 counties in China.[24] The *New York Times* called the study, "the Grand Prix of epidemiology."[25]

"IGF-1, Insulin-like growth factor-1," said Dr. Klaper, "is one of the most, and may well be *the* most spectacularly powerful promoter of growth in the mammalian body. It's in all mother's milk, which is a good thing. IGF-1 is a wonderful thing to give an infant animal or human.

"However, once a person is an adult, there's a lot of growth you do not want to promote. Heaven forbid there is a malignant growth in the ovaries, the prostate, or the testicles, because if you stream IGF-1 through that cancer, oh boy, you will promote its growth.[26]

"Cow's milk is full of IGF-1," Dr. Klaper continued. "Meat has it. Eggs have it. As a result, cancer is rampant in our society. Plants don't make IGF-1, and for that reason, the incidence of cancer in plant-based eaters is much, much lower."

"IGF-1 is a cancer-promoting growth hormone involved in every stage of cancer cell growth, spread, and metastases," Dr. Greger said. "Any animal protein boosts IGF-1 in the body. By reducing our animal protein consumption, we reduce our levels of IGF-1, and that reduces cancer cell growth."

Sometimes we are blind to stunningly simple things. Of course a fluid meant to stimulate rapid growth in an infant animal would stimulate the uncontrolled growth of cancer cells (and—I'm still getting over this—we're all producing tumors all the time). It's like throwing rocket fuel on a fire.

Thirty-five different hormones and 11 growth factors have been found in cow's milk, organic or otherwise.[27]

A study comparing cancer rates and diets in 42 different countries found that eating cheese and dairy products is strongly correlated with testicular cancer. The highest rates of cancer were in countries like Switzerland and Denmark, where cheese is consumed frequently, while the lowest rates were in countries like Algeria, where dairy is less common.[28]

The Physicians' Health Study, which tracked over 20,000 men over 11 years, discovered that prostate cancer risk jumped by over 30 percent in men who ate 2.5 servings of dairy a day.[29] Two to three daily servings of dairy are recommended by the federal nutrition guidelines[30] and the American Heart Association.[31]

Many, many other studies have shown powerful correlations between dairy—low-fat or otherwise—and prostate cancer,[32] the second leading cause of cancer deaths in American men.[33]

The tangible effects of dairy on prostate cancer was illustrated when scientists dripped organic cow's milk onto human prostate cancer cells in a petri dish. The cow's milk fuelled prostate cancer cell growth in fourteen experiments by over 30 percent. The scientists did the same experiment with almond milk—which inhibited the cancer growth rate by over 30 percent.[34]

Eating cheese and other dairy products is also linked to feminization in men. This is ironic, considering that men often refuse soy, as we've seen, out of fear it will take the edge off their masculinity. Yet they have no qualms about Philly cheese steaks, whey protein shakes, and three-cheese pizzas, loaded with the sex steroid hormones of a pregnant female bovine mammal.

A group of young men, ages 19-21, were asked to drink a quart of cow's milk in 10 minutes. Within the hour, their estrogen levels shot up 60 percent, while their testosterone levels plummeted dramatically.[35]

Another study was titled, "Dairy food intake in relation to semen quality and reproductive hormone levels among physically active young men." The "physically active young men" ate a large amount of cheese in particular, and regardless of their overall dietary patterns, the researchers saw a significant decline in the ability of their sperm to, uh, get around, and also a decline in the quality of their semen.[36]

Women, obviously, have different concerns. Dairy consumption in women is linked to breast cancer,[37] endometrial (uterine) cancer,[38] and ovarian cancer, among other health issues.

Over 29,000 post-menopausal women were studied over 10 years through the Iowa Women's Health Study. The women who consumed more than a single glass of milk a day had a 73 percent greater risk of developing ovarian cancer than the women who drank less than a glass of milk daily.[39]

A Swedish study followed over 60,000 women, ages 38-76, over 13 years, and found that women who consumed four or more dairy products a day *doubled* their risk for ovarian cancer, compared to women who consumed less than two dairy servings daily.[40]

The five-year relative survival rate for ovarian cancer is 45 percent,[41] meaning, on average, that 55 percent of women do not survive beyond five years of their diagnosis.

***

Take a breath and we'll go on.

Your milk could very well be radioactive.

"One of the many pollutants that come out of nuclear reactors, even when they're operating normally, is Strontium-90, an unstable radioactive element," Mike Ewall, director of Energy Justice Network, explained to Keegan and I when we met in Washington D.C. EJN is a national support network for grassroots groups fighting dirty energy and waste industry facilities.

"Strontium-90 falls on farm fields, crops, and grass," Ewall said. "Cows that eat that grass or those crops will ingest the Strontium-90, which acts like calcium in the body."

In the periodic table (remember high school chem?), strontium (Sr) is just below calcium (Ca), indicating their similar properties. Strontium-90 is the radioactive form of strontium, which in its natural state helps build healthy bones.[42]

"Because Strontium-90 is mistaken for calcium in the cow's body, it ends up in the milk," Ewall went on. "And when people eat dairy products, our bodies think it's calcium as well, so we store it in our bones. But Strontium-90 gradually breaks down, and can cause bone cancer and leukemia."

"If Strontium-90 falls out over farm fields," I said, "then shouldn't we be worried about eating vegetables?"

"You'll get a lot more exposure from dairy than you'll get from eating Strontium-90-exposed vegetables," Ewall said, "precisely because Strontium-90 acts like calcium and accumulates in milk. Our main dietary source of radioactive pollutants is in the milk supply."

"How many nuclear reactors are there in the US?" Keegan asked.

"There are 99 remaining nuclear power reactors, commercial scale, in the country," Ewall replied. "There are also research reactors on university campuses that emit radioactive pollution."

"Where are they?"

"They're scattered throughout the US. More so on the East Coast and the Midwest. Illinois is the number one state for nuclear reactors. But also, the West Coast is downwind from Japan, with their fifty-some nuclear reactors. Most of them are now shut down since the Fukushima disaster, but radiation from Fukushima is continually being found on the California coast."

Then there's dioxin.

"Any incinerators, including trash incinerators, generate some of the most toxic chemicals known to science called dioxins,[43]" Ewall said. "They're toxic at such small doses they're measured in pictograms and nanograms, which are invisible. The minutest amounts of dioxins can disrupt cells and cause health problems."

Dioxin is the toxic contaminant in Agent Orange,[44] the chemical exfoliant used in the Vietnam War. When people talk about the horrifying long-term effects of Agent Orange, they're talking about dioxin exposure.[45]

"Dioxin exposure is connected to a myriad of health problems," Ewall said, "including cancer, birth defects, diabetes, developmental disabilities, lower testosterone levels, impaired immune system, allergies, low birth weights, dental defects, loss of intelligence and learning ability, ADHD, depressed behavior, small penis size, low sperm count, delayed puberty, sexual reproductive disorders such as endometriosis, and malformed and mixed sex genitalia.[46]"

"I'm sorry, did you say... small penis size?"

There is an actual medical condition called "Micropenis" that has been scientifically shown to be associated with dioxin exposure.[47] About 1 in 200 males are diagnosed with the condition—a penis measuring 2.8 inches or less when erect.[48]

I know a lot of men who would cling to their nachos despite threats of cancer and early death, but Micropenis... that might shake them up.

Ewall waited for me to re-focus. "93 percent of our exposure to dioxins comes from eating dairy and meat products."[49]

"How does that happen?" I asked.

"It's similar to Strontium-90. Dioxins come out of incinerators and fall across farm fields. Cows eat the grass or the crops. A cow standing in the shadow of an incinerator will ingest, through the large amounts of food it eats, more dioxin in one day than it would take you fourteen years to breathe, if you were standing right next to that cow, breathing the same air. The dioxin accumulates in the cow's fat, which includes the milk and the meat. Anyone eating meat or dairy will receive that dose of dioxin."

"And dioxins are generated by any incinerator?" Keegan asked.

"That's right. There are currently about 80 trash incinerators commercially operating in the US, but there are others for medical waste, hazardous waste, and various things. Some of the worst dioxin pollution in the country has been in Pennsylvania, near Harrisburg's incinerator, which was the largest source of dioxin for many years. That's right next to the dairy region. Pennsylvania is the fourth-largest dairy state. There are also a lot of incinerators in Minnesota and Wisconsin, the largest dairy state. And it's a global problem. There are places throughout Europe, in Belgium and France for instance, where dairy producers were told they couldn't sell their dairy because dioxin contamination from incinerators is getting so high. Japan, too, has huge concentrations of incinerators."

In some ways, though, it doesn't matter where you—or dairy cows—are, in relation to dioxin-spewing incinerators.

"There's no safe place to run if you're looking to find clean animal products to eat on this planet," Ewall said. "Dioxins travel incredibly far because they're light. Incinerators in Iowa and Harrisburg, Pennsylvania were pegged in a 2000 study as the largest single contributor to dioxin contamination at eight sites in the Canadian arctic. The indigenous people there were so concerned they wrote to the mayor of Harrisburg asking him to shut down that incinerator."

"What about organic?" I asked.

"Going organic doesn't help you avoid contaminants like dioxins, Strontium-90, or mercury, because when they fall out, they don't skip the organic fields. It has nothing to do with the conventional versus the organic process. These pollutants are falling on farm fields and water bodies everywhere. It makes no difference whether you're eating dairy, chicken, fish, pork, or beef.

"How long do dioxins stay in your body?" Keegan asked.

"Dioxins have a half life of seven and a half years [the WHO estimates a dioxin half life of 7-11 years[50]]. This doesn't mean it's gone from your body in fifteen years. It takes seven and a half years for any amount of dioxin in your body to be reduced by half. If you were to stop consuming dioxin-contaminated food right now, it would take 7.5 years for your dioxin levels to be cut in half. It would take another 7.5 years for that amount to be cut in half, and so on."

Keegan and I also talked with Dr. Goldhamer about bioaccumulation.

"If you compare your typical plant-based foods, even with their various residual chemical by-products," he said, "to an equivalent number of calories of animal-based foods, the animal foods are going to be dramatically higher in toxicity, as much as 1,000 fold, depending on the circumstances."

The WHO states, "Although formation of dioxins is local, environmental distribution is global... The highest levels of these compounds are found in some soils, sediments and foods, especially dairy products, meat, fish and shellfish. Very low levels are found in plants, water and air."[51]

"If animal food is a dominant part of your life," Dr. Goldhamer said, "toxicity will be a dominant part of your life as well.

Other toxic pollutants like PCBs and organochlorine pesticide (a class of mostly banned pesticides including DDT) also accumulate in dairy and other animal products.[52] The brains of patients with Parkinson's disease have been shown to have high levels of these toxins.[53]

A meta-analysis looking at over 300,000 people found that overall dairy consumption is tied to a substantially higher risk for Parkinson's, a chronic, progressive disorder of the nervous system that causes the malfunction and death of vital nerve cells in the brain.[54] There is no cure. Scientists estimated that every cup of milk consumed daily could increase the risk for Parkinson's by 17 percent.[55]

Another study, following 7,504 men over 30 years, found a 2.3-fold increase in Parkinson's in men who consumed more than 16 ounces of milk a day, compared to those who consumed none. "Contamination of milk with neurotoxins may be of critical importance," the scientists wrote.[56] A 2013 editorial in the journal *Nutrition* was even more emphatic, stating, "The only possible explanation for this effect is the evidence of the contamination of milk by neurotoxins."[57]

And then there's the pus.

Cows today are genetically manipulated to produce 6 to 7 times more milk than cows from a hundred years ago.[58] Their bloated, overloaded udders are extremely susceptible to infection. Mastitis is an endemic disease of dairy cows.[59] The udders become inflamed, usually from bacteria like *Staphylococcus aureus*.[60] According to the USDA, about 1 in every 6 dairy cows has clinical mastitis.[61] The infection can be detected by visible abnormalities in the milk, like clots or flakes.[62] That milk is discarded, because the bacteria present a threat to food safety.[63]

But there is also subclinical mastitis, in which the udder is infected but the cow shows no symptoms. The milk from a cow with subclinical mastitis—which can affect 5 to 75 percent of cows on a farm[64]—is visibly no different from uninfected milk.[65] And it is legal for dairies to sell milk produced by cows with subclinical mastitis.[66] Many dairy cows live with chronic mastitis during their relentless cycles of pregnancy and lactation.

One of the most common ways to test for subclinical mastitis is to do a Somatic Cell Count (SCC). The higher the SCC, the more inflammation there is in the udder.[67]

Somatic cells are not pus cells, as many on the Internet claim. But the majority of somatic cells are leukocytes, or white blood cells.[68] And pus, which builds up at sites of infection and inflammation, is made up of accumulated dead leukocytes.[69] When a cow is infected with mastitis, over 90 percent of the somatic cells in her milk are the leukocytes that create pus.[70]

"Dairy products have a lot of other products associated with it, not the least of which is pus," Dr. Goldhamer told us flatly. "There are laws limiting how much pus you can have in milk and still sell it—something like 750,000 pus cells per CC.[71] Because you wouldn't want too much pus in milk. People might object. You could think of cheese as coagulated cow pus."

But the milk is pasteurized, so no worries, right?

"You may comfort yourself by thinking that the pus is pasteurized," Bob and Jenna Torres write in their book, *Vegan Freak*, "and certainly, pasteurization will prevent you from becoming ill, but you're still eating pus. Look at it like this: you could stick a dog turd in an autoclave and render it biologically harmless with significant pressure and heat. Yet, we're willing to wager that you'd not be anxious to eat it unless you have some very strange proclivities indeed."[72]

"Cheese is our number one source of saturated fat,"[73] Dr. Greger said.

I groaned. For years, I lived on what could be called a high-cheese diet. Not merely cheese every day, but cheese at every meal. "People think the number one source of saturated fat in our diet is steak or something like that," said Dr. Greger, "but no, it's dairy."

Over half the calories from most cheeses come from fat.[74] One cup of diced cheese has over 530 calories. Three hundred eighty-five of those are fat calories, including about 28 grams of saturated fat. That single cup of cheese will give you 139 percent of your recommended daily limit of saturated fat. You'll also pack away 139 mg of cholesterol and 820 mg of sodium.[75]

"There's a study going around right now saying cheese might be good for your heart," Dr. Davis said. "Guess who sponsored it? The dairy industry. They took 15 people for two weeks, and either fed them diets high in 1.5 percent milk fat, or high in cheese, or butter with no other dairy. Did they then wait to see who had a heart attack? No, they didn't look at the heart at all. They looked at the TMAO metabolite associated with heart disease and found the milk and cheese eaters had less TMAO than the butter people, and so therefore cheese is better for your heart.[76] It's utterly ridiculous.

Why didn't they include a non-dairy group? They would have had the lowest TMAO.

"Dairy is loaded with saturated fat," Dr. Davis said. "It causes inflammation, oxidative stress, vessel contractility—the clamping down of vessels. There have been many legitimate studies. A Swedish study recently caught the news because it showed that the more dairy people ate, the higher their risk of early death."[77]

Most people I know choose low-fat dairy, thinking that will give them the benefits of dairy—calcium, for instance—without the ill effects. Low-fat dairy, though, is a fraud.

What does low-fat 2 percent milk really mean? It's reassuring to people that it's 98 percent fat-free. If you divide a carton into 100 parts, and two of those little parts are fat, that's not very much, right? But you've got to understand that "98-percent fat free" refers to the *weight* of the milk, not the caloric percentage. Ninety-eight percent of a container of 2-percent milk is water weight. Two percent of the *weight* is from fat.

Now let's look at the calories. *Thirty-five percent* of calories from "low-fat, 2-percent" milk are from fat. But nobody would buy anything labeled "low-fat, 35-percent milk." It's low-fat only when you compare it to the 49 percent of calories from fat found in whole milk.[78]

McDonald's tried this in the early 1990s when it marketed its McLean Deluxe burger as 91 percent fat-free. That figure, of course, was by weight. By calories? Forty-nine percent of calories from the McLean burger were from fat.[79] Just like milk.

Things are not looking so hot for dairy consumption and our health, between the cancer acceleration, natural sex steroid hormones, natural growth hormones like IGF-1, bioaccumulation of radioactive isotopes, neurotoxins, and the most lethal component of Agent Orange, along with plain old pus, and 35-percent-fat milk masquerading as a low-fat health product.

Cue the question: *"But where will I get my calcium?"*

Here in America, calcium and milk are synonymous, just like protein and meat. It's another nursery school belief, inculcated in us as toddlers and never examined since.

As Colleen Patrick-Goudreau puts it in a lecture, "What is calcium? It's a mineral. And where are minerals found? In the ground, in the earth, in the soil. And why do cows have calcium in their milk? Because they eat the grass... [But t]hree out of four cows raised specifically for dairy are not consuming grass,[80] and so that the dairy industry can live up to the marketing claims that it's a high-calcium food, what do they do to [the cows'] feed? They supplement their feed." She pauses and looks at her audience. "You could supplement *your* feed. We'd skip a lot of problems. You don't even have to supplement your feed; you could go right to the source and get your calcium from the green leafy vegetables, the highest source of calcium."[81]

Cow's milk has 189 mg of calcium in every 100 calories. Romaine lettuce has 194 mg per 100 calories, kale has 257, tofu has 287, collard greens have 539, turnip greens 685, and bok choy has 775 mg.[82]

Milk, at 189 mg, just fell off the calcium throne. It never belonged there in the first place.

Calcium, of course, is vital for strong bones. Osteoporosis is a disease in which bones become brittle and weak,[83] and is most common in older women.[84] Doctors commonly advise post-menopausal women to consume more dairy, to build calcium stores and stave off osteoporosis.[85]

Dairy, however, does not seem to be the answer to osteoporosis. Hip fractures and osteoporosis are strongly linked. One of the world's highest rates of hip fractures belong to US women, ages 50 and up.[86] And yet Americans, on an individual basis, consume more dairy than most countries in the world.[87] The only countries with higher rates of hip fractures are in Europe, Australia, and New Zealand—where people consume even more dairy than in America![88]

I asked Dr. Barnard about osteoporosis and dairy.

"It's not entirely clear from the scientific literature that milk causes osteoporosis," Dr. Barnard said, "but it sure doesn't stop it. Harvard researchers looked at 72,000 older women, over an 18-year period, and found that the milk drinkers had zero protection from fractures.[89] Researchers who studied bone development in children found that kids who drink the most milk have zero protection from stress fractures.[90] Milk does not build strong bones."

Dr. Mills gave us the most graphic illustration of the non-essential nature of dairy.

"How tall are you?" he asked me.

"Uh…about 6-2."

He assessed me. "Okay. If I could flay all the skin off you and boil the flesh off your skeleton, all the bones in your body would weigh about 35 pounds."

I don't know if I looked as alarmed as I felt.

"A bull moose grows a full rack of antlers in three months," Dr. Mills continued, ignoring me. "They're made of solid bone. A mature bull's antlers weigh 80 pounds, more than twice the amount of your entire skeleton. That moose grows his rack of antlers while eating nothing but green, leafy plant foods."

Jane Chapman, 61, is from Washington State. She can only move painfully and slowly with a walker. When Keegan and I visited her, she told us her story.

"Not too long ago," she said, "I finally got some X-rays of my hips and back. It was severe, bilateral, osteoarthritis of the hips, and I'm scheduled for two hip replacements. That's bone on bone. It's the grinding of the joints. I can't pivot. I hold onto the walls or there's a good chance I'll fall. I use a walker. I have one of those disability parking things, but I've gotten to the point where it's easier to just stay home."

"What other conditions are you dealing with right now?" I asked.

"I'm on two different high blood pressure medicines, six asthma type medicines—even after four years of shots—and then another medicine to help take care of side effects from some of those medicines, high level anti-depressants, hormone replacement therapy, a couple of different pain meds for my back and hips, several muscle relaxants and over-the-counter anti-inflammatories. Then supplements for adrenal fatigue. I have 28 bottles of medicines and supplements that the doctors said I should take."

"According to your doctors, what are all these problems from?" Keegan asked.

"They say, 'You didn't take care of yourself,' and I got heavy, and 'It's in your genes,' or 'What do you expect? You're getting on in age.' The outlook that doctors have painted for me is, have the hips replaced, take the meds, take the joint compounds. Just manage the pain. A lifetime of trips to the pharmacy and limited mobility. I'm afraid of this hip replacement. And there's still the degenerative back stuff, my scoliosis—how many times are they going to have to take the knife to me to put things back together—and do I really want that?"

She paused.

"This summer, the kids were playing Twister and they wanted me, Grandma, to play. It wasn't going to happen. I can spin the dial. I want to do so much more than that, and I just feel very... I'm sad. Robbed. To think that this is all that's left..." Her words trailed off, disbelief and sorrow struggling on her face. "One of my daughters, she said, 'There is nothing left of you, mom.' And she was right."

CHAPTER 8

EGGS: CRACKED

The most interesting thing to me about eggs is not that the cholesterol in a single egg, eaten daily, can shorten a woman's life as much as smoking 5 cigarettes a day for 15 years (that's 27,300 cigarettes).[1] Nor is it that those who ate the most eggs in a 2012 study had two-thirds the arterial plaque of the heaviest smokers in the study, with habits comparable to a pack a day for 40 years or more.[2] Eating only 3 eggs a week was shown to substantially increase plaque build-up.

Those are pretty striking results. But the most interesting thing to me about eggs is the behavior of the egg industry, which, mirroring the two studies above, has remarkable parallels with the behavior of the tobacco industry.[3]

The egg industry has been slapped on the wrist repeatedly for decades, by institutions like the USDA, the Federal Trade

Commission (FTC), the US Court of Appeals and the Supreme Court, for "false and misleading advertising that eggs had no harmful effects on health."[4]

In 1977, the National Commission on Egg Nutrition, a major trade group, was convicted of false advertising by the US Court of Appeals and ordered to "cease and desist from disseminating any advertisement" which "represents that there is no scientific evidence that eating eggs increases the risk of heart attacks, heart disease, atherosclerosis, arteriosclerosis, or any attendant condition."[5]

The FTC has twice brought cases against Eggland's Best, Inc., in 1994 and 1996, for making "deceptive" advertising claims like:

> *"Imagine eating delicious, real, whole eggs and not raising your serum cholesterol. People did. In clinical tests of Eggland's Best eggs. They ate a dozen a week while keeping within the limits of the Surgeon General's low-fat diet. And... their serum cholesterol didn't go up."[6]*

The USDA has reminded the egg industry repeatedly that due to laws against false advertising, "you can't couch eggs/egg products as 'healthy' or 'nutritious'...Nutritious and healthy carry certain connotations, and because eggs have the amount of cholesterol they do, plus the fact that they're not low in fat, these words are problematic."[7]

This is a list of advertising claims about eggs that the USDA has told the egg industry they *cannot* use, because...they're not true:

- o "A rich source of protein"
- o "Nutritional powerhouse"
- o "Relatively low in calories"
- o "Relatively low in fat"
- o "Low in saturated fat"
- o "Eggs contribute nutritionally"
- o "Healthful"

o   "Eggs contribute healthful components"

See, under the FDA, a food can only be labeled "healthy" if it is low in saturated fat and contains 90 mg or less of cholesterol per serving.[8]

The egg scorecard on healthy: fail-fail.

But a little thing like that doesn't stop the American Egg Board (AEB).

"AEB devised an integrated, 360-degree media approach to surround moms...wherever they are," declared AEB's 2008 Annual Report.[9] The AEB newsletter, *Eggstra!*, shows a photo of a young mother and her daughter. Images of marketing tactics—TV, radio, billboards, Internet, women's magazines, parenting magazines, lifestyle magazines, and egg cartons—are arranged in a tight circle "surrounding" the pair, with arrows aiming in towards them.[10]

The crosshairs are on moms, "because they are the primary shopper, food decision maker, and meal preparer for the household."[11] In other words, mom is the gateway.

In 2014, Hellmann's Mayonnaise, which makes over $64 billion a year and is the world's largest producer of food spreads,[12] sued Hampton Creek, a small $50-million-a-year[13] start-up that makes egg-free mayonnaise. Hellmann's claimed Hampton Creek was guilty of false advertising, because you can't call something "mayonnaise" if it doesn't contain eggs. Is that like how you can't call eggs "healthy" when they aren't?

Internal AEB emails were leaked to *The Guardian*, revealing that the egg industry had been trying for months to destroy Hampton Creek, because the egg-free company, as AEB president Joanne Ivy wrote, is "a crisis and major threat to the future of the egg product business."[14]

Apparently Hampton Creek presents such a "major threat" to the egg industry that some senior AEB officials were fantasizing about murder.

"Can we pool our money and put a hit on [Josh Tetrick, Hampton Creek CEO]?" emailed one senior AEB member. "[I could]" contact some of my old buddies in Brooklyn to pay Mr. Tetrick a visit," wrote AEB's executive VP in another email.[15] Tricky thing about emails, you can't always tell when someone is joking.

This is all fascinating to me, because there would be no reason for this behavior if the egg industry had a healthy product to sell in the first place. And it seems like they know it.

But there's been a lot of media attention on research claiming eggs and cholesterol are not so bad for you after all.

"As a cardiologist actively involved in looking at people's arteries, heart disease, and heart attacks, cholesterol is still very much an issue," Dr. Joel Kahn told us. "Many egg and cholesterol studies were done in people eating diets already overloaded with animal-based fats. Their cholesterol is 230, 240—the average American cholesterol—and when you add in several eggs a week, you don't see much change.

"If you're smoking 20 cigarettes a day, smoking 19 or 21 will probably not make a profound difference to your lung cancer risk."

In 2015, a meta-analysis examined 40 studies on dietary cholesterol, ranging from 1979 to 2013. The authors found that consuming cholesterol in the diet significantly increased both the level of total cholesterol in the blood, as well as the levels of unhealthy (LDL) cholesterol.

The Guardian, in an article subtitled, "The US government has removed suggested caps on cholesterol consumption in a victory for an egg industry keen to dissociate its product from heart disease," writes:

> *"The discrepancy between research saying eggs do not have an effect on cholesterol and research saying they do might boil down to a single point....: 'Increases in LDL [unhealthy] cholesterol were no longer statistically significant when intervention doses exceeded 900 milligrams per day.'*

That's about five eggs.

Put plainly, said [Dr. J David] Spence [one of the authors of the study comparing arterial plaque in smokers and egg-eaters], the American diet already contains so much that could cause harm, it's hard to measure the effect of a single potentially unhealthy food."[16]

"An egg has about two hundred mg of cholesterol in the yolk," said Dr. Kahn. "It's also about 20 percent saturated fat. The government tells you to limit saturated fat, but we've taken our bull's-eye off cholesterol. What do you do with that information? Do you quarter the yolk? Do you eat the rim of the yolk? Or do you throw your hands up and say, 'I'm confused'? Nobody at dinnertime can separate the cholesterol from the trans fat, from the fat, from the carbs. It's a plate of food."

It's difficult to pinpoint whether it was the cholesterol or the saturated fat in eggs, or maybe the effects of both, but the Physician's Health Study found, looking at over 21,000 men over twenty years, that eating one egg a day increased the risk of dying by 23 percent.[17]

A scientific study on eggs and cholesterol in the *American Heart Journal* stated, "We found no evidence of adverse effects of daily egg ingestion on any cardiac risk factors in adults with CAD [coronary artery disease] over a span of 6 weeks."

But halfway through the report, I read this:

"Disclosures. This study was conducted with funding from the Egg Nutrition Center/American Egg Board and the Centers for Disease Control and Prevention."

Close reading of the study's tables reveal that 90.6 percent of the subjects were taking cholesterol-lowering medication.[18]

"AEB-funded research continued to provide strong evidence that eggs do not contribute to heart disease," declared the American Egg Board 2008 Annual Report.[19]

That doesn't seem right.

But regardless of funding, scientists can't just *lie* in their reports.

What can a scientist funded by the egg industry do when they're confronted with a study like one from France, showing that as the dietary fat and cholesterol content of their subjects increased, so did the fat and cholesterol in their bloodstream?[20] Or another well-designed study, published in *The Lancet* and conducted by the Harvard Medical School, which found that adding only one extra-large egg a day to the diets of healthy young vegetarians for three weeks, caused their cholesterol levels, including their dangerous LDL cholesterol, to shoot up?[21]

You can get around these inconvenient results by only measuring fasting cholesterol levels in the *morning*, seven or eight hours after the previous meal, as Dr. Greger explained to me.

Because, as the authors of the study comparing the risks of eggs and smoking wrote in an editorial, "Fasting LDL cholesterol levels… have little to do with what the patient consumed the previous day."

So if you wait an entire night to measure cholesterol, there won't be a big difference between people who had eggs for dinner and those who didn't. Pretty clever.

"Diet is mostly about the postprandial state," continues the editorial. Post-prandial means the period after eating a meal. "Dietary cholesterol increases cardiovascular risk, probably mainly because of postprandial effects: for several hours after a high-cholesterol meal there is an increase in oxidative stress, vascular inflammation and adverse effects on endothelial function, and oxidation of LDL cholesterol is increased by nearly 40 percent. Dietary cholesterol is permissive of the harmful effect of saturated fats."[22] Meaning, cholesterol in your food can make the destructive effects of saturated fat even worse.[23]

The only foods containing cholesterol are derived from animals.[24] And one of the most concentrated sources of dietary cholesterol in the US population, by far, is eggs.[25]

"How many hours are there between meals?" Dr. Greger asks in a NutritionFacts video. "Maybe four hours between breakfast and lunch? So if we had eggs for breakfast we'd get that big spike, and by lunch, start the whole cycle of fat and cholesterol in our arteries all over again. Most of our lives are lived in a postprandial state, in an after-meal state, and this shows that the amount of cholesterol in those meals—they actually used eggs in this study, so the amount of egg in our meals makes a big difference when it really matters—after we've eaten, which is where we spend most of our lives. So that's why when the Egg Board funds a study, they only measure fasting cholesterol levels the next day."[26]

"The yolk of a hen's egg is the most concentrated glom of saturated fat and cholesterol on the planet," Dr. Klaper said. "It is made to run a baby chicken for 21 days with no outside energy. It is pure fat and cholesterol. When we put that into our bloodstream, it coats our red blood cells. Our blood gets thicker and more viscous. It changes our hormone levels and raises our cholesterol levels. Two scrambled eggs for breakfast sends a wave of fat and animal protein through your bloodstream first thing in the morning."

In 2016, the average person in the US ate 263 eggs,[27] far ahead of the global average.[28] Apart from the build-up of artery-clogging plaque that can lead to cardiovascular disease, heart attacks, stroke, and death, eggs are also associated with much higher risks of heart disease and death for people who have diabetes, as well as recurrence or progression of prostate cancer.

The Physicians' Health Study, the Nurses' Health Study, and the Health Professionals Follow-Up all demonstrated that people with diabetes who eat more than one egg a day double their risk of heart disease and death, compared to people with diabetes who eat less than a single egg per week.[29]

Twice the risk of death is bad enough, but in a study from Athens, Greece, "two findings are consistent across genders and models: a striking positive association between egg intake and diabetic mortality, implying that increased daily intake by one egg (40g) *increases the risk of death overall threefold and the risk of coronary death more than fivefold.*"[30] (Italics added.)

In other words, one egg a day for people with diabetes can triple their risk of death, and quintuple their risk of dying from heart disease.

Eggs can also double the health risks for men with prostate cancer, which, if you recall, is the second most common cancer in American men.

Every 20 minutes a man in the US dies from prostate cancer, which after a year totals over 26,000—enough to fill a baseball stadium with dead men. Every year. One out of every seven American men will get prostate cancer. And while the five-year survival rate for men diagnosed while the cancer is still within the prostate is over 99 percent, the survival rate plummets to 28 percent if the cancer spreads to the bones, organs, or lymph nodes. This is why it's vital, for the nearly 2.8 million men currently living with the disease, that prostate cancer not be allowed to progress.[31]

Harvard researchers monitored about 1,300 men with prostate cancer for two years, looking for links between their diets and the progression or recurrence of their cancer.

The scientists found that men who ate even the smallest amount of eggs—less than one a day—doubled the risk of their cancer coming back or worsening, compared to men who very rarely ate eggs.[32]

This may have something to do with choline, a concentrated substance in eggs. A higher risk for prostate cancer is linked to high levels of choline in the bloodstream.[33] And the same research team from Harvard, examining almost 48,000 men in the Health

Professionals Follow-Up Study, found that "choline intake was associated with an increased risk of lethal prostate cancer." Men who ate the most choline increased their risk of dying from prostate cancer by 70 percent.[34]

Another study found that "men who consumed 2.5 or more eggs per week had an 81% increased risk of lethal prostate cancer compared with men who consumed less than 0.5 eggs per week."[35]

The thing about eggs, even if you never crack a single one, is that they're frequently hidden in items like baked goods, canned soup, artificial and natural flavoring, frosting, pasta, pretzels, and salad dressing. You can get plenty of egg in your diet without ever knowing it, especially if you're allowing yourself a "small" number of eggs per week.

The choline found in eggs, just like the carnitine found in red meat, metamorphoses into Trimethylamine[36] with the help of bacteria in the intestines of meat-eaters.[37] And Trimethylamine is oxidized in the liver to become TMAO, aka The Molecule From Hell.

A research team from the Cleveland Clinic fed their study subjects two large, hard-boiled eggs. Their TMAO blood levels jumped after eating the eggs. These were all healthy adults with no chronic illness, no active infections, and low-risk cholesterol levels.[38] All it took were a couple of eggs to flood their bodies with a toxic metabolite strongly correlated with heart attacks, strokes, and death.[39]

Eggs, like dairy, are potent little grenades of bio-accumulated contaminants. Let's just look at dioxins, the incinerator pollutants that Mike Ewall told us about. The dioxin levels in eggs[40] may be the reason why one study showed that consuming more than half an egg daily was connected to doubled or tripled risks for cancers of the breast, prostate, mouth, colon, and bladder, over people who ate no eggs.[41]

Dioxins get into chickens and eggs the same way they get into cows and their milk. It spews out from incinerators around the world and falls on crops, which are then fed to animals. A Netherlands study found a "clear linear" relationship between chicken feed containing a moderate amount of dioxins eaten by laying hens, and a rapid spike in dioxin levels of their eggs. "The current EU dioxin limit for feed cannot guarantee egg dioxin levels below the EU-limit," the scientists warned.[42]

And then there's *Salmonella*, which sickens about 1.2 million Americans every year and kills around 450.[43] Eggs are a major source of *Salmonella* poisoning.[44]

Eggs leave a hen's body through the same passage as her feces.[45] Eggs contaminated that way tend to contain *Salmonella* in the egg white.[46] Bacteria inside the hen's ovaries can also colonize an egg before the shell is formed.[47] If the ovary is infected, then the yolk tends to contain the pathogen.[48]

The largest egg recall in US history—over half a billion eggs— took place in 2010, due to a massive *Salmonella* outbreak.[49] About 1,500 people were sickened,[50] with classic *Salmonella* symptoms of bloody diarrhea, fever, cramps, and vomiting.[51] Ironically, the recall took place one month after the FDA released a 71-page "egg safety rule," hoping to prevent exactly that kind of outbreak.[52]

This was not good PR for the egg industry.

But bacteria can be cooked to death, can't it? Hard-boiled eggs are recommended as the safest cooking method, but *Salmonella* can survive even in eggs boiled for 8 minutes.[53]

The egg industry, probably sick of the bad press, decided to do a little research of their own. So the Egg Nutrition Center/ American Egg Board funded a study looking into the safest ways to cook eggs and get rid of that pesky *Salmonella*.

They most likely anticipated positive results.

But the scientists on the egg industry payroll firmly concluded that scrambled, over-easy, and sunny-side-up eggs, due to bacterial concerns, were *not safe to eat*.[54]

Now that's incredible.

CHAPTER 9
FISH: POLLUTION SPONGES

Fish is often considered the healthiest of meats. (Some people don't even think it's meat.) People who have long stopped eating red meat and poultry will still eat fish. We're told it's a great source of lean protein and Omega 3-fatty acids, which has been shown to help prevent heart disease and stroke,[1] and that fish is "brain food."[2]

I asked several doctors about fish and received a landslide of warnings.

Fish are one of the most polluted foods on the planet.[3]

"Fish have become mercury sponges," said Dr. Goldhamer. "Perhaps the biggest concern with animal products is biological concentration. When you eat an animal, or the byproducts of its body, you get a biologically concentrated dose of toxin—the animal's lifetime accumulation of toxic exposure.

"Fish have very high levels of biological contaminates. In many parts of the country they warn, 'Don't have more than so many of these fish per week'. My recommendation is to avoid all fish."

"There are so many limits on animal foods," I said. "'Don't eat too much fish,' or 'eggs,' or 'limit red meat.' Are there vegetables you need to limit?"

Dr. Goldhamer laughed. "Too much water and you can call it drowning. If you drink too much carrot juice, your skin might turn a little orange. The difference between carrots and fish is that orange skin goes away when you stop eating too many carrots. But too much mercury can kill you."

In Minamata, Japan, a plastics factory discharged industrial waste, including mercury, into the local bay for many years. Fish and shellfish were a major part of the local diet.

A strange disease began to afflict Minamata and the surrounding areas. Between 1932 and 1968, at least 50,000 people exhibited symptoms like convulsions, slurred speech, spastic limbs, loss of motor function, brain damage, paralysis, and delirium. Thousands of people deteriorated over decades and died from this mass mercury poisoning.[4]

"Welcome to the 21st century," said Dr. Klaper. "For the past 100 years, we've used our oceans as sewers. Mercury from coal power plants rains down on oceans. The pesticides and herbicides we pour on our fields to raise corn and soybeans for flesh production eventually find their way into the oceans. Fish are eaten by bigger fish, which are eaten by bigger fish, and the amount of mercury, pesticides and herbicides in their flesh is shocking. Mercury poisons the brain and kidneys. The pesticides and herbicides have estrogenic and cancer-promoting properties. For this reason alone I would not eat fish."

"What about farmed fish?" I asked.

"When you pen thousands of salmon in a cage," he answered, "it's an ecological and health disaster. They're raised in confinement, like chickens and pigs, and the fish get fungal and bacterial infections.

They get sea lice. You have to feed them antifungals, antibiotics, and these substances accumulate in the flesh.

"Salmon are carnivorous animals," Dr. Klaper pointed out. "Farmed salmon are fed wild-caught fish, along with grains sprayed with pesticides, herbicides, and antibiotics. This organic material is deposited into the salmon cages, and the salmon then generate enormous clouds of nitrogen-heavy waste that accumulate around the fish farms and suck up oxygen, turning the surrounding ocean into dead-zones."

Dr. Davis used to be a fish-eating vegetarian. "I cut out the meat because the science shows the meat is bad for you, but the fish looked okay, so I kept eating it," he told us. "But I've got a lab in my office—my mercury level was through the roof at 14. It's supposed to be zero. I stopped eating fish. Now my mercury level is zero. I prefer it that way."

Dr. Davis is lucky he stopped in time. Richard Gelfond, the CEO of Imax, is a high-powered executive who often ate fish for lunch and dinner as part of a low-calorie, low-cholesterol diet. One day, while running, he suddenly felt he was about to fall over. He had also been experiencing baffling symptoms like numb lips and tingling feet. Gelfond consulted doctors from one coast to the other. No one could help him, despite a battery of tests. His symptoms got worse.

"It got to the point where I really couldn't cross the street," Gelfond told CBS News. "I had to hold my wife's hand."

A neurologist finally asked Gelfond if he ate a lot of fish. A mercury blood test was ordered. Gelfond's mercury levels were 13 times higher than the level considered safe.

"I never suspected it was caused by all of those tuna steaks, swordfish tacos, sushi lunches, and other fish meals I was eating as part of what I thought was a healthier diet," Gelfond told *Consumer Reports*.

Over a decade has gone by since his mercury poisoning diagnosis. "I am still probably only 75 percent of what I was before,"

Gelfond said. "I can't run, for example. I assume I am never going to be able to do the things I did before."[5]

Mike Ewall, who told us about Strontium-90 and dioxins in dairy, also warned us about fish.

"The largest concentrations of dioxins and other toxic pollutants in food were found in farm-raised fish, because they're fed meat," Ewall said. "They're at the top of the food chain. Mercury, once it hits a water body, turns into methylmercury, which loves to accumulate in fatty tissue. Mercury climbs up the food chain. It's the same process as dioxins and related chemicals like PCBs."

PCBs were once used as coolants and lubricants in electric equipment. Like dioxins and mercury, they're stored in animal fat,[6] and have no taste or smell.[7] General Electric dumped about 1.3 million pounds of PCBs into the Hudson River between 1946 and 1977, when they were finally banned.[8]

PCBs are tremendously concentrated in the tissues of fish, our primary source of PCB exposure.[9] You'd have to drink water from the Great Lakes for 100 years to build up the same PCB levels you'd get from eating half a pound of salmon or trout from those waters.[10]

PCB exposure in humans has been linked to higher rates of cancers of the skin, liver, gall bladder, biliary tract, gastrointestinal tract, brain,[11] and breast.[12]

In 2003, independent lab tests found that 70 percent of farmed salmon from supermarkets in San Francisco, Washington, D.C., and Portland, Oregon had PCB levels "that raised health concerns." Sixty percent of the fish tested were so contaminated they would be unsafe to eat more than once a month. There are roughly 23 million Americans who eat salmon more than once a month.[13]

The same tests showed that farmed salmon may be the most PCB-contaminated protein source in the United States.[14] Nevertheless, the farmed salmon industry persists in saying that all kinds of salmon can be safely enjoyed more than once a week, citing outdated contamination limits from the FDA.[15]

Here's another simplistic dietary equation we've been taught: Omega 3s = Fish. Just like Protein = Meat, and Calcium = Dairy, this one is false.

"What's good about fish is the Omega-3s," Dr. Davis said. "For a fish to get Omega-3, it needs to eat algae. Algae are the true source of Omega-3s. But now we're eating farmed fish, which grow in these big tanks, get sea lice, are loaded with PCBs, dioxins, and other chemicals, and don't contain natural Omega-3s because they're no longer eating algae."

Dairy cows, too, used to graze, getting calcium from the earth. Now they're fed grain and calcium supplements. Same system.

Instead of eating fish, "You can go to the source," Dr. Goldhamer said. "You can supplement with an algae-based product, or eat plant-based sources of Omega-3 fatty acids, like ground flax seeds," (available in convenient, ready-to-sprinkle packages), "walnuts, and dark green vegetables."

All green, chlorophyll-rich vegetables contain Omega 3s in their chloroplasts.[16] Canola oil, pumpkin seeds, soybeans and soy products like tofu and tempeh also offer Omega-3s. No mercury, dioxins, PCBs, antibiotics, or sea lice medication included.

"Sick populations" is a brilliant concept in preventive medicine.

In a "sick population," bad health is so widespread that the perception of "health" is completely skewed. Studies done within a "sick population" often show that what should be called ill health is "normal" only because everyone is sick.[17]

Here's an example:

"There is plenty of evidence that people who eat fish regularly are less likely to have cardiovascular disease," states the American Heart Association.[18]

Let's unpack that statement.

The saturated fat in your diet can raise your cholesterol dramatically, leading to fatty plaque build-up in the arteries.[19] When the plaque ruptures, a blood clot can form on the surface of the plaque, inside the artery.[20] That clot can grow until it mostly or completely obstructs the blood flow, leading to a heart attack or stroke.[21] Almost all heart attacks and strokes are caused by blood clots.[22]

Here's where the fish come in. The Omega-3 fatty acids in fish help reduce blood clotting. If you are part of our country's "sick population" eating the standard American diet, and your arteries are already congested with plaque, putting you at risk for forming dangerous blood clots, then yes, one or two servings of fish per week can help protect you, to a small degree, against your high-risk diet.[23]

But if we began eating plant-based, another reality would emerge. Our arteries would be clean and smooth on the inside. And for a truly *healthy* population, eating fish wouldn't matter[24]—apart from getting a juicy morsel of PCBs, dioxins, mercury, and other concentrated toxins with every bite.

If everyone in the country smoked a pack of cigarettes a day, you could say, "Those who use a bronchodilator drug are less likely to suffer from the symptoms of emphysema."[25] Bronchodilators would become a health item. Like fish.

And after all that, the high mercury content in fish may outweigh any protective benefits. Fish polluted with mercury—and 84 percent of fish contain unsafe levels[26]—have been shown to *heighten* the risk of heart attacks.[27] Ironic.

Fish oil is the country's third most popular supplement, after vitamins and minerals.[28] Americans buy into the fish oil industry, which is projected to grow to $1.7 billion in 2018,[29] because again, they believe fish oil will help prevent heart disease.[30]

"But there is one big problem," wrote the *New York Times* in 2015. "The vast majority of clinical trials involving fish oil have found no evidence that it lowers the risk of heart attack and stroke."[31]

Dr. Andrew Grey, from the University of Auckland in New Zealand, compiled results from 24 rigorous, well-designed studies on fish oil, published in the world's most prestigious medical journals between 2005 and 2012. Most of them looked at the ability of the supplement to prevent heart disease in high-risk groups. All the studies, save two, found that fish oil had no more benefit than a placebo.[32]

This information apparently didn't get out to the public, as global sales of fish oil soared by over 100 percent from 2005-2012.[33]

Science once indicated possible heart-protective benefits from fish. In 1989, researchers worked with over 2,000 Welsh men who had suffered a heart attack. Some men were asked to eat more oily fish. And over the next two years, that group was 29 percent less likely to die.

But in 2003, some of the same scientists conducted a follow-up. This time they looked at 3,000 Welsh men with angina (chest pain caused by heart disease) and asked some of them to either eat oily fish or take fish oil supplements. This time, the fish-eating group— particularly the fish oil group—was more likely to die. "The excess risk [of cardiac death] was largely located among the subgroup given fish oil capsules," wrote the scientists.[34]

Numerous studies have been published recently showing no protective benefits, or unclear benefits at best, from fish oil against heart attacks and strokes.[35]

Dr. Gianni Tognoni, the lead author of one of these studies, examining 12,000 people, told the *New York Times*, "I think that the era of fish oil as a medication could be considered over now."[36]

But as Peter Whoriskey of the *Washington Post* writes, "While the persistent popularity of fish oil may reflect the human weakness for anything touted as a life-extending elixir, it also reflects that, even among scientists, diet notions can persist even when stronger evidence emerges contradicting them."[37]

"Most of the fat in fish is not Omega 3," Dr. Barnard told us. "It's a mixture of saturated fat and various kinds of unsaturated fat that do nothing good for you. Typical Atlantic salmon is 40 percent fat.[38] It's like a sponge filled with grease. That's one of the reasons why people who really tuck into fish tend to get heavy.[39] It's also part of the reason why fish eaters have more diabetes compared to people who follow a totally plant-based diet.[40]"

I thought of animals who live on a fish-based diet: seals, walruses, whales, penguins. A thick layer of blubber for these animals is a good thing. For human beings, not so much.

Fish protein also increases blood cholesterol in the same way that beef, chicken, and pork do. In fact, if you compare calories, fish is higher in cholesterol (50 mg cholesterol/100 calories) than pork (24 mg/100 calories), beef (29 mg/100 calories), or chicken (44 mg/ calories).[41]

And there is new evidence from UC San Diego's Scripps Institution of Oceanography that environmental pollutants in fish are not only poisonous in and of themselves, but actually inhibit the human body's natural ability to eject dangerous contaminants.

Humans, along with almost all other animals and plants, possess a cellular protein called P-gp. It binds to foreign chemicals and expels them from the cell. Scientists found that 10 common pollutants in wild-caught tuna hindered the capacity of P-gp to protect the cells of the body, by actually attaching themselves to P-gp, causing it to malfunction. The pollutants then enter the cells freely, sort of like a gang of violent drunks flooding into a bar after a couple of them have handcuffed themselves to the bouncer, dragging him to the floor.[42]

In the 1970s, two Danish investigators, Hans Olaf Bang and Jørn Dyerberg, gave birth to something called "The Inuit Paradox." The Inuit, living in Arctic regions, traditionally survived on large amounts of fish, along with meat from animals like caribou, walrus, and whales, with very few plants.[43]

Bang and Dyerberg published a series of studies linking the high-fat, high-protein diet of the Inuit (called Eskimos then) to a low rate of heart disease.[44] The Inuit Paradox asks, "How can a people living on meat and blubber have no heart disease and enjoy such robust good health?"[45]

The short answer is, they can't.

"These hardy people survived living at the edge of the nutritional envelope, but not in good health," Dr. John McDougall writes.[46]

But scientists and doctors have cited the Bang and Dyerberg studies for decades.[47] They're the basis for nutritional recommendations that persist to this day ("Consume fatty fish regularly!" "Take your fish oil!"), but no one had thoroughly examined their findings until 2014. The Inuit Paradox, like a non-vegetarian Frankenstein's monster, had come to roaring life, rampaging around for decades, despite its parts being put together all wrong.

In 2014, a Canadian research team, led by Dr. George Fodor of the University of Ottawa Heart Institute, took a closer look at Bang and Dyerberg's scientific methods. Their findings were published in the *Canadian Journal of Cardiology.*

Fodor and his team found a couple of problems.

"[Bang and Dyerberg] actually never measured the frequency of heart disease in [Inuit]," Dr. Fodor told the CBC. "They relied upon some [public health records] in Greenland, and also relied on hearsay. People told them that [heart disease] was very rare. So this is very soft, from the point of view of science."[48]

The Bang and Dyerberg studies were based on speculation.

The Danish researchers only studied the tiny town of Uummannaq, population 1,300. It's roughly 2.3 percent of Greenland's population. Some of the Uummannaq settlements are very remote, with the nearest medical facilities over 100 miles away.[49]

This becomes particularly significant when you realize that Bang and Dyerberg's findings depended heavily on mortality statistics from Greenland's chief medical officer. As the Canadian research team wrote:

> *[At the time of Bang and Dyerberg's studies,] 30 percent of the total population lived in outposts and small settlements where no medical officer was stationed...*
>
> *Thus, 20 percent of death certificates were completed without a doctor having examined the patient or the body...there was a specific concern with mortality data and hospital admission statistics in Greenland, because doctors had limited diagnostic facilities and the study population was widely scattered with few possibilities of communication during certain seasons. Therefore, the reported data are likely an underestimation of the true magnitude of the disease in this area.*[50]

In 1986, a decade after Bang and Dyerberg's studies, only one in seven people in Greenland died in a medical facility properly equipped to verify whether heart disease was the cause of death.[51]

The Canadian team also reviewed 40 years of new medical evidence, finding that "Eskimos have a similar prevalence of CAD [coronary artery disease] as non-Eskimo populations, they have excessive mortality due to cerebrovascular strokes, their overall mortality is twice as high as that of non-Eskimo populations, and their life expectancy is approximately 10 years shorter than the Danish population."[52]

An earlier study from 2003, led by a highly experienced scientist from the National Institute of Public Health in Greenland, examined numerous autopsy studies, finding that heart disease was indeed prevalent among the Inuit, even among the young.[53]

Yet decades later, Bang and Dyerberg's studies are cited repeatedly as "proof" that, thanks to their fish-heavy diets, the Inuit have very little heart disease. Dr. Fodor and his colleagues gently hypothesize that this may be "an example of confirmation bias." In other words, if a particular piece of data bolsters your belief, you are far less likely to examine it thoroughly. The Canadians also noted "a trend of applying less rigorous standards of scientific evidence when reporting about non-pharmacological (i.e. lifestyle) interventions."[54] Translation: if expensive drugs and invasive medical procedures are not involved, then soft science is good enough.

Heart disease among the Arctic tribes dates back at least 2,000 years. In 2013, mummified bodies from the Aleut,[55] another polar people who lived on fish and meat, were examined using whole body CT scans. The mummies had significant hardening of the arteries in their hearts, brains, arms, and legs.[56]

Two Inuit women, one in her 20s and one in her 40s, were frozen for 500 years before being freed from the ice, *National Geographic* reported. Scientists found they both had advanced osteoporosis (weak, brittle bones) as well as widespread clogging of the arteries. The researchers noted that these conditions were "probably the result of a heavy diet of whale and seal blubber."[57]

Fish is a highly acidic protein, which can lead to the formation of kidney stones and osteoporosis.[58] This appears to play itself out in the Inuit population. Inuit over the age of 40 have a 10 to 15 percent greater loss of bone mineral density compared to non-Inuits. A 1974 study examining 107 elderly Inuit showed that "Aging bone loss, which occurs in many populations, has an earlier onset and greater intensity in the Eskimos."[59]

The Arctic peoples, whose diet puts them at the top of a contaminated food chain, carry an enormous toxic burden. The toxins trapped in the fat of the animals they eat are transferred directly to the fat on their own bodies.

The fatty tissues of Arctic marine mammals contain concentrations of pollutants 8 to 10 times higher than animals elsewhere. This corresponds to toxin levels 8 to 10 times higher not only in the bodies of the Inuit, but in the breast milk of Inuit mothers, with PCB milk levels five to ten times higher than women in southern Canada.

The levels of contamination are "so extreme that the breast milk and tissues of some Greenlanders could be classified as hazardous waste," according to BlueVoice, an ocean conservation group. The Inuit, due to their diet, are the most intensely concentrated human packages of environmental toxins on earth.[60]

The Inuit people have survived for thousands of years in one of the harshest climates on our planet. For thousands of years, they ate food forged of necessity and ingenuity. But serious health consequences come with that diet.

There is no Inuit Paradox. There is only a simple truth, articulated in a quote by Francis Bacon, which Dr. Fodor and his team, after deflating the Bang/Dyerberg studies, present in their report:

"Man prefers to believe what he prefers to be true."

CHAPTER 10
BLOOD VESSEL DISEASE: THE TREE OF LIFE

Heart disease, for those who have never faced it, can seem a little boring. It doesn't have the strange terror that cancer can induce. It appears to be some kind of plumbing problem.

Heart disease = Aging runs another cultural assumption. It's comforting to put the blame on something none of us can control. Grandpa's got a bad heart—the old ticker's running down. No big deal.

In Joan Didion's *The Year of Magical Thinking*, the reality of "a sudden massive coronary event" is far more honest. Didion and her husband John sat down to dinner one evening in their apartment, as they had for years:

> I only remember looking up. His left hand was raised and he was slumped motionless. At first I thought he was making a failed joke...
>
> I remember saying *Don't do that.*

116

When he did not respond my first thought was that he had started to eat and choked... I remember the sense of his weight as he fell forward, first against the table, then to the floor. In the kitchen by the telephone I had taped a card with the New York-Presbyterian ambulance numbers...in case someone in the building needed an ambulance.

Someone else.

Life changes fast.
Life changes in the instant.
You sit down to dinner and life as you know it ends.[1]

***

My dad didn't die from his life-threatening heart problems. He was one of the lucky ones. My mom, my sister, and I were lucky too—we didn't lose him.

For most Americans, the first indication they have heart disease may be the heart attack that kills them. Death, for these people, happens within an hour of the first symptom.[2]

Cardiovascular disease is the leading cause of human death on the planet. Over seventeen million people are killed by heart attacks, strokes, and other cardiovascular events every year. By 2030, that number is predicted to swell above 23.6 million. In the US, one person dies every 40 seconds from cardiovascular disease. And it's not just men. Heart disease is the top cause of death for women. Cardiovascular disease kills more people than all forms of cancer combined.[3]

These are almost entirely preventable deaths.

"You can identify heart disease years before the first chest pain," Dr. Joel Kahn told Keegan and I, "or the first heart attack, or God forbid, the first dropping dead. We can save so much pain for individuals and loved ones. Very strong data from the past fifteen years shows that a certain lifestyle drops your risk of heart attack by about 85 percent."

"Eighty-five percent?" I echoed with disbelief. Like diabetes and cancer, my family's heart disease has been heavy on my shoulders since I was a teenager.

"Yes," said Dr. Kahn. "When I find individuals with silent early heart disease—no symptoms—who have no clue what they're walking around with, I tell them about Vitamin L: Lifestyle, the secret to avoiding chronic disease. Not smoking; maintaining a healthy weight; exercising. And what also comes out constantly from the scientific data is, 'If you're not getting 5 or 6 servings of fruits and vegetables every day, you're denying yourself the greatest protection from cardiovascular disease.'"

I have been awed over and over, while speaking to these doctors and health professionals, by the human body and the complex, intuitive processes within us—especially the interfacing of our bodies with the food we eat. There are ingenious systems at work that most of us are oblivious to.

"Cardiovascular disease," Dr. Esselstyn explained to Keegan and I, "has its inception when you injure the endothelium, that delicate single layer of cells that lines the innermost wall of our arteries.

"The endothelium makes nitric oxide. Nitric oxide is the strongest vasodilator—a substance that opens blood vessels—in the body. When you climb stairs, the arteries to your heart and your legs widen because of nitric oxide. Nitric oxide prevents our artery walls from becoming thickened, stiff and inflamed, and protects us from high blood pressure. And—this is key—a normal level of nitric oxide will protect you from ever developing arterial blockages. Every person with cardiovascular disease has thoroughly injured the capacity of their endothelial cells to make nitric oxide—they can no longer make enough to protect themselves.

"Now," he went on, "if you stop consuming every last smidge of any nutrient that will further injure your endothelial cells, *they recover*. As they recover, they make more nitric oxide. As you make more nitric oxide, the disease is halted. We've often seen striking evidence of disease reversal.

"When endothelial cells are beaten down, not only are they not making enough of the vasodilator nitric oxide, they also begin to make vaso*constrictors*, which narrow the blood vessels. Arteries, on plant-based nutrition, stop making the bad vasoconstrictors and start making the good vasodilator. With cardiovascular disease, all the blood vessels are diseased—not necessarily with plaque, but because the endothelial cells have been so injured they can't make this wonderful vasodilator to revive their health.

"But suddenly," he continued, "when these thousands of blood vessels once again start making nitric oxide, they all dilate. Even a tiny increase in diameter leads to a huge increase in blood flow. That happens throughout the entire vascular tree in the body. That's what makes these people suddenly feel so much better."

It sounded faintly miraculous. I loved Dr. Esselstyn's image of the "vascular tree in the body." I could picture the branching blood vessels, from the tube-like aorta to the tiniest capillaries only one cell thick.[4]

"People start to feel better, even within just a few weeks of eating a plant-based diet," said Dr. McMacken. "Are those blockages dissolving right away? No, it's because you're removing the foods that cause inflammation in your body, that promote cholesterol deposits in your blood vessels. You're removing foods that interact with your gut bacteria to make more toxic substances, like TMAO. And you're taking in antioxidants, phytonutrients, foods that further reduce your blood pressure and cholesterol, and help your blood vessels heal so they function properly.

"My own experience with patients," she recalled, "and the studies also show, that when people adopt a fully plant-based diet, their cholesterol levels plummet within a few days. If you do blood tests after a couple weeks, there are dramatic improvements. By the same token, after several days of eating animal products, you can actually see inflammatory markers and cholesterol rising. Within just a few days."

***

Before World War II, the death rate in Norway from circulatory diseases was steadily rising. Then in 1940, the Nazis invaded. The Germans confiscated the country's livestock, forcing Norwegians to live on grains, fruits, and vegetables. Almost instantly, the number of deaths from heart attack and stroke plunged. It was one of the most dramatic mass reversals of heart disease in history. But in 1945, with the end of the war, the Norwegians recovered their farm animals. They got their meat, milk, and eggs back. And they got their strokes and heart attacks back, too.[5]

Atherosclerosis, the medical term for plaque accumulation in artery walls, is ground zero for many heart attacks and strokes. *Athera* in Greek means "gruel,"[6] while *atheroma* in medical Latin means "encysted tumor."[7] *Sclirosis* in Medieval Latin is "a hardness, hard tumor."[8]

This hardened gruel on artery walls is made up of many things, primarily cholesterol, fat, cellular waste, calcium, and clotting material.[9] High blood cholesterol levels can powerfully increase your risk of developing atherosclerosis and heart disease.[10]

And what causes high blood cholesterol levels? According to the National Heart, Lung, and Blood Institute of the National Institutes of Health, eating foods containing cholesterol (like eggs, cheese, and meat), saturated fat (meat, dairy, fried and processed foods), and trans fat (fried and processed foods) will do the trick. Eating the saturated fat found predominantly in animal protein will raise your LDL (bad) cholesterol levels more than anything else in your diet.[11]

Now let's go to North Karelia, Finland.

Early in the 1970s, Finland had the highest death rate on the planet from cardiovascular disease.[12] In one distressingly ordinary example, 38-year-old Seppo Holttinen, a svelte, blond father of three who loved to dance, crumpled on the dance floor and died of his third heart attack. Holttinen's father, one month earlier, was also killed by a heart attack.[13]

Seppo Holttinen lived and died in North Karelia, a Finnish region where 1,000 heart attacks occurred every year in a population of 180,000. The local diet was loaded with pork and dairy, especially butter,[14] fatty milk, and cream.[15] Over half the men also smoked.[16] Fifty percent of the heart attacks struck men younger than 65, and 40 percent led to death, despite the fact that most men were getting plenty of physical labor as loggers and farmers.[17]

The situation became so severe that the Finnish government stepped in. In 1972 the North Karelia Project, a national pilot program aimed at halting cardiovascular disease by reducing cholesterol, lowering blood pressure, and cutting smoking, was launched.[18]

Dr. Pekka Puska was director of the Project, going on to become WHO's director for Non-communicable Disease Prevention.[19] He and his small team must have felt like a crew in a rowboat charged with reversing an ocean liner, bearing down on them at full steam.

"The whole environment had to change," Puska said. "The food industry, restaurants, cafeterias, supermarkets."[20]

An immense cultural overhaul was required.

Puska and his staff doggedly spread their message—replace meat with vegetables, butter with vegetable oil, and cut back dramatically on smoking and salt—at churches, schools, community centers, supermarkets, and town meetings. The North Karelian community, thick with dairy farms, was not happy at first. The cold climate also meant that fruits and vegetables frequently had to be imported, a prospect that met with considerable resistance from people who had survived economically on milk from their cows and meat from their pigs.[21]

The North Karelia Project needed help. So they went in, as Puska described it, "boots deep in the mud."[22]

The Project enlisted the powerful help of the Martha Organization, a women's group. Together they hosted hundreds of "Parties of Long Life," Sunday gatherings where families could listen to talks on the whys and hows of replacing meat with vegetables, and the importance of cutting back on salt and smoking. Recipes adding vegetables to traditional dishes were handed out, and the families were served the new, healthier versions. North Karelian stew, originally made with water, fatty pork, and salt, got a makeover, with rutabagas, potatoes, and carrots swapping out some of the pork. The results were delicious and popular—the new version was dubbed "Puska's Stew."[23]

The North Karelia Project was a true grassroots movement. Puska recruited 1,500 ambassadors from numerous villages, educating and urging them to speak to their neighbors.[24]

Things began to turn around. Dr. Puska persuaded bread companies to reduce salt and use vegetable oil instead of butter.[25] He also convinced the local sausage maker to cut down on salt and use mushroom filler instead of pork fat.

"The sausage industry said in the beginning they couldn't make the sausage with lower salt," said Dr. Aulikki Nissinen, who worked with Puska. "Somehow they managed it when people started to demand it."

Sausage sales went up.

To deal with the fruit shortage, the Project worked with cooperatives to gather and freeze the berries that grew for a short time in the region.

Puska and his team also swayed lawmakers and businesses to provide smoke-free workplaces.[26]

Cholesterol-lowering competitions sprang up between towns. Winning towns received cash and prizes like new bicycle paths. Cafeteria chefs collected unused salt and displayed it proudly in enormous glass jars. Puska and his team even appeared regularly on a proto-reality TV show that followed people as they changed their lifestyles. The country was riveted. The show ran for 13 years, and 25 to 50 percent of the country tuned in during any given season.[27]

After five years, the North Karelia Project expanded to all of Finland. Food-labels were changed to make it easier for Finns to find low-fat, low-sodium foods. School cafeteria menus were overhauled. Dairy subsidies were dropped, though dairy farmers were encouraged to produce canola oil from rapeseed as a butter replacement.[28]

The North Karelia Project was a stunning success. Death from cardiovascular disease in North Karelia plummeted by 73 percent, and by 65 percent throughout Finland, over the 25 years of the Project.[29]

"The Finns have a very pragmatic, non-ideological approach to life," said Dr. Derek Yach, director of the Rockefeller Foundation's program on global health, who worked with Dr. Puska at WHO. "They see a problem and they don't have a big long debate about what's the philosophical reason or individual responsibility. They recognized that these lumberjacks were dropping dead and that it was because their food was not optimal."

"Heart disease need never occur," Dr. Greger told us. "There are millions living in rural China, rural Africa, eating traditional plant-based diets where heart disease is almost non-existent. When doctors like Nathan Pritikin, Dean Ornish, and Caldwell Esselstyn put people with end stage heart disease on the diet that these heart-disease-free populations were eating, hoping to slow the disease, something amazing happened. Arteries were opening up without drugs, without surgery. Our bodies can bring us back towards health if we stop damaging ourselves at every meal.

"If you whack your shin on a coffee table," Dr. Greger continued, "it will get red and swollen. If you stand back and let your body's healing properties work, you'll be fine. But what if you whacked your shin three times a day, every day, at breakfast, lunch, and dinner? It would never heal. You'd say to your doctor, 'My shin hurts,' and your doctor would whip out his or her pad—'No problem, I'm trained for this'—and write you a painkiller prescription. You'd resume whacking your shin three times a day, but boy, does it feel better with the pain pills. Thank god for modern medicine."

Nathan Pritikin, mentioned by Dr. Greger, was actually an inventor, who ate 3 eggs every morning and a pint of ice cream after dinner. He loved butter and bowls of whipped cream. He was diagnosed with substantial coronary heart disease at the age of 41. His cardiologists gave him the textbook advice of the day: no exercise, no stress, no exertion. But Pritikin noticed in his own research that, as in Norway, heart disease dropped dramatically during World War II, despite the considerable stress. He also noticed that indigenous cultures eating mostly vegetarian diets had very little heart disease. Against the advice of his doctors, who told him flat out that he couldn't control his cholesterol, he embarked on a low-fat, plant-based diet.

Within 3 years of his diagnosis, an electrocardiogram showed that his heart disease was gone. And for the next 25 years, he helped thousands of other people achieve the same results. When Pritikin died, his autopsy revealed arteries completely free of heart disease.[30]

Dr. Dean Ornish in 1990 published a landmark study, "The Lifestyle Heart Trial," in *The Lancet*, the most prestigious medical journal in the world. Ornish and his research team put people with heart disease on a low-fat, plant-based diet, along with a program of moderate exercise, stress management, group support, and no smoking. They found that "comprehensive lifestyle changes may be able to bring about regression of even severe coronary atherosclerosis after only 1 year, without use of lipid-lowering drugs."[31] No drugs, no surgery.

"[There's] a cartoon," Dr. Ornish told the *Washington Post*, "of doctors busily mopping up the floor [around] a sink overflowing without also turning off the faucet. And it's a great metaphor—that if you don't turn off the faucet, if you don't treat the underlying cause, even if you mop up the floor, even if you do a bypass graft or put a stent in, you're not changing the underlying condition that led to it and so more often than not, those clog up as well...when people get put on cardiac drugs or cholesterol-lowering drugs... when the patient says, 'How long do I have to take this?' And what does the doctor say? 'Forever,' right? How long do I have to mop the floor? Forever. Well, why don't I just turn off the faucet?"[32]

But that's not how our medical system works.

"Preventive medicine as it exists today in America typically revolves around secondary prevention," said Dr. Mills. "Mammograms, colonoscopies—we're trying to detect diseases after they've developed. What we need is true primary prevention, in which we reduce the risk of developing disease in the first place.

"Take heart disease. We have a business of bringing people in after they've had a heart attack, doing the catheterization, putting in a stent to open up the blood vessels, the coronary artery bypass graft where we crack your chest open, take veins from various parts of your body and re-route the circulatory system to your heart. We also know that a plant-based diet significantly reduces or eliminates the risk of developing heart disease at all. Which is the better approach?"

Building on the work of Pritikin, Ornish, and his own pioneering efforts, our friend Dr. Caldwell Esselstyn published a startling study in July 2014.[33]

"We worked with 198 patients," he told us. "To show you how sick they were, 119 had already had a bypass or a stent. Another 27 were told they'd have to get bypasses or stents. After they went through our program, they didn't need them. Of the people with significant heart disease who adhered to our plant-based program over the next 3.75 years, 99.4 percent avoided any further cardiac event. Of the 21 patients who didn't stick with our program, 62 percent had progressive cardiac events."

"Wait," I said. "Only 0.6 percent of the people who stayed with the plant-based diet had any more heart problems? But 62 percent of the people who didn't follow the plant-based diet had more heart attacks and other issues?"

"That's right," nodded Dr. Esselstyn. "Heart disease is nothing more than a toothless paper tiger that need never exist. And if it does exist, it need never progress. Coronary artery heart disease is a completely benign, food-borne illness."

The diet that Dr. Esselstyn used in his study was simple: whole grains, legumes, lentils, fruits and vegetables, along with a multivitamin, a B_{12} supplement, and flax seed meal for essential fatty acids. There were no added oils or processed foods with oils, nor was there meat, poultry, dairy, sugary foods/drinks, avocados, nuts, or excess salt. Unlike Dr. Ornish's study, exercise, meditation, yoga, or psychosocial support were not required.[34] It was all about the food.[35]

"Do people ever say your approach is too severe?" Keegan asked Dr. Esselstyn.

"A doctor in Texas told me that," he laughs. "He said, 'I think your approach is extreme, though I do think it works. I'm 38. I don't have vascular disease. Why shouldn't I eat what I want on the weekends?'

"I said, 'You can eat whatever you want, but let's look at the data. The autopsies of people who die of accidents, homicides, and suicides between the ages of 17 and 34 show they're already loaded with cardiovascular disease. You're 38, so you're loaded with cardiovascular disease. Not yet enough for that first cardiac event. You want to continue destroying your endothelial cells for 104 days out of every 365. I don't think that's very smart. You may postpone your heart attack until you're 65 instead of 55. You may delay your erectile dysfunction, you may delay your dementia, but you are still destroying your endothelial cells, and your disease is going to progress.'"

"What did he say to that?" I asked.

"Not much."

"Erectile dysfunction is related to heart disease?"

"For males, the canary in the coal mine is often erectile dysfunction," Dr. Esselstyn said. "The penile artery is tiny compared to the coronary artery going to the heart, so not infrequently, before somebody ever comes down with symptoms of heart disease, they're going to find they can no longer raise the flag. Yet all is not lost. When I've counseled somebody for heart disease, perhaps ten or eleven months later, I'll often get a phone call. 'Dr. Esselstyn? This is Mr. So-and-So. I'm wondering if I don't owe you another check, because recently something has...come up again.'"

Just as with dioxins in dairy causing Micropenis (you do remember Micropenis, don't you?), erectile dysfunction may be the thrust behind convincing a lot of guys to take cardiovascular disease seriously:

> *Heart attack? Whatever. Pass the wings.*
> *Floppy penis? Whoa, tell me again about plant-based...*

"Before being a Chief of Cardiology, I was the director of a nuclear lab," said Dr. Kim Williams. "We did a study that showed if a man checked 'Yes' on the erectile dysfunction box, the odds that he had blood vessel problems were much, much higher. Stroke, heart attack, erectile dysfunction—they're manifestations of the same thing. Blood vessel disease. You need to improve blood flow to the organ itself. Any organ."

"Erectile dysfunction can be a warning three or four years before a heart attack," said Dr. Kahn. "If that's happening to you and there's no explanation, adopt a plant-strong diet right now. Do it years before you need to have your chest cracked open. Get your heart health back, and get your sexual function back."

I looked up the American Heart Association's diet recommendations. I wasn't surprised at what I found, after the websites of the American Diabetes Association and the American Cancer Society. Recipes for Grilled Chicken and Vegetables, Pork Tenderloin Stuffed With Spinach,[36] and Steak Stroganoff;[37] recommendations to eat low-fat dairy and skinless poultry and fish,[38] and to buy cuts of beef labeled "choice" or "select" rather than "prime."[39]

These suggestions made me think of a doctor who doesn't tell his or her patients to stop smoking, "because I know how much you love it." Maybe switch to e-cigs…

To the AHA's credit, there's a link in small font near the bottom of the "Making Healthy Choices" page: "Vegetarian Diets." If you click on that, the AHA concedes, "Many studies have shown that vegetarians seem to have a lower risk of obesity, coronary heart disease (which causes heart attack), high blood pressure, diabetes mellitus and some forms of cancer."[40]

They don't make that information easy to find.

Another phenomenon I wanted to investigate was the Maasai. Like the Inuit Paradox, the Maasai Paradox belongs to the romantic "Noble-Savage-Eats-Primitive-Meaty-Diet-And-Remains-Free-of-Corrupting-Disease" ideal that is so beloved by industrialized, privileged, and primarily white cultures.

The widely-circulating rumor is that the Maasai, an East African semi-nomadic people in Kenya, traditionally consume only meat, milk, and blood, while retaining excellent heart health. A 1964 study, led by Dr. George Mann, reported no heart disease in Maasai men, who were also very slim, with low cholesterol. But the only methods to detect heart disease available to the scientists in the study were physical exams and EKGs.[41]

"As any physician can attest," writes Dr. Thomas Campbell, "a patient can have a normal EKG and physical exam and still drop dead a week later of a heart attack related to atherosclerosis that has been progressing for decades."[42] Not only that, but the researchers were primarily examining young men. Roughly 60 percent of their 400 subjects were under the age of 44, and only three men were older than 55.[43]

That might be because Maasai men, even in 2015, have a life expectancy of 61.1 years, with a Healthy Life Expectancy—years of full health—of only 55.6 years.[44] The average life expectancy of an American male is over 76 years old.[45] (Imagine what it would be if the average American man ate a health-promoting diet…)

Nor were Mann and his researchers able to measure the diet of the Maasai. They wrote,

"The accurate measurement of dietary intake of these people proved extraordinarily difficult…because of the erratic intake of food, there being no fixed meal patterns in the families, because there are no uniform units of measurement or utensil and because of the disruption of usual behavior in the presence of an observer."[46]

That makes it tough to accurately assess the link between diet and disease.

In the early 1980s, the International Livestock Centre of Africa (ILCA) found that even though Maasai women and children drank large amounts of milk, they only ate meat 1-5 times a month. The men's food consumption again proved too difficult to track.[47]

And then there's the fact that the Maasai are so active (sedentary Americans would have to walk almost 12 miles more every day to be as active[48]) that ILCA calculates the women and children were only taking in 50 to 70 percent of their estimated caloric requirements.[49] That could account for the overall slimness of the tribe.

A few years after his initial study, Dr. Mann went back and performed autopsies on 50 Maasai men. He found "extensive atherosclerosis" comparable to older American men, busting the myth he himself had helped generate. Yet there were no heart attacks, and the Maasai men retained functional blood vessels. Mann and his researchers speculated that "the Masai are protected from their atherosclerosis by physical fitness which causes their coronary vessels to be capacious"[50]—in other words, their extreme physical activity made their blood vessels a lot roomier, able to accommodate more "hardened gruel."

So it's not that the Maasai have no heart disease. They do. But there are radical factors that seem to keep the disease from striking the Maasai as it does Americans. Perhaps it's simply that the Maasai, with their 55 years of healthy life expectancy, just don't live long enough for their "capacious" blood vessels to get completely congested.

Alzheimer's disease is another blood vessel disorder. It's the sixth-leading cause of death in the US, killing more people than breast and prostate cancers combined. Every 66 seconds, someone in the country develops Alzheimer's.[51]

"Alzheimer's has been going up all around the world," said Dr. Greger. "In Japan, for example, they switched from a traditional rice-based diet to more meat. Animal fat was the number one risk associated with their skyrocketing rates of dementia.

"We know a plant-based diet cleans out the blood vessels. Guess what? We have blood vessels in our brain, our kidneys, our spine. One of the leading risk factors for dementia as we get older is the lack of oxygen and nutrients getting to the brain. The same artery-clogging fat and cholesterol build up in arteries of the brain, just as in the heart. That's why a plant-based diet can affect all organ systems at once, whether you're trying to reverse erectile dysfunction, heart disease, or get blood to the most important organ of the body, the brain."

"We've got over 5 million Americans with Alzheimer's now— figures are going through the roof," said Dr. Barnard. "There's a lot of evidence that the fat in meat and dairy is a big contributor. The Chicago Health and Aging Project reported in 2003 that people who ate the most saturated fat had 2 to 3 times the risk of Alzheimer's compared to other people.[52] It's not the only study to show that. A plant-based diet is key to preventing Alzheimer's disease. Whether it could reverse it, that's not known. If a person is in the early stages, there's some evidence that lifestyle changes might help, but I do think there comes a point when the brain is too far assaulted by diet and lifestyle factors. There is a point where you're not going to go back."

***

Amy Resnic is from Swampscott, Massachusetts, north of Boston. She's 51 years old, a large woman with short dark hair.

"I recently went to my doctor for asthma," she told Keegan and I. "While there, she did some blood work, and one of the tests was C-reactive protein. On a scale from 1 to 3—1 being low for a cardiac event, 3 being high—my number was 10.82."

"What does that mean?" I asked, startled.

"That means I am on the road for a heart attack, probably within the next 30 days."

"Thirty days?!"

"Thirty days, if I'm going the way I'm going."

"Did your doctor say what's causing this?"

"She said maybe genetics. Doctors always say to lose weight, but that's easier said than done. I know I need to do something. I am so exhausted. I'm tired when I wake up, tired during the day, I take a nap and still I'm tired. I can't breathe. I've been using a CPAP machine to help me breathe at night, and sometimes during the day, for about 5 or 6 years."

"Are you on any medications now?" Keegan asked.

She led us over to a table cluttered with pill bottles. She held up an inhaler. "This is a steroid that helps me breathe." She held up another. "This is the rescue inhaler I use more than once a day. Both of these have an effect on my heart. I take Diltiazem, for my heart. Ibuprofen, 800 mg three times a day for the pain in my neck and hands. Also Cyclobenzaprine, a muscle relaxer. Oxycodone for pain. Lorazepam for anxiety. Topamax. Prozac. That's it."

She tidied up the bottles.

"I know I need to make a change for my health, or else I'm not going to be here very long."

CHAPTER 11
OUR CHILDREN

I took a desperately needed break from my research. I shoved away from the desk and opened a window. It was a glorious spring day in San Francisco. The wind was blowing in from the bay.

Down the street I could hear the happy shrieks of kids. School had just gotten out.

Children remind me of new leaves. Have you ever looked at a freshly unfurled leaf? Tiny, light green, super shiny. Exposed to the world for the first time. A friend of mine, Tara, told me that as she held her newborn son, looking at his toes and his sea shell ears, she thought to herself, "I will do everything I can to keep him as perfect as he is now."

A lot of parents feel that way.

Which is why, as I looked out my window, seeing the kids and their grown-ups, I felt a pang of urgency.

A paper called "The Pediatric Aspects of Atherosclerosis" had pushed me in disbelief away from my computer. Scientists had examined autopsies of accidental death victims, ages 3 to 26. Fatty streaks in blood vessels leading to the heart were found in *almost every child by the age of ten years old*.[1]

Fatty streaks are the first indication of heart disease—the "first grossly visible lesion[s]"[2] of atherosclerosis. They are irregular, yellowish discolorations on the "luminal surface" of an artery.[3] The inside space of an artery is called a "lumen." The word originates in Latin, meaning "an inner open space."[4] But the same Latin word also means "light."[5]

Fatty streaks are the first obstruction of the light in our children.

In 1953, 300 autopsies were performed on young American soldiers killed in the Korean War. The average age was 22.1 years. "In 77.3% of the hearts, some gross evidence of coronary arteriosclerosis was found," researchers wrote. "The disease process varied from 'fibrous' thickening to large atheromatous plaques causing complete occlusion of one or more of the major vessels." Several of the young men's arteries were over 90 percent blocked.[6]

"This widely cited publication," wrote a follow-up, "dramatically showed that atherosclerotic changes appear in the coronary arteries years and decades before the age at which coronary heart disease (CHD) becomes a clinically recognized problem."[7]

A later study, examining the hearts of thousands more young US soldiers killed in Korea, reinforced these findings.[8]

Children's bodies are impacted by the same things as adult bodies, only more so. Blood cholesterol levels in kids correspond to the amount of plaque in their arteries, just as in adults.[9] And like adults, reducing, or better yet, eliminating from their diet saturated fat, trans fat, and dietary cholesterol will lower the cholesterol levels of kids.[10]

Ninety percent of caloric intake for American kids comes from dairy products, white flour, sugar, and oil. Fruits and vegetables form less than 2 percent of their diet.[11] In fact, roughly a full quarter of toddlers between the ages of 1 and 2 eat absolutely no fruits and vegetables. For kids 15 months of age, the most common vegetables are French fries.[12] Over 80 percent of American preschoolers, ages 2 to 5, eat more total fat, saturated fat, and cholesterol than is recommended. The top fat source for kids is whole milk.[13] (Incidentally, the top source of lead for preschoolers is dairy.[14]) The leading cholesterol sources are eggs and whole milk.[15]

These are the foods we give our kids to make them strong. What we do not know is that we are feeding them the foundations for chronic, life-shortening diseases. These diseases take root while our children sleep under our roofs, and are budding by the time they enter fifth grade.

Keegan and I sat down with Dr. Paul Porras, a pediatrician in Maryland. He's a young man with dark hair and Clark Kent glasses.

"Do you think children should be consuming dairy?" I asked.

"Milk is a risky food for human consumption, particularly for children," Dr. Porras said bluntly. "As a pediatrician, I see on a daily basis children suffering from conditions linked to dairy consumption: eczema, acne, constipation, acid reflux, iron deficiency. Pretty much every major organ in the body can show symptoms of dairy intolerance: the skin, digestive tract, respiratory tract, circulatory system.

"Milk in its natural state has almost 50 percent of calories from artery-clogging saturated fats. And all the kids I see with iron deficiency anemia, the culprit is excessive dairy intake, which inhibits iron absorption and causes microscopic blood loss through the bowels. Iron deficiency anemia can also cause cognitive problems in a child.

"Cow's milk protein is one of the most allergenic foods in nature," he went on. "About once a week I see a newborn with allergic colitis, presenting with bloody stools, a reaction to cow's milk protein, either through formula or passing through breast milk. Within days, you see an improvement by switching to nondairy formula, or by removing dairy from the mother's diet. So there is even a danger of the mother drinking milk or eating cheese and yogurt while lactating."

"How do parents react when you suggest removing dairy?" Keegan asked.

"Usually they look at me like I have three heads," said Dr. Porras. "They ask me about calcium."

"Why do so few parents know the health risks of dairy?" I asked.

"The dairy industry and the government have very successfully pushed the message that kids need dairy," he said. "My son's public school gym has posters: 'Dairy is important for strong bones and teeth.'"

"Would you like to see dairy taken out of school lunch programs?" I asked.

"Yes," Dr. Porras said simply.

"If an obese child comes to you, what do you recommend?" I asked.

"About a third of the children I see in my practice are obese," he said. "Exercise is important, but it is very difficult to attain a healthy weight if there is no dietary change. Boiling it down to one thing, I would increase fiber-rich foods: fruits, vegetables, whole grains, beans. Fiber is bulky and gives us a feeling of satisfaction. We have stomach receptors that, once they stretch to a certain point, our brain gets the signal we have eaten enough. But with animal foods, we have to eat a lot more for the same satisfaction. Meat is not necessary for health and definitely plays a role in obesity."

In 2012, more than 1 in 3 children were obese or overweight.[16] Childhood obesity has more than doubled in the last 30 years,[17] while adolescent obesity has quadrupled.[18] American kids win the sad prize of being the heaviest in the world, and they continue to gain weight more rapidly than children in other countries.[19]

Justin Painter, a North Carolina boy, weighed 250 pounds when he was 7 years old. A local newscast shows Justin walking on his family's porch. He can barely move. He clutches a Scooby Doo ball in one hand, limping and rocking from side to side. His breathing is labored. Then the camera pans down to his white-socked feet. They're tiny baby doll feet. That's when you understand he's just a little boy, suffocating in layers of fat.

Justin's weight began ballooning when he was three. His mother, Joyce, took him to numerous doctors, only to be told she needed to "watch his diet." She doesn't feed him chips, cookies, or snacks.

"If I'm doing something wrong, show me, show me what I'm doing," Joyce Painter pleads in the newscast. "If there is something in [my kitchen] that I don't need to have, show me! So I can throw it out!" She is close to tears.

I don't know what the doctors told Mrs. Painter to feed her son, but the camera lingers on Joyce's open notebook, revealing one day's meals for her seven-year-old:

Breakfast
4 Scrambled Eggs
1 slice Cheese
1 tsp. Ketchup
1 ¾ glass Diet Sprite

Lunch
5 Vienna Sausages
1 Cup Popped Popcorn
1 glass Diet tea
Nutr. Bar Snack

Supper
Hamburger Steak

1 tsp. Ketchup
1 Glass Diet Pepsi
¾ cup Sweet Potato
½ tsp butter
Splenda[20]

Joyce Painter had contacted the news station in desperation, after the Department of Social Services threatened to take custody of Justin if his weight didn't drop. To the DSS, it was a situation in line with child abuse. Mrs. Painter wanted to show the public she was doing all she could to help her son.[21] After consulting many doctors, she feeds him as healthfully as she knows how.

Something is wrong here. Knowledge is not getting through.

Children and teenagers who are obese or overweight are far more likely to be obese as adults,[22] skyrocketing their risks for heart disease, Type 2 diabetes, stroke, and joint problems.[23] They will also have higher risks for many cancers, including cancers of the breast, cervix, colon, endometrium, esophagus, gall bladder, kidney, pancreas, prostate, and thyroid, along with multiple myeloma and Hodgkin's lymphoma.[24] Over 300,000 deaths every year are caused by unhealthy weight gain.[25]

As a bariatric surgeon specializing in weight loss surgeries, Dr. Davis is well acquainted with the problems of obesity.

"Obesity, it's a death sentence," he said to us, shaking his head. "It's an instigator for other diseases. We know that weight is strongly tied to cancer, so the future is going to contain more cancer, not less. The vast majority of diseases I see in the hospital are due to what people are eating."

"Everyone blames the overweight person. But in many ways it's society's fault. In the doctors' lounge at the hospital, some other doctor will say to me, 'Why don't you just tell those fat people to push away from the table.' And he's eating a cheeseburger. That doctor is no different than my patient. He's still going to get the heart attack like everybody else."

By the time an obese child turns six, the likelihood that he or she will be obese as an adult is over 50 percent. Seventy to 80 percent of obese teenagers will remain obese into adulthood. But more alarmingly, the Harvard Growth Study demonstrated that "being overweight during the adolescent years predicts adult morbidity from several chronic diseases and mortality from all causes *regardless of adult body weight.*"[26]

Another study confirmed that "Overweight in adolescence was a more powerful predictor of these risks [heart disease, colorectal cancer, gout, and arthritis] than overweight in adulthood... Because body-mass index appears to be programmed early in life, the prevention of overweight in childhood and adolescence may be the most effective means of decreasing the associated mortality and morbidity in adults."[27]

About 85 percent of people with diabetes are overweight or obese.[28] Remember Dr. Barnard's analogy of fat gumming the lock, preventing the insulin key from working? Sugar is locked outside the cells and builds up dangerously in the bloodstream.

Type 2 diabetes used to be called Adult Onset Diabetes. In 1980, there were no documented cases among American adolescents aged 8-19. Thirty years later, 57,638 cases of "Adult Onset diabetes" were seen among children and adolescents.[29] The name had to be changed to Type 2 diabetes. There are about 3,600 new cases every year in children.[30]

This alarming increase in Type 2 diabetes correlates with the equally alarming surge in childhood obesity.[31]

The first large study looking at Type 2 diabetes in children didn't occur until 2012, "because this didn't use to exist," said Dr. Robin Goland, a member of that study's research team.

The results, after following almost 700 overweight or obese children with Type 2 diabetes for 4 years, are troubling. The disease was shown to progress far more quickly in children than adults. It's also harder to treat. The researchers hypothesized that the rapid growth of children and hormones in puberty could be the reason. Oral medications became ineffective in half the patients after only several years.[32] This could mean a much sooner onset of diabetic complications like heart disease, amputation, kidney failure, eye problems, and nerve damage.[33]

"I fear that these children are going to become sick earlier in their lives than we've ever seen before," Dr. David Nathan, one of the authors of the study, told the *New York Times*.[34]

"People need to understand," emphasized Dr. Greger, "that if their child gets [Type 2] diabetes, you've just taken 19 years off their life span.[35] That's what we may be exposing them to when we feed them the standard American diet. Who wouldn't go to the ends of the Earth to give their children another two decades of life?"

We haven't even talked about Type 1 diabetes, which used to be known as Juvenile, or Childhood Onset diabetes. In Type 1 diabetes, the body doesn't make insulin.[36] This form of the disease is usually diagnosed in children or young adults, representing about 5 percent of diabetes cases,[37] although the incidence of Type 1 is rising around the world,[38] particularly in affluent countries.[39]

"In Type 1 diabetes," Dr. Barnard said, "the insulin-producing cells have been killed. Blood tests show that these cells are destroyed through an autoimmune reaction by antibodies that have somehow formed in the body. What triggers that? One of the biggest culprits under scientific study right now is cow's milk protein.[40] Some kids are genetically at risk, but if they are not exposed to the protein that causes the disease to manifest, they will never get it."

I had never heard of a link between Type 1 diabetes and cow's milk.

"Cow's milk protein is foreign," Dr. McDougall said. "It is meant for baby cows. For some people, when cow's milk protein gets into the blood, the body says, 'Hey, this isn't supposed to be here.' Then the body makes antibodies to the cow's milk protein, and the antibodies attack and destroy the pancreas, along with the ability to make insulin.

"You want to ruin a family?" he continued. "Have one of the children develop Type 1 diabetes. The life of your family changes. The whole focus is on that child: insulin shots, blood sugar levels, trips to the hospital."

"Why doesn't everybody know this? There's something called the dairy industry. They hire scientists to tell a different story or give you reason to doubt. But this overwhelming research—at least 200 articles—is published in our major [medical] journals."

The risk of developing Type 1 diabetes, for a genetically vulnerable kid who eats or drinks milk products, is greater than a smoker's risk of developing lung cancer.[41]

Keep that in mind as you read the following story.

Daniella Meads-Barlow was a healthy 17-year-old who spent one particular evening doing homework and watching *X Factor*. She said goodnight to her parents at 10:30. Daniella had been living with Type 1 diabetes since she was 5, and her dad asked what her blood sugar readings were. She replied that her readings were 12.2—normal.

That was the last thing she ever said to her parents.

Her mother found her dead the next morning. Her blood levels had plummeted silently during the night, and at some point while her parents slept, her heart stopped. The paramedics said she had been dead for hours.[42]

Dead-in-Bed syndrome is a recognized medical term for one of the most harrowing consequences of Type 1 diabetes. A child or young adult with the disease, often having managed it well for years, goes to bed healthy. They are found dead the next morning.[43] The cause is unknown. As many as 1 in 20 young people with Type 1 diabetes die this way.[44]

Infants who are fed cow's milk-based formula in their first 3 months have a 52 percent higher risk of developing Type 1 diabetes. Drinking a lot of cow's milk after infancy also raises a child's likelihood of developing the disease.[45] Cases of Type 1 diabetes have been increasing rapidly 3-5 percent every year.[46]

"Dead in bed numbers will rise with that," said Dr. Neville Howard, an endocrinologist at the Children's Hospital at Westmead (Sydney, Australia). Dr. Howard treated Daniella Meads-Barlow for 12 years before she died.

"A parent with a child with diabetes never sleeps with the door closed," Daniella's mother said, "and never sleeps properly through the night ever again." She paused, remembering. "She did say to me: 'How will I survive, Mummy, unless I live up the road from you? How can I live?'"[47]

One of the most treacherous fallacies in our society may be this: Milk = Childhood Health.

Keegan and I met Michele Simon, a public health attorney, at her home in Oakland. She's been writing about the food industry's marketing tactics since 1996.

"Marketing to children is probably the most egregious problem we're facing in the realm of public health," Simon said to us. "It's a huge problem in schools. Milk gets a pass, because our culture believes that dairy is a health food.

"The National Dairy Council promotes a school-based program called 'Fuel Up to Play 60.' Ads for milk are all over schools, under the guise of encouraging kids to exercise. Exercise is used as a distraction. The food industry wants you to think you can eat anything as long as you exercise. Science tells us you'd have to run many miles to burn off, say, one sugary milk beverage. And 70 percent of milk consumed in schools now is flavored, so kids are getting a heavy dose of sugar along with their milk.

"The dairy industry is also all over the Women, Infants and Children food assistance program (WIC)," Simon continued, "because of this idea that mothers and young children need dairy for nutrition. When there was an attempt to include fruits and vegetables in the WIC package, the dairy industry actually lobbied against it because they feared fruits and vegetables would displace dairy. That's the kind of undermining of public health that the industry engages in."

Princeton, New Jersey's public school system is ranked number 1 in New Jersey[48] and fifth in the nation.[49] The school district spends an average of $24,368 on every child,[50] more than double the national average of $10,658.[51]

Parents often move to Princeton specifically to enroll their kids in the public schools.[52] I was curious about Princeton's lunch programs. If there are healthy school lunches around, they're much more likely to be found in a prosperous, top tier district.

With local help from an intrepid, eight-year-old insider named Konrad H., I got my hands on the May and June Lunch Menus for Princeton elementary schools.

The menus, organized like a calendar, are decorated with brightly colored balloons, stars, a beach umbrella, and a smiling red crab. The days are themed—All American Monday! Fun Flavors Tuesday! Wacky Wednesday! Chicken Lover's Thursday! Pizza Lover's Friday!

A clown in a top corner holds a bunch of balloons: "BALLOONS For a Balanced Lunch!" Each balloon is labeled Milk, Protein, Grain, Veggie, or Fruit.

Balloons and exclamation marks aside, these are the meals being served in one of the most highly ranked, affluent public school districts in the country:

Philly Cheese Steak, Cheeseburger with Waffle Fries, Mozzarella Sticks, Grilled Cheese, Turkey Ham & Cheese, Mac n Cheese, Big Daddy's Cheesy Pizza, Nachos Grande, Chicken Quesadilla, Popcorn Chicken, BBQ Chicken Tenders, Chicken Ranch Patty with Turkey Bacon, Pancake with Turkey Sausage, Pasta & Meat Sauce, Spinach/Egg/ Bacon Salad, and Hot Dogs, among other healthy options.

In a little rectangle, the Gluten-Free and Vegan options for the entire month are listed. In May, those were Chex Cereal & Yogurt (GF), or SunButter & J[elly] Sandwich (V). In June, those were... Chex Cereal & Yogurt, or SunButter & J[elly] Sandwich.

Milk choices include skim white (which, as we now know, is 35 percent fat), Chocolate, Strawberry, and White Lactaid,[53] so any kids who experience bloating, nausea, diarrhea, and stomach pain from dairy can still join the milk party.

"With the National School Lunch Program, which is run by the USDA," Susan Levin said, "historically you had to take a carton of cow's milk for that meal to be reimbursable. So you're imparting upon all these children the 'necessity' of this product. You had no choice. Now, you don't have to take the cow's milk for most programs, but the damage is done. We're convinced we need dairy."

"We have got to conquer the USDA hammerlock on school nutrition," Dr. Esselstyn stressed. "They can't dictate this epidemic of illness in our children. It's unacceptable for them to declare meat and dairy mandatory, which will establish a foundation of disease while you're a teenager."

The Princeton Public School lunch menu is similar to kids' menus at family restaurants. Dr. Davis tells us, "A lot of my patients ask for a card saying, 'I've had gastric bypass surgery and cannot eat much; please allow me to order from the kid's menu.' No, I'm not giving you that! The kids' menu is the worst: cheeseburgers, hot dogs, chicken strips. There's no question kids are eating too many calories from too much meat and too much fat."

Parents around the country, from Mrs. Painter and her 250-pound boy in a tiny North Carolina town, to Wall Street executives commuting daily into Manhattan from Princeton, are unaware that the meat, egg, and dairy-heavy diets of their children may be generating—cell by cell, molecule by molecule—fertile breeding grounds inside their young bodies for chronic disease and early death. If parents have an uneasy hunch about this, they don't know what to do about it. Their children are used to the stream of grease, sugar, salt, and animal tissue, and refuse anything else. So parents resign themselves: *Everyone's kids are eating this way. They'll grow out of it by college.*

But very few moms and dads realize, "the first ten years may be the most critical," according to Dr. Joel Fuhrman in his book, *Disease-Proof Your Child.*

"The most recent scientific evidence is both overwhelming and shocking," Dr. Fuhrman writes. "[W]hat we feed (or don't feed) our children as they grow from birth to early adulthood has a greater total contributory effect on the dietary contribution to cancers than dietary intake over the next fifty years...We could not have designed a cancer-causing environment more effectively if we scientifically planned it. We feed our children a diet high in saturated fat, add lots of processed foods ... and combine it with an insufficient intake of unrefined plant foods...and presto, we have created a nation rich in autoimmune illnesses, allergies, obesity, diabetes, and finally, heart disease and cancer."[54]

While parents might despair at the "impossibility" of changing their kids' mac'n'cheese-pizza-sketti-with-meatballs diet, Dr. Fuhrman notes, "My medical practice over the last thirteen years has proved to me that children are willing and able to change dangerous habits more readily than adults."[55]

Kids might be more adaptable than you think. Sometimes a simple explanation—which hopefully affirms what they've been taught all their lives—about not hurting or killing animals when we don't need to, will resonate much more powerfully with a child than lectures on saturated fat, carcinogens, phytochemicals and antioxidants.

"There is no good time in life to eat animal products," Dr. McMacken said to us, shaking her head. "The most important thing, perhaps, is that the habits formed in childhood are incredibly important for risks later on, especially cancer risks."

If your children refused to wear their seat belts or brush their teeth, would you look the other way? Why not? Because you love them. Ultimately, moving your family from the standard American diet of meat, eggs, and dairy to a health promoting, disease-cutting, plant-based diet is an act of love.

***

It starts in the womb.

"People say, 'Don't you want to have a little bit of milk because you're pregnant? Don't you want to have some fish because you're pregnant?'" Dr. Barnard said. "Who do you think is going to receive the hormones in the milk and the pollutants in the fish? An Australian study showed that women who are heavy in early pregnancy, indicating a poor diet, can give birth to babies who have thickened arteries.[56] These newborns developed the beginnings of heart disease *in utero*. Can you imagine heart disease beginning before you're even born?"

In another startling study, Italian scientists found that high cholesterol levels in a pregnant mother can lead to fatty streaks—remember, the first sign of heart disease—in the arteries of her unborn child.[57]

Pregnant women are regularly warned against fish,[58] and for good reason. One weekly serving of fish during pregnancy can build up more mercury in your unborn baby than injecting a dozen mercury-containing vaccines straight into their fetal bodies.[59] And fetuses are far more sensitive to mercury than adults.[60] Mercury in the diets of pregnant women is linked to birth defects, intellectual and developmental disabilities, seizures, and cerebral palsy.[61]

Then there's meat. Scientists discovered that pregnant women who ate grilled meat—or were even exposed to the cooking smoke—in their third trimester were shown to give birth to babies with birth weight deficits, as well as smaller heads, an indication of brain size. This is probably the consequence of ingesting carcinogens, like heterocyclic amines and polycyclic aromatic hydrocarbons, which form when meat is cooked.[62]

And women who eat the smallest amount of vegetables while pregnant had a higher risk of giving birth to babies who would go on to develop Type 1 diabetes. Women who ate vegetables only 3 to 5 times a week had a 71 percent higher chance of having a child with diabetes than pregnant women who ate vegetables every day.[63]

The bodies of pregnant women, on average, contain up to 50 potentially toxic chemical pollutants.[64] The levels of some pollutants in women's blood can drop by almost half during pregnancy[65]—those pollutants are being offloaded through the placenta,[66] and then of course to the developing child.[67]

"Men have no way of getting rid of the dioxins in their bodies, but women have two ways," Mike Ewall told Keegan and I. "One: the dioxin crosses into the placenta and then into the growing infant, and two: it comes out from the breast milk." Not surprisingly, of all humans, developing fetuses are the most sensitive to dioxin exposure.[68] So when a pregnant or breastfeeding mother eats cheese, yogurt, milk, meat, eggs, or fish, she is passing her dioxin load directly to her baby.

There is a healthier, safer way to nourish your children, born or unborn.

"You can be an infant, toddler, pregnant, lactating, and you can get all your nutrients from plants," said Levin. "It's not just adequate. It's healthful. That's a positioned statement from the Academy of Nutrition in Dietetics."

Levin is 39 weeks pregnant—it's a boy. She's been vegan for twenty years. She stood to show us her belly.

"It's been a very easy pregnancy," she said. "Many people go through pregnancy on a plant-based diet, and they do really, really well. You can have a wonderful, and in fact a better pregnancy by adopting a plant-based diet.

"During lactation, a vegan diet is also completely adequate. Your nutrient needs will go up, like any breastfeeding woman, so you eat more. If you're vegan, you're probably getting very nutrient dense calories, so your baby will benefit.

"Anything a breastfeeding mother eats," she continued, "transfers into the milk, so you want to be very cautious about toxins and hormones. If you eliminate animal products, you're not getting that exposure, and neither will your baby. Ultimately, as a pregnant or lactating mother on a plant-based diet, your baby will be the biggest beneficiary."

"The one thing I will mention for all pregnant and lactating mothers on plant-based diets," cautioned Dr. Goldhamer, "is a reliable source of Vitamin B_{12}, so your breast milk will contain adequate amounts of the vitamin." (More on B_{12} later, but a great resource for plant-based pregnancy/breastfeeding is *The Everything Vegan Pregnancy Book*, by Reed Mangels.)

"Human breast milk is the fluid designed by evolution over millions of years as the perfect food for human babies," Dr. Greger said. "It has the lowest protein content in any mammalian milk—rat milk, donkey milk, any milk that's ever been tested. That gives you a sense of human protein requirements. Protein overload is one of the reasons formula is not optimal." One cup of human milk contains 2.5 grams of protein, compared to 7.9 grams in cow's milk, and 8.7 grams in goat's milk.[69]

"A plant-based diet is perfect at every stage of life," said Dr. Barnard. "Adults and children should be eating vegetables, fruits, whole grains, and beans. There is no stage of life where you need a pork chop, cheese, animal fat or cholesterol in your food.

"A lot of people ask me if a child will grow stronger by eating meat and dairy. Well, you might theorize that if I eat more brains, I'll get smarter. But that doesn't work. 'If I eat more muscle tissue, more meat, I'll get bigger muscles.' That doesn't work either."

"Kids do not need to drink milk to grow big and strong," Levin said. "Kids who don't consume dairy can get plenty of calcium from more healthful foods, like beans and greens. Greens have twice the absorbable calcium as cow's milk, along with other nutrients that promote health. If milk is easier for you, there are products like soy and almond milk supplemented with the same nutrients that cow's milk is supplemented with."

Scientists at Loma Linda University confirmed that children on plant-based diets have no problems growing—they're taller than meat-eating kids by roughly an inch on average, and they're leaner as well.[70]

Now here's something really intriguing. Tufts University showed that vegetarian, and especially vegan kids, measure higher on IQ tests—about 16 points higher, on average—than their meat-eating playmates. Their "mental age" was more mature by a year than omnivore kids. And vegan kids were the smartest of the vegetarian children.[71]

I know, I know, what are you supposed to do with that information? Obviously genetics plays an enormous role in intelligence, as well as family environment and educational opportunities. But it's interesting, isn't it? Maybe smarter people choose to adopt plant-based diets. Another study followed 8,000 children in Britain, testing their IQ at age 10. Twenty years later, the researchers came back to find out which of the subjects by age 30 had become vegetarian or vegan. The kids with the higher IQ scores were much more likely to become vegetarian as adults.[72]

It seems clear, whether you're concerned about pregnancy, breastfeeding, infancy, or growing children and adolescents, that the only animal product a child should consume is the milk of her or his own mother.

"A plant-based diet," nodded Dr. Klaper, "is absolutely compatible with glowing health and growth in humans. I've seen two generations of infants raised as pure vegans. They grow up into strong, healthy, intelligent adults."

***

If mass killers like heart disease, diabetes, and cancer can be prevented, or even reversed, by eating a plant-based diet and avoiding animal protein—even "healthy" chicken, fish, and dairy—and if science has shown that no more than 10-20 percent of risk for the primary causes of death come from our genes,[73] then health, in a vast majority of cases, lies within our grasp.

It's no longer up to chance. A family's medical history, disfigured perhaps by massive heart attacks by age 50, early death from breast cancer, or crippling diabetes, is stripped of the dread it casts over the next generation. Moms and Dads can help protect their kids against disease well into their children's adult lives.

I felt like the clouds were parting. For myself, for those I loved, and for all of society.

But then one day, while I was looking something up on the WHO website, I stumbled upon a phrase I had never heard before. It sent chills up my spine.

Post-antibiotic era.

Part Two

THE WORLD

Chapter 12
Post-Antibiotic Era

On World Health Day 2011, Dr. Margaret Chan, Director-General of the World Health Organization (WHO), made a measured but harrowing statement to the global community:

"The world is heading towards a post-antibiotic era, in which many common infections will no longer have a cure and, once again, kill unabated... We cannot allow the loss of essential medicines—essential cures for many millions of people—to become the next global crisis."[1]

The next global crisis. How had I not heard of this phenomenon? In March 2012, Dr. Chan spoke in Copenhagen:

"A post-antibiotic era means, in effect, an end to modern medicine as we know it. Things as common as strep throat or a child's scratched knee could once again kill."[2]

October 2015, in Berlin:

"If current trends continue, sophisticated interventions, like organ transplantation, joint replacements, cancer chemotherapy, and care of pre-term infants, will become more difficult or even too dangerous to undertake."[3]

Antimicrobial resistance, in the words of Dr. Chan, was "a cross-border slow moving tsunami."[4]

What is propelling this global tidal wave?

"Compelling evidence shows," Dr. Chan said, "that [antibiotic] resistance is driven by the total volume of antibiotics used... [The] growing demand [for meat], especially when met by intensive farming practices, contributes to the massive use of antibiotics in livestock production."[5]

Intensive farming practices. That's a polite label for factory farms.

"[M]assive quantities of antibiotics are used to promote growth, not to treat sick animals," Dr. Chan continued. "Routine use of antibiotics at sub-therapeutic levels kills the weakest bacteria, but lets the more resistant ones survive... Human consumption of food carrying antibiotic-resistant bacteria can lead to the acquisition of a drug-resistant infection."[6]

Dr. Chan touched on the discovery in China of a gene that had "sent shockwaves through the medical and scientific communities." She called it a "horizontal transfer of [antibiotic] resistance, and it is frightening."

I didn't know what a horizontal transfer of resistance was, but I was definitely frightened. Especially after Dr. Chan's summary:

"The Chinese findings, which have been replicated in several other countries, solidify the links between the agricultural use of antibiotics, [antibiotic] resistance in slaughtered animals, resistance in food, and resistance in humans. All of the dots are connected."[7]

There's a tendency in the general public—and I'm guilty of this too—to mentally shut down, maybe move on to the Sports section or clickbait, when confronted with a concept that is too abstract, technical, or just too plain overwhelming to get your head around. After all, we think, there's nothing I can do, the good scientists will take care of it, and besides, there's this very interesting article over here comparing Donald Trump to 8 evil comic book presidents.

But I felt compelled now to understand. I'm no scientist, but I wanted to know how these dots were connected.

This particular story of antimicrobial resistance begins with an antibiotic called colistin, which was approved for use in 1959. But it turned out the drug can damage the kidneys, so it was quickly shelved. It wasn't used much for half a century. Most importantly, bacteria didn't have a chance to develop resistance to it.[8] Colistin still works.

But safer drugs have begun to fail, especially in the face of super-virulent strains. More and more, these pathogens are invulnerable to most antibiotics available.[9]

So colistin has been brought back to the front lines, as a "last resort" weapon against these complex infections.

"[Colistin has] really been kept as the last drug in the locker when all else has failed," Dr. Jim Spencer, of the University of Bristol (UK), said on NPR.[10]

But what about colistin's damaging effect on the kidneys, the reason it was retired in the first place?

"Drugs that we previously discarded because their toxicity was too high now don't look so bad if the alternative is death," Lindsay Grayson, editor of the medical text *Kucers' The Use of Antibiotics*, said on Bloomberg News.[11]

I can't argue with that.

And colistin, because it was introduced over a half century ago, is very cheap. That makes it especially attractive for "intensive farming practices." As Dr. Chan mentioned, enormous amounts of antibiotics are routinely given to factory-farmed animals in their feed and water, to make them grow bigger faster[12] (and more profitable), as well as to simply keep them alive in the severely overcrowded, unrelentingly stressful, and filthy conditions of industrial-scale animal production.[13]

Agricultural colistin use in China is among the world's highest.[14] And in 2013, Chinese researchers found colistin-resistant *E.coli* in a pig from a factory farm near Shanghai.

Dr. Chan's "shockwave" had hit. What happens when a last resort drug begins to fail?

In November 2015, the new resistance to colistin was announced in *The Lancet Infectious Diseases*. MCR-1 is the catchily-named gene responsible for the colistin resistance, and here's the thing about MCR-1: it's located on a plasmid, a tiny piece of free-floating DNA. This means that plasmids carrying MCR-1—and colistin resistance—can easily move from one bacterium to another, allowing resistance to hopscotch rapidly around the world.

MCR-1 was found in slaughterhouse animals, in meat sold for human consumption, and in hospital patients with infections.[15] So the gene has already crossed species into human beings.

"It's almost like it [MCR-1] possesses a universal key," Dr. Lance Price, of the Antibiotic Resistance Action Center at George Washington University, told Maryn McKenna, who has reported extensively on this issue.[16]

The medical community can only wait helplessly to see which strains of bacteria MCR-1 will jump into—benign ones that live quietly in intestinal flora, or into aggressive, malignant "superbugs" that cause complicated infections in multiple systems of the body, and are already invulnerable to other drugs.[17]

"You're looking at the last line of defense against antibiotic resistance falling," said David Plunkett, of the Center for Science in the Public Interest, on NPR. Plunkett has worked for years on the problems of excessive antibiotic use in farmed animals. "And the potential for it now to spread not only in China but around the world—you're looking at the potential for untreatable epidemics."[18]

MCR-1, after the initial discovery in China, has been found in Malaysia, Portugal, Denmark, France, the Netherlands, Algeria, Laos, and Thailand.[19] And on May 27, 2016, I opened up the *New York Times* to read:

> *"American military researchers have identified the first patient in the United States to be infected with bacteria that are resistant to an antibiotic that was the last resort against drug-resistant germs."*

The antibiotic was colistin.

Colistin resistance had landed on our shores.

"We now have all the pieces in place for [bacterial strains] to be untreatable," Dr. Lance Price said in the *Times*.

"The medicine cabinet is empty for some patients," Dr. Thomas R. Frieden, director of the Centers for Disease Control and Prevention, said at a D.C. press conference addressing the crisis.[20]

"The emergence of *mcr-1*," The Lancet Infectious Diseases reported, "heralds the breach of the last group of antibiotics…with the advent of transmissible colistin resistance, progression of [many disease-causing bacteria] from extensive drug resistance to pan-drug resistance is inevitable and will ultimately become global."[21]

Pan-drug resistance means resistance to all known drugs. Nothing known to medical science will treat those infections.

I was completely shaken.

This was not about what I chose to eat. This was not about choice at all. This was about a broken food system, global agricultural policies, massive abuse of drugs, and the menace of rapidly evolving microbes, all of which affected everyone, regardless of how they ate.

For my own sanity I had to talk to someone about this. Keegan and I packed our bags and made the long trip to Baltimore, Maryland.

Bob Martin is the director of Food System Policy at Johns Hopkins Center for a Livable Future. He has a kind face, with blue eyes that droop at the corners, and graying, light brown hair. He looks like a classic American farmer. All he needs is a straw hat, overalls, and a pitchfork.

Before Johns Hopkins, Martin was executive director of the Pew Commission on Industrial Farm Animal Production. The commission investigated Concentrated Animal Feeding Operations (CAFOs, another abstract name for factory farms), relating to public health, the environment, animal welfare, and rural communities.

Keegan and I met Martin in his office.

"These large-scale intensive animal operations represent an unacceptable level of risk to public health," he told us. "Eighty percent of antibiotics sold in the US go to food-animal production. Our number one concern is the daily low-level doses of antimicrobials given to animals in these containment facilities, to offset poor environmental conditions and overcrowding. That is one of the major drivers of antibiotic resistant bacteria.

"MRSA (Methicillin-resistant Staphylococcus aureus), a multi-drug-resistant bacteria," Martin continued, "started out vulnerable to antibiotics. It got into the swine operations. Because of the routine low-level use of antibiotics in those operations, it re-emerged into the human community as a super pathogen. It usually manifests with high fevers and pus-filled blisters. Internalized, it grows as a white, pus-filled mass and leads to life-threatening complications like blood poisoning."

The human infections from MRSA in this country more than doubled between 1999-2005: from 127,000 to 288,000.[22] More people in the US die from MRSA than from AIDS.[23]

In 2008, a researcher from the University of Iowa showed that 70 percent of farmed pigs tested in Iowa and Illinois carried the MRSA virus. A strain of the bacteria was also discovered on a nursery school teacher, who had never set foot on a hog farm, though there were farmers' kids in the school. This proved that there is no need for a human being to be in contact with infected animals, or live with people who work with infected animals, in order to carry—and spread—the bacteria.

Every thirty minutes, *Staphyloccus aureus* reproduces. A colony of more than 1 million bacteria can grow in 12 hours from a single bacterium. And every time a staph cell reproduces, there is an opportunity for it to shape-shift into a drug-resistant super pathogen. If a staph cell encountered MCR-1, it could develop colistin resistance without ever coming in contact with the drug.[24]

I asked Bob Martin the burning question in my brain, about a post-antibiotic era. I was hoping he'd have news about, oh, some powerful antibiotic that was discovered last week, or a global ban on antibiotics in animal feed. No such luck.

"If a post-antibiotic era in medicine happens," Martin said quietly, "infections like MRSA will be impossible to treat. You'll be at risk in minor surgeries to have a fatal infection. You'll be at risk having a tooth extracted. We'll be back to Civil War medicine. You get an infection in your leg and you have to cut your leg off. It's a very serious potential outcome."

Keegan cleared his throat. "What about viruses?"

"These overcrowded animals become a perfect engine for generating a new flu virus," Martin said. "The military learned there has to be a certain amount of space between bunks. You can't overcrowd people because it fosters transmission of viruses. Same for animals.

"Pigs and people can contract all four types of flu viruses: swine, avian, equine, and human. A pig is the perfect petri dish for combining a strain of avian flu with a strain of swine flu. Then the workers carry it back out into the human community. It's aggravated when a swine operation is located near a poultry operation. That's happening more and more in North Carolina.

"The most virulent avian flu repository is migratory waterfowl," he continued. "Many swine operations are in the major migratory pathways of ducks and geese. It creates the potential for an explosive flu epidemic. The great 1970 influenza outbreak started as an avian flu that mutated in pigs—and this was before animals were heavily concentrated. There is a health threat no matter how we raise animals.

"A new virus in 2014 ravaged the swine herd in the United States—Porcine Epidemic Diarrhea Virus. No one had ever seen it before. The first suggested treatment was to grind up baby pigs who had the virus and feed them to the older pigs to protect them."

Keegan and I almost retched. We later found an undercover video showing this cannibalistic vaccination at a Kentucky pig farm.[25]

I tried to get back on track. "Are there numbers on antibiotic use by species?"

"No," Martin answered. "The industry has always opposed collecting that information. And the FDA always lets them get away with it."

Speaking of the FDA letting the industry get away with things, I discovered that the agency's big plan for halting antibiotic use in industrial animal feed—one of the drivers of a global health crisis—is a *voluntary* phase-out of non-illness-related antibiotics. Running across the top of the FDA paper outlining the phase-out plan is a header in bold:

Contains Nonbinding Recommendations.[26]

So the FDA is simply suggesting that antibiotic use be curbed in industrial animal production. They're suggesting that drugs be reserved for sick animals; they're suggesting that the pharmaceutical companies make a veterinarian's prescription necessary to obtain these drugs; and maybe the drug labels should be changed as well. But these are just suggestions, encouragements, non-binding recommendations.

Because, as they declare on their website, "FDA believes that the collaborative approach is the fastest way to implement the changes...We have worked with stakeholders, including animal pharmaceutical companies, to encourage their cooperation on this important public health issue, and we are confident in their support."[27]

They're going to give it three years,[28] and if things don't change, they'll figure something else out.

What could possibly happen in three years? Well, in 1999, there were 11,200 deaths from antibiotic-resistant infections. Just six years later, in 2005, there were 23,000 deaths.[29] That's an increase of more than 100 percent.

The FDA has known about antibiotic resistance since at least 1977, when it tried to withdraw important human medications from use in animal agriculture. But the pharmaceutical and animal agriculture lobbies were enraged. Both the Senate and the Congress commanded FDA "to hold in abeyance any and all implementation of the proposal," insisting that more testing was needed. So FDA studied antibiotic resistance for almost twenty years. The results were the same as the initial findings in the 1970s, but still the FDA did nothing. In the meantime, the Centers for Disease Control and Prevention, the National Academy of Sciences, the USDA, the American Academy of Pediatrics, and WHO all targeted low-dose, routine antibiotics as the driving force behind the rise of drug-resistant bacteria.[30]

The FDA was finally sued in May 2011 by a group of non-profits, including the Natural Resources Defense Council, the Union of Concerned Scientists, the Center for Science in the Public Interest, Food Animal Concerns Trust, and Public Citizen.[31]

In March 2012, a federal judge declared that the FDA must address the gratuitous use of antibiotics in animal production. Margaret Mellon, a senior scientist with the Union of Concerned Scientists, responded:

"For the past 35 years, while advocates and citizens alike have been urging FDA to take action, the problem has steadily worsened and FDA has sat on its hands, which begs the question of whose interests the agency is protecting...The glacial pace of the FDA response on animal antibiotics is unacceptable. The agency needs to curb the unnecessary uses of vital antibiotics in animal agriculture. Peoples' lives depend on it."[32]

A few months later, a federal court ordered the FDA, which it called "arbitrary and capricious," to take action and reconsider two citizen petitions, which FDA had denied, that urged the agency to ban sub-therapeutic antibiotic use in livestock.[33]

So the FDA devised this voluntary phase-out plan.

"I don't think voluntary is going to work when so much money is at stake," Bob Martin said. "And the fact is, most drugs approved for growth promotion are co-labeled as appropriate for disease prevention."

Meaning, antibiotics can be administered for "disease prevention," but—gee whiz!—the drugs still have that convenient upshot of making animals grow abnormally fast!

According to the FDA's 2014 Annual Summary, domestic sales of antibiotics approved for use in food-animals increased between 2009 and 2014 (which covers the implementation of the voluntary phase-out plan), sometimes drastically:

- Aminoglycoside: ↑ 36 percent
- Cephalosporin: ↑ 57 percent
- Penicillin: ↑ 28 percent
- Lincosamide: ↑ 150 percent[34]

"Regulate at the consent of the regulated, it's crazy," Martin said. "FDA is a captured agency. They'll say, 'We work in a political environment and we do what we can.' One entity in the country can balance the power of these major corporations and that's the federal government. If they don't do it, nothing will stop this abuse."

Bob Martin had said, *There is a health threat no matter how we raise animals.* I thought that was an extreme statement.

I was wrong. Sixty percent of human pathogens, and 75 percent of emerging diseases, come from the animal kingdom.[35] Eighty percent of potential bioterrorist microorganisms have their origins in animals.[36]

The scientific term for a disease that can be transmitted between animals and humans is "zoonosis." The plural is the deceptively endearing "zoonoses."

The domestication of animals, beginning about 12,000 years ago,[37] marked a momentous turning point in human infectious diseases. That's when close, extended contact with animals opened the door for a flood of zoonoses to jump the species barrier into humans. Measles appears to have come from sheep and goats. Whooping cough—pigs and sheep. Smallpox—camels. Influenza—ducks. Leprosy—water buffalo. The human rhinovirus (the common cold) came not from rhinos, but from cattle.[38] Anthrax, tuberculosis, brucellosis, *campylobacteriosis*, *Salmonella*, haemorrhagic colitis, listeriosis, streptococcal sepsis, trichinellosis,[39] *E.coli*, and bovine spongiform encephalopathy (Mad Cow Disease),[40] are just the tip of the zoonotic iceberg.

And within the congested, massive animal slums/prisons that are factory farms, manned by a constant rotation of stressed human workers—the annual employee turnover rate is 95-100 percent, one of the highest in the country[41]—the already great risk of disease explodes exponentially. Of course they were pouring all kinds of drugs into these animals. It makes a perverted kind of sense.

Those drugs are, of course, ending up in the meat on dinner plates throughout the country.

Back in San Francisco, Keegan and I visited the Center for Food Safety (CFS). We met with Cristina Stella, a Staff Attorney, and Paige Tomaselli, a Senior Attorney.

"There are currently at least 450 different drugs administered to animals," Stella, a young woman with brown corkscrew curls and glasses, told us, "either alone or in combination. These drugs are given for a variety of reasons—very few of which are beneficial to the animal or to consumer health."

"How many drugs are there in one animal?" I asked.

"Part of the problem in this field is the lack of data," said Stella. "The government and the industry work together to keep the public in the dark."

"Why?"

"Because people don't want to eat meat that's on drugs, that's why," she answered. "They don't want to know that, in order to survive the horrific conditions on factory farms, animals have to be pumped full of drugs, sometimes *in utero*, right up until slaughter."

"What drugs are used besides antibiotics?" Keegan asked.

"Arsenicals have been used since the 1960s," Stella said. "They've been prohibited since the end of 2015, but we'll feel the effects of arsenical use for a long time."

"Isn't arsenic poisonous?"

"Yes," said Paige Tomaselli. "But it's also an antimicrobial. And it helps animals gain more weight on a smaller amount of feed, and gives their meat a 'healthy' color."[42]

Great. A poisonous carcinogen's been added to our food supply for over fifty years so that chicken meat can have a nice tint.

"What other drugs are there?" Keegan asked.

"Beta agonists are fed to cows, pigs, and turkeys, in the days leading up to slaughter, to increase their weight right at the end of their lives," Stella said. "These drugs can cause cows' hooves to fall off, or increase their risk of being downers—that is, cows that can't rise to their feet."

"One beta agonist is ractopamine," Tomaselli added. "There's no therapeutic purpose to it whatsoever. What it does to pigs is horrendous. Sometimes the animal gains weight so fast its limbs break under it. Animals can even die from it. Residues of beta agonists have been found on the meat we eat."[43]

"But we don't know what this is doing to human beings," said Stella. "Only one study has been done on humans. It was only 6 people, and one dropped out because of increased heart rate."

"Why doesn't the FDA do more tests?" Keegan asked.

"FDA doesn't really test drugs, period," Stella said.

"To get an animal drug approved through FDA," explained Tomaselli, "the pharmaceutical company is supposed to show the safety of the drug—on animals, not on humans. But the manufacturer of the animal drug does all the safety testing. Not the FDA or independent scientists. FDA just reviews information provided by the pharmaceutical company."

"That's ridiculous," I said.

"And it's an entirely confidential process," Tomaselli continued. "It's protected by the Trade Secrets Act and by confidential business information regulations. The public, independent scientists, and public interest organizations are not allowed to comment on the process. CFS, for instance, can't provide science we may have on a drug or a similar drug to the FDA, until after the drug has been approved. If we know there's a problem with it, we have to petition or sue the FDA, to try to get them to withdraw their approval."

That doesn't seem beneficial to human health.

"These drugs are tested for a particular purpose," said Stella, "like beefing animals up or how it affects their reproductive systems. We know if they cause weight gain, but we don't know whether they're safe. They show that it's safe *enough* for their intended uses. If 100 percent of animals administered a drug don't drop dead, then FDA considers it safe."

That's absolutely crazy. The FDA claims they are "responsible for protecting the public health by assuring the safety, efficacy and security of human and veterinary drugs..."[44]

"Who is the FDA working for?" I ask. "The public or these companies?"

"They would say they're working for the public," answered Stella, "and that they can only do as much as the information they have allows them to do."

"That's what Bob Martin said too," Keegan said.

"But from the consumer's perspective," Stella went on, "they are definitely on the industry's side. I do not trust them, as a consumer, to protect me and my health at all."

Keegan let out his breath. "That's a powerful statement from an attorney who works in food safety."

"Consumers have *no idea*," Stella said emphatically, "what are in the products they consume. Packaged meat should carry warnings that these animals have been on drugs their whole lives. Consumers absolutely have a right to know that. It would change their purchases if they did know."

Cristina Stella told us the CFS has been submitting FOIAs (Freedom of Information Act requests) for "years and years and years." FOIA grants the public the right to request records from any federal agency. These agencies are bound to divulge the requested information, unless it falls under 9 exemptions, including national security, law enforcement, and personal privacy.[45]

But Stella told us the FDA often wouldn't disclose the requested material to the CFS. When they did respond, the information seemed to be a very small slice of what should be in the agency's possession.

After our meeting with Stella and Tomaselli, Keegan and I talked to Jaydee Hanson, a senior policy analyst with CFS. He told us more about the stonewalled FOIA requests.

"When we try to get information from federal agencies," Hanson said in his raspy voice, "we get back page after page of blacked-out information, because the company claimed confidential business information. The company secret is how sick a product makes me or how badly it pollutes the environment. That's wrong. We should have the right to know. We don't in this country. Greedy chemical and drug companies control what we eat."

Hanson showed us on his computer some of the federal documents CFS received in response to FOIA requests. He scrolled down, shaking his head. Page after page was covered, sometimes entirely, with black blocks obscuring the text.

"Confidential business information," he muttered. "Twenty-two pages removed. Seven pages removed, ten pages removed. At least they're nice enough to let you know they're removing them."

He clicked the document closed in disgust.

"We have about 3,000 people die every year in the US from things they eat[46]—*Salmonella, E.coli*," Hanson said. "That's more than the number of people killed in 9/11 in the Twin Towers of New York, every year. If we had some terrorist organization killing 3,000 people a year, we would be all over it! If you add the antibiotic-resistant bacteria deaths on top of that, you get over 26,000 people dying a year.[47] That's over eight 9/11s every year!

"*Can you imagine?!*" he exclaimed, his voice cracking with astonishment. "We consider it *normal* that a town the size of the town I grew up in, gets wiped out *every year*. If that many people were being killed by some terrorist group in the United States every year, we would find them."

Bob Martin, Paige Tomaselli, and Cristina Stella had all touched on the disease-breeding conditions of factory farms.

"Animals are literally living in their own waste," Tomaselli told us. "They're stuck in cages with sick or even dead animals. Stressed animals tend to shed more bacteria. Pathogens are created in these filthy conditions, and the public is exposed to them."

I know a bit about factory farms. I know that "broiler" chickens raised for meat are jammed together by the tens of thousands in a single building, usually without windows, sitting in a thick layer of their own excrement for their entire short lives. Sometimes the caked excrement won't be cleared before the next batch of chickens comes in.[48] They breathe air clotted with ammonia, dust, and feces 24 hours a day.[49]

The vast majority of "laying hens," who produce eggs, live lives far worse than broilers. They are often kept in "battery cages," about five to ten chickens per cage, with each individual hen given a space roughly the size of a piece of printer paper to live her whole life in.[50] These cages are so small that hens cannot stretch their wings. Paul Shapiro, from the Humane Society of US (HSUS), calls battery cages, "the most severe form of factory farming in the country."[51] Long-dead, rotting hens are frequently found in the cages by investigators with the living birds, sometimes trampled or mummified.[52] [53]

Long rows of battery cages are stacked on top of each other, usually four or five tiers high. The feces and urine of the hens on upper stories fall through the cage floors onto the animals below.[54]

"If you haven't been in a hen plant, you don't know what hell is," said an undercover activist in *Rolling Stone*. "Chicken shit is piled six feet high, and your lungs burn like you took a torch to 'em."[55]

There have been movements around the country to ban battery cages, led by consumer outrage and groups like HSUS. Cooperation from certain companies is market-driven, with corporations scrambling to keep their customers from boycotting their products in disgust.

Cage-free, though, isn't a pastoral paradise. Cage-free means that laying hens will be kept like broilers—in packed, indoor, life-long confinement, while living and laying eggs in their own waste. The switch to the cage-free system is expected to take fifteen years or more.[56]

And fierce opposition to legislation increasing living space for hens has emerged from an unexpected source: the pork industry. Pork producers are terrified that federal laws mandating larger cages for chickens will set a profit-destroying precedent for pigs.[57] You'd understand if you were to visit a swine operation.

Female sows, kept continually pregnant, live their lives in "gestation crates." These are metal cages roughly the size of the pig's body. The sow cannot turn around, or even lie down in comfort.[58] These are large, heavy, pregnant animals.

The floors are slatted concrete, without straw or bedding. The urine and excrement of the animals fall through the slats into a large collective pit below.[59] Like chickens, pigs stand above their own feces and urine every day of their lives, constantly breathing the heavy ammonia fumes rising through the floor.[60]

Cattle, by comparison, have it pretty good, except for the whole getting-killed-and-eaten part. They're still raised outdoors generally,[61] and are brought to feedlots—huge open-air pens where they are confined by the thousands—at the very end of their lives to pile on massive amounts of lucrative weight before being killed.[62]

They eat huge amounts of food for the 3-6 months they are there, gaining between 2.5 and 4 pounds every day.[63] With tens of thousands of animals, each eating about 4,500 pounds of food while in the feedlot,[64] farmers are constantly looking for economical feed. There's grain, but that gets pricey. Luckily, there's "protein concentrate." Sounds like something you'd add to your smoothie after a tough workout.

Protein concentrate, though, comes from a process known as "rendering."

"Rendering is a $2.4-billion-a-year industry, processing 40 billion pounds of dead animals [per] year," Howard Lyman, who came from a line of four generations of cattle ranchers, wrote in *Mad Cowboy*. "There is simply no such thing in America as an animal too ravaged by disease, too cancerous, or too putrid to be welcomed by the all-embracing arms of the renderer."

A renderer is an enormous grinding machine that turns entire bodies of diseased farm animals, as well as road-kill, euthanized pets, and animal blood and feces, into a slurry which is 25 percent fecal material.[65] The protein component of this paste is dried and pounded into a brown powder. This "protein concentrate"—packed with protein, calories, and marvelously cheap—is added liberally to animal feed.

Chicken excrement is also a popular additive to livestock feed. What a great idea! There's literally tons of it, it's cheap but expensive to dispose of, and it's got protein! In the states of Maryland and Delaware alone, there are 523 million chickens producing enough manure to fill the dome of the US Capitol about once every week.[66] The FDA estimates that 1 to 2 million tons of chicken feces is fed to cattle every year in this country.[67]

Lamar Carter, a rancher in Arkansas, boasted to *U.S. News & Report,* "My cows are as fat as butterballs. If I didn't have chicken litter, I'd have to sell half my herd. Other feed's too expensive."[68]

"If you are a meat eater," Howard Lyman writes, "understand that this is the food of your food."[69]

Disease runs rampant on factory farms. At least most animals are still intact while alive.

But the day comes along when each animal is taken to the slaughterhouse. And there, all these animals who have lived their lives in unspeakable filth and disease are carved open, spilling the incubated pathogens in their bodies out into the world, as their flesh is packaged and sent by truckloads to feed the country.

The slaughterhouse is the last stop before the supermarket. Keegan and I wanted to learn what happens there from someone who knows the system well.

We met with Dr. Lester Friedlander on a sunny day outside. He's an unusual looking man in burgundy scrubs, with a stocky figure and a round, mottled face. His straight gray hair came down in a fringe to his eyebrows. Dr. Friedlander is a celebrated Doctor of Veterinary Medicine who was awarded the USDA Veterinary Trainer of the Year Award after only two years of work with the USDA, as well as USDA Certificates of Merit and Commendation.[70] He was Supervisory Veterinary Medical Officer for the USDA Food Safety Inspection Service for ten years, serving as Chief Veterinarian at the country's biggest, single-building slaughterhouse and hamburger production plant, as well as exposing the illegal use of steroids in veal calves at a different plant. In 1991 he discovered a new disease in cows, and published his discovery in the *Journal of Veterinary Pathology*.[71] He was on the Board of Directors for the National Association of Federal Veterinarians in Washington, D.C., and was recognized in the Who's Who in Veterinary Science and Medicine.[72]

And then the USDA forced him to retire.

"What happened was," Dr. Friedlander told us, in a voice like a Brooklyn cabbie, "I was one of the first veterinarians in the country taking cow brains out to test for Mad Cow disease. Back in 1991, Dr. Paul McCloskey, Chief Pathologist for the Food Safety and Inspection Service, called me up to his office, and told me, 'We just had a big meeting in D.C. about Mad Cow disease. Lester, do me one favor.'

"'What's that?' I said.

"He said, 'If you ever find it, don't tell anybody. That's what we discussed in Washington. We export beef to over 90 countries; if we find Mad Cow disease, our export partners will not want our beef.'"

Dr. Friedlander didn't listen. He became a whistleblower, warning the American public about Mad Cow disease, and after appearances on *48 Hours* and *Prime Time Live*, the USDA asked Friedlander to leave.[73]

"They called me into Washington, D.C. and said I had to quit. They said, 'We don't like you because you cause too many problems. You don't need a lawyer. We'll agree upon something. What do you want?' I said, 'I'd like to have federal insurance for my kids. I don't want to pay any state or federal taxes, and I want my salary.' One guy gets on the phone and said, 'This is what Dr. Friedlander wants.' He hangs up the phone and says, 'Sign the dotted line.' So now, for over twenty years, I pay no state tax, no federal tax, I get my pay, and I have federal insurance. I love America," he deadpans.

"Luckily there wasn't a gag order," he adds. "I would never have signed it. The USDA operates like the military. When I got on TV, right away they sent out memos to all the veterinarians and food inspectors—'If anybody from the media contacts you, do not talk to them. Refer them to Washington, D.C.' It shut up everybody. If they don't listen, they can get fired just like in the military because you didn't follow orders."

"What's going on with Mad Cow disease today?" Keegan said. "Isn't collecting brains the only way to test for it? They don't do that anymore?"

"That's right," Friedlander said. "Because of money. A recommendation was made to stop slaughtering cows with a captive bolt, which goes directly into the brain and can spread Mad Cow prions to the following cows—and instead they should slice the jugular, without touching the brain.

"The industry thought it over, but they would lose money, losing 10-15 cows an hour. They decided not to do that. Industry dictates what they want, and the USDA goes along with it.

"One of the biggest mistakes USDA ever made," Friedlander continued, "was to let the slaughter plants do their own HACCP (Hazard Analysis Critical Control Point) program [an in-house food safety inspection]. The Quality Assurance people in the plant told me, 'Dr. Friedlander, our supervisor said to never fail the HACCP program.' 'Why?' I asked. 'Because then we have to rewrite it, so the best thing is to falsify it.'"

Timothy Pachirat, who worked undercover at a Nebraska slaughterhouse for five months, confirms many of Friedlander's statements in his book, *Every Twelve Seconds*. Pachirat rotated through several jobs there, including QC (Quality Control) for the plant.

"If Jill [another QC worker] or I do find contamination..." Pachirat wrote, "the implicit and explicit expectation from the kill floor managers is that we will not document it. Instead, we are to write "No FMI" [acronym for Fecal, Milk, Ingesta] on the entry for that hour's inspection and orally notify one of the trim-rail red-hat supervisors about the contamination. He, in turn, will tell the employees on the trim rail to 'be more careful' [and look for contaminants on upcoming carcasses to trim off]."[74]

Pachirat describes an incident in which he fails a piece of meat because he found ingesta [straw on the carcass that was in the cow's mouth at slaughter]. When he and his co-worker Jill were alone, Jill exploded, berating him for documenting a contaminant when the inspector was too far away to see, saying he should have put the contaminated meat back in the box, burying it under other pieces.

"When I asked her directly how she felt about lying in the paperwork we fill out," Pachirat writes, "her first reaction was hostility: 'What do you mean we lie?' After I pointed out several recent examples of contamination that we failed to document she became more resigned and shrugged her shoulders: 'If we reported this stuff how long do you think we could stay in our jobs?'"[75]

"What sorts of things are found in the meat we eat?" I ask Dr. Friedlander.

"Tumors, cancers, deep-seated abscesses. It was more than enough times I had to go, after inspectors had missed it, back into the cooler and condemn a carcass for cancer or some other condition. That stuff gets through to the consumer, for sure.

"If there's an abscess under the hide, pulling the hide off will usually let the pus out. If it's deep-seated, inspectors or employees might stick their knife into it, and then it explodes all over the place.

"Then everything is supposed to be sanitized, to make sure no other carcasses have pus on them. Doesn't always happen. I remember an incident in the boning room, a worker stuck his knife into a deep-seated abscess, and the pus went all over the piles of meat on each side. They just put it all into the box and shipped it out."

I swallowed. "And as a USDA inspector, how much time do you get with each...carcass?"

"When I got there, the production line speed was 147 cows per hour. After a couple years, they increased it to 160. Two years later, they increased it to 170. The line speed is now going about 220 cows an hour. That gives you 15 seconds per cow."

"What are you looking for as an inspector?" Keegan asked.

"A big one is fecal contamination on meat. That causes *E.coli*. We grind up maybe 12 carcasses at a time [to make hamburgers]. Just one cow with feces on it will contaminate the whole batch. Then it goes into the patty machine."

"How much meat has fecal matter on it?"

"A lot. It's a shame when you hear somebody ate hamburger with fecal contamination and the kid died or somebody was hospitalized. That should have been taken care of in the slaughter facility. The USDA says there's zero tolerance for fecal matter, but in reality, they allow 5-10 percent fecal matter on carcasses, because they're going by so fast and you can't really see the fecal matter. Another problem is if inspectors aren't looking carefully, the company might take a high-pressure hose and spray the feces off. That just contaminates other parts of the carcass.

"When cows come to the slaughter plant, there's balls of feces on their sides. Same thing happens with poultry and pork."

Pachirat also describes the near-impossibility of pinpointing contaminants on the bodies whizzing by:

"I had very little sense of what these contaminants actually looked like on a cattle carcass. But when I asked Jill to describe what I should be looking for, her retort was a short and sarcastic: 'Don't you know what shit looks like?'

"Spotting these contaminants as the carcasses move past at high speed is extremely difficult. The QC must make a rapid visual scan of the carcasses and sort between discolorations and small splotches that are a natural part of the carcass and anomalies that might signify contamination... Unfortunately fecal material is the hardest contaminant to spot and identify. Black grease and rail dust can be seen on the pale carcasses; fecal matter blends in with the carcass and is often so tiny that the eyes can miss it even when the QC is looking directly at it."[76]

Earlier in the book Pachirat describes the cows coming down the line to be killed:

> "Already caked in feces from their time in the feedlot, the transport truck, and the slaughterhouse holding pens, the cattle are packed so closely together as they push their way up the chutes that the defecation of one animal often smears the head of the animal immediately behind. The impact of hooves against concrete splatters feces and vomit up over the chute walls, covering our arms and shirts, and sometimes hitting us in the face."[77]

"A lot of people are cutting back on red meat, and switching to chicken," Keegan said. "Can you tell us about poultry slaughter?"

"The birds come through on hooks," said Dr. Friedlander, "and then a mechanical arm goes up the cloaca [a chicken's only posterior opening for urine, feces, and eggs] and pulls out everything inside the cavity. Unfortunately when the mechanical arm pulls the intestines out, they often burst. Then all the fecal contamination is inside the bird. At the end of the poultry slaughter line there's a big chill tank to cool the birds down quick so they can get packaged and shipped out. If you have just one of those chickens with broken intestines and fecal contamination, the whole chill tank is contaminated. They call the water in the tank, 'fecal soup.' All the chickens throughout the day, if they don't change the water, are contaminated with feces. Hundreds of thousands of chickens go through that water. And while they're in the tank the chicken flesh soaks up that fecal soup. That's what they call 'retained water' on the chicken label."

I felt nauseous, thinking of the chicken nuggets I ate as a kid. "What about feeding chicken excrement to cattle, is that still happening?" I asked.

"That's still happening."

"How often?"

"Any chance they get. They feed chicken shit to cows. You can only put manure on the field so many times. Fields get saturated and when it rains the shit flows into the waterways. Scientists examined the chicken feces, and told the USDA there was nutritional value in it. So the FDA and USDA approved it as cattle feed."

He laughs drily.

"The cows didn't like the taste of the shit. So guess what the farmers did? They poured molasses over it. Made it sweet and sticky, and now the cows clean it off the troughs."

So rude.

"Does organic or grass-fed matter at the slaughterhouse?" Keegan asked.

"It's all the same slaughterhouse. Same contamination problems. There's no such thing as a grass-fed, organic slaughterhouse.

"'Organic' is just a label. The organic association visits maybe once a year. They call up the farmer first and let them know they're coming. So if the farmer has any drugs, steroids, antibiotics on the shelf, he puts it in the closet. The organic guy checks everything out and says, 'You got a nice place here. You're certified organic.'

"And even if an animal has never been fed any antibiotics, hormones, or steroids, natural hormones end up in the meat."

I thought of the growth hormones and reproductive hormones in dairy.

"Cows come into the slaughter plant pregnant—I've seen this a lot, the calf is right in her birth canal," Dr. Friedlander continued. "Because the cow is pushing her calf out, there's a dangerous increase of oxytocin in her body. When inspectors see that, they should condemn the whole carcass. Instead, they pull the calf out, or, if it's still in the uterus, they cut the fetus out, and hang it up on a hook. They drain the fetal blood and bottle it for research, and send the mother's carcass on for human consumption.

"Other natural hormones like adrenaline or cortisone, the stress hormone, are increased in the animals' bodies and then retained in the meat. Animals are smart. They're sentient beings.

They feel pain. They see what's going on. They hear the noise, other animals vocalizing. Why wouldn't they be scared? It's almost like the Holocaust, you hear people screaming on the other side of the door, right? The animals before them are making all kinds of noise, stamping their feet, trying to back up and get out of there."

"Then, in their flesh—are people eating...fear?" I asked.

"Yeah. You could say that. They're eating all those naturally occurring stress hormones. They're eating the fear."

We were silent for a short time. Then Dr. Friedlander spoke up.

"If you eat meat, you're playing Russian Roulette because you never know when that bullet will come out and kill you."

CHAPTER 13
A CIVIL RIGHTS ISSUE

The massive community health risk of factory farms is invisible to most of the nation. It is an alternate universe, of horrific suffering, epidemic pathogens and disease, and toxic contamination of inconceivable proportions, concealed beneath the fabric of America. And animal factories are all over the country, often in extreme concentration.[1]

Where are they hiding? Who lives near these operations? And what must it do to their communities, and their health?

There are more factory-farmed pigs in North Carolina than there are people: 10.1 million pigs and 9.4 million people.[2]

"An adult hog produces 8 to 10 times more feces than an adult human,[3]" Larry Baldwin of the Waterkeeper's Alliance told us. He picked Keegan and I up at the airport, and was driving us to talk with some locals. Baldwin was a burly guy with wrap-around mirrored sunglasses and a gray goatee. He looked like an off-duty Hell's Angel in his clean white polo shirt. "With over ten million pigs, you're looking at the equivalent of 100 million people producing waste in this state."

That's equivalent to the populations of North Carolina, California, New York, Texas, Pennsylvania, New Hampshire, and North Dakota flushing their toilets into North Carolina.[4]

The topic of animal excrement seemed inescapable.

The scenery rolling by outside Baldwin's pick-up truck was a flat, parched greenish-brown. There were clusters of trees and small white houses. Where were the factories?

"The hogs poop through slats in the floor, which collects underneath and is then drained into what the industry refers to as a lagoon," said Baldwin. "It's an open pit of hog feces and urine. Some lagoons can be the size of a football field, and there can be several lagoons for one facility. Then the raw, untreated waste is sprayed onto an open field. But we've got too much waste concentration for the area. On top of that, more and more chickens are being raised here, with the same waste issues. There's a sprayer right there."

I looked out the window. Baldwin pointed to an irrigation jet. What was being flung in a high, far-reaching arc over the fields was brown.

Keegan quickly rolled up his window.

I found out later that the sprayers are called "manure cannons." The manure cannons essentially aerosolize the feces-urine slurry and blast the mist high over the fields. They send the manure as far as possible, in a futile attempt to keep the ground from becoming sodden with pig feces.[5] The cannons spray hundreds of gallons of manure every minute. Lawn sprinklers, by comparison, average 2-3 gallons of water a minute.[6]

"Does that sprayer mean there's a pig facility nearby?" Keegan asked.

"It does," Baldwin said.

"Can we see it?" said Keegan.

"Sure."

We turned off the main road. I couldn't see anything that looked like an industrial-scale operation.

"Most people are familiar with *Charlotte's Web*," Baldwin said as we drove. "Wilbur the pig doing back flips in the barnyard. That's not the way we do things anymore. The meat in this country is primarily—percentage in the upper 90s—from factory farms. They're usually a number of long, low buildings—the industry calls them barns—where you have hundreds or thousands of animals crammed together. They don't see the light of day. They never step on grass. All they do is eat and produce waste."

Now I saw what Baldwin was talking about. Five large, white, non-descript buildings, long and low, side by side, with gently sloping metal roofs. They could have been anything—warehouses, equipment storage, indoor ice rinks. On the ends of the buildings were big turbines, their blades revolving.

Keegan asked Baldwin if we could stop and get a few exterior shots. He pulled over and we got out.

The smell was stomach churning. I felt my lunch rise up in my throat. It smelled like—well, it smelled like sour mountains of pig excrement in the scorching North Carolina sun, combined with something sweet I couldn't place.

Keegan, holding his breath, set up the camera and zoomed in for a closer shot.

Between the buildings and us was a lake. The water was an odd maroon, pinkish color. A few large pipes sloshed a chocolate brown stream into the lake.

We quickly got back in the truck. The smell clung to our clothes and our hair.

"From an environmental standpoint," Baldwin said as we drove away, "from a community standpoint, North Carolina is in a state of emergency.[7] I've seen creeks the color of Pepto-Bismol, running miles downstream."

"Why does the water turn pink?" Keegan asked.

"Bacteria in the water," Baldwin replied. "What's really moving is talking to people in these communities, who will tell you what this industry has done to their lives."

"That's why we're here," I said.

"What kind of farmers run these animal factories?" Keegan asked.

"We don't call them farmers," Baldwin said. "They're either contract growers or producers. In some ways I feel for them. They're probably on land that's been in their family for generations, and they may have been trying to raise animals in the traditional way. But then they had to decide, 'I'm either getting out of the agricultural business altogether, or become a contract grower for an industry like Smithfield foods.' Smithfield is the largest integrator in North Carolina. When someone becomes a contract grower, whether it's hogs, poultry, whatever, they basically become an indentured servant. They no longer have control over what happens on their property.

"Smithfield Foods will use them," Baldwin continued. "Smithfield owns the hogs, they own the feed. As a grower, you sign a contract that says, 'I will babysit your pigs. I'll feed them, get them to grow, then I'll give them back to you and get paid.' Even if these family farmers, as they still want to be called, don't agree with how they're raising the hogs, very few of them say anything, because if they do their contract can be nullified. Then they're out of business altogether. All the control is in the hands of large corporations like Smithfield. What the corporation does not take responsibility for is the land, the buildings, the mortgage, and the millions and millions of gallons of waste."

"What kind of health threats are we looking at?" I asked.

"The hog waste itself is composed of pollutants, or 'nutrients,' like nitrogen, phosphorus, ammonia," Baldwin said. "Also bacteria. These pollutants and bacteria are spread into the open environment, impacting surface and groundwater, as the waste percolates through the soil. Then there's the airborne issues. Whether it's evaporation from the lagoons, or from wind as the manure spray is blown off site, or the large ventilation fans at the ends of the barns, that's all being discharged into the air that people breathe. And there's the proximity to communities. If you fly over these facilities, it's astounding how close they are to houses, schools, churches, municipal buildings."

We drove in silence for a few minutes.

Baldwin cleared his throat. "Just on this trip, we've passed 5 hog facilities. Most people on this road don't know they exist because they can't be seen. Unless the prevailing winds come from that direction, you'd never think about it."

Baldwin turned down a dirt drive in Stantonsburg, North Carolina, population 788. We pulled up to a one-story structure that resembled a homemade craft project; some horizontal white siding, some vertical panels of old unpainted wood, numerous doors of different colors and windows of different styles.

"Here we are," Baldwin said. "This is Don Webb's place. He built it himself."

"Hello!" yelled Don Webb, coming out of one of the many doors. A former pig farmer, he is still tall and unbent at 76, with fringes of white hair under his baseball cap. He often raises his southern drawl with belligerence, pumping his arms for emphasis.

"Don Webb!" he shouted, by way of introduction. "Chip?" he said, peering at me.

"Kip."

"Kip? I'll forget it. And you, young man?" Webb said to Keegan.

"Keegan."

"Deegan? I'll forget."

We decided to film outside. "If it gets hot," Webb said, "I faint and y'all drag me back inside."

The words came out of Webb like a flood.

"I owned three hog places," he said. "One day I stopped at Mr. Baysmore's little store—he sell bologna, crackers, Pepsi Colas. He says, 'Don, I think the world of you and I need to talk to you. Can't you do something about that odor? People smell it and drive over to the IGA instead. I lose a lot of business. Ain't there something you can do?'

"Less than 3 days later, Mr. Lewis, he's African-American, he stops me and says, 'Don, we havin' a hard time. The smell is somethin' awful. We can't set out on our front porch. In the house we got to shut the windows and it's too hot and we don't have air conditions.'

"I heard yeast in the cesspools would stop the stink, so I got out there in a little aluminum boat and stirred the yeast in. But Mr. Baysmore and Mr. Lewis said, 'We in the community thank you for trying, but please, whatever you did, please don't do it no more. It stinks worse than ever.'

"I got to thinking, 'They can't be much to me if I'm stinking their homes up to make a profit.' All of a sudden it hit me: 'How would I feel if somebody were doing this to my mother and father?' I went back and told the two gentlemen, 'Tell the neighborhood to give me a year. I'm going to solve this problem.'

"I sold out of the business. It didn't take me a year. I couldn't live with myself knowing I was forcing other people to smell my feces and urine. It come out of the hog, but I owned the hog. I couldn't drive by their homes and know I was making them unhappy. It takes a sorry human being to do that to another human being.

"The rich people stink up your home, with the feces, the flies, the buzzards, the death trucks full of rotting hogs," Webb thundered. "In Duplin County, they spray their feces on the Black churches, on people's homes. They say, 'We feed the world.' No, if you take the money away they'll let folks starve. You could feed the world using corn and wheat more than you can meat. And you don't see big hog operations by country clubs because you don't mess with the rich and powerful."

Larry Baldwin was listening with folded arms.

"A number of years back," Baldwin said, adjusting his sunglasses, "we built our own little mock hog farm on the lawn of the general assembly in Raleigh. We filled a child's swimming pool with 55 gallons of hog waste. A pump in the middle shot it up in the air, so Raleigh could get an idea of what people in eastern North Carolina are living with. The manager of facilities came out and said, 'If you spill one drop of hog waste on the ground, it will be considered hazardous waste. I will call in the hazmat team to clean it up and your organization will be charged thousands of dollars for that cleanup.' My question right back was, 'Why is hog feces considered hazardous waste in Raleigh, but in eastern North Carolina, it's fertilizer?' He got back in his vehicle and left."

"Look," Webb said, pointing beyond his house. "There's a blue-line stream that comes right across my property. I've seen that stream filled with feces and urine from the hog pen over there. If I pumped my feces out over my yard from my septic tank, what would the neighbors say? What would the government do? If someone had a diesel truck running 24 hours a day, we'd do something about it. Why do you flush your commode every time you use it? Why not save water, let it pile up? We teach our children to use the bathroom, and we teach them to wash their hands so they don't spread germs. But it's all right to let it pile up in a cesspool, next to where people live and children go to school? And now look, the chickens and turkeys are coming!"

"That's right," Baldwin nodded. "We're getting more and more poultry production in North Carolina. At full capacity, these slaughterhouses will process 1.25 million chickens every week. Each chicken produces several pounds of waste in their very short lifetimes. Where does that waste go? At some point, Mother Nature is going to say, 'I can't handle this.'"

"We Americans," Webb continued, jabbing his finger, "we get warnings but we wait like it's the Titanic. Our government in North Carolina has given the corporate hog people the right of eminent domain over our air, our land, and our lives. A virus is going to come sooner or later. Then people go hollering, 'We didn't know this was going to happen to us.' It'll be a hog virus, a chicken virus. Worse than the ones we have already. It's going to spread like wildfire."

***

The incestuous mingling of business and politics is epitomized in the career of former North Carolina Senator Wendell Murphy—the man who, in Don Webb's words, "started this factory hog thing." Murphy was the owner of Murphy Family Farms, which became the world's largest pork production system.[8] Smithfield Foods bought Murphy Family Farms in 2000 for almost half a billion dollars.[9]

About 20 years ago, Don Webb took Senator Murphy on a tour to see the harm that Murphy's hog farms were having on the community. They visited black neighbors in their trailers who had tuberculosis and lived with 30,000 hogs right across the road, and they visited white neighbors in their colonial brick homes who had to wear masks because their eyes burnt and their throats were raw from the noxious air. Every family, black or white, begged the Senator to do something about the swine operations.

Not a lot changed.

Senator Murphy started out as a high school agriculture teacher. Soon he opened a feed mill, and raised a few pigs behind the mill. In less than 25 years, Murphy Family Farms was the largest pork producer in the country, with gross revenues of over $72 million. In 1982, Murphy was elected to the North Carolina House of Representatives, where he served until 1988, when he was elected to the State Senate.

The multi-million dollar hog farmer-turned-Senator helped pass "Murphy's Laws"—legislation that paved the way for industrial-scale hog production, along with industrial-scale pollution and profits.

Tax breaks in the millions were handed out to companies (including Murphy Family Farms) to build massive "barns" and buy equipment to run them. The fuel used by these companies' vehicles were subsidized by tax dollars. The authority to halt the unchecked sprawl of CAFOs was taken away from local governments.[10] And Murphy was instrumental in exempting hog farms from monitoring what they spew into waterways.[11]

As Keegan and I packed up our gear, Don Webb said to us, "As a kid I used to hear, 'Money is the root of all evil.' I didn't understand it. I understand it now."

We piled back into Baldwin's truck. Next stop: Warsaw, Duplin County.

Senator Murphy is a native of Duplin County. When he was elected to the House of Representatives in 1982, there were about 172,000 pigs raised there.[12] There are now more than 2.2 million hogs raised in Duplin County,[13] the highest pig population in any US county.[14]

As we drove, I thought of what Don Webb said about manure cannons spraying on Black churches in Duplin County.

"A disproportionate number of hog facilities are located near communities of color: predominantly African-American, Hispanic, American Indian, and low-income communities," Baldwin said. "It's a human rights issue as much as an environmental one."

A 2014 study from the University of North Carolina at Chapel Hill found that African-Americans in the state are one and a half times as likely to have their homes within three miles of a hog CAFO as Caucasians. American Indians were two times as likely, and Hispanics 1.39 times as likely to live by these operations. "This spatial pattern," noted the authors of the study, "is generally recognized as environmental racism."[15]

***

Warsaw, North Carolina. Population 3,000, sitting on roughly three square miles. Almost 60 percent of the town is African-American.[16]

We pulled up to a modest white house with black shutters. A narrow green lawn separated the house from the road.

We were there to speak with René Miller, a tall African-American woman in her mid-sixties. Her hair was cropped, and she wore what looked like pediatric scrubs, blue with tropical fish. She had the bearing of a queen and spoke in a soft, deliberate voice. In her arms was her great-niece, a baby girl with a halo of brown hair, chubby arms, and an unsnapped pink onesie. Just down the road from Miller's house is an industrial pig operation.

"My mother had this house built," Miller told us as we stood outside her front door. The air was hot and stagnant. She hugged the baby girl. "When I was growing up, this was all forests. When the flood came in 1999, the hog house had just been built. The sheriff built it. That's why it's so close to the road."

"Did they warn you they were going to build it?" I asked.

"Nope. They figure, hey, I'm the sheriff, I ain't got to get your permission for nothing. The hog house is where that sprayer come from." She pointed to a field directly across the road from her front door. "They spray to my house." The manure cannon wasn't turned on that afternoon. "If he'd be spraying right now, it'd be shooting right here in the yard. All in you all face. He always spray Sunday."

"Just Sunday?"

"No, other days too. I don't use this door because it hit you right in the face."

"What does it smell like?"

"It smell worse than a decomposed dead body."

The little girl cooed. I wiped my forehead. Miller told us how the winds would sometimes bring the liquefied feces down on her property like rain. She stopped hanging laundry outside because it would get drenched with manure water.

"What health problems do you and your family have?" Keegan asked.

"I have asthma," Miller answered. "I have sinus, sarcoidosis from the bacteria. I have a pacemaker for sick sinus syndrome. My sister, she have asthma." Miller held up the baby girl's chubby fist. "This little one, *her* brother have asthma. He's three." She cuddled the girl. "And we don't know yet what she might have. Most everybody in this neighborhood got asthma or cancer. My neighbor died from cancer last year. My nephew, he's got terminal cancer at stage four. Not a smoker, not a drinker. It's in his lymph nodes."

"Has it affected your well water?" Keegan asked.

"Yes. Our well water got contaminated, so we had to go to county water. I have a monthly water bill now, which I didn't have before. Don't make no sense, do it? It's all about making money."

"Doesn't seem like they have decency," said Keegan.

"No," Miller replied. "They don't have decency. They don't have pity, they don't have love, they don't have faith, they don't have nothing. They might as well take a gun and shoot us because they're killing us slow."

A ten-wheeler livestock truck roared by, twenty feet from where we stood. It sent a hot blast of grit over us. The baby girl in Miller's arms was startled. She wobbled her head and held her hands up before turning to stare, open-mouthed, after the truck.

"I don't eat pork because I know where it come from," Miller said after the dust settled. "They put the dead hogs and the chicken in hog boxes by the road, the sick ones, the ones they can't sell. They stay in there, in the heat, all day. They swell up and they burst. A truck picks them up, takes them to a processing plant in Rose Hill, grind them up and feed them back to the hogs and cows. See, that's what you eat. If you knew where the bacon come from, you wouldn't eat no pork."

I paused, wanting to gag. "Do you know that for a fact? They grind them up and feed them back..."

"I know that for a fact. Here, come on, I'll show you the boxes. We can walk down to my family's graveyard too."

The little girl was starting to fuss, eating her fists, her forehead beaded with sweat.

"I imagine she's as hot as we are," I said.

"Yeah, I'll take her in."

Miller brought her great-niece inside the house to her mother, and rejoined us on the road. "Here we go," she sighed. "We can pass out before we get there. I'm not a heat person."

We walked down the asphalt.

I soon began to smell something awful.

There, down the road, were two large gray containers. Bloody fluid pooled under one. Both were piled high with large, decomposing pigs. Their legs stuck stiffly over the sides. The eyes were swollen, and the lips had begun to pull back from the teeth. Flies swarmed. A turkey vulture perched on a snout. It stretched its wings and pecked at the pig's dead eye.

"These ones ain't burst yet," Miller said in a muffled voice, holding her hand over her nose and mouth. "In a day, a truck will come, take them to Rose Hill, they'll get ground up into pig feed."

I pulled my T-shirt up over my nose as we walked by the boxes.

"The hog and chicken houses are right beside the graveyard," Miller said, after the smell had subsided enough to talk again. "They built the chicken houses last year."

The cemetery was a small, overgrown patch in the shade of a few large trees. The crooked white crosses didn't even come up to my knees. Next to the graveyard was a field. Long, low hog barns stood in the distance.

"You can tell where the graveyard start because it's where they stop cutting the grass," Miller said. "This is our cemetery. This is all my family. This is my uncle here. My brother. My sister. My nephew. He died 2012."

"How did he die?"

"Kidney failure. And that's my niece," Miller pointed to another marker. "They were twins. She died 2013; heart attack. All her artery was clogged. She loved pork. Her heart burst, collapsed on the floor. She was dead before they got her help."

In the distance, next to one of the barns, a Hispanic man shaded his eyes to peer at us.

Miller jerked her head at him. "He's the one gonna call the boss. The boss told me not to ever go on his land."

"Where's his land?" I asked.

"Right there." Miller pointed at where I stood.

"Oh." I moved back into the tall grass.

"When we have a funeral here," Miller said, "he spray."

"During the actual funeral he would spray?" Keegan asked.

"During the funeral, yeah."

"Does he do it on purpose?"

"He might not think so, but I do. Because he know he can."

"René," Keegan said, "people might say you're making trouble, but you're not making trouble at all. The hog operations are making trouble."

Miller beamed at Keegan, a remarkably bright smile. "I agree with that! People call me, 'Always starting trouble.' I talk on what I see."

The biting flies were vicious, and it was hot, even in the shade.

"Most of these hog and turkey houses is in a Black or Hispanic area," Miller said.

"Do you think it's a civil rights issue?" Keegan asked.

Miller paused. It was clear nobody had ever asked her that before, but she answered decisively. "Yes. Yes, I do. The white people, if they got farms, it's either a Hispanic living on it or African Americans. The white people might live in Raleigh or in Garner. They live wherever the hog houses stops."

"René, I'm sorry your family has to go through this," Keegan said.

"Yeah," Miller said. "I pray to God every day. I'll wear God's ear out. If he have an ear. I'll wear his spirit out."

"Does the government know about this?" I asked.

"Oh, they know. People been to Raleigh many times to tell them. Everybody in Duplin County's paid off by Smithfield. Ain't nobody here going to help us. People afraid to come forth."

"Are you concerned about speaking up?"

"No."

"Why not?"

"Maybe I can make a difference for my kids, my grandkids. I'm not saying anything will happen while I'm living—I might be dead, but at least I did something. I'll tell the truth if it's killing me—and that right there," she nodded at the hog farm, "that right there is killing me and my family."

***

Steve Wing, a professor from UNC at Chapel Hill, has been studying the impact of factory farms on neighboring communities since 1996. His research found that people living near CAFOs inhale microscopic particles of toxins such as endotoxins, molds, bacteria, and yeasts deep into their lungs, along with toxic gases like hydrogen sulfide, which is produced by anaerobic decomposition of pig feces, and ammonia, which can be absorbed in the upper respiratory tract, as well as burning the eyes and mucous membranes.

People living near a factory farm suffer far more headaches, diarrhea, coughing, sore throats, runny noses, and burning eyes than people who live elsewhere. Children at a school within three miles of a CAFO had significantly higher percentages of wheezing and asthma, asthma-related symptoms, and asthma-related medical visits.

Factory farm odors, either outside or inside their homes, spiked the blood pressure of subjects, and when smells were stronger, people felt more stressed, anxious, depressed, angry, and unable to focus. These people were confined, often without air conditioning, in their houses by the odors and the mists of fecal spray. They couldn't mow their lawns, garden, play, socialize, sit on their porches, use their well water, or have cookouts.

The water in these neighborhoods was teeming with parasites, fecal bacteria, viruses, nitrates, and other toxins from CAFO manure, particularly downstream from a factory farm, or after rain, which can carry fecal waste from spray fields into streams.[17]

Hurricane Floyd, the "flood" in 1999 mentioned by René Miller, washed *one hundred and twenty million gallons* of industrial fecal slurry—raw pig feces, urine, and the attendant mega-colonies of bacteria, viruses, pharmaceuticals, insecticides, hydrogen sulfide, methane, ammonia, phosphorus, and nitrates, just to name a few primary ingredients—into the Roanoke, Neuse, Tar, Pamlico, New and Cape Fear rivers. Marine life and human communities were decimated.[18]

One hundred and twenty million gallons of pig excrement. The amount of oil spilled by the Exxon Valdez was between 11 and 12 million gallons.[19]

"We do have a practical problem here," Governor James B. Hunt Jr., in a stunning understatement, admitted about the hog lagoons.[20]

But there's no need to wait for a natural disaster to be flooded by animal excrement. In 1995, a manure lagoon in North Carolina burst and heaved 25 million gallons of feces into the surrounding land and rivers.[21]

"It came through the woods," Celia Weston told the *New York Times*. Her three acres of tobacco and soybean crops were glazed with the sludge. "You could see the dark stuff. It made me sick. I thought, 'Oh, there goes our crops.'"[22]

The Cape Fear River suffered a 2 million gallon lagoon spill into its waters. One and a half million gallons was spewed into the Persimmon Branch. Another million into the Trent River, and

200,000 gallons into Turkey Creek. All within North Carolina, in the space of four years.[23]

These are waterways that human communities depend on to survive. Perhaps the most tangible signs of this foul contamination are the deaths, in the millions, of the fish who live in the water.

Ten million fish were killed in the 1995 lagoon rupture.[24] In 1996, forty CAFO waste spills killed close to 700,000 fish in Iowa, Minnesota, and Missouri.[25] In 1998, 100,000 gallons of industrial animal waste spewed into Minnesota's Beaver Creek, which killed almost 700,000 fish.[26] Between 1995-1998, there were at least 1,000 lagoon ruptures or other pollution resulting from industrial animal production across ten states, and 200 fecal-contamination-related fish kills that destroyed 13 million fish.[27]

Jeff Tietz in *Rolling Stone* memorably describes the catastrophic fish kill caused by the 1995 rupture:

> *"The sludge was so toxic it burned your skin if you touched it, and so dense it took almost two months to make its way sixteen miles downstream to the ocean. From the headwaters to the sea, every creature living in the river was killed. Fish died by the millions.*
>
> *"...Within a day dead fish completely covered the riverbanks, and between the floating and beached and piled fish the water scintillated out of sight up and down the river with billions of buoyant dead eyes and scales and white bellies—more fish than the river seemed capable of holding."[28]*

The burning, suffocating, gasping deaths of these fish are a magnification of what happens to the people who live every day with the poisonous air, water, and land near an industrial animal operation.

"The poor people," said Kemp Burdette of the Cape Fear River Watch, "they literally get shit on."[29]

Contaminants, particularly for people of color, are not just in the environment.

"When I was in my early 20s," Dr. Mills told us, "I would go with my colleagues and get frozen yogurt for lunch. By about 3 o'clock in the afternoon, I was sick as a dog. Gas, bloating, diarrhea, stomach cramps. I said to my mother, 'Mom, I may have colon cancer.' And she said, 'Oh, you just can't drink milk anymore.' She was well aware of lactose intolerance in African-Americans."

Lactose intolerance is the inability to digest lactose, the sugar found in milk. Just as Dr. Mills experienced, digestive problems like abdominal pain, bloating, diarrhea, nausea, and gas rear up soon after eating dairy products.[30]

"Now," Dr. Mills continues, "in my clinic work, an African-American man or woman will tell me they think they have irritable bowel syndrome or a spastic colon. From their symptoms, they're more likely lactose intolerant. I ask them to do two weeks of no dairy.

"In at least 80 percent of the cases, the symptoms disappear. But some of the patients say, 'I knew I was lactose intolerant, but the government dietary guidelines tell me I have to eat dairy for my health." Dr. Mills grunted angrily. "That pisses me off."

Dr. Mills was pissed off because up to 75 percent of African-Americans and Native Americans are lactose intolerant.[31] So are up to 80 percent of Latinos and Latinas,[32] as well as up to 90 percent of Asians.[33] Compare that with about 5 percent lactose intolerance in people of North European ancestry.[34] Researchers at Cornell found a wide range of lactose intolerance across the globe, from 2 percent in Denmark to 100 percent in Zambia.[35]

Dr. Greger told us, "Most people in the world are lactose intolerant. That's the normal state. It is actually lactase *persistence*, the ability to digest milk proteins after infancy, that is an unnatural state. A mutation allowed Caucasians in Northern Europe to survive during the winters by eating butterfat, and that gene spread. That's relatively recent in our evolution. For the majority of the world, most Asians and Africans for example, they can suffer gastrointestinal side effects from dairy, which may be a good thing because dairy consumption is associated with increased cancer risk, increased bone fracture risk, and shorter lifespans."

(A 2009 study declared that "Lactose Intolerance Rates May Be Significantly Lower than Previously Believed," citing only 10.05 percent lactose intolerance in Hispanics and 19.5 percent in African Americans. The catch? The study came from the National Dairy Council.[36])

"The government is telling me, as an African-American, to eat food that's going to make me ill, for no health benefit, and why?" Dr. Mills demanded. "Not for the calcium. You can get calcium in all kinds of non-dairy foods. It's primarily because of the lobbying power of the dairy industry. If that's not institutional racism, I don't know what is."

After one too many of his lactose intolerant African-American patients told him they were just following government guidelines, Dr. Mills went to Physicians Committee for Responsible Medicine in the late '90s and proposed an article on nutritional racism. PCRM was immediately on board, deciding to examine not just lactose intolerance, but also other diseases prevalent in communities of color.

PCRM published a two-part article in 1999 called "Racial Bias in Federal Nutrition Policy." The paper set off a storm of controversy, but Dr. Mills was pleased that it helped pull dietary guidelines towards plant-based foods.

MyPlate, a visual depiction of the most recent government guidelines, makes it clear that vegetables and fruits should make up larger portions of what we eat. The chart is circular, like a plate, with sections labeled for different food groups. And yet MyPlate, which is meant to cover recommendations for every American, still has a circle, like the footprint of a glass on a placemat, marked "Dairy." That circle represents the daily 2-3 servings of dairy, per person, endorsed by the government.[37]

"What do you think about that little dairy circle on MyPlate?" I asked Dr. Mills.

"It's a bird dropping," he says shortly. "It shouldn't be there. We should not be consuming the milk of another species. There's a very strong link between dairy and prostate cancer, for example. That's particularly significant for African-Americans and other people of color because we know heart disease, cancer, diabetes, kidney stones, and other diseases tend to strike ethnic minorities to a greater degree and with greater lethalness, when they eat a Western diet."

African-Americans in the US have a 26 percent higher incidence of cancer, compared to white Americans. African-Americans also have 53 percent higher rates of lung cancer, 40 percent higher rates of hypertension, and a 36 percent higher incidence of prostate cancer. An African-American woman is 67 percent more likely to die of breast cancer than a Caucasian American woman. Obesity in African-American and Mexican-American women, compared to white women in this country, is 45 percent greater. Latinas have twice the rate of heart disease as white women in the States. Diabetes in Latinos is 53 percent higher, and 69 percent higher in African-American men, than in white men. Rates of diabetes among African-American women are more than twice as high as among white women. Diabetes rates in Native American women are more than triple those in white women.[38]

Dick Gregory, the African-American civil rights activist, entertainer, and vegan, was way ahead of his time when he said, decades ago, "[T]he quickest way to wipe out a group of people is to put them on a 'soul-food' diet. One of the tragedies is that the very folks in the Black community, who are most sophisticated in terms of the political realities in this country, are nonetheless advocates of soul food. They will lay down a heavy rap on genocide in America with regard to Black folks, then walk into a soul-food restaurant and help the genocide along."[39]

Soul food is the traditional diet of southern African-Americans, the descendants of slaves. Deep-fried, battered chicken, pork and gravy, vegetables slow-cooked with animal fat, and tons of butter, cream, and sugar are all typical of soul food. It's also known as "heart-attack on a plate."

"Black people think these foods constitute our ethnic identity as African Americans," Dr. Mills said, "but when you look at traditional West African diets—and I talk about West Africa because that's where the slaves who became African-Americans were taken from—those diets are typically plant-based diets, very low in fat, containing very little meat and no dairy.

"When a population that is adapted to a low-fat, plant-based diet, is suddenly exposed to high levels of fat, animal protein, and not enough fiber and antioxidants, they're much more likely to develop chronic diseases, the way you see in the African-American population today. People in West Africa did not eat all this crap that we call soul food.

"When blacks were brought to the plantation, they were forced to eat the garbage. That's why they had to eat the entrails, the pig intestines full of shit—those became 'chitlins'; the hooves became 'pig's feet'; the bones of the neck and the tail became 'ox-tails' and 'neck bones.' This is not our true heritage," Dr. Mills said quietly. "This is the legacy of the plantation. It is plantation food. It's killing us. We need to realize that we are still carrying the vestiges of slavery on our dinner plates. We need to get back to our true heritage, and that is a plant-based, low-fat diet."

I got chills. "Soul food. It's slave food."

"That is exactly what it is."

Decolonizing poor people of color through diet was a new concept to me. It's about wresting power back from those who have dominated so many for so long—whether they are corporations who have been the puppet-masters of our government and society for decades, or slave masters and colonial oppressors who began kidnapping and raping other peoples centuries ago for their own gain.

Our unquestioning consumption today drapes us in heavy chains. Those chains are frequently invisible to us. They would seem weightless too, were it not for the grave burden of illness they inflict. Corporations deliberately stoke our unthinking consumption. They feed on it, growing bloated with wealth from our diseases, our disabilities, and our desperation. All social injustice is linked. Our country's unspeakably broken food system, our broken medical system—these are health issues, environmental issues, animal welfare issues, civil rights issues, and they are human rights issues.

"When Americans become truly concerned with the purity of the food that enters their own personal systems," Dick Gregory said, "when they learn to eat properly, we can expect to see profound changes effected in the social and political system of this nation. The two systems are inseparable."[40]

"I understand," A. Breeze Harper writes in *Sistah Vegan*, "that many of us have our ethnic and racial identities embedded in the foods that we and our families have been eating since colonial times. We are scared to lose these... [and] I've met many people of color who are misinformed that eco-sustainability and plant-based diets are a "white thing"; that it goes against what makes them Black, Asian, Chicano, Native Americans, and so on...However, I do ask you, How did our ancestors eat *before* colonization?"[41]

Lauren Ornelas understands that food is a political tool. She also knows too well that healthy food is often an unattainable luxury. A Latina with a T-shirt that proclaims "BROWN AND PROUD," she is the founder of Food Empowerment Project (FEP), a food justice organization based in Northern California.

"Not consuming animal products is one way to reject colonialism," Ornelas told me. "The reason so many people of color cannot digest the milk of another species is because colonialism, a relatively recent phenomenon, brought many of the animals in our diets today—cows and goats, for example—into Latin America. Our diet, before colonizers came in, was mostly squash and beans and foods like that."

For many people, though, turning away from animal products is not as simple as deciding to do so.

"Today, across the US and globally," Ornelas said, "access to healthy foods is a privilege and not a right. Communities of color often have no super markets, no urban gardens, and what's more readily available are liquor stores masquerading as grocery stores, which mainly sell alcohol and chips. There's probably more fast food. And the reason people living in these neighborhoods can't afford or don't have access to healthy foods is because maybe they work two or three jobs, and the grocery store closes at 8pm and they don't get off work until midnight. What's open to them are convenience stores, where the fruit and vegetables are rotten. Even if they have canned fruits and vegetables, they'll often be expired. They may have to take two buses to get to a place that sells fresh produce.

"It's important to understand," she said emphatically, "when you hear about high rates of diabetes, obesity, or other health problems plaguing communities of color, it's not that they don't care about their health. Many of them want to eat healthier, but there are many barriers in the way."

I nodded. "But maybe they could take that extra bus ride to a good store on a day off?"

"A lot of these people don't have days off," Ornelas said gently. I felt like an idiot. "They'll work seven days a week. Farm workers, they pick our fruits and vegetables but don't have access to the same fruits and vegetables they're picking. They work from sun up to sun down, and if they get a day off, all they want to do is sleep. Their bodies are exhausted. They want to spend that short time with their families.

"But it's more than proximity," she continues. "It's the fact that people aren't making living wages. We're not even talking about a budget. We're talking about people who *have no money.* We have to fight for living wages so it's not a privilege but a right, for human beings to have access to healthy foods."

Addiction is another plague of low-income communities. A lot of well-meaning people shake their heads over addiction. Parents educate their kids on the dangers of marijuana, meth, cocaine, and heroin, and make sure there's always a designated driver.

But another addiction, just as lethal, is often ignored. It is the addiction to killer foods.

"Think about the proliferation of junk food in Black communities," bell hooks writes in *Breaking Bread: Insurgent Black Intellectual Life*. "You can go to any Black community and see Black folks of all ages gobbling up junk food morning, noon, and night. I would like to suggest that the feeling those kids are getting when they're stuffing Big Macs, Pepsi, and barbecue potato chips down their throats is similar to the ecstatic, blissful moment of the narcotics addict."[42]

The addiction to killer foods coils around the whole nation, from inner cities to the most affluent gated communities. And the roots of this addiction are lodged deep in our prehistoric past. Our cravings are a mutation of survival instincts that helped *homo sapiens* endure for millennia.

We evolved in an environment of scarcity. Our ancestors, living in the wilderness—without agriculture, domesticated herds, grocery stores, or 24-hour Mickey D's—were much more likely to die of starvation than anything else.[43]

Occasionally though, our ancestors would get a windfall of animal meat and the attendant fat, brains, and bone marrow. Time to celebrate! Hurray for super concentrated calories! It was a vacation from foraging. Our early human predecessors glutted themselves—it could be a very, very long time before they had a feast like that again.

Our bodies, always looking for a survival edge, evolved to seek out food with the most extreme caloric density for the least amount of effort.[44] Meat has about 1,200 calories per pound while raw salad vegetables have about 100 calories per pound.[45] Guess which meal our ancestors would have lunged for?

Things continued like this for the first 99 percent of human history.

But then you transplant that human animal—who has survived for thousands of years thanks to a cunning radar for fat, sugar, and salt—into the 21st century United States of America. They're now deluged by mounds of grease, animal tissue, and cascades of sugar and salt. It's more than anyone could possibly eat, although we do try our best.

That's the situation we're in now. Our brains are still hard-wired for scarcity and famine. We still have those primordial instincts to seek out fat, though we can walk into any diner and order bacon cheeseburgers, chicken parmesan, pulled pork sandwiches, egg salad, and shrimp scampi.

"These fascinating functional MRI studies look at areas of the brain associated with addiction and pleasure," Dr. Davis told us. "Overweight patients have a brain that looks very similar to an alcoholic, or a cocaine addict.[46] Specifically, they don't have as many dopamine receptors in the pleasure centers of their brain. And if you talk to any of my overweight patients, they never feel satisfied. They eat, but they don't get the same satisfaction that someone else might."

This is called "tolerance" in drug abuse. The first hit of a drug can be orgasmic. Both addictive drugs and a high-fat, salty, sugary meal can release large amounts of dopamine—a pleasurable, oh-yeah-baby-give-me-more neurotransmitter—in the brain. The higher the caloric density, the more dopamine is secreted. But if the drugs or the high-fat meals become a habit, and routinely bathe the brain in unnaturally high amounts of dopamine, then the dopamine receptors are overwhelmed. The brain takes action by producing less dopamine, or even removing the receptors.[47]

When this happens, the body requires a higher and higher dosage, be it heroin or triple-cheese pizza, to achieve the same "high."[48] The scientific term is neuroadaptation[49]—literally, the adaptation of your nerves to the addictive substance.

"Scientific investigation," writes Dr. Goldhamer in *The Pleasure Trap*, "has confirmed this astonishing fact: Human beings show evidence of neuroadaptation to modern processed foods in much the same manner that drug addiction involves acquired tolerance to pleasure-triggering drugs."[50]

"You are just as addicted as somebody who is addicted to drugs," Dr. Goldhamer told us in person. "It is the same neural chemical in cascade."

And as if the primal early human screaming in our brain wasn't enough, "food manufacturers have entire laboratories to manipulate the chemistry of food so that it can bang on the dopamine circuitry in people's brains most effectively," Dr. Goldhamer continued.

Compounds that trigger our pleasure centers are isolated, added, and artificially enhanced in food to more efficiently ensnare us. Wild animals, the kind our ancestors occasionally ate, had maybe 15 percent fat. Now, animals bred for food are genetically engineered and fed diets, as well as drugs and hormones, designed to push the fat percentages of their flesh up to 50 percent or more.[51] This extra fat is what causes the "marbling" in steak. According to culinary experts, the more marbling, the tastier.[52]

I know firsthand about cheese addiction.

"The casein protein," Dr. Barnard told us, "is the main protein in dairy, and particularly in cheese, which is very concentrated. Casein breaks apart in the human digestive system to create casomorphins. These are casein-derived, morphine-like compounds that attach to the very same brain receptors as heroin. Don't get me wrong, they're not as strong, but they're strong enough to make you come back again and again to dairy, to cheese, despite the fact that you're gaining weight, despite the fact that you're unhealthier than you've ever been. I've had hundreds of people come here and adopt plant-based diets. Their diabetes improves or goes away, they lose weight, their cholesterol comes down, all kinds of benefits. But then a few say, 'I really miss cheese.' I think, 'Why? It smells like old socks.' Well, casomorphins is why."

Casomorphins are found in human breast milk as well.

"It triggers a very calming dopamine release," Levin said. "Whether you're a baby calf or a baby human, you need to crave milk from your mother. So it makes sense that milk is a bit addictive, for the survival of that species."

Ever seen the look on a breastfeeding infant in the arms of his or her mama? They're blissed out. And then they nod off. Kind of like… well, you know where I'm going with this. And then consider that cow's milk has twice the amount of casein as human breast milk.[53] That's potent stuff.

"Dairy truly is an addiction," Dr. Davis said. "One of the most recent meds that I've been using with my patients blocks the opiate receptor, so when they eat cheese they don't get the high. And then they don't want the cheese. Many of the medicines we're using now for weight loss can be used with addiction."

"If I had to pick one food to eliminate from America today," Dr. Kahn told us, "I would be extremely unpopular, and probably pick cheese. It causes a chemical addiction similar to drugs."

"Cheese is almost the perfect food to compromise health," said Dr. Goldhamer. "It's an animal product, so you've got all the issues of biological concentration. It's a highly processed food that naturally has a lot of saturated fat, and then you put a lot of sodium into it. Cheese is something we wouldn't use with any patient, at any time, for any reason."

"About 100 years ago," Levin said, "most Americans were eating about 3 pounds of cheese per year. Now, we're each eating about 34 pounds per year. We are consuming excessive amounts of something that is mostly saturated fat."

"What would you tell a patient trying to wean themselves off cheese or dairy?" I asked. I was thinking of my own cheese habit.

"Go cold turkey, pardon the pun," she said. "Give yourself 3 weeks. Don't even think past 3 weeks. That liberates your mind.

Don't get near whatever you're craving. Don't let it in your house. Often if you don't touch it for three weeks, there may be some new health benefit to keep you motivated. 'My skin's clearer.' 'My energy is higher.' 'I've lost those pounds I wanted to lose.' 'My allergies are better.' Once you see the benefit, it's hard to go back.

"It's not funny to me that people are addicted to cheese," Levin said. "I think it should be treated the way we treat tobacco addiction—it's real and it can make you sick."

The problems of sugar, unlike cheese, have been common knowledge for decades. When I was a kid, my mom was always telling me to eat less sugar. And there's been a spate of movies tackling the issue of excess sugar in the American diet. Sugar, to be sure, is not a health food, and we need to rein in our outrageous intake. But at least there is awareness about the impact of sugar on health. You don't hear so much about the dangers of meat, dairy, and eggs.

I wanted to know how these two megaliths, sugar and animal protein, stack up when it comes to promoting disease. A kind of dietary Celebrity Death Match.

There was unanimous agreement among the health experts we talked to, ranging from cardiologists to dietitians to critical care physicians.

Animal protein thrashed sugar.

"When it comes to the health threats that put Americans in the hospital, on the operating table, and on the autopsy table," Dr. Klaper said, "it's by far the animal flesh-based diet that is the number one culprit. The sugar is an accomplice, but it's the animal flesh that's really killing us."

"Research shows that animal products are definitely more damaging to health than sugar," Levin told us. "High-fat diets, including diets high in animal protein, contribute more calories, leading to excess weight. A gram of sugar has 4 calories whereas a gram of fat has 9, so you're more than doubling your caloric intake when you're eating fat. Fat builds up plaque in your arteries, causing your blood flow to slow down. It's going to jack up your bad cholesterols. That all contributes to heart disease. High fat diets are associated with diseases like Type 2 diabetes and different types of cancer, especially hormone cancers like breast and prostate cancer. Animal products are definitely riskier."

"Dr. Walter Kempner at Duke University, back in the 1940s, was one of the first to reverse some of our killer diseases with diet alone," Dr. Greger said. "The diet he used was not only strictly plant-based, it was extremely restrictive: rice, fruit, and table sugar. You don't hear a lot about Kempner these days because it came out later that he was really abusing his patients to get them to adhere to this insane diet. But the study is sound. These patients basically had death sentences, went to Kempner, and were given sugar. On this diet they were able to reverse their high blood pressure, diabetes and many of its complications like blindness and retinopathy, heart disease, malignant hypertension that had an average life expectancy of six months. (This was before modern blood pressure pills.) Kempner was producing dramatic reversals of chronic disease. It was a horribly deficient diet, but it just shows that what's to blame is the animal protein, the fat, the sodium."

And no, the study was not funded by the sugar industry. Good question, though.

"Show me a single study," said Dr. Esselstyn, "where somebody continues to eat all this beefsteak, butter, gravy and the typical Western diet, but you stop the sugar—when has that ever reversed heart disease? Is there a single study? No."

If the world cut back on sugary soda, about 300,000 lives around the globe would be saved.[54] Processed meat, however, is responsible for the deaths of over 800,000 people. Which also happens to be about four times as many people who die from illegal drug use.[55]

This is according to the Global Burden of Disease Study, the most comprehensive risk analysis of the causes of death ever performed. It was published in 2012 in one of the world's most respected medical journals, the *Lancet*, and funded by the Bill and Melinda Gates Foundation. Close to 500 researchers from 300 different organizations in fifty countries assessed almost 100,000 data sources.[56] It's hard to argue with.

The animal proteins are killing us. But the pleasure center of our brains still ping like crazy when we eat things that increased our ancestors' chances of survival in the wilderness. *More, more, more,* our brains moan, as the fat stimulates floods of dopamine through our neural circuitry.[57] Our hearts fail, our little children get diabetes, we die from cancer in epidemic proportions, our obesity rates skyrocket, and still our primordial brains yearn for, and almost always get, the next dietary dopamine fix, stockpiling the fat and calories and sodium for a long winter famine that never comes.

Addiction can be exhibited in at least three ways. The addict craves the addictive substance. The addict loses self-control over the addictive substance. And the addict continues to use the addictive substance in spite of severe consequences.[58]

Hello, my name is America, and I am an addict.

And who's the biggest pusher of them all? Look no farther than the one and only—your very own—Uncle Sam.

CHAPTER 14

HENS IN THE FOX DEN

The year was 1977.

An extraordinary thing happened.

An American politician, on January 14, stood up before the press and declared, "The simple fact is that our diets have changed radically within the last 50 years...These dietary changes represent as great a threat to public health as smoking. Too much fat, too much sugar or salt, can be and are linked directly to heart disease, cancer, obesity, and stroke, among other killer diseases. In all, six of the ten leading causes of death in the United States have been linked to our diet."

Then most astoundingly:

"Those of us within Government have an obligation to acknowledge this."

That was Democratic Senator George McGovern of South Dakota. He was chairman of the Select Committee on Nutrition and Human Needs, which had just released the first edition of *Dietary Goals for the United States*. The Select Committee was sometimes called the McGovern Committee, and the paper soon came to be known as the McGovern Report. It was the first comprehensive statement ever made by the US Federal government on the risk factors of the American diet.[1]

McGovern hoped the *Dietary Goals* would "perform a function similar to that of the Surgeon General's Report on Smoking."[2]

"The purpose of this report," he wrote in the Foreword, "is to point out that the eating patterns of this century represent as critical a public health concern as any now before us."[3]

Dr. Mark Hegsted, Professor of Nutrition from the Harvard School of Public Health, helped prepare the report.

"The diet of the American people has become increasingly rich—rich in meat, other sources of saturated fat and cholesterol, and in sugar..." Dr. Hegsted said at the January 1977 press conference. "It should be emphasized that this diet which affluent people generally consume is everywhere associated with a similar disease pattern—high rates of ischemic heart disease, certain forms of cancer, diabetes, and obesity...[These] are the diseases that kill us. They are epidemic in our population...We have an obligation to inform the public of the current state of knowledge."[4]

Let me just say again that these statements were made in 1977.

The McGovern Report was based on years of hearings and scientific reviews. The National Nutrition Policy Study Conference in 1974, which brought together nutritionists, physicians, public health officials, consumer advocates, farmers, and food industry executives, was an important resource for the Committee. The conference examined the relationship between meat and chronic disease, as well as malnourishment—including overconsumption.[5]

Ted Kennedy, in his opening remarks for the conference, said, "America stands in ironic contrast [to the children of West Africa] as a land of overindulged and excessively fed. In many ways the well-being of the overfed is as threatened as the undernourished."[6]

The McGovern Committee believed that millions of American consumers wanted better information on food and health issues,[7] and it worked passionately to deliver that information. After the 1974 conference, the Committee held hearings in a quest to reverse diet-related disease.[8]

Subterranean rumbles, in response, were beginning to rock the meat industry.

David Stroud, president of the National Live Stock and Meat Board, which represented beef, pork, and lamb producers, knew the McGovern Committee was highly esteemed. Its reports were the highest in demand among government publications. When Stroud heard of the Committee's new diet/disease hearings, he sent a confidential message in February 1976 to Meat Board members, warning of beef's "serious erosion in market position" if the link between beef and disease were pursued in the public arena. For several years already the meat industry had "been the focus of serious and sustained criticism on moral, economic and health grounds." Stroud advised meat producers to be on guard against "tough questions about the necessity of the meat industry at all."[9]

The McGovern Committee's hearings, "Diet Related to Killer Diseases," began in July 1976. Senators heard from scientists and other experts on the relationship between the American diet and diseases like heart disease and cancer.

Six months later, *Dietary Goals for the United States*—the McGovern Report—was released.

The report urged Americans to reduce overall fat, saturated fat, and cholesterol consumption.[10] Meat, eggs, and dairy provided almost 45 percent of the country's total fat intake, 60 percent of saturated fat, and 100 percent of its cholesterol.[11] The message of the McGovern report was, essentially, "Eat fewer animal products."

To make it really clear, the report stated explicitly that Americans should "Decrease consumption of meat," and "Decrease consumption of butterfat [dairy fat], eggs, and other high cholesterol sources."[12]

The meat, egg, and dairy industries went insane.

"The [1977] dietary goals," Jane Brody wrote in the *New York Times*, "provoked loud opposition from major sectors of the food industry, particularly the producers of meat, eggs, and dairy products."[13]

"The Meat, Milk, and Egg Producers were very upset," Dr. Mark Hegsted said later in an interview. "[T]he beef people were complaining vigorously."[14]

David Stroud, definitely one of "the beef people," said, "much of the poor advice has come from zealots with a good deal to say but little to no scientific evidence supporting their positions."[15]

Meat Board Reports, an industry journal, accused the Select Committee of having "listened only to the clique of promoters holding this point of view, whose motives are questionable."[16]

The National Dairy Council wanted the report withdrawn and rewritten to have "the endorsement of the food industry."[17]

The meat and egg industries demanded additional hearings to present their case. The hearings were granted in March and July.[18] Wray Finney, president of the American National Cattlemen's Association, crowed that now the McGovern Committee could "conduct a truly unbiased examination of all the facts," so Americans would receive "a balanced, correct view of this whole matter."[19]

A week before the March hearings, the National Live Stock and Meat Board sent a list of 24 Meat-Board-approved experts[20] to the McGovern Committee to stand as witnesses, including David Stroud and Wray Finney.[21]

Those speaking for the meat industry insisted there was no "proof" of the connection between diet and disease, and that therefore one could not make a statement linking the two.[22]

In a typical exchange, Senator McGovern questioned Dr. E.H. Ahlers, a nutrition researcher and one of the Meat Board's experts, about an international survey conducted by the University of Oslo. The survey polled 209 specialists who were called by the *Los Angeles Times* a *"Who's Who* of nutrition researchers, physicians, nutritionists, epidemiologists, geneticists, and others who are studying lipids and atherosclerosis."[23]

Senator McGovern: *92 percent of these doctors surveyed [in the Oslo report] have changed their own dietary patterns [reducing fat and cholesterol in response to knowledge about diet and heart disease]... Because we are dealing with probabilities, rather than scientific fact, if you wanted to follow the prudent course, where you minimized the danger of risk, would you generally follow the recommendations for dietary goals set by our committee, or would you say to ignore them?*

Dr. Ahlers: *The proof is not there yet...It is a matter of balancing the risks and the benefits. I truly believe the risks and the benefits are both very small. I think your report should emphasize the uncertainties that still exist and should not imply that by heeding these recommendations the public will reduce its risks of suffering the several diseases identified in this report.*[24]

The proof was not there yet, the powerful meat industry insisted.

So *Dietary Guidelines for the United States* was rewritten.

A second edition, that "had the endorsement of the food industry," was issued in December 1977.

"[A]fter the sustained outcry from the meat industry..." wrote the *New York Times*, "the committee changed its specific recommendation that Americans 'decrease consumption of meat and increase consumption of poultry and fish' to one that urged they 'decrease consumption of animal fat and choose meat, poultry and fish which will reduce saturated fat intake.'"[25]

The second edition hastened to add, "the 300 mg per day [cholesterol] recommendation does not mean eliminating egg consumption... Eggs are an excellent, inexpensive source of protein, vitamins and minerals."[26]

And since the risk of heart disease is lower among pre-menopausal women, and children and the elderly require especially good sources of protein, vitamins and minerals, the report suggested that those groups might want to include *more* eggs in their diet, "even to the point of easing the cholesterol recommendation to increase egg consumption."

The paper goes on schizophrenically to warn that for the last quarter century, steadily mounting evidence has shown that dietary cholesterol is a risk factor for heart disease, and that heart disease is the number one killer in the country. Therefore, the report reiterated the importance of limiting cholesterol to 300 mg a day.[27]

Right. Limit your cholesterol. But don't stop eating eggs. Women, children, and the elderly should eat even more eggs. Watch out for that cholesterol though.

The second edition also made it clear that the Select Committee never recommended a reduction in protein, and certainly never favored vegetable protein over animal protein. "In fact," the second edition declares, "meat, poultry and fish are an excellent source of essential amino acids, vitamins and minerals."[28]

Included in the second edition was a Foreword written by Republican Senator Charles Percy of Illinois. Senator Percy admits, "I have serious reservations about certain aspects of the report... I have become increasingly aware of the lack of consensus among nutrition scientists and other health professionals."[29]

In another mollifying gesture, testimonies of the Meat Board experts were printed in their entirety in *Dietary Goals for the United States—Supplemental Views.*[30]

The meat, egg, and dairy industries had won.

And shortly after the second edition of *Dietary Goals* was released, the McGovern Committee was no more.[31]

"[M]isshapen and bent by a number of powerful interests," wrote the *New York Times*, "a proposal…would eliminate the Select Committee on Nutrition and Human Needs and tuck its functions into a subcommittee of the Agriculture Committee. It's not exactly sending the chickens off to live with the foxes, but the image will do… The Agriculture Committee looks after the producers of food, not the consumers, and particularly, not the most needy."[32]

That's the situation we are in today.

George McGovern, by the way, lost his Senate seat in 1980, three years after the McGovern report. He lost to Republican James Abdnor, a cattle rancher[33] who had the best interests of the cattle industry at heart.[34]

***

Welcome to the United States Department of Agriculture.

This is where, today, the chickens live with the foxes.

"The US Department of Agriculture was created to support agriculture," Susan Levin told us. "They make sure that farmers—well, now they're usually corporations—are successful at pushing their product. Then later, the USDA became responsible for making nutrition recommendations. This conflict of interest is so obvious. The USDA is pushing milk, eggs, cheese and beef on the public, while telling them they need to reduce their saturated fat and cholesterol. And what products are those found in?"

"The USDA has two conflicting missions," said Dr. Davis. "It's supposed to protect us, the consumers, and it's supposed to protect the producer. Guess what, when those two interests come head-to-head, they usually choose the producer. It takes a lot to convince them that we need to eat less meat because if we eat less meat, the USDA is failing on one of their primary goals, which is to protect the meat industry."

One of the major tools used by the USDA to influence American consumers is the *Dietary Guidelines for Americans.* This federal report has been issued every 5 years by the USDA and the Department of Health and Human Services (HHS) since 1980, shortly after the McGovern report was introduced.[35] The *Guidelines* advise Americans on what to eat, according to the latest medical, scientific, and nutritional research.

But there's a disturbing pattern when you look at the members, through the years, of the Dietary Guidelines Advisory Committee (DGAC), the group selected by the USDA and HHS to provide an Advisory Report:[36]

⇒ 1995: **3 out of 11** members of the DGAC had current or previous ties to food and/or drug industries, including the National Dairy Council, Bristol-Myers Squibb, International Life Sciences Institute (lobby group funded by food, drug, and chemical companies[37]), Proctor & Gamble;

⇒ 2000: **7 out of 11** members with current or previous industry ties, including the National Dairy Council, National Live Stock and Meat Board, Dairy Management, Inc., the Egg Nutrition Center;

⇒ 2005: **11 out of 13** members with current or previous industry ties, including the American Egg Board, National Dairy Council, National Dairy Board, Wisconsin Milk Marketing Board, Proctor & Gamble, Bristol-Myers Squibb;

⇒ 2010: **9 out of 13** members with current or previous industry ties, including the Dannon Institute, Kraft General Foods, Campbell's Soup Company, McDonald's, Novo Nordisk, Eli Lilly, Chocolate Manufacturers Association, and GlaxoSmithKline.[38]

Here's a closer look at the industry ties of just the 2000 Committee, ties that existed during or before their tenure on the DGAC:

⇒ American Meat Institute
⇒ National Live Stock and Meat Board
⇒ National Dairy Council
⇒ National Dairy Promotion and Research Board
⇒ National Dairy Board
⇒ Wisconsin Milk Marketing Board
⇒ American Egg Board
⇒ Mead Johnson Nutritionals
⇒ American Council on Science and Health (lobbying group[39])
⇒ International Food Information Council (PR arm of the food and agriculture industries[40])
⇒ International Life Sciences Institute (which the WHO barred from participating in setting global health standards because of their financial stakes in the outcome[41])
⇒ Gatorade Life Sciences Institute
⇒ The Dannon Company
⇒ Kraft Foods
⇒ Nestlé
⇒ Slim-Fast
⇒ Sugar Association
⇒ Grain Foods Foundation
⇒ Kellogg Company
⇒ Campbell Soup Company
⇒ Miller Brewing Company
⇒ Health Valley Foods
⇒ Weight Watchers
⇒ Peanut Institute
⇒ Chocolate Manufacturers Association
⇒ American Pharmaceutical Association
⇒ National Association of Chain Drug Stores

And because enough paper has been wasted on this list, here are all the pharmaceutical companies connected to the 2000 DGAC: GlaxoSmithKline, Bristol-Meyers Squibb, Procter & Gamble, Merck, Hoffman-La Roche, Johnson & Johnson, King Pharmaceuticals, Knoll Pharmaceuticals, Abbott Laboratories, Wyeth Ayerst Laboratories, Eli Lilly, AstraZeneca, BreathQuant, Critical Therapeutics, Warner Lambert, Pharmanex, Dey, Genetech, Janssen, MedImmune, Novartis, Oridion, Pathogen Scientific, Schering-Plough, Verus, Boehringer Ingelheim, Novo Nordisk and Sanofi-Synthelabo.[42]

That was just one incarnation of the Dietary Guidelines Advisory Committee.

Mind: blown.

But that was back in 2000. The 2015 DGAC released their Advisory Report in February 2015. It had some unusual recommendations.

"[T]he U.S. population," wrote the 2015 DGAC, "should be encouraged and guided to consume dietary patterns that are rich in vegetables, fruits, whole grains, seafood, legumes, and nuts; moderate in low- and non-fat dairy products and alcohol (among adults); **lower in red and processed meat**; and low in sugar-sweetened foods and beverages and refined grains."[43] (Italics added.)

"Consistent evidence indicates that, in general," continued the Advisory Report, "a dietary pattern that is higher in plant-based foods, such as vegetables, fruits, whole grains, legumes, nuts, and seeds, and **lower in animal-based foods is more health promoting**...than is the current average U.S. diet."[44] (Italics added.)

This was a revolutionary report.

The DGAC, however, does not determine the *Dietary Guidelines*. The USDA and HHS ultimately write the *Guidelines*.[45] They are advised not only by the DGAC, but also by lobbyists, industry interests [you have to check out this footnote],[46] and other politicians who may be swayed and made to dance like marionettes on a string.

In a stunning reversal of history, in March 2015, shortly after the release of the DGAC's Advisory Report, Republican Senator John Thune of South Dakota—in the Senate seat once occupied by George McGovern—led 29 other Republican Senators in sending a letter to USDA Secretary Tom Vilsack and HHS Secretary Sylvia Burwell. The letter urged the USDA and HHS to "reject the [DGA] committee's inconsistent conclusions and recommendations regarding the role of lean red meat in a healthy diet," which "is alarming to the livestock, pork, and poultry industries."[47]

I read this letter on Senator Thune's website, my heart aching for George McGovern, who, sitting in the same Senate seat, had tried to tell the truth to the American public almost four decades earlier.

The thirty senators speaking for the "alarmed" livestock industries received over one million dollars from the food industry between 2013-2014—half of which came from the beef and cattle industry.[48]

When the 2015-2020 *Dietary Guidelines for Americans* was released in January 2016, there was no mention, despite the explicit advice of the DGAC, of reducing meat consumption.[49] The 2015 *Guidelines* recommend just over two pounds a week of meat, poultry, eggs, and seafood—exactly the same as the 2010 *Guidelines*.[50]

"This is virtual proof that the USDA is not allowed to say anything negative about red meat," Walter Willett, chair of the department of nutrition at the Harvard School of Public Health, told the *Boston Globe*.

Perhaps in Willett's indignation could be heard the echo of Dr. Mark Hegsted, his predecessor at the Harvard School of Public Health, who had assisted George McGovern with the McGovern Report.

"The basic censorship of the report from the Advisory Committee," Willett continued, "is deeply troublesome."[51]

Can you hear the foxes whispering to the chickens?

Come on chickens, we'll take good care of you, we have lots of tasty food here, very healthy for you...

***

"The craziest thing in the work I do is the checkoff program," Mark Kennedy, legal director for PCRM, told Keegan and I. Kennedy is a soft-spoken man, though as he talks, he grows animated.

"Checkoff programs are created by the USDA," he said. "These programs tax all the producers of a particular industry. For instance, beef, pork, dairy, and eggs all have their own checkoff program. The milk producers might be charged by the gallon, or the beef industry might pay $1 per cattle. All that money goes into a big fund overseen by the USDA, and pays for marketing campaigns for that industry as a whole. Everyone has seen these government advertising schemes: *Milk: It Does a Body Good.* Or *Beef: It's What's For Dinner.*

"In the last fifteen years," Kennedy went on, "the USDA has begun using checkoff programs to advertise for 'industry trendsetters.' McDonald's, for instance, is an industry trendsetter in the beef, dairy or pork field, because they sell so many burgers, milk products, or can put bacon on a burger.

"This is the USDA, the government, jamming as much crap on food as they can," he said. "Those ads for Pizza Hut, the stuffed crust, a pound of cheese: that's a government program. A few years ago, the dairy checkoff program gave $12 million [actually $35 million, according to recent research[52]] to Domino's Pizza to market new, cheese-heavy products, so that other restaurants can look to Domino's and say, 'Wow, the pound of cheese worked for them, we'll do it too.'"

The dairy checkoff promotes what it calls "cheese-demand enhancement" by working with Domino's.[53] Since the start of their partnership in 2009, 10 billion pounds of extra milk have been used by the pizza industry.[54]

"At McDonald's," said Kennedy, "you have the McCafé, which is in theory a coffee, but it's more than 50 percent milk. Again, you have the promotion of the milk industry through this product. McDonald's has six people staffed full-time, whose salaries are paid for by [the government dairy] program.[55] These six people come up with how to put more cheese on beef, how to put more milk in a coffee, anything to drive up the consumption of these unhealthy products.

"The Wendy's Bacon Double Cheeseburger: government program," Kennedy continued. "Angus Steak and Egg sandwich at Dunkin' Donuts: government program! You'd never think that this— pure garbage from a food standpoint—is coming from a federally funded program."

I had never heard of checkoff programs, though of course I'd seen the milk mustache commercials, and I knew all the slogans— Pork: The Other White Meat, The Incredible Edible Egg—better than nursery rhymes.

Keegan and I went to talk with David Robinson Simon, author of *Meatonomics*. Simon reminded me of a silver-haired David Duchovy from the original X-Files days.

"One reason checkoffs are so creepy," Simon said, "is because it's our government telling us, 'Eat more beef.' 'Drink more milk.' 'Eat more cheese.' These checkoff programs bombard us with messages all day long, in every single medium. They inculcate the belief that these products are necessary. 'Beef: It's What's for Dinner' gets into our subconscious and people wandering around the grocery store looking for dinner suddenly think: beef! That's the impact of these messages being presented to us over and over again."

"It's kind of Orwellian," Keegan noted. "Or maybe Huxley."

"Actually, several years ago," Simon said, "the Supreme Court made a decision that—because a checkoff program is so heavily influenced by the USDA and was created by Congress—that a checkoff program speaks the message of the federal government and is a tool of the government. It speaks what the court calls 'Government Speech.'"

Government Speech. People start raging about the Nanny State when Michelle Obama teams up with Elmo telling us to eat more fruits and vegetables, or Michael Bloomberg tries to take our jumbo sodas away. But in fact it's Big Brother we live with on a daily basis, who's been pushing the most addictive, killer foods on Americans for decades. And we are cheerfully unaware.

"The invasion of one's mind by ready-made phrases...can only be prevented if one is constantly on guard against them, and every such phrase anaesthetizes a portion of one's brain," George Orwell wrote in 1946.[56]

There are, admittedly, more checkoff programs dedicated to non-animal products than to animal products. There's a checkoff for blueberries, popcorn, watermelons, mushrooms, avocados, and others. But I've never encountered catchy ads for mushrooms plastered all over the media.

Why? You get one guess.

Ka-ching.

The combined fruit and vegetable sectors annually raise about $55 million through checkoff programs.[57] (I'm not including soy or sorghum, because those crops are mainly subsidiaries of the animal agriculture industry.[58] Ninety-eight percent of US soy meal feeds pigs, chickens and cows.[59])

The animal-based checkoffs, in comparison—beef, dairy/fluid milk, eggs, lamb, and pork—raise, annually, over $550 million.

Of all the checkoffs, dairy/fluid milk leads with $389 million, while popcorn brings up the rear: $600,000.[60]

"The research I've done," Simon said, "suggests there is about an 8 to 1 return on investment for that $550 million dollars of spending. That means the animal-based checkoff programs generate an additional $4.6 billion in sales each year."[61]

That's a lot of extra meat, eggs, and milk that people are buying and eating.

Theoretically, all the money funding the checkoffs is coming from the food industries themselves.

But in reality, "It's the consumers who are paying these taxes in the form of higher prices," Simon told us.

"We're paying $550 million to promote meat, dairy, and eggs to ourselves?" I asked.

"That's correct."

I wrestled with the logic. I had read that historically, meat and dairy are cheaper than ever.[62] I asked Simon about that.

"Yes, that has more to do with the overall externalization of costs that these producers are shoving onto the backs of American consumers and tax payers," he said.

"What's 'externalization'?"

"Economists use the term, 'externalized cost,' to describe offloading a cost onto somebody else who is not a party to the transaction. If I take my garbage to the front curb for a garbage service to collect, I internalize my collection costs. That's appropriate. I generate the garbage, I pay to have it collected. But if I drive my garbage to a public park and dump it there, I externalize my garbage collection costs. I impose those costs on society. American meat and dairy producers are externalizing the vast majority of their production costs onto society, which allows them to lower their prices."

"Which keeps people buying their products," Keegan said.

"Yes. It's common for producers to say, 'People want meat and dairy and we're just meeting that demand.' The research shows something different. It is in fact *producer* behavior, particularly this practice of keeping prices very low, which is driving the market. Retail chicken prices, for example, have fallen by about 74 percent since 1935, adjusting for inflation. During this period, annual chicken consumption has gone from about 9 pounds to about 56 pounds [per person].[63] Prices go down, consumption goes up."

"Exactly how much money is being externalized?" Keegan asked.

"Over $414 billion in production costs are being externalized on American consumers and taxpayers every year by the American meat and dairy producers,"[64] Simon replied. We gaped. "To put that in perspective, $414 billion is nearly one quarter of Canada's gross domestic product.[65] It's also half of what we spent on social security payments in 2012."

"$414 *billion*? How does that break down?"

"The biggest category is about $314 billion in associated health care costs to treat diseases like cancer, diabetes, and heart disease related to consumption of animal foods.[66] ($314 billion, by the way, would represent three-fifths of annual Medicare spending.)[67] There's about $38 billion in subsidies.[68] About $37 billion in environmental damage/cleanup costs. There's roughly $20 billion in costs associated with animal cruelty (the willingness of consumers to pay to end animal cruelty)[69] and about $5 billion in fishing related costs."[70]

My head was reeling with numbers. Luckily, Keegan was keeping up.

"What kind of subsidies?" he asked.

"Crop insurance, disaster payments, counter-cyclical payments which most non-farmers have never heard of," Simon said. "Water subsidies. I pay full price for my water in Southern California, but in the Central Valley, water is heavily subsidized for farmers. For every dollar I spend on water, they spend 2 cents.[71] Our tax dollars are paying that subsidy."

Amazing.

Agricultural subsidies were part of President Roosevelt's New Deal, a response to the Great Depression, when the prices of crops and other farm products were decimated. They were meant to bring some price stability and assist small farmers who were struggling.[72]

Today, subsidies don't help small farmers much. Subsidies, wrote James B. Stewart in the *New York Times*, "flow overwhelmingly to the wealthiest farmers and agribusinesses. While the wealthiest farmers collect over $1 million a year each in insurance subsidies, and 10,000 get over $100,000, the lowest 80 percent of policy holders collect on average just $5,000 each."

"Right now, the federal government favors the big guy over the little guy," then-Congressman Paul Ryan of Wisconsin, told the *Times*. "We subsidize large agribusiness and the wealthy at the expense of the family farmer and the taxpayer."[73]

But in the end, *why* is the US government doing this? Running multi-million dollar Federal programs to push harmful, addictive foods onto (and into) its citizens, driving up health care, disability, and environmental costs, and handing out billions of tax dollars to the corporate industries producing these foods? Why does it matter to the politicians running our country?

Again, you get one guess.

It's expensive to get elected and to stay in office.

"The meat, egg, and dairy industries," Simon said to Keegan and I, "spent, in one year, at least $138 million dollars lobbying Congress alone." This amount is based on the annual spending of lobby groups who file tax returns.[74] Some groups aren't required to file returns, and some big trade groups' financial statements aren't public. The amount of spending for those groups is unknown to the public, so it's very likely that $138 million is a low estimate.

It's money well spent for these industries. A $1 industry contribution usually results in a $2,000 return as federal subsidy payments.[75]

So the meat, dairy, and egg industries slam the American consumer with a three-part wallop: artificially low prices, made possible by the $414 billion offloaded onto the consumer; aggressive, often misleading advertising campaigns; and millions of dollars spent wooing the government to hand out subsidies and pass legislation to wrap the industries in a cocoon of legal protection.

Take the Cheeseburger Bill.

Also known as the Commonsense Consumption Act, or the Personal Responsibility in Food Consumption Act, it blocks lawsuits "by any person against a manufacturer, marketer, distributor, advertiser, or seller of food, or a trade association, for any injury related to a person's accumulated acts of consumption of food and weight gain, obesity, or any associated health condition."[76]

Translation: if you become obese or develop diabetes, cancer, heart disease, or any other condition from long-term consumption of any particular food, you just have to live with it. (Or die from it.) The courts don't want to hear your story. Twenty-five states—half the states in the nation—have passed these laws and they continue to be introduced.[77]

"As one judge put it, if a person knows or should know that eating copious orders of super-sized McDonald's products is unhealthy and could result in weight gain, it is not the place of the law to protect them from their own excesses," said Republican Congressman James Sensenbrenner of Wisconsin.[78]

My first reaction was, gross, who would eat copious amounts of McDonald's? Wasn't everyone traumatized by *Super Size Me*? But then, I thought of the people that Lauren Ornelas works with, the ones who don't have the money, time, transportation, or choice to eat anywhere else.

A law to protect some of the wealthiest corporations in the world against some of the poorest, most vulnerable people—who would come up with such a thing?

"The importance of the American Legislative Exchange Council (ALEC) in US legislation," Simon said to us, "cannot be overstated. ALEC is an incubator for business-friendly legislation. It brings together state legislators and corporate lobbyists. They typically meet over some fun event, like a trip to Disneyland. The lobbyists pay for everything; the legislators go for free. They mutually develop 'model legislation' that the legislators then introduce in their home states. Each year, ALEC is responsible for introducing about 1,000 bills in state legislatures. About 200 of those pass."

"The ALEC," said Democratic Congressman Mark Pocan of Wisconsin, "is a corporate dating service for lonely legislators and corporate special interests [and] eventually the relationship culminates with some special interest legislation and hopefully that lives happily ever after as the ALEC model. Unfortunately what's excluded from that equation is the public."[79]

The Cheeseburger Bill, surprise surprise, is a brainchild of ALEC.[80]

It's pretty shrewd, when you look at some of the companies and trade groups who've been associated with ALEC: McDonald's, Wendy's, Coca-Cola, Molson Coors, Frito Lay, Kraft Foods, Dr. Pepper, Outback Steak House, Pepsi-Cola, Sara Lee, Walgreen's, Wal-Mart, YUM! Brands (owner of Kentucky Fried Chicken, Taco Bell, Pizza Hut, Long John Silver's and A&W), National Association of Convenience Stores, National Pork Producers Council, and National Soft Drink Association (now wisely renamed American Beverage Association), among many others.[81]

"These Cheeseburger Bills are preemptive?" Keegan asked Simon.

"Yeah. The proponents of these laws have been very upfront that they're a direct response to the large damage settlements awarded against Big Tobacco. Tobacco companies have had to pay over $400 billion to state Medicaid programs to reimburse them for costs associated with tobacco related diseases."

"But it's not limited to cheeseburgers, right?"

"No, they cover any food that can contribute to obesity and related health conditions. They're called Cheeseburger because they were developed in response to a lawsuit filed against McDonald's that involved cheeseburgers."

"So, under ALEC," said Keegan, "these businesses came up with this...what's the official name? Common Sense Consumption?"

"Yeah. And the fact that these laws are based on a model template called the Common Sense Consumption Act is really funny. What they're actually saying is, 'You, the consumer, should have the *common sense* to know that our food is bad for you, and you shouldn't eat a lot of it.'"

"That is funny."

"Yeah. Hilarious."

After we said goodbye to David Robinson Simon, Keegan and I walked in the bright sunshine down a busy LA street.

My head felt like it was going to explode. It was swimming with sums of cash in the millions and billions, numbers I couldn't even begin to conceptualize, money surging like a river beneath the animal agriculture industry. My mind couldn't untangle how our Federal and legislative bodies were basket-woven with industry interests. Our own government, using agencies tasked with the explicit mission of protecting us, is peddling the most damaging, debilitating, and lethal food substances to us. It's called *Government Speech*. Staggering amounts of our own tax dollars are used to keep us sick and addicted—and convinced it's all for our own good health. The American public has been turned into a moneymaking commodity, just as surely as the hens jammed in their battery cages, the pigs in their gestation crates, and the dairy cows in their continual cycles of impregnation, giving birth, and lactation. Our illnesses and addiction to what makes us ill generates revenue for massive corporations, and indirectly, reliable funding for our government officials.

And just in case any of us figure out what's going on, the corporations and our government have teamed up to lay down a barricade of preemptive laws to protect themselves from We The People.

I was lost in thought.

Keegan turned to me.

"You know," he said, "the Cheeseburger Bill is kind of benign compared to Ag-Gag."

"Ag" stands for agriculture. "Gag" means to silence. Ag-Gag Laws have nothing to do with suppressing the agriculture industry. They have everything to do with silencing whistleblowers and undercover investigators by making it a criminal act to photograph or film abuse of animals or workers at any animal enterprise, including factory farms, slaughterhouses, and laboratories. The work of undercover activists, in an overwhelming majority of cases, is the only way the American public can know what is happening at these facilities.

North Carolina passed a new law that took effect January 1, 2016. It's an Ag-Gag law on steroids. Whistleblowers, under the law, are gagged not only in agricultural facilities, but in all workplaces. This means, among other things, that it is illegal to film abuse of animals in factory farms, toddlers in day care, or the elderly in nursing homes, and then share those recordings with the media or activist groups. A sponsor of the law told a Senate Committee that the whole idea was to stop people from "running out to a news outlet."[82]

If Keegan and I went back now to see René Miller in North Carolina, and took our cameras over to the industrial hog facility next to her family graveyard, we could be prosecuted as criminals. If we visited her great-niece's day care center, covertly filmed a teacher molesting a child, and then alerted the media with our footage, we could, again, be prosecuted as criminals.

The new North Carolina law provides a revealing glance into the current priorities of our country. Corporate interests are steam-rolling not only the welfare of animals, but also the welfare of human beings, including the most vulnerable among us. You will be criminalized, the law says, if you attempt to find out and share the truth, if that truth damages the profits of a business.

Jake Conroy was sentenced to four years in federal prison. He served 37 months, spent six months in a federal halfway house, had three years of federal probation, and owes a restitution fine of one million dollars.

He was convicted, along with five others, of running a website.[83]

"We were the target of government repression," Conroy told Keegan and I. "The SHAC7, as we came to be known, was an organization designed strictly to close down an animal testing laboratory. The government alleged that we used our webpage to conspire with others on the Internet, to encourage them to engage in a campaign, Stop Huntingdon Animal Cruelty (SHAC). We never encouraged anyone to engage in illegal activity. And we were very specific about not harming humans or animals."

It was a David-and-Goliath story.

Huntingdon Life Sciences (HLS) was the largest contract animal-testing lab in Europe. They tested drugs, pesticides, food additives, household cleaners, and other products on roughly 75,000 animals a year, ranging from mice to wild baboons. SHAC held nonviolent protests and pressured the customers, investors, and stockbrokers of HLS to sever their connection with the laboratory.

"We had over 100 companies pull out from the laboratory because of our campaign," Conroy said. SHAC was able to bring HLS close to bankruptcy several times.[84]

Goliath freaked out.

"The FBI investigation on SHAC was the largest FBI investigation for its time," Conroy told us. "They recorded 555 ninety-minute cassette tapes of telephone conversations. That covered conversations about demonstrations, but also conversations with family members and loved ones. They were following us sometimes 24 hours a day. Monitoring our Internet connections. They paid people posing as activists to infiltrate SHAC and report to the FBI. The pharmaceutical industries spent $250,000 to have our webpage taken down for a couple days. They put everything they had into convicting us."

"This was really about silencing you guys," I said.

"Absolutely. They want to silence people through passing laws, and throwing people in prison. They want you to fear becoming the next whistleblower. It's telling that these industries are working so hard and spending so much money to criminalize people for simply recording what's going on inside these facilities and making it known to the public. They spent hundreds of thousands of dollars in legal fees to come after us. They spend millions prosecuting activists for putting out photographs or video from inside the laboratory.

"Sometimes the Ag-Gag Laws will stretch to even having copies of that footage or photography. That's why it's such a big issue for the media. If I film something undercover, and give it to you as a person of the media, you could potentially be charged under these Ag-Gag laws as a felon for simply possessing the footage. They want to terrify you into not doing anything."

Conroy and the rest of the SHAC7 were convicted under a federal bill called the Animal Enterprise Protection Act (AEPA), which has now become the Animal Enterprise Terrorism Act (AETA). Like state Ag-Gag Laws, these federal bills make illegal an extensive selection of First Amendment-protected activities—undercover investigations, whistleblowing, protests, boycotts, picketing, and more—if they cause a loss of profits for any animal enterprise.

The Animal Enterprise Terrorism Act is, once again, a creation of ALEC.[85]

As of June 2015, there were eight states with versions of Ag-Gag Laws: Kansas, Montana, North Dakota, Iowa, Missouri, Utah, North Carolina, and Wyoming.[86] They have been introduced in almost 30 states.[87]

But there is hope. In 2013, 11 states introduced Ag-Gag bills and, thanks to pressure from the public, every bill was defeated.[88] In 2014, Ag-Gags were defeated in 9 states,[89] passing only in Idaho.[90] And then remarkably, wonderfully, in August 2015 a federal district court in Idaho struck down that state's Ag-Gag Law as unconstitutional.

The Idaho decision could be the precedent needed to strike down other Ag-Gag Laws.

"This is an issue outside of the animal rights or the environmental community," Conroy said to Keegan and I, "because this is about keeping secret the source of our food. People want transparency. They want to know where their food is coming from."

Ag-Gag Laws, on the surface, may seem designed to thwart "extremist" animal rights activists.

But in fact these laws pose an incalculable public health risk.

An undercover video of a California slaughterhouse, Hallmark Meat Packing (also known as Westland/Hallmark), was filmed by the Humane Society of the US (HSUS) and released on January 30, 2008. *The Washington Post* reported the story.[91]

The video showed "horrendous abuse of downed cows too sick and injured even to stand," Wayne Pacelle, HSUS President, testified before Congress. "The Hallmark footage showed workers ramming cows with the blades of a forklift, jabbing them in the eyes, applying painful electrical shocks often in sensitive areas, dragging them with chains pulled by heavy machinery, and torturing them with a high-pressure water hose to simulate drowning [in humans this is called waterboarding] as they attempted to force these animals to walk to slaughter."[92]

Cows too ill to stand (unless, of course, they are tortured, dragged by chains, electro-shocked, or stabbed by forklift blades) are called downers. The federal government has banned them from being used as human food.

These animals present a heightened risk of Mad Cow disease, a fatal illness that eats away the brain, and which has a long incubation period with an average of thirty years.[93] An overwhelming majority of Mad Cow cases in North America have been tracked to downer cows.

Consuming the flesh of these cows also poses much higher dangers of *E. Coli* and *Salmonella* poisoning, since, unable to stand, they frequently wallow in feces.[94]

The downer cows at Hallmark, however, were considered "dollars on the hoof," and the plant manager didn't want a single one to go to waste.[95] Defying the risk of introducing potentially fatal disease into the country's food supply, the manager and the slaughterhouse workers tortured the exhausted dairy cows until they struggled to their feet and were slaughtered for ground beef.[96]

The release of the shocking HSUS video set into motion the largest beef recall in the country's history. In less than 3 weeks after the HSUS video emerged, Westland/Hallmark Meat Company recalled 143 million pounds of beef. The recall affected meat dating back over two years. Most of it had already been eaten.[97]

One hundred forty-three million pounds of beef is enough to make two hamburgers for every single man, woman, and child in the United States.[98] Eating any of those burgers, made from the combined flesh of countless cows, would be playing Russian Roulette, as Dr. Friedlander said, for Mad Cow, *E. Coli*, *Salmonella*, and other potentially fatal pathogens.[99]

And the proportion of children who had eaten the Westland/Hallmark meat was distressingly high. Fifty million pounds of the recalled beef had gone to school lunch programs, or federal programs for the elderly and poor.[100] Over the previous five years, Westland/Hallmark had sold roughly 100 million pounds of frozen beef, with a price tag of $146 million, to the USDA for school lunches and food for the needy.[101]

"Where were the inspectors who should have been preventing downed cattle from entering the food supply?" Caroline Smith DeWaal, from the Center for Science in the Public Interest, demanded in *The Independent*. "Where were the safeguards to make sure that meat from sick animals didn't end up on school lunch trays from coast to coast?"[102]

Well, actually, the official "safeguards" were right there at Hallmark. USDA inspectors were "continuously" present at the slaughterhouse.[103] Hallmark also passed 17 independent food safety/humane handling audits in 2007.[104] Two of those audits took place in the same weeks the undercover video was shot. And on the exact date that operations at Westland/Hallmark ground to a halt, an auditor wrote, "I have reviewed the records and programs you have at your plant [which] are the best I have ever seen in any plant... Your plant has passed numerous audits on humane handling of animals in this plant in the year of 2007 and has no failures, which you should to [sic] be very proud of."

That particular auditor boasted 25 years of working with the USDA.[105]

In 2004-2005, Westland won the USDA's Supplier of the Year award for the National School Lunch Program.[106] It was discovered later that Westland/Hallmark had been selling downed cow meat for four years before the HSUS video triggered the massive recall.[107] Those four years of egregious food safety failure and vicious animal brutality stretched back to encompass the year Westland was crowned USDA's Supplier of the Year for the country's school children.

It took one undercover investigation less than three weeks to put a stop to what four years of official oversight could not, or would not.

This information is what the Ag-Gag laws and their federal counterpart, the Animal Enterprise Terrorism Act, are designed to smother.

What's in your meat? What's in your milk and eggs? Without whistleblowers, you will almost certainly never find out, unless you or someone in your family wakes up in the hospital.

CHAPTER 15
PHARM TO TABLE TO PHARM

A health-promoting diet is in direct competition with the pharmaceutical industry.

There are billions of dollars to be made from illness.

"We sometimes joke that when you're doing a clinical trial, there are two possible disasters," Alex Hittle, a stock analyst, told the *New York Times*. "The first disaster is if you kill people. The second disaster is if you cure them.

"The truly good drugs," Hittle said, "are the ones you can use chronically for a long, long time."[1]

"Conventional medical treatment dictates that you must take drugs," Dr. Goldhamer told Keegan and I, "for conditions of dietary excess like high blood pressure, diabetes, high cholesterol, or autoimmune diseases. Not just for a week, a month, or a year. You are told you have to take drugs forever. If you follow your doctor's advice, you will never get well. Because drugs do not address the underlying cause of disease."

The public's willingness to endure lifelong pharmaceutical use is called, in industry lingo, "compliance."[2] And we are compliant. In 2014, the US spent $374 billion on pharmaceuticals.[3] That's more than the combined gross national products of New Zealand and Bangladesh.[4] It's also well over 200 percent of what the US federal government spent on education in 2015.[5]

Of course we're racking up a bill like that. New cancer drugs, for example, average about $10,000 a month, with some costing $30,000 a *month*.[6] And, for cancer patients, there are chemotherapy and surgery costs, which vary. Colon cancer is the most expensive chemo, with one round of treatment running about $46,000. Tack on colon cancer surgery at almost $32,000,[7] and it's no surprise that, even for the lucky ones with health insurance, "many cancer patients are facing severe financial strain, even bankruptcy in some cases," according to Dr. Richard Schilsky, of the American Society of Clinical Oncology, in the *New York Times*.[8]

Pharmaceutical companies hold sick people and their families hostage. In 1990, Congress held hearings on the industry's promotional tactics. David C. Jones, a former pharmaceutical executive, was one of the witnesses. Jones revealed that drug companies take far more than the cost of research into account when setting the price of a medication.

"[T]he fewer the options, the higher the price," Jones testified. "The greater the desperation, the greater the suffering, the higher the price. These are routine conversations that occur with virtually every drug that is introduced."[9]

Jones recounted a company meeting, held after scientists discovered that a particular drug could be produced much more economically, allowing the price to be dropped from $10,000 per patient to $2,000.

"But marketing executives [at the meeting] asked why we would want to do that," said Jones. "Someone even said that we should not worry about the price because neighbors would hold garage sales to raise money for those [who needed the medication]."[10]

And yet independent reviews spanning the last 35 years have shown that only 11 to 15 percent of new drugs have substantial benefits over existing drugs.[11] Some medications, new and old, don't work at all.

"The vast majority of drugs—more than 90 percent—only work in 30 or 50 percent of the people." That's a 2003 statement from Dr. Allen Roses, a top executive at GlaxoSmithKline. In 2001, scientists from Abbott Laboratories appraised the effectiveness of medications for fourteen diseases. They found the drugs worked in as few as 25 percent of the people who took them.[12]

In 2006, Mara Aspinall, president of Genzyme Genetics, stated that 30 to 70 percent of people taking statins to reduce their cholesterol get no benefit.

"If you look across all drug categories today," Aspinall said, "an average of 50 percent of people treated with individual drugs are receiving treatments that are not efficacious for them." [13]

I asked Dr. Klaper about the effectiveness of medications. Both my dad and step-dad take statins. My step-dad says, "I would rather just take these cholesterol pills the rest of my life and eat whatever I want."

"I've been a physician for over 40 years," Dr. Klaper said, "and it hurts my heart to see the medical and pharmaceutical industries generating billions by treating symptoms, without being honest with the patients.

"There's a commercial, this lady who's all happy because she's got lower numbers on some statin drug. 'I got the numbers I'm looking for!' But is she healthier? If she has a pizza and takes her statin pill thinking now she's okay, this is a fraud of massive proportions. This woman is still going to develop diabetes, still going to have her heart attack.

"People think, 'I've had my stents, my bypass. I'm okay now.' No, you're not. Your arteries are still getting clogged. You think you're cured of heart disease, so you get your next helping of chicken cacciatore. I'll say it again, this is a fraud perpetrated on the American public. Many people in these industries are good people, but they are locked in by this money machine. People are deceived on a daily basis."

Dr. Esselstyn confirmed Dr. Klaper's words. "You have a $5 billion stent industry. A $35 billion statin drug industry. They don't want that to go away. Look, if I'm in the middle of a heart attack, there's no question that I want a man or a woman with great expertise in stents by my side. They will save my life and a lot of my heart muscle. But the 90 percent of stents being done electively? There is zero evidence that you can prolong life or protect against a future heart attack with stents."[14]

Angioplasty, the medical procedure used to open blocked or narrowed blood vessels, often with stents, has not been shown to extend life expectancy by a single day.[15] There is a 15 to 50 percent risk of suffering permanent brain damage from bypass surgery,[16] although the operation prolongs life only for the sickest patients.[17]

And within six months of an angioplasty or bypass operation, there is a 25 to 50 percent chance that the blood vessels will become obstructed again.[18] Unless, of course, the patient switches to a plant-based diet.

"Medicines have become a crutch to allow our unhealthy behavior," Dr. Davis told us. "Statins reduce your cholesterol, but they don't help the inflammation that occurs every time you eat animal protein. They don't help the saturated fat, the endotoxins, the carcinogens. They have no effect on the fact that when you eat meat, your blood vessels constrict, which is why people get heart attacks right after meals, usually after a fatty meal."

Great. Your cholesterol is lower, but you're still dead.

The drugs themselves, in fact, kill a shocking number of people. About 128,000 people a year in this country die from prescription drugs. That number only includes properly prescribed and administered medications, not overdoses or mis-prescribing.[19] To steal a parallel from our friend Jaydee Hanson at Center for Food Safety, that's equivalent to over forty-two 9/11 attacks.

Can you imagine.

Because of drugs that often have little or no benefit, serious side effects, and astronomical costs, the equivalent of forty-two Twin Towers come crashing down every year. This makes prescription drugs the fourth leading cause of death, running neck and neck with strokes. Another 1.9 million people are hospitalized due to these same, properly prescribed, properly taken medications.[20]

What's an industry to do?

Orwell again: "Advertising is the rattling of a stick inside a swill bucket."

Inside a *pill* bucket is more like it.

Nine out of ten major pharmaceutical companies spend more—sometimes over twice as much—on marketing than on research. Some numbers from 2013: [21]

Company	Research & Development ($ billion)	Marketing & Sales ($ billion)
Johnson & Johnson	8.2	17.5
Novartis	9.9	14.6
Pfizer	6.6	11.4
GlaxoSmithKline	5.3	9.9
AstraZeneca	4.3	7.3

Those billions of marketing dollars are going to your doctor.

Because doctors have the power to prescribe. In 2012, drug companies spent over $3 billion advertising to consumers. But they spent eight times that amount advertising directly to health care professionals—roughly $24 billion.[22]

That money covers everything from the click pen emblazoned with a drug name that you fill out your forms with, to free lunches, travel, nights out, to thousands of dollars in return for sponsored lectures and promotional appearances.[23] In 2005, drug and medical industries covered between 65 and 80 percent of the cost of accredited continuing education courses for doctors.[24]

In 2014, pharmaceutical companies reported making payments to more than 607,000 doctors in the country. There are only about 700,000 American doctors.[25] That's 87 percent of US physicians who received drug payments.

And like the lobbying expenditures of the animal agriculture industry, Pharma gets a good return. American doctors who receive payments from pharmaceutical companies—meaning 87 percent of them—are two times as likely to prescribe their drugs.[26]

"There's a direct inducement for physicians to promote the drugs because they're getting essentially paid to do so," Dr. Mills said to Keegan and I. "The pharmaceutical industry will tell you they're not paying you to enroll this patient in a study looking at drug X; rather, they're providing a stipend to cover associated costs and time. The effect is the same. If I'm getting $100 for every patient I enroll in a drug study, that's a strong inducement to enroll a lot of people."

Ask your doctor today about pharmaceutical money, and whether it's right for you...

Both the animal agriculture and pharmaceutical industries use scientific studies to convince people their products are safe, effective and necessary. But given the huge amount of medical evidence to the contrary, these industries have to take a little extra initiative with these reports.

In 1980, drug companies paid for 32 percent of the country's medical research. Twenty years later, they were covering 62 percent.[27]

But it wouldn't do to write the reports themselves. So pharmaceutical companies enlist teams of academic scientists and private doctors to prepare their reports for them. Take a look at many of the clinical drug trials published. There are usually four or five researchers listed as authors. At the bottom of the page in fine print, however, you might learn that the drug manufacturer paid for the study.

"The industry," Melody Petersen writes in *Our Daily Meds*, "was using the names of the professors as ornaments, hanging them on their studies like shimmering glitter on a Christmas tree."[28]

In the animal agriculture industry, checkoff programs are used not only to advertise, but to create "scientific" studies—which are really the same thing.

"Checkoff programs both promote their goods and fund research," David Robinson Simon said. "Often, the lines are blurred, because the research is carefully designed to show that, contrary to other research, these foods are good for us."

"They say, 'Statistics don't lie, but liars use statistics,'" Dr. Goldhamer deadpanned. "You can find people who will tell you, 'Eighty percent of smokers never get lung cancer. How dangerous could it be?' You could make a cigarette so toxic that you die from heart disease very quickly, and that would effectively cut down the lung cancer rates. The company could then market it as a cigarette that doesn't cause lung cancer."

"It's not that their data is bad, it's the conclusions they draw," said Dr. Davis. "There is simply no question that if there is money funding a study, it biases that study.

"A report in *Journal of American Medicine* concluded that metabolism drops the least with a high-protein diet, the supposed significance being that it will lead to fat loss. There was a very slight increase in metabolism from eating meat compared to not eating meat. But when you actually start reading the data—something the layperson and the journalists are not going to do—you see the authors neglected to mention that the cortisol levels, stress hormones, and inflammation in the high-protein group went sky high. This did not happen in the low-protein group.[29] Why wasn't that mentioned anywhere in the study? Why was the conclusion that meat increases your metabolism slightly, rather than that high-protein diets cause dramatic amounts of inflammation and stress to the body?"

I wanted to know about the studies declaring that saturated fat and cholesterol are not-so-bad-for-you-after-all, and the beautiful curl of butter on the cover of *Time* magazine.

Dr. Davis snorted. "It's so distressing to me, all this 'fat isn't bad for you.' It's based on two very flawed studies. I've got a *thousand* studies showing saturated fat is bad for you, but apparently they're not sensational enough to make the cover of *Time*. Of the two, the big one was the Siri-Tarino study. The authors received significant amounts of money from the meat, dairy, and egg industries.[30] Go take a look.

"So what did they do? The Siri-Tarino researchers decided, 'We're taking everyone with high cholesterol out of the study because cholesterol is an independent cause of heart disease.' The problem, of course, is that saturated fat causes heart disease partly by raising cholesterol, so they're removing the people who are actually affected by the saturated fat, focusing instead on a few people who have the good genetics to be able to withstand saturated fat's heart-damaging effects.[31] It's an over-adjustment bias to eliminate a correlation that actually exists.

"The other study, the Chowdhury paper, actually used people who were on lipid-lowering medication, so the scientists concluded that saturated fat doesn't cause heart disease by looking at people who were taking medications that specifically block the effect of saturated fat.[32] It's insane."

I did take a look at the Siri-Tarino study. Three out of four researchers had industry ties. Patty Siri-Tarino received an honorarium and was supported by a grant from the National Dairy Council. Ronald Krauss belongs to the Merck Global Atherosclerosis Advisory Board, and received grants from the National Dairy Council and the National Cattleman's Beef Association.[33] And Qi Sun was supported by a fellowship from Unilever Corporate Research.[34] Unilever is a major supplier of frozen fish to the US and European markets,[35] as well as the owner of brands such as Hellmann's Mayonnaise, Knorr, and ice cream companies like Magnum, Ben and Jerry's, and Klondike.[36]

It's also important to remember that, as Dr. McMacken said, even with these industry interests, "Not a single saturated fat study ever showed that saturated fat was good for you."

And cholesterol?

Dr. Davis snorts again, exasperated. "A lot of these studies botch their methods. They'll look at cholesterol and heart disease, but they look at people when they die. A lot of these people have been hospitalized for months before they die from heart disease. In late stages of life, especially when infirm, cholesterol levels will drop. Really sick people often can't eat and are fed liquid nutrients through IVs. Then they die from a heart attack, and people conclude, 'Look at their cholesterol when they died, it was normal.'[37] It wasn't normal all their life."

The Framingham Heart Study studied tens of thousands of people over several generations, and the researchers never saw a heart attack in anyone with a total cholesterol level less than 150.[38]

"Another problem is that scientists will compare a high cholesterol group to a slightly lower cholesterol group," Dr. Davis continued. "They won't see a difference in heart disease, so they conclude, 'Cholesterol doesn't kill you.' Dr. Esselstyn has a great analogy for this: it's like comparing people who die in a car wreck going 100 miles an hour versus people dying in a car wreck going 80 miles an hour. There are an equal number of deaths, so the conclusion is that speed doesn't kill. That's crazy. If people drove 30 miles an hour, there'd be far fewer deaths.

"This is what's going on in the cholesterol research. And it is being shaped by lobbyists up at the USDA level."

In February 2015, the Dietary Guidelines Advisory Committee (DGAC) recommended dropping the cholesterol limits in the next Dietary Guidelines for Americans, stating that cholesterol is no longer "a nutrient of concern for overconsumption" and that "available evidence shows no appreciable relationship between consumption of dietary cholesterol and serum cholesterol."[39]

But if you look closer at the 2015 DGAC, as we did for earlier incarnations of the committee, you'll notice a few things. The American Egg Board directly nominated one DGAC member. Another was the active recipient of egg-industry research grants. Two more were employed by a university that received over $100,000 from the American Egg Board to fund research challenging dietary cholesterol limits.[40]

And about 90 percent of scientific studies on dietary cholesterol are currently paid for by the egg industry.[41] I wonder if those studies provided any of the "available evidence" cited by the DGAC.

Because of these egregious conflicts of interest, the Physicians Committee for Responsible Medicine sued the USDA and the DHHS.[42]

But the day after PCRM filed their lawsuit, the USDA released their 2015 Dietary Guidelines, which remarkably included an even stronger warning against cholesterol than before: "[I]ndividuals should eat as little dietary cholesterol as possible...Dietary cholesterol is found only in animal foods such as egg yolk, dairy products, shellfish, meats, and poultry."[43]

It's a heartening outcome, but industry interests drove the protective cholesterol limits awfully close to the edge of the cliff. And the damage has been done: there's now a big question mark over cholesterol lodged firmly in the minds of the American public.

All this talk about industry-funded science brought me back to something Dr. Greger said:

"You can learn about eggs from the egg industry. You can learn about the benefits of chewing gum from the Wrigley Science Institute."

No, he didn't make that up. "The Wrigley Science Institute," according to their website, "is the first organization of its kind

committed to advancing and sharing scientific research that explores…
the role of chewing gum in health and wellness."[44]

For real.

Dr. Greger went on. "The studies trying to vindicate saturated
fat are very explicitly a campaign by the dairy industry. The number
one source of saturated fat is dairy, not meat. In 2008, the global
dairy industry got together in Mexico City. One of their primary
goals was to 'neutralize the negative impact of milk fat…as related
to heart disease.'"

I thought of how three of the four authors of the Siri-Tarino
saturated fat study were funded by either the National Dairy Council
or Unilever, owner of a slew of major ice cream brands.

Martijn Katan is an emeritus professor of nutrition at the Vrije
Universiteit Amsterdam, a world-renowned expert on diet and heart
disease, and a member of the Royal Netherlands Academy of Arts
and Sciences. He spoke about the Mexico City dairy conference in
2014 to *Nutrition Action*, a publication of Center for Science in the
Public Interest:

> *[The global dairy industry] set up a major, well-funded
> campaign to provide proof that saturated fat does not
> cause heart disease. They assembled scientists who were
> sympathetic to the dairy industry, provided these scientists
> with funding, encouraged them to put out statements on milk
> fat and heart disease, and arranged to have them speak at
> scientific meetings. And the scientific publications we've seen
> emerging since the Mexico meeting have helped neutralize
> the negative image of milk fat… I do not mean that the data
> were fabricated. But the methodological limitations of
> observational studies make it easy to get the result that you
> think beforehand should be correct—namely, that saturated
> fat is not associated with heart disease.*[45]

***

It's a demonic feedback loop.

Let me see if I can get this straight.

Pharmaceutical companies sell mountains of drugs to factory farms, which depend on them to maintain their abnormally intensive systems.

The animals develop antibiotic resistance that spreads to humans. Humans need stronger drugs.

In the meantime, the animal industries flood the government with cash in exchange for subsidies. The government, invested in keeping the generous animal food lobbies flush, runs federal programs pushing people to eat increasing amounts of animal-based foods.

People oblige.

People get sick, requiring medication for the rest of their lives, along with expensive medical procedures. The drugs and procedures falsely assure them that they can continue to eat the food that made them sick in the first place.

People continue to support the animal agriculture industry by buying their products, which pay for studies to further convince the public that animal products are an essential part of a healthy diet.

People continue to support the pharmaceutical companies because they are tethered to their prescription drugs. This allows drug companies to pay for the "education" of our doctors who prescribe more drugs to us.

Then pharmaceutical companies sell mountains of drugs to factory farms…

It was all coming together. I could see the convergence in our nation between the food, medical, and pharmaceutical industries, and our government. It is an immense and intricate braid bound together by greed. And it is wrapped around the neck of the American public.

When I got back to my apartment that night, I sat down in front of my computer.

In the search engine, I typed:

American Diabetes Association Sponsor

CHAPTER 16
EXPLODING MYTHS

And there it was.

The American Diabetes Association has taken money from, among others, Kraft Foods, makers of Velveeta processed cheese, Oscar Mayer processed meat, and Lunchables, processed kids'meals; Campbell Soup Company; Cadbury-Schweppes, the world's largest confectioner and producer of foods like the Cadbury Crème Egg and Dr. Pepper; Coca-Cola; Hershey's;[1] Dannon, one of the largest dairy yogurt producers; Kroger, a supermarket chain; Walgreens,[2] which also sells groceries and in 2015 made 66 percent of its sales through its pharmacy division;[3] and Bumble Bee Foods, makers of processed canned meats.[4]

American Diabetes Association also flirted seriously with Burger King for almost a year, until BK came out with a burger with more fat than had ever been seen on the fast food market.[5] Now that's just going too far.

But wait, there's more. In the ADA's 2016 "Banting Circle Elite" level of corporate sponsorship, which requires a gift of at least $1 million, you'll find AstraZeneca, Eli Lilly, Merck, Novo Nordisk, Sanofi, Janssen Pharmaceuticals, and Boehringer Ingelheim Pharmaceuticals. In the next tier down, requiring a gift of only $500,000, is GlaxoSmithKline and Pfizer.[6]

These drug companies are in the booming business of helping people manage the symptoms of their Type 2 diabetes. Dr. Ratner, the doctor I interviewed at ADA, only wanted to talk about people living longer *with* diabetes. Once I mentioned eliminating diabetes or prevention, it shut down the conversation. Diet and cure? Whoa, let's not go there.

I typed in another one:

American Heart Association Sponsor

American Heart Association has received money from the National Cattlemen's Beef Association, National Live Stock and Meat Board, Subway, Walgreens,[7] Texas Beef Council, Cargill, South Dakota Beef Industry Council, Kentucky Beef Council, Nebraska Beef Council, Tyson Foods, AVA Pork, Unilever, Trauth Dairy, Domino's Pizza,[8] Perdue, Idaho Beef Council,[9] and fistfuls of pharmaceutical companies—the usual suspects like AstraZeneca, Bristol-Myers Squibb, GlaxoSmithKline, Novartis, Pfizer, Sanofi, and Merck, which spent $400,000 to fund an AHA program teaching 40,000 doctors to "treat cholesterol according to guidelines."[10]

Whose guidelines, I wonder?

Both AHA and American Cancer Society take money from Walmart,[11] which was called in 2011, "the most powerful force in our food system, more dominant than Monsanto, Kraft, or Tyson." In 2010, Walmart got a full 25 percent of the $550 billion spent on groceries in the US. In many markets around the country, Walmart scored more than 50 percent of grocery sales.[12]

One more:

Susan G. Komen Sponsor

Here you've got Kentucky Fried Chicken (eat a breast to save a breast...?);[13] Eggland's Best; Yoplait, the world's leader in fruit yogurt;[14] Dietz Watson, maker of "premium deli meats and artisan cheeses;" Trident Seafoods, and Walgreens.[15]

"I have no doubt," Dr. Klaper said to us, "that the major health-related organizations have the best intentions of the American public at heart. But once these groups say, "The best thing to reduce your risk of cancer, heart disease, and diabetes is to reduce or eliminate your consumption of meat, dairy, and egg products"—that would be the end of their funding. That would bring the entire catastrophe down upon their heads, and they would essentially disappear as organizations. That means you are not going to be hearing the truth, as far as nutrition goes, from these organizations. He that pays the piper calls the tune."

"The Academy of Nutrition and Dietetics (AND) is the nation's largest trade group for registered dietitians, representing some 75,000 nutrition professionals," Michele Simon told us. "One of AND's major sponsors is the National Dairy Council. They give AND money every year, and they get to have a huge booth at the annual expo. So you walk in, and there's the National Dairy Council promoting itself to nutritionists who are telling Americans how to eat. They also sponsor scientific sessions, so dietitians can learn why lactose intolerance is no big deal, sponsored by the National Dairy Council. And they offer continuing education units so nutritionists can continue to hear about the wonders of dairy."

McDonald's sponsored and catered the 2014 annual conference of the California Dietetic Association, an affiliate of AND. The California Beef Council, Hershey's, Walmart, and many other industry groups were there to educate the congregated dietitians.[16]

AND also publishes "Nutrition Fact Sheets" to help people make healthier choices. Guess who writes those "Fact Sheets"? The food industry. Not only that, but they pay $20,000 per "Fact Sheet" to AND.[17]

"What's really sad," Simon went on, "is that we cannot trust the information from these leading health organizations, because they're taking money from the very industries that are causing the problems these groups are supposed to be helping to prevent."

I stood on my building's roof, looking out over the neighborhood. All these people, living their lives around me, were being fed false, dangerous information about their diets and their health. Most of them would think I was "extreme" if I told them that, to protect their health and the health of their families, they should switch to a plant-based diet. (And I live in San Francisco!) Even my own family would think I was taking it too far. I could hear the questions now—protests, really. I had already learned the answers to basic questions about going plant-based: *Where will I get my protein? Calcium? Iron? Won't soy give me man-boobs?*

But there were others. *I knew someone who was vegan who got really weak and her hair fell out. Aren't we supposed to be meat-eaters? People on meat-based diets like Paleo look really great. Isn't "plant-based" expensive?*

I was going to find out. Let's go explode some myths.

The "Tired, Sick Vegan"

I've known people who try a plant-based diet, but then say, "I got so weak. I couldn't get out of bed." The insinuation is always that the absence of animal protein—*real* protein—sapped them.

"Your body does not use protein for energy," Dr. Davis told us. "Your body uses carbohydrates or fat for energy. This idea that a person becomes weak and tired because of protein deficiency is absolutely not true. There's no biochemical explanation for that. Most of my patients, in fact, feel fantastic when they shift their diet."

"I've been doing this for 30 years," said Dr. Goldhamer. "I've had 15,000 people on an in-patient basis, and I haven't yet come across someone whose symptoms were caused by a deficiency of dead flesh, coagulated cow pus, or any other animal products. Physically, human beings are able to adopt a plant-based diet and thrive. Psychologically? It might be like an alcoholic saying, 'I can't quit drinking because of my constitution.'"

"Not eating enough calories is one of the problems sometimes experienced by people new to a plant-based diet," said Dr. Greger. "Whole plant foods are much less calorically dense than animal foods. If your caloric intake suddenly drops, people can feel lousy. So you need to eat more to get the same number of calories. Good news for people who like to eat."

"One of my friends was plant-based for 3 years, and then felt really weak," I said. "She had a sip of bone broth and felt better."

"Come on."

"No, I've heard it a few times: 'I had some chicken and I felt all better.'"

"That is crazy psychological placebo nonsense. It's actually not possible. Now, if she said, 'I started eating meat again, and a couple months later I felt much better,' then maybe she was iron-deficient. But there is no disease on the planet where you eat a piece of chicken or a can of tuna, and the clouds part and the sun comes out."

"Or," I said, "what about people who say, 'I know my body, I just need meat'?"

"That's like saying, 'I need meat because I'm a Capricorn.' It makes no biological sense."

Dr. Kim Williams was a little more philosophical. "Are there people who simply can't change their diet?" he mused. "There certainly are. Now, you have to ask, 'Are they given all the information? Are they given all the motivation? Do they have the opportunity and the environment to support this?' Most of the time, when I have a patient who can't change their diet, it's because of their surroundings. Environment is huge. Culture is huge."

"Going vegan is a significant dietary change for a lot of people," said Dr. McMacken. "As with any change, you're probably going to notice some different feelings. But if your idea of a plant-based diet is Oreos, French fries, diet coke, and lots of processed meat alternatives, you're not going to feel great."

The same would be true if you ate nothing but kale and broccoli, shunning grains, legumes, nuts, and seeds.

Both those diets would certainly turn you into a tired, sick vegan. What you need in your meal plan is a dash of knowledge.

Going Paleolithic

The Paleolithic diet is based on the idea that many diseases today are due to our modern eating habits. I'm down with that. But if you're going to go Paleo, you eat only what a caveman (supposedly) ate.[18] Never mind, as Dr. Davis writes in *Proteinaholic*, that "prehistoric man was an obligate consumer. He ate what was available because otherwise he starved. He made decisions on food based not on optimal health, but rather survival. Second, there's no such thing as 'the' Paleo diet; patterns of eating varied tremendously from region to region and season to season. The idea that there existed one specific Paleo diet is pure fiction."[19]

Regardless of what a true Paleolithic diet consisted of, John Durant, author of *The Paleo Manifesto*, concedes that it should most likely include human flesh.[20] You don't hear too much about that from Paleo proponents today.

There are some really good things about the Paleo diet. The 21st century Paleolithic human doesn't eat dairy (cavemen didn't raise cows), processed food (cavemen didn't have Doritos), or added sugar and oils.[21] Salt is used sparingly, and lots of vegetables are included.

But the Paleo diet also bans grains and legumes (cavemen didn't have agriculture).[22] It prescribes eating large amounts of saturated fat, like beef tallow (rendered fat), lamb tallow, lard, and duck fat, stipulating that it must come from healthy, happy animals. Paleo proponents also, famously, advocate eating lots of animal protein: red meat, pork, chicken, eggs, internal organs, wild fish and shellfish.[23]

"As Dr. McDougall says, 'People love to hear good news about bad habits,'" said Dr. Klaper. "People like to eat flesh, so they love to hear, 'You should eat flesh every day,' which is what most Americans do. Not even mountain lions eat flesh three times a day. Yet Paleo tells us we're carnivorous apes, as though every caveman had a mastodon in the freezer.

"There's a major health concern for Paleo folks," he continued. "People consuming this flesh-based diet may lose weight, because they don't eat dairy, oils, or refined carbohydrates. But what's happening inside your arteries, Paleo friends? The plaque is building up. These are the lean and fit folks who drop dead at the gym at 39."

"Where is the research?" Dr. Esselstyn asked. "I'm unaware of any hard data on the Paleo diet, where you take patients with illness—hypertension, diabetes, heart disease—and you reverse the disease or prevent it from developing. Because when you follow Paleo, you're eating the very foods that destroy the vascular system."

Dr. Kahn agreed. "You're going to be hard put to come up with a scientific answer other than, 'Go back to plant-based,' if you're desiring clean arteries that affect your brain, your central function, and your heart function throughout your life span."

Paleo's got such a great story, though. Tarzan cosplay, anyone?

"Paleo presents this fantasy of some muscular caveman running through the forest, tearing their kills apart like a tiger: 'Ahhh, I am caveman, hear me roar,'" said Dr. Davis. "That wasn't at all what was going on back then! The anthropologists laugh at the Paleo people."

A two-million-year-old hominid fossil from South America, *Australopithecus sediba*, recently had a dental exam. *Australopithecus* lived in an open savanna with abundant opportunities for animal food,[24] and yet isotope analysis on the fossil teeth showed that our early ancestors were heavy plant eaters—primarily leaves, fruits, and bark.[25]

"No matter what region of the world is studied," Dr. Davis writes in *Proteinaholic*, "analysis of Neanderthal teeth proves that these humans ate mostly plants."[26]

"When you look at the anthropological literature on modern Stone Age people," Dr. Mills said, "typically only 15-20 percent of their diet was made up of animal food. Most of the hunts were unsuccessful. Even when a hunt was successful, the meat was quickly divided, so any person only got a relatively small amount of animal tissue, which had to be eaten right away, before it started to rot. We were not efficient enough as hunters, with Stone Age technology, to have a meat-centered diet."

"How about the theory," Keegan said, "that a high-protein, high-fat diet like Paleo allowed us to evolve our big brain?"

"Yeah, right," laughed Dr. Mills. "If eating meat led to larger brains, then the carnivores should be the most intelligent creatures on the planet. We know better. The dog still drinks out of the toilet."

In fact, a 2015 study from the University of Chicago shows that it was carbohydrates, especially starch, that were critical for the incredibly fast growth of the human brain over the last million years. Human brain function uses 25 percent of our body's energy stores, and up to 60 percent of our blood glucose. The most efficient source of glucose comes from carbohydrates, and it's very unlikely that our high glucose demands could have been met with a low-carb diet.[27]

This research supports what doctors like John McDougall have been saying for decades.

"The Mayans and Aztecs are civilizations that existed for 1,300 years," Dr. McDougall told us. "They were known as the people of the corn. They lived on a starch-based diet. People tell me, 'Potatoes will make me fat.' Yeah, fat like Inca warriors. Or look at Asia—extremely successful civilizations for thousands of years. Before they switched from rice to a Westernized diet of animal foods and oils, there were almost no overweight Asians.

"The bulk of your calories should be rice and other grains, corn, potatoes, sweet potatoes, beans, lentils, peas, as well as fruits and vegetables. Pasta and marinara sauce, lasagna, bean burritos, vegetables and rice, these are the foods your body is designed to live on. These foods will restore your health.

"You have to get the starch concept," Dr. McDougall emphasized, "otherwise you won't be satisfied and you won't have the energy you deserve. Look at historical records. You will find consistently that large populations of successful people lived on starch-based diets."

Even our spit can attest: the primary enzyme secreted in human saliva is amylase, which specifically breaks down starch.[28]

Dr. Davis told us a story from his own practice. "I have a patient from Ghana, a very smart lady. She's lived in the US for many years, and for many of them, she's had a serious problem with obesity. She's on medication for weight loss, she's got a trainer, but her diet is eggs, bacon, chicken, sausage. 'What do you think is wrong?' I ask her. She said, 'My issues are at night, when we eat more carbs from our traditional diet from Ghana. The carbs make me fat.'

"I had just read a study about Ghana, and people in Ghana are not overweight. I asked her, 'When you go back to Ghana, are people overweight?' She says, 'I'm one of the biggest people there.' I ask, 'What do you eat there?' 'Traditional Ghana meals: lots of starches, sweet potato stews, maize, corn, fruit. The funny thing is that's the only place I lose weight!'"

Analyses of fossil teeth also show that early humans ate legumes, a great source of both carbohydrates and protein. But the Paleo diet argues, against mountains of evidence, that beans are poisonous to humans.[29]

"Paleo advocates say, 'Don't eat legumes, they didn't have legumes in Paleo times,'" Dr. Davis said. "Number one, they had legumes in Paleo times. Number two, legumes are the one food associated with longevity in every single long-lived culture. Not one scientific study shines a bad light on legumes, and there's a thousand studies showing they're good for you. But instead, the Paleo people are opting for a Paleo coconut bar, like the kind the Paleo people ate back in the day when they went to the Paleo store."

"The Paleo effect may actually create sicker people," continued Dr. Davis in another vein. "We're seeing higher cholesterol levels in Paleo followers, the same or worse insulin sensitivity, and frankly I'm seeing weight gain in them. They say to me, 'I'm on Paleo and I gained weight.' 'What are you eating?' 'I'm eating lots of steaks and chickens.'"

"Paleo folks," Dr. Klaper said to us, "are setting themselves up for an epidemic of clogged arteries, colon cancers, and autoimmune diseases. It's not a healthy diet. We are not carnivorous apes. If we eat like that, the consequences are going to be very severe."

The British Dietetic Association's list of "Top 5 Celebrity Diets to Avoid in 2015" included the Paleo Diet at number 2.

It lost out to the Urine Therapy Diet.[30]

Carnivores, Herbivores, Omnivores, and Evolution

I hear it all the time. "Human beings have evolved to eat meat. Look at our eyes. Look at our canine teeth!"

Look at the canines on a panda.

"When your cat yawns," said Dr. Barnard, "you see protruding razor teeth used to kill prey, to scrape hide and pull meat off bones. Our canine teeth are no bigger than our incisors. That happened at least 3 and a half million years ago. Our teeth are designed for grinding, which is good for vegetables, fruits, grains, and beans. Not so good for killing and eating a raw animal. Try eating road kill without tools."

"Lots of herbivores have canines," Dr. Mills told us. "The canines in hippos are gigantic. The canines in several primates are very long, almost like the canines in carnivores, but they're used for defense and fighting each other. Human canines have become small and rounded. They're utterly useless for ripping anything other than an envelope."

Dr. Esselstyn said, "With our 30-foot-long gastrointestinal tract, there's no question that humans are herbivores. From an evolutionary standpoint, we might have had to eat meat in times of scarcity. But look at our bodies. Can you imagine eating a dead elephant? Are you going to go through his hide with your fingers, with your teeth?"

I wondered why a carnivorous animal like a cat doesn't get the same cancers that humans get from eating large amounts of meat.

"The human body has a very long digestive tract, with extra surface area to extract nutrients, and process all the fiber in plants," Dr. Barnard explained. "If you eat a high-fiber diet—by which I mean a plant-based diet—fiber will carry out the carcinogens and the excess hormones. An animal like a cat is built for a meat-based diet. They have a very, very short intestinal tract, so the carcinogens don't stick around. It's a completely different system."

Cats and other carnivores move food through their intestinal tracts in under 4 hours. But food stays in our human bodies for 18 hours or more.[31]

"And take a look at our eyes," Dr. Barnard said. "A human being can detect antioxidants at 300 yards. I'm talking about the orange beta-carotene of a carrot, the red lycopene in a tomato, or the dark purple anthocyanins in blueberries. Cats don't have the same color vision we have. They're looking for motion. They're hunters.

"Research clearly shows that meat-eating for humans began as scavenging,"[32] he continued. "With stone tools, we could scavenge from a lion, and scrape the meat off the bones. Then once you've got fire, you're on to something. Humans became honorary carnivores. Some might say we're omnivorous—if we find meat, we'll eat it. But our bodies are herbivorous bodies. We still have pre-Stone Age coronary arteries, and we still get heart disease when we eat animal protein."

I could see how the question might shift from "Could we?" to "Should we?" You *could*, for instance, put a nail in the wall with the wooden handle of a hammer. But it wouldn't be the best way to use it.

"We are omnivores with choice," is how Dr. Klaper put it. "Yes, we can digest small amounts of animal flesh, and I'm sure that scavenging carcasses probably got us through our early years, but we are not obligate canivores. There's a big difference."

Of all the doctors Keegan and I spoke with, Dr. Mills had spent the most time exploring the anatomical and physiological distinctions between herbivores, carnivores, and omnivores. He gave us a master class on the topic:[33]

- ✓ Carnivores prey on animals who run away, so their joints are permanently flexed in a runner's crouch in order to explode into a quick burst of speed. They don't, however, have much stamina.
- ✓ Herbivores tend to have straight limbs. When they stand, it is the skeleton, rather than the muscles, that resists the force of gravity. That means little muscular energy is required to stand and travel for long distances. Humans are optimized for foraging. We are some of the most efficient long-distance movers on the planet,[34] able to cover very large areas looking for food at a low energy cost.
- ✓ Herbivores tend to have small openings to their oral cavities. They have cheek muscles that push the food back to the molars so they can grind and swallow soft, chewed balls of food. Our teeth slide across each other in a horizontal plane. The herbivore jaw is very mobile, which allows rotary motions of chewing, but if an herbivore tries to crush bones or wrestle an animal down with its mouth, it's probably going to dislocate its jaw, which in the wilderness would mean starving to death.
- ✓ Carnivores don't chew their food. They have a very strong, stable jaw. They have reduced facial musculature, they can open their mouths extremely wide, and their teeth are shaped like steak knives that slide past each other in a vertical plane

to slice meat off bone, and cut through tough tendons and hides. Their esophagus (the tube connecting the mouth to the stomach) is very stretchy and wide—food rarely gets caught. Human beings frequently choke to death on animal tissue. Ninety percent of people that choke to death every year choke on meat.[35]

✓ Herbivores have to eat multiple meals every day to get enough calories.

✓ A typical carnivore can eat 30 percent of their body weight at a single meal. A 300-pound lion can eat 90-100 pounds of flesh at one go. Why? Because hunting is very inefficient. Ninety to ninety-five percent of their hunts are unsuccessful. The average wild carnivore eats once every 7-10 days.

✓ Carnivores can eat rotting tissue, which allows them to eat, for example, 100 pounds of flesh from a buffalo and still come back the next day to eat another 100 pounds of now-decomposing flesh.

✓ The pH of a carnivore's stomach acid, after eating a meal, is less than or equal to 1.0.[36] The pH of car battery acid also ranges from about 0.8 to 1.0.[37] That's necessary because, again, they're eating rotting tissue loaded with bacteria and pathogens. This powerful stomach acid kills the bacteria and also dissolves bone and tough connective tissue.

✓ When plant-eaters (including humans) have food in our stomach, the pH is around 4.5—if it's a healthy stomach environment.[38] Just strong enough to kill certain bacteria found in soil and plants, but not good at killing virulent pathogenic bacteria.

✓ Plant-eaters need a source of Vitamin C because our bodies don't make it. Vitamin C is widely distributed throughout plant foods. Carnivores make their own Vitamin C.

✓ We, on the other hand, can take an abundant plant pigment called beta-carotene (which gives color to vegetables like carrots) and convert it into Vitamin A. We can make as much

Vitamin A as we need. Carnivores cannot do this. They have to ingest pre-formed Vitamin A, often from animal livers.

✓ Too much pre-formed Vitamin A is toxic to us. Carnivores can detoxify pre-formed Vitamin A. Herbivores can't.

✓ Along the same lines, carnivores can detoxify nitrogenous waste from excess protein. We can't do that.

✓ Some plant substances that are extremely beneficial to herbivores are toxic to carnivores. For instance, garlic, onions, and other plants in the allium family have compounds that essentially cause the red blood cells of a cat to explode, and potentially kill them.[39] They can't detoxify these compounds the way we can. But we not only detoxify them, they actually boost our immune function and help protect us against diseases like cancer.

✓ Only herbivores have an innate drive to seek out salt. Sodium is a necessary nutrient, and plant tissues are very low in sodium. That's why we love potato chips, and why cows and deer love saltlicks.

✓ Carnivores have no innate drive to seek salt.[40] They get plenty of sodium from animal flesh and bodily fluids like blood.

"That's amazing," Keegan said, fascinated. "But a lot of people argue that we're not herbivores, we're omnivores."

"Sure," Dr. Mills said. "We are *behavioral* omnivores. But that doesn't tell you whether we are *physiologically designed* as omnivores. A true, by-design omnivore is an animal designed to hunt, kill, and dismember prey, but also has the capacity to use plant foods for energy.

"Bears and raccoons fit the bill. They retain the jaw structure, teeth, claws, stomach and intestinal structure of carnivores, but they also have slightly modified molars that allow them to pulp plant foods. Yet they're able to eat rotting flesh, they have giant stomachs, and their livers can process enormous amounts of calories without becoming diseased.

"Human beings," Dr. Mills continued, "unlike bears or raccoons, do not have that mixed anatomy and physiology that you see in true omnivores. Because we are *not* true omnivores."

"How can we eat meat then?" Keegan asked.

"Great question. Digestion is done by enzymes, which break apart amino acids. All proteins, plant or animal, are made of the same 20 amino acids. Think of a boat or a plane. Very different vehicles, but they're both composed of metal, screws, rivets, bolts.

"It doesn't matter to a screwdriver whether a screw is on a boat or a plane. If it fits, it will turn it. Likewise, the protein-digesting enzymes will break apart the amino acids, and that's what allows you to digest animal tissue.

"The problem comes when the tissues are absorbed. That's when your risk for heart disease, diabetes, cancers of the colon, breast, and prostate, among others, is significantly raised.

"Animal tissue is also more difficult for us to digest than plant proteins. That's why, after a huge meat meal, the food tends to sit in the stomach for a very long time. People get acid reflux, indigestion, and it can actually make them feel ill."

Dr. Kim Williams told us a personal story about the difficulty of digesting meat. "I was playing tennis for the University of Chicago," he said, "and I was vegetarian at the time. We were at a dual meet and they forgot to get me something vegetarian. So I had a choice: play singles-doubles, eat nothing, then play another singles-doubles match. I said, 'I'll eat the hamburger.' Four-four in the first set of the second singles match, and I was in the corner throwing up. So many people have had that experience." He shook his head at the memory. "Meat is very difficult to digest."

Even if it doesn't make you ill, meat can make you smell bad and cramp your sex life. A 2006 study, using 2 groups of men divided into meat-eaters (eating an average amount of red meat), and non-meat eaters, showed that women significantly preferred the body odor of the men who had *not* eaten meat for two weeks. To make sure the guys in the meat group weren't just naturally stinky, the researchers switched the diets at a later date with the same men. The meat-eating group became vegetarian, and vice versa. The women still preferred the smell of the men—a different group this time—who did not eat meat.[41] (There are fascinating studies on smell and partner choice in homosexual men and women,[42] but none dealing with diet, as far as I know.)

The choice of heterosexual partners is a driving force behind conventional evolution. "The guy who smells like plants is more desirable than the guy who smells like rotting flesh," said Dr. Mills, "because the plant guy is more likely to produce healthy children, and survive long enough to help the mother raise the children."

"Can you tell us about pathogen disgust?"[43] Keegan asked.

"Yes, there are certain things that elicit a disgust response in humans from all cultures," Dr. Mills said. "For instance, things that are moist, slimy, bloody, things covered with flies, worms, or animal hair, things that are rotting. That partial list I gave you pretty much describes raw animal tissue. Of course, there are cultural and individual variations, but in general, most humans have a disgust response to raw animal tissue."

"Why would we have a disgust reaction if meat is part of the human diet?" I asked.

"Well, we're not meant to eat it, and that's why we're disgusted. Raw animal flesh is often loaded with pathogens that can kill us. Our feelings about raw meat are called 'pathogen disgust.' Even the mere texture of raw meat can cause it to lodge in our throats and choke us to death. But a carnivore will eat a piece of bloody, rotten, raw flesh without hesitation. They will eat from a rotting carcass for days until it's completely consumed. Wild animals in war zones dig up corpses because, to them, decomposing bodies smell like food.

"Everybody loves a smoothie made with fruit and some vegetables," he went on. "But if you put a fish in a blender and grind it up, it's absolutely repulsive. Or put rotting beef in a blender, covered with maggots, and grind that up. Decaying tissue induces a vomiting reflex in us, which is indicative that we shouldn't eat it. If you smell a decaying body, you actually have to stifle the impulse to throw up. It's a reflex mechanism designed to protect us. The body is programmed to expel rotten flesh in an effort to keep you from getting sick."

But there are cultures around the world who eat raw meat—Steak Tartare from France, for instance, Kibbeh nayeh from Lebanon, or, most commonly, Japanese sashimi.

Putting aside the inherent health risks ("Steak Tartare is delicious partly because it is dangerous," swoons one admirer in *Newsweek*[44]—pardon me if I don't find the prospect of bloody diarrhea from *E. coli* appetizing[45]), the raw meat in these dishes is always cleaned (no gristle or hair, please), drained of blood, eaten as fresh as possible, and seasoned or mixed with things like onions, garlic, cloves, nutmeg, peanuts, bulgur, lemon and lime juices, and other herbs and spices.[46]

"What we call 'seasoning' are plants and plant parts," Dr. Mills said. "We rub herbs and spices on animal tissue to give them the flavor and smell of plants. Our brain finds those flavors delicious. Without them, meat is bland and tasteless to us. Has your dog ever said to you, 'I'm not eating that meat until you season it with pepper and basil, and cover it with a garnish'? He's happy to eat stringy, bloody, rotting animal tissue."

Even a Steak Tartare aficionado might balk at that.

The scientific community hasn't settled the question of why human beings have forward-facing eyes. "Humans are predators because their eyes are on the front of their heads," is what you normally hear. But what about gorillas, koalas, orangutans, and pandas? And there are many predators, like sharks, tree shrews, killer whales, sperm whales, robins, mongooses, and snakes, with eyes on the sides of their heads.

My favorite eye-position theory is X-Ray Vision.

Try this: hold one finger vertically in front of your nose. Close one eye. Your finger blocks everything behind it. Open both eyes, and you can see through it like Superman.

Now hold your out-spread fingers a short distance in front of your face. Close one eye. Your fingers block a good deal of your vision. Open both eyes. You now get a much fuller spatial picture of what's behind your hand.

A study done at Rensselaer Polytechnic Institute[47] examined 319 species and found that eye position depends on 1) the clutter in the animal's habitat, and 2), the animal's size in relation to the objects creating the clutter.

They're not talking about the mess in your living room. Animals with eyes on the sides of their head—for example, fish, horses, buffalo, insects, reptiles, birds, and rabbits—tend to be found in non-cluttered environments like fields, plains, deserts, open stretches of water, or an environment where the cluttering objects are bigger than the separation between an animal's eyes—like a mouse making its way through leaves in a forest. Large animals with eyes in the front of their heads tend to evolve in a cluttered environment like a jungle—apes, tigers, koala bears, pandas, or lions hunting in tall grass. And like other primates, we first evolved in a leafy, cluttered jungle.

The depth perception afforded by our forward-facing eyes would also have been invaluable as we judged distances while swinging rapidly through trees.[48]

Mark Changizi, the leading Rensselaer researcher, muses intriguingly on the future evolution of human eye placement.

"In today's world," he said, "humans have more in common visually with tiny mice in a forest than with a large animal in the jungle. We aren't faced with a great deal of small clutter, and the things that do clutter our visual field—cars and skyscrapers—are much wider than the separation between our eyes, so we can't use our X-ray power to see through them.

"If we froze ourselves today and woke up a million years from now...it might be difficult for us to look the new human population in the eye, because by then they might be facing sideways."[49]

Isn't being vegan expensive?

No. Being sick is expensive.

Keegan and I visited a grocery store with Toni Okamoto, founder of the blog, "Plant-Based on a Budget." The site has been up for only 4 years, and already it's had over 4.5 million views. It's been showcased on *Huffington Post*, *US News World and Report*, *Reader's Digest*, and many other media outlets.[50]

"A common misconception about eating plant-based is that it's expensive, but it can be just as cheap, if not cheaper than the standard American diet, and much more nutritious," Okamoto tells me, as we grab a shopping cart outside.

"I originally created 'Plant-Based on a Budget' for a few reasons. My family was having health issues related to the meat and dairy they were eating. I wanted to give them a resource on plant-based eating.

"The blog was also my response to the SNAP (Supplemental Nutrition Assistance Program) challenge, better known as the Food Stamp challenge. It challenges families who are financially well off to keep their food budget within the parameters of what a low-income family the same size would spend with food stamps, for a short time. In 2015, for example, a family of four's monthly allowance through SNAP, with maximum benefits, would be $649. On the SNAP challenge you have to stick within those budgetary guidelines.[51]

"I felt there was something disrespectful about the challenge. The website was posting pictures of privileged people in front of discount grocery stores, saying, 'I'm eating on a budget!' But for them it's a temporary thing. I grew up in a low-income household, and it's not a temporary thing for a lot of people.

"My Plant-Based on a Budget challenge is $100 a month, per person. Maximum SNAP benefits for one person allows $194 a month. So you can do this on food stamps, and still have money left over. A family of four receiving SNAP benefits can do this with even greater savings."

We walked into the supermarket.

"So where are we going first?" I asked.

"Produce section," she answered. "I'll get the cheapest apple, which today is the Golden Delicious."

We were selecting in-season produce, as well as food from the bulk bins.

"That really cuts down on cost," Okamoto said. "You also eliminate a lot of expense by not buying meat and dairy."

We pushed the rattling cart down the aisles.

Lettuce. A tomato. Two carrots. A lemon. Half a pound of pinto beans. Half a pound of pasta. Barley. Granola. A pound of oats. Corn tortillas. Soymilk. Frozen broccoli.

Frozen vegetables, in addition to being cheaper, are usually more nutritious than fresh vegetables. Fresh vegetables often lose nutrients while they're being transported from the field to the store, while frozen ones are flash-frozen right after they're harvested, preserving their vitamin content.[52]

I looked at the growing pile of food in the cart.

"Can a person really thrive while spending this little money on food?" I asked Okamoto.

"Definitely," she said. "I've had hundreds of people give me feedback. I've done it myself. Our meal plan for a family of four is $25 per person per week, which adds up to $400 a month for the whole family."

Okamoto checks her shopping list. "My favorite on this meal plan is the tofu-ricotta lasagna."

"So you're not just eating rice and beans every day," I said.

"No," she laughs. "On my site, I have a lot of contributors who focus on different cultural cuisines. I'm Japanese-Mexican, so I created a lot of plant-based Mexican dishes. Other writers focus on Asian cuisine, Indian, even Soul Food. There's an amazing Southern Style Collard Greens recipe."

"What desserts are there?"

"On this plan...peanut butter cookies."

"You have a good recipe for peanut butter cookies?"

"I do. I'll send it to you."

We walked around a bit more, selecting unsalted sunflower seeds, bouillon cubes, bananas, kale, and cilantro.

"Even if the food is affordable," I said, eyeing the vegetables in the cart, "people will say, 'I don't have time for chopping all those vegetables or cooking, it's easier to grab a roast chicken.'"

"When I did my own challenge," replied Okamoto, "I was working 40 hours a week, with a 3 hour commute, and I was still able to prepare the food. Now, I probably work over 70 hours a week. I also live an hour from where I work. I do not want to be chopping vegetables when I get home.

"So I cut all my vegetables at once on the weekend, and store them in the fridge. It takes a lot less time than you would expect. When I need them, they're ready.

"I cook my beans that day too, and put them in the fridge or freezer. You can cook food overnight in a crockpot, which you can get at Goodwill for a few dollars.

"Anyone can eat this way. Families on food stamps. Busy parents with young children. Our four-person meal plan includes recipes for kids. If my dad, the biggest barbecuer ever, can do it, then anyone can."

We rolled up to the cashier.

"$20.64 is your total," said the gentleman behind the counter.

"$20.64?!" I looked at the receipt. It was right. "That's an entire week of food!"

"Goodness!" said the cashier. "A lot of customers spend over $100 at a time."

"What are they buying?" Okamoto asked.

"Oh, a lot of everything. Milk, chicken, cheese."

Keegan took home the groceries. He was psyched to try Okamoto's challenge, especially the lasagna.

I had the receipt though, and I kept looking at it. Twenty dollars and sixty-four cents for a week's worth of meals.

I thought of something Dr. McMacken had said to me: "I take care of patients who are on public assistance, as well as patients with a lot more financial resources. I have never had anyone tell me that the advice I gave them on eating a plant-based diet was too expensive. Because I focus on foods that are affordable. Fruits and vegetables, especially when purchased in more economical forms, like frozen, or at a farmer's market, and items purchased in bulk like beans. There's also a tremendous pay-off when you think about people coming off their medications, and saving themselves from procedures, surgeries, doctor's visits—these foods pay for themselves a thousand times over. I would challenge anyone who said that a whole foods, plant-based diet is too expensive."

The biggest question is this:

How much is your health worth to you?

CHAPTER 17
THE NEXT STAGE IN HUMAN EVOLUTION: VEGAN ATHLETES

I challenge anyone to watch Timothy Shieff in action without jaw-dropping astonishment.

Shieff, whose professional nickname is "Livewire," is a two-time World Freerunning Champion, and a professional Parkour athlete. He was also captain of Team Europe in the competition, "American Ninja Warrior, USA vs. the World." Shieff led Team Europe to victory.

Parkour comes from the French *parcours*, which means "through[1]-run,"[2] or "the path." The art of Parkour, strictly speaking, involves getting from Point A to Point B, using the obstacles in between—for example, walls, trees, buildings—to increase your efficiency.[3] Freerunning is the same idea, except that flips, twists, handstands, and other forms of creative expression are thrown in.

It's a mix of gymnastics, rock-climbing, breakdancing, and martial arts, bound together with seemingly super-human agility, flexibility, and strength.

Keegan and I met Shieff at a Parkour gym in Concord, California. It was a large, windowless area with concrete walls and fluorescent lighting. Dominating the space was an enormous, industrial obstacle course, constructed from metal scaffolding, wooden "buildings," staircases, crash mats, metal rings, heavy ropes, and walls with ledges just deep enough for a fingertip grip.

We watched Shieff run the course. It was insane. He was doing what looked like computer-generated stunts from a Marvel summer blockbuster—Spiderman came to mind—but Shieff was right there in the flesh, running up walls with muscular elegance, leaping like a jaguar from one "building" to another, handstanding on top of scaffolds, and performing "the flag": after getting a wide grip on a vertical pole with both hands, he effortlessly lifted his body until it was horizontal to the floor, like a human windsock in a full breeze.

Back on the ground, Shieff looked like an average guy, with a topknot of blond hair and remarkably clear, pale skin. Passing him on the street I'd never suspect that he could do, as he does in one of his videos, a one-handed handstand on the edge of a roof, high over an urban street.

"For something like Ninja Warrior and Parkour," he told us in a soft British accent, "you need to have a good strength to bodyweight ratio. When I went vegan, I lost 15, 20 pounds. I became more agile and more efficient. I had more stamina. It was just that extra bit of pop. I'm a 100 percent better athlete than I was before."

"How did you feel when you first went vegan?" I asked.

"Once I learned you could get your protein without eating animals, I thought, 'Okay, I'll try it for a week,'" Shieff recalled. "Within a week, I had more energy and noticeable improvement in my recovery. The biggest cause of fatigue is dehydration, and a lot of repetitive strain injuries come from inflammation in joints and ligaments. A vegan diet is more hydrating, anti-inflammatory, and more alkalizing, so you aid your recovery tremendously. My tendonitis went away. I could train for longer hours. And once I noticed these things, I thought, 'What have I been doing all these years?'

"Back then, I still wanted to taste animal flesh," he admitted. "But I made a choice for the greater good that went against my desires, and when you do that, you challenge yourself to grow mentally. You apply that to your training, and you become a stronger person in every way."

"You lost weight when you first went plant-based," I said. "What about athletes who need to keep their weight up?"

"I know bodybuilders who have put on bulk and muscle mass after becoming vegan," said Shieff. "I stayed just as strong, but I lost body fat. It enhances whatever athleticism you're working towards.

"For me, I felt stale in my training. Becoming vegan unlocked the next chapter in my progress. It's not always a question of how you're training. You need to look at yourself as a complete person, which includes what you eat and how you live.

"And then beyond my physical abilities, I evolved as a person. I've always been against animal cruelty. But I actually started living in alignment with that truth."

"What's your definition of health?" Keegan asked. Good question for a guy who can scale the inside of a 20-foot chimney without equipment.

"Longevity," Shieff replied. "There are people on the Paleo diet who are just as strong as vegans, but in the years to come, the plant-based lifestyle will pay dividends. We'll still be doing this stuff when we're 50, 60, and beyond.

"I feel like I've not peaked yet. I eat clean, I feel fresh, and every day I'm reaching new heights. I don't know where the end is going to be.

"Experiencing being vegan is the key to understanding it. You can read all these blogs, arguing pros and cons, but until I experienced the difference myself, that's when I realized that this is a very vibrant way to live. I'm not stuck in these desires that aren't serving me.

"Once you know better, you have to do better," Shieff said. "Veganism for me is about evolution. It's about the next chapter of humanity."

That's a convincing statement from a man who is almost super-human in his physical abilities. If Timothy Shieff is a preview of the next stage of human evolution, we are on the right track.

About 0.5 percent of the American population is currently plant-based.[4] "Large" percentages of vegans can be found in Israel[5] and China,[6] where 4-5 percent of both countries' populations eat a wholly plant-based diet.

There are surprisingly high numbers of vegans, though, among top-tier, professional athletes. Check out this far-from-complete list:

> **Mac Danzig**, MMA (Mixed Martial Arts) and UFC (Ultimate Fighting Championship) fighter, winner of season six of The Ultimate Fighter
> **Venus and Serena Williams**, both of them ranked #1 in the world at some point in their superstar tennis careers
> **Jehina Malik**, competitive bodybuilder (and vegan since birth), winner of the 2013 NPC Eastern USA Bodybuilding Championships
> **Patrik Baboumian**, winner of Germany's Strongest Man in 2011, winner of the European Powerlifting Championship in 2012
> **Steph Davis**, one of the world's greatest rock climbers, and the only woman to free-solo climb (no ropes or harnesses) a 5.11 mountain face (very, very steep)
> **Scott Jurek**, ultra-marathon runner who broke the record in 2015 for the fastest thru-hike of the Appalachian Trail, which stretches from Georgia to the top of the highest mountain in

Maine (Jurek did the trail in 46 days, 8 hours, and 7 minutes, averaging 50 miles a day)

➢ **Tia Blanco**, American pro surfer who won gold during the 2015 ISA World Surfing Games

➢ **Brendan Brazier**, Canadian professional Ironman triathlete

➢ Paralympics British rower **David Smith**, who won gold at the 2009 World Rowing Championships and the 2012 Summer Paralympics

➢ UFC fighters, brothers **Nick and Nate Diaz**

➢ **Meaghan Duhamel**, Canadian figure skater and Olympic silver medalist

➢ **Cam Awesome**, an 8-time national super heavyweight boxing champion, and captain of the USA National Boxing team

➢ **Claire "Fury" Foreman**, a Muay Thai (Thai kickboxing) martial artist from Australia who won the Australian title in 2015

➢ Track star **Carl Lewis**, named "Olympian of the Century" and holder of 10 Olympic medals and 10 World Championship medals.[7]

Athletes, perhaps more than any other segment of the population, are besieged with the myth that you cannot be a high-performing human being without eating animal protein. Tofu and chickpeas, many think, might "sustain" a tie-dyed civilian strolling to the natural foods co-op, but a bruising powerhouse like a football player needs "real" protein.

It's true that athletes need more protein than non-athletes, but how much depends on a lot of things: for example, the sport, body weight, age, and the intensity and duration of training sessions.

Strength and power athletes, like weightlifters and sprinters, need about 1.2 to 1.7 grams of protein per kilogram of body weight (1 kg = 2.2 lbs). Endurance athletes like marathoners need about 1.2 to 1.4 g/kg of body weight.[8]

Athletes, use this to figure out your weight in kilograms:

(Weight in lbs) ÷ 2.2 = (Weight in kg)

Then, to determine the upper range of protein requirements for either a strength athlete or an endurance athlete:

Endurance Athletes: Daily protein requirements in grams	**Strength/Power Athletes**: Daily protein requirements in grams
(Weight in kg) × 1.4g protein/kg	(Weight in kg) × 1.7 g protein/kg

An NFL player weighing 300 pounds would need a colossal 232 grams of protein daily. For many athletes, that means reaching for steaks, eggs, chicken breasts, and quarts of whey protein shakes.

But not for David Carter, NFL Defensive Lineman—also known as The 300 Pound Vegan.

Dave Carter is a big guy. He towered over me (and I'm 6'2"). He's about twice my width, a wall of solid muscle. His biceps are the size of my thighs. His demeanor, though, is soft-spoken and modest.

"All my life," Carter told Keegan and I, "I was all about meat. My family owned a BBQ restaurant. A year and a half ago, I was playing with the Dallas Cowboys, and I had a lot of pain from tendinitis, from football injuries. I had nerve damage in my right arm. I couldn't feel three of my fingers and couldn't make a full fist to grab guys on the field. My bench press was weak.

"My wife has been vegan for six years, and I'd heard about the health benefits, but I was like, 'Honey, I can't be vegan and play football. I'll be skinny and feeble.' But the injuries started adding up. The pain was incredible. I couldn't lift myself out of the tub—it felt like somebody took a bat to my elbows. Team doctors were giving me Celebrex for the inflammation. It didn't do anything.

"Then I watched the documentary *Forks Over Knives*," Carter recalled. "And I finally realized, 'Man, my *diet* is what's contributing to all the pain I'm experiencing.' Milk was causing inflammation in my joints. And I was drinking milkshakes every night to gain weight. I was killing myself from the inside out. So I thought, screw it. I may as well try the vegan thing."

"What happened?" I asked.

"At first, I had no energy," said Carter. "But a month later, I started feeling improvements. I did start losing weight, but I thought, 'I have more energy, I'll keep going.' The grip in my hands was coming back. The tendinitis inflammation was going away. My blood pressure was down. My strength, speed, agility, my recovery time—all that was improving."

"Wow."

"My weight started going back up when I added more legumes, seeds, rice, millet, and other grains into my diet. I was running 7-minute miles, which was good for me at my weight. Before I was vegan, I was only bench-pressing 315 about five times. Two, three months after going vegan, my bench press went up to 465. I was like, 'Oh my god! I'm vegan and I'm bench-pressing 465 pounds? This is ridiculous!'

"I was doing the leg press machine with my trainer one day, and it had 1,000 pounds on it. I told him, 'I'm feeling good. Put another 45 pounds on each side.' We kept adding weight, doing sets of 10, again and again. We were at 1,380 pounds, and there was no more room for weights. So my trainer gets on top of the machine. He's 200 pounds. I was doing sets of ten like that. Then we had to get creative. I said, 'Let's push my car.' We were pushing my Cadillac Escalade around. We pushed it up a hill. Then I'd slowly walk the car back down the hill, and push it up again."

"Holy crap," I said. "All of a sudden you had super powers." First we had Spiderman with Timothy Shieff, and now here was the Incredible Hulk. Except that our Hulk was green on the inside, and much more loveable.

"Yeah!" said Carter. "The 300 Pound Vegan is my super hero name! My trainer wasn't vegan at first, but seeing my strength and my cardio improve, he ended up going vegan. In fact, about 20 people in the gym went vegan from watching us."

"And your recovery time improved too?" Keegan asked.

"Oh yeah. Before becoming vegan, at the end of a long day of practice, my joints hurt. My soreness lasted a lot longer.

"After becoming vegan, my coaches have been telling me, 'Stop working out so much!' My energy level is through the roof. My recovery time is, like, non-existent. I'll just drink a beet juice or some dates after a workout, and I'll be ready to go again. Little or no muscle soreness. I can run forever."

"Why is that?" I asked. I was training for a marathon, and was really curious.

"Well, you only get clogged arteries due to the saturated fats in meat, dairy, in eggs. Your heart needs to deliver oxygen (via your blood) through your arteries to your extremities for you to perform your best. But by eating dairy and meat, you make it very difficult for your heart to pump oxygen for your arms and legs to move as fast as they can."

"That makes a lot of sense," I said. "You're not creating blockages in your body. What's your daily workout schedule like now?"

"I lift weights 5 days a week, 2 to 3 hours each day. The other 2 days I'm doing cardio, or when I'm in Costa Rica I carry a huge bag of rocks up a hill. I do that until I've had enough.

"I also do 500 push-ups. When I was in Costa Rica, I was working with this 76-year-old guy, Viktoras Kulvinskas, a nutritionist and former bodybuilder. He was doing 200 push-ups every day, and he has scoliosis [curvature of the spine]. And he's vegan.

"I was like, 'Oh hell no. Here's a 76-year-old vegan guy, and I'm 27. I've got to catch up.' So I worked up to it, and now a few times a week I do 500 push-ups within an hour."

"Holy crap." That was Keegan this time. "Did you get any pushback from the NFL about being vegan?"

Carter paused. "Let me just say, I was on a team, and they weren't very comfortable with my being vegan. I was 300 pounds, running with the wide receivers and the DBs, and the other players were asking, 'Man, what are you eating? How are you staying this big on plants? How are you still working out after this crazy workout we just did?'

"I asked the team chefs if they could make some vegan food. I wanted something simple: rice and beans, peanut butter, nothing fancy. The chefs were excited, and started creating vegan lasagna, and all this other amazing stuff.

"Meanwhile, the strength coach was telling us to drink milk protein shakes. But then we got inflammation from the milk, so he'd tell us to drink a shot of concentrated cranberry juice to help with the inflammation. It made no sense. Then a nutritionist told me being vegan wasn't healthy. She said I wouldn't get my protein, and that soymilk causes cancer. She didn't like me because I was telling all the other players that milk causes inflammation, and meat gets caught in your intestines, bringing toxic chemicals into your body. I think she told the coaches about me.

"So then," Carter continued, "the coach called me into his office, and said, 'What's going on, man? Can you not be vegan?' I said, 'No, I'm vegan for life. I'm not going to stop because of you.' He had called me into his office just to tell me to stop being vegan.

"The next day, all the vegan food was gone from the menu. The chef told me, 'Someone high up said we can't do that anymore.' I was like, '*Wow.*' The next day, I was released from the team. I wasn't forcing it down anyone's throat. And I was performing at my best. I was running with the top players, keeping up with guys who were 100 pounds lighter than me."

"Why would they let you go when your performance increased?" Keegan asked.

Carter paused again. "Teams are sponsored by companies like Muscle Milk," he said carefully. "Every other Superbowl commercial is for chicken wings. In my opinion, the meat and dairy industry have a lot to do with professional sports. Imagine if all the other guys on the team started going vegan. It causes controversy."

"So day after day," I said, "professional football players are wolfing down huge amounts of animal protein. Does that affect their health?"

"One of the things that pushed me to change my diet is that the average football player dies at 56 years of age," said Carter. "That's because they're constantly drinking milk and whey protein shakes, eating steak and chicken. I was eating 4 pieces of chicken in one sitting and big 20-ounce steaks.

"We thought, 'We're big dudes, we need to eat meat to be men.' I thought that too. But you're screwing your insides up. You're taking advantage of a helpless animal. You're killing a life that you don't need to take. With dairy, you're stealing breast milk that's meant for the baby cows and drinking it yourself. How is that manly? Men are supposed to be protectors. If you feed it to your kids, you're killing your kids.

"You can't be your strongest if you're eating the wrong foods. You're clogging your arteries and intestines. It takes 3 to 5 days to digest meat. Some guys don't take poops for three days. That stuff is rotting inside your body. You look big and strong on the outside, but you're dying on the inside. That's not strong, that's weak. Your heart is crying for help. You're dying."

***

Brendan Brazier is known not only for being a professional Ironman triathlete, but also for his expertise on vegan nutrition, particularly for athletes—much of it developed by using himself as a guinea pig.

There are two major elements that constitute an athlete's practice: training and recovery. Training is the component that usually gets the attention. Brazier noticed early in his career, however, that most training programs differed only in minor ways. This was true for both professional aces and mediocre players. Recovery was something of an afterthought. Brazier spoke with many professional athletes, and, like Dr. Greger and Dr. Davis, read scores of medical journals, dietary studies, and health and nutrition publications. The biggest distinction amongst athletes, he discovered, was diet.

"Knowing that training is little more than breaking down muscle," he wrote in *Thrive: The Vegan Nutrition Guide to Optimal Performance in Sports and Life*, "I figured that what rebuilds that same muscle must be a major factor for recovery and therefore quicker improvement. If I was able to recover from each workout faster, I would be able to schedule them closer together and therefore train more than my competition. I would improve faster. As I suspected, food was the answer—high-quality, nutrient-dense, alkaline-forming, easily digestible food in proper proportions... Nutrition has a dramatic effect on recovery—that was unmistakable."[9]

Brazier experimented with various performance-enhancing diets, and began eating plant-based. His words confirm those of Tim Shieff and Dave Carter:

> *The result was astounding. Not only did my recovery time plummet but my energy level, strength-to-weight ratio, and endurance shot up... On the cellular level, this diet was able to speed the renewal of muscle tissue. That meant that following this diet would actually help the body regenerate more frequently, suggesting that it could help reduce biological age.*[10]

Brazier's optimum performance diet revolves around the concept of "high net-gain nutrition." "Net-gain" refers to the energy and nutrients that remain in the body after digestion. Many foods in the typical American diet—meat and dairy for instance—take almost as much energy for the body to process as the foods contain. Those foods provide a very low net-gain. Whole fruits and vegetables, and grains like wild rice, quinoa, amaranth, and buckwheat are high net-gain foods.[11]

Brazier also focuses on alkaline-forming foods. Alkaline foods correct excess acid in the body, or acidosis. Every illness occurs when the body is in an acidic state.[12] Kidney stones, bone weakness, heart disease, diabetes, fatigue, weight gain, sleep disorders, digestive problems, inflammation, arthritis, even cancer—these are all conditions that thrive in an acidic environment.[13]

Athletes are particularly susceptible to acidosis. Rigorous activity creates lactic-acid build-up, and the meat-and-dairy-based diets of many athletes push their acid levels dangerously high.

The solution is to eat more alkaline-forming and less acid-forming foods. Alkaline foods include asparagus, beets, broccoli, carrots, onion, zucchini, sweet potatoes, oranges, mangos, avocados, bananas, pineapple, almonds, wild rice, and quinoa.

Acid-forming foods include dairy, chicken, beef, pork, shellfish, and fish.[14] These are the foods that contribute to inflammation and pain that significantly delay athletic recovery time.

And as any exceptional athlete knows, athletic performance is only partly physical. Clarity of thought and split-second, strategic thinking is essential for high performance.

Brazier discovered, on a plant-based diet, not only improvements in his strength, energy, and speed, but also in the sharpness of his mental acuity.

The brain, like the rest of the body, is nourished by the food we eat. When we eat food that is difficult to digest, our bodies divert extra blood to the stomach to help digestion. This means that blood, along with the attendant nutrients and oxygen, is drawn away from the brain, resulting in slower, more lethargic thinking.[15]

Lara Heimann knows how deeply the fibers of our body, our mind, and our emotions are bound together. At 47 ("I want credit for every year and every month," she tells us), she is a tall, striking master yogini. Heimann combined functional mobility training from her background in physical therapy, athletics, and eight years of practicing Vinyasa yoga to create YogaStream, a vigorous, challenging style of yoga characterized by intense core work, classical asanas sometimes modified to prevent common yoga injuries, strength drills, plyometric segments, and, at higher levels, many, many inversions—handstands of all variations, forearm stands, and arm balances. The connection to the mind and the spirit, along with attention to safe physical alignment, is always paramount.

We met with Heimann at her studio in Princeton, New Jersey, a large open space flooded with natural light.

When we arrived, Heimann was teaching the most advanced class offered at the studio. At this level, she practices along with her students. We watched as she seemed to float slowly, without using momentum or perceptible effort, into an assured handstand, before wrapping one leg around another into an "Eagle" leg bind. Heimann turned her head to survey her students (upside down), occasionally calling out "Pull your ribs in, Julie," or "Mike, wrap your triceps back!"

This was not, as many people still think of yoga, an hour of stretching to a New Age soundtrack.

"Is this hot yoga?" I asked after the class, as Heimann's students, dripping with sweat and beaming, filed out. There were puddles of perspiration on the studio floor.

"No, the room is only heated to about 78 degrees," she replied. "Hot yoga turns it up to 90 or 100. We heat the body internally using the core muscles."

"How did you get involved with yoga?" Keegan asked.

"I was a runner first," Heimann said. "I ran cross-country Division 1 at Duke University, where I studied physical therapy and anatomy. I encountered yoga in one of my running clubs. I was already teaching hip-hop, spinning, and aerobics, but I never felt the same marriage of physicality and discipline of mind that I found in running until I practiced yoga."

"Do you still run?" I asked.

"No, running creates an imbalance around my hips that affects my yoga practice, so I haven't done that in years. But my resting heart rate is the same as when I was running long-distance. I surf—Costa Rica is one of my favorite surfing spots. I teach a lot internationally—leading retreats, workshops, trainings, and video shoots in beautiful tropical locations—so I surf as often as I can. And last summer, my family and I hiked 205 miles from one coast of England to another. We climbed over 30,000 feet in elevation, carrying our gear. It took 17 days. But yoga is the only exercise I do regularly."

"How often do you practice? Can you describe it?" I love yoga and am fascinated by its enormous diversity.

"I practice 5 to 6 days a week, for about one and a half hours," Heimann said. "My most rigorous practice is usually one where I spend more time on my hands and upper body strength than anything else. I'll incorporate as many inversions as possible. I'll focus on long holds upside down in some handstand variation, push-ups in a variety of ways, and sprinkle in some high intensity interval training and strength drills. Right now I'm working on pressing up into a handstand from various arm balances."

An arm balance is a group of yoga poses in which only the hands are planted on the mat, and the entire body hovers above the floor, supported on one or both upper arms.

They're hard.

Heimann demonstrates a "Firefly" arm balance, in which her hands are planted flat on the ground, her arms are straight, and her legs—the backs of her thighs contacting the backs of her upper arms—are extended in a straddle. The only parts of her body touching the ground are her palms and fingers. Again, some crazy super hero creature flashes into my mind. "Firefly" is wild enough, but then Heimann presses down even further into her hands. She tucks her chin in towards her throat, while her abdominal muscles visibly contract, her belly button suctioning inwards. Slowly, with intense control, she unfurls her spine and lifts her pelvis up, stacking it over her shoulder girdle. Her legs slowly come together and point straight up at the ceiling, suspended in an elegant living column of a handstand.

It's incredible to watch, and I find myself holding my breath. After a few moments, she lowers herself back into "Firefly," again with focus and deliberateness.

"I've conquered lowering into an arm balance from a handstand, but pressing up is a whole other beast," Heimann said, rejoining us on the floor.

"How long have you been vegan?" Keegan asked.

"I became vegan when I was 32. I'm 47 now. I feel as good, if not better, than I did in my late 20s, running over 60 miles a week. My yoga practice gives me a realistic gauge for how I'm growing. I continue to be able to do more every year than I did the year before. I know my diet and lifestyle has everything to do with it. I truly believe that food can be medicine and that plant-based is the healthiest diet. And health for me means being able to wake up each day with energy and purpose that is not hindered either physically or mentally."

"What would you say to a high-performance, high-intensity athlete who was skeptical about a plant-based diet?" Keegan asked.

"Look at all the amazing vegan athletes who are thriving and competing at an even higher level since they've become vegan," Heimann said. "Our bodies run best on clean, whole foods. They contain all the nutrients we need and they're easy to digest, whereas protein from dead animals and animal secretions are highly acidic and put a lot of strain on the body. When we place high athletic demand on the body, we need all our energy directed to the task at hand, whether it's lifting weights, running long-distance, or engaging in a team sport. Experiment with what works best for you and your training—some might need extra vegan protein powder, while others feel best eating whole foods on a regular basis. Think of a vegan diet as an opportunity for increased possibility in your performance."

"What does strength mean to you?" I asked.

Heimann paused.

"For me, strength is clarity. It is finding the balance where I can exert the perfect amount of energy without struggle. In the physical sense, this means that I feel fully connected and clear—uncongested—in my body, breath, and core center, so that I can practice in a challenging and sustainable way. But true strength, to me, is not physical. True strength is about being clear on what matters in life, and standing firmly rooted in your values. Physical strength only enhances true strength, which is when your actions and words are aligned with your core beliefs. Kindness requires strength. Compassion requires strength."

She stops, and looks over at a small bronze Buddha in the studio corner.

"Acting against the cultural norm requires strength."

***

Brendan Brazier writes about the incredible, almost sci-fi idea of "growing a younger body":

Biological age refers to the time that has passed since body cells last regenerated. When we exercise, the body must regenerate its cells more rapidly than when idle. Depending on activity level, six to eight months from now our bodies will have regenerated nearly 100 percent of their tissue at the cellular level. This new tissue will literally be made up of what we eat between now and then. The body of an active person is forced to regenerate rapidly; therefore, it consists of more recently produced—younger—cells, making for a younger body.[16]

Mu Jin Han, a bodybuilder based in Los Angeles, is the perfect example of growing a younger body. We hung out with him at a gym while he was working out.

"I've been vegan since I was 45," he tells Keegan and I. "I'm 52 now, but I feel like I'm 32. I have many friends on medication who look older than they are."

The guy is totally ripped. His muscles look like they were cut with lasers.

"When I was 45," he said, "I had aches and pains in my neck, shoulders, and knees. Later I found out these were all inflammations caused by eating acidic foods and animal products. It took about two months to cut out animal products, and when I did, all the aches and creaks went away. People tell me I look younger now than when I was 45."

"Did your weights go down at all?" I asked.

Han laughed. "I *started* working out when I was 47. All the muscles you see on me, I gained as a vegan. The youngsters at the gym told me, 'Old man, you've got to eat meat or whey to build muscles.' I said to them, 'I'm eating like a gorilla—straight from Mother Earth. I get everything I need and nothing I don't."

"Were the 2 months of transition difficult?" Keegan asked.

"Well, in the beginning," said Han, "I didn't know anything about vegan food. After a month, I made friends with other vegans who gave me lots of tips. I got information on the Internet and from books. Like everything, it's much easier when you have knowledge."

"What about people who say that meat is for real men and vegetarians are wimps? I'm sure you hear that all the time—or, maybe you don't," I said, acknowledging his muscles.

"There is a reason there are so many commercials for erectile dysfunction drugs. Heart surgeons will tell you, if you have ED, there's a one in four chance you will have a heart attack. It's a clear sign of blockage in your arteries, and that blockage is also clogging your manhood. Also, what is a real man? A real man is one who stands up for the truly defenseless, whether humans or animals."

"And what does health mean to you?" I asked.

"Health is a marathon, not a sprint," Han replies. "A lot of younger guys say, 'I eat a lot of meat and dairy, and I'm healthy.' I say, 'When I was your age, I ate junk, and I looked healthy. But when you get to be my age, you start to feel the effects of your lifelong diet.' True health is how you feel when you're in your 60s, 70s, 80s, 90s.

"We're entering the *Star Trek* age, that's what I like to call it," Han went on.

"The what?"

"The *Star Trek* age. Vegan meat and cheese will surpass the real thing."

"Hey, yeah!" I said. "You know they're all vegan in *Star Trek*, right? Except for the Klingons and a few others."

I love *Star Trek*. Especially *The Next Generation*. I'll always remember when Commander Riker said, "We no longer enslave animals for food purposes." Make it so, Number One.

Sorry. I have to let the geek out for air every once in a while. Between me, Keegan, Han, and the Enterprise, the whole interview could have gotten derailed.

Let's bring it back.

"What supplements do you take?" I asked.

"The only thing I take is B_{12}," Han said. "Vitamin D in the winter, sometimes a few iron pills. That's it."

"No protein powder?"

"Only if I'm going to miss a meal after a workout. Otherwise, I have no need of it. If you eat enough calories, you get all your protein."

We left Han to finish his workout.

"It's a beautiful life!" he called out as he waved goodbye.

The protein myth has been effectively busted, and we already looked at iron, calcium and Omega-3 fatty acids. But there were still a few other nutrients—particularly the ones Han mentioned—that people typically use as a reason not to go plant-based.

References to Vitamin B_{12} have popped up regularly through this journey—vegan moms must be sure to have it while pregnant and breastfeeding, and the Adventists and Dr. Esselstyn include it in their plant-based regimen. This vitamin helps convert nutrients into energy, assists in creating DNA, and also sustains the protective coverings around nerves.[17] In *Becoming Vegan*, the gold standard reference for plant-based nutrition, dietitians Brenda Davis and Vesanto Melina write, "Lack of vitamin B_{12} is responsible for the lion's share of bad press that vegan diets receive."[18]

So what's the deal with this nutritional "hole" in a plant-based diet?

"The only vitamin you cannot get from plants is B_{12}," Dr. Greger told us. "It's not made by plants or animals. It's made by bacteria."

"If you pull up a carrot growing in organic dirt," said Dr. Davis, "and you eat it right there, you'll get B_{12}."

B_{12} deficiency isn't a plant-based problem. Almost two-fifths of the American population could have marginal B_{12} levels, even those eating animal products.[19]

Becoming Vegan suggests a daily B_{12} supplement of at least 25 micrograms (mcg). Some experts recommend as much as 250 mcg daily for adults up to age 65, and 500-1,000 mcg for seniors.[20]

"Unless you're eating bacteria-contaminated foods on a regular basis," Dr. Greger said, "the healthiest, cheapest source is B_{12} fortified food—a lot of cereals and non-dairy milks are B_{12} fortified—or a supplement. Don't get it from bugs, dirt, and feces like the other primates, and don't get it from meat, dairy, or eggs. Animals eat dirt and feces, and then it diffuses into their flesh and secretions."

To get just 47 mcg of B_{12} from eggs, you'd have to eat 200 to 400 eggs a day.[21]

I'll take the B_{12} supplement, thanks.

And Vitamin D?

"It's a hormone created by your body when you're exposed to sunlight," said Dr. Greger. "You can get all the Vitamin D you need from sunshine or a supplement."

Like B_{12}, vegans and non-vegans alike suffer from Vitamin D deficiency.[22] There are a few plant sources, like mushrooms and tofu, while animal sources include egg yolks, fatty fish, beef liver, and dairy.[23] It's safer and more effective to take a supplement—or go out in the sunshine!

When shopping for supplements, you'll find D_2 and D_3. Generally, D_2 is from plants and D_3 is from fish skin or lanolin, a waxy secretion of sheep glands.[24] But there are also vegan D_3 supplements from lichen. Both D_2 and D_3 are effective, though you might need a little more D_2 to get the same concentration as D_3.[25] I say go for vegan D_3.

Other vitamins and minerals of particular importance to vegan athletes are riboflavin (B_2), zinc, and magnesium.

Riboflavin helps with energy production. As training increases, so do riboflavin requirements. You can get plenty of riboflavin from soy foods, fortified cereals, nutritional yeast (don't be scared of the name, it's delicious and not at all yeasty), almonds, avocados, bananas, broccoli, leafy greens, mushrooms, whole grains, and other plant foods.[26]

Zinc is also important for energy production, as well as muscle repair. Rigorous exercise causes zinc loss through urine and sweat. To get your zinc, eat legumes, tofu, nuts, seeds, whole grains, and wheat germ.[27]

And like zinc, magnesium can be lost through urine and sweat during exercise. Magnesium is vital for muscle function. So eat it in nuts, legumes, greens, and whole grains.[28]

***

Rich Roll, when he was 39, was walking up a flight of stairs in his house. He stopped halfway, buckled over, chest tight, and covered in a cold sweat. He thought he was dying.

"From that moment I decided I was going to change how I ate, how I moved my body, and the stress levels in my life," Roll told Keegan and I. "That's what propelled me towards a 100 percent, whole foods, plant-based diet."

Roll, until the age of 39, lived on junk food—nachos, pizza, fried chicken. He was the kind of guy that Cheeseburger Laws were designed for. He carried a 50-pound spare tire of fat around his midsection. He was lethargic and depressed. "This is how you're supposed to feel in middle age," he thought to himself.

Today, twelve years later, at the age of 51, Roll is a celebrated ultra-endurance, plant-powered athlete. In 2010, five years after Roll became vegan, his friend Jason Lester, a plant-based disabled athlete with only one functional arm, concocted a physical endurance challenge that had never been done before. He called Roll up and invited him along.

"He called it Epic Five," said Roll. "It was five Ironmans on five Hawaiian islands in five days. I said, 'Knock yourself out.' But then I started thinking about all the amazing things that human beings have done in the world of endurance and adventure. No one had done this. And I knew I had to attempt it."

"What exactly is an Ironman?" I asked.

"An Ironman is widely considered the ultimate test of human endurance. It's a 2.4 mile swim, followed by a 112 mile bike ride, then a 26.2 mile marathon immediately afterwards. We did five of those in a row in a little under a week. I was 44."

"Five full Ironmans?"

"Five full Ironmans."

I gawked. "You almost die?"

"No," Roll laughed. "Didn't die. You should try it."

"I don't know about that."

Roll has gone on quite a journey since that panicked, crisis moment, unable to climb the stairs to his bedroom. He told Keegan and I his story.

"I actually didn't want the plant-based diet to work, so I could happily go back to eating cheeseburgers. But within seven to ten days of eating nothing but plants close to their natural state, I experienced a monumental resurgence in my vitality and energy levels. I couldn't remember feeling that good since I was a young child.

"I had so much energy I was compelled to start exercising again for the first time in many, many years.

"Swimming and athletics were a big part of my childhood, but I always thought, 'It's time to be an adult, that's in your past.' I was reconnecting with that lost part of me.

"I had abused myself with drugs, alcohol, junk food, a high stress job. But in a very short time after adopting a whole food/plant-based diet, my vitality returned, I lost weight, my skin cleared up, I slept better, my mental acuity improved.

"My initial goals were simple," Roll recalled. "I wanted to lose weight and have the energy to enjoy my children. That was it.

"But with every week, I saw my own transformation, and realized how resilient the human body is. I became obsessed with the idea of human potential.

"After 4 months of eating plant-based, I went out one day for a run. My goal was 45 minutes. But it was one of those days where I was just in the zone. I ended up running 24 miles that day. I'd never done anything like that in my life.

"The truth is, I'm not some crazy gifted athlete. I was a benchwarmer at Stanford. I was never a big point scorer. I was never a competitive runner. But through a rigorous training program and a plant-based diet, I was able to do things I never thought possible.

"After that 24 mile run, I wanted to test the outer limits of what I was capable of—physically, emotionally, mentally, and spiritually. That led me to the world of ultra-endurance. 'What am I truly capable of?' Ultraman, this crazy, double, three-day Ironman race seemed at that point to be the most frightening and ultimate answer to that question.

"I was 42 when I did my first Ultraman. My only goal was, 'Don't die.' I ended up finishing eleventh overall.

"I did it again the following year, twice the athlete I was the year before. I finished sixth overall despite crashing my bike and working with a swollen knee that could barely bend."

I asked Roll about his recovery time.

"As an athlete, the Holy Grail is recovery," he said. "You don't get better during your training sessions. You get faster and stronger *between* them. If you can speed up your body's ability to repair itself, you can train harder, longer, and further with less likelihood of over-training, or missing sessions because you're sick or injured. When you extend that over time, it translates into tremendous performance gains. Eating plant-based is a great way to expedite your recovery.

"On the other hand," Roll went on, "meat and dairy are very acid-forming and inflammatory, which impede your body's ability to recover. You're living in a state of chronic inflammation."

"What about 'real men eat meat'?" I asked.

"Going to the grocery store," Roll said, "picking up a side of beef in Styrofoam, and putting it on the barbecue—what does that have to do with being a man? Being a man means being strong, but you have to match that strength with compassion. You have a responsibility to take care of those who are weaker. We are not obligate carnivores and do not need to kill or torture animals. A man protects the health of his family. And when I grow old, I want to be vital and disease-free so I can take care of my children and my wife."

"Did people ever say you couldn't be a real athlete while eating a vegan diet?" Keegan asked.

"Oh, all the time," Roll said. "Our culture has this entrenched, outdated idea that you cannot perform as an athlete without eating animal products. When I was training on a plant-based diet, people said I was crazy. All I can tell you is that I have the energy and strength of somebody in their early 20s. I'm 51 years old. I've maintained this physique for twelve years now. Every aspect of my life has been improved by adopting this lifestyle."

"What would you say to someone who is contemplating the change?" I asked.

"It can be scary, because it's different than what we're used to. There's sometimes a period of getting over cravings. People think they can't live without cheese, steak, fish, or whatever, but the truth is, you can. It's a choice. Give it a month. Once you get to the other side, you're free."

"Were there foods you were addicted to?" I asked.

"I know a lot about addiction," Roll replied. "I went to rehab for alcoholism. This is something I understand deeply. Food addiction is real. If somebody like me, who has a profound problem with addiction, can break free of the chains that kept me eating foods that I knew were killing me, and embrace this lifestyle—I love the nutrient-dense foods that make me feel amazing—if I can do that, I know that anybody can."

"What does breaking free of food addiction feel like?" I asked.

"Completely liberated. Quitting dairy was the hardest. I couldn't go a day without cheese. You've got to weather that storm. You've got to get to the other side. Put enough distance between you and those foods in order to break free. People ask me, 'What's wrong with moderation?' Well, if I ate cheese occasionally, I'd just walk around wondering when I was going to get the cheese. Now, I don't even think about it. I can't be moderate with drugs and alcohol, and I can't be moderate with food.

"That doesn't mean my lifestyle is bland. My life exploded into this incredible experience. Your taste buds come alive. You start to crave these foods that make you feel good. Then you want to feel strong and healthy all the time, and that supports your enthusiasm for taking it to the next level."

I smiled. "So now, I guess, the famous question. Where do you get your protein?"

Roll stared at me for a split-second in disbelief. Then he opened up into a terrific laugh. "From *plants*!!!"

***

Human beings have been testing their physical limits for thousands of years. A cemetery dating back to the 2nd and 3rd centuries AD was discovered in Ephesus, Turkey, in 1993.[29] The graves contained thousands of bones, as well as tombstones that depicted gladiators. The cemetery contained at least 67 people, almost all of whom died between the ages of 20 and 30. Many of them had healed wounds, as well as mortal ones.

For the first time, an ancient gladiator graveyard had been uncovered.[30]

In 2014, scientists from the University of Bern, Switzerland, and the Medical University of Vienna used stable carbon, nitrogen, and sulfur isotope analysis to examine the 1,800-year-old gladiator bones from Ephesus.[31]

The analysis revealed that these professional fighters lived on barley, wheat, and beans. There was little or no meat or dairy in their diets. Two of the individuals analyzed had much higher levels of animal protein and lower levels of legumes. The researchers believed that these two were originally from a different area, with a different diet.[32]

The scientists also discovered that the bones of these ancient warriors were incredibly strong, with very high levels of calcium and strontium (not to be confused with radioactive strontium-90). Strontium, like calcium, promotes bone health.[33] The gladiator bones contained almost twice as much of these minerals as the bones of non-gladiator Romans from the same era.[34] At first, the researchers were not sure why.

Pliny the Elder, the ancient Roman author, writes of a drink—a kind of Gatorade-of-antiquity—made of ashes that was used by gladiators after fights and training. Plant ash, often mentioned in Roman texts, was used medicinally and as a spice.[35] Although barley is already calcium-rich,[36] the scientists theorized that the high levels of strontium and calcium in the gladiator bones came from a plant ash sports drink, like the one described by Pliny.[37]

Nor was the grains-and-legumes diet necessarily an economic decision to feed, as cheaply as possible, prisoners of war and slaves, who were often used as gladiators. About 100 years before the existence of the Ephesus cemetery, many free Romans, including upper class men, knights, and senators, began voluntarily enrolling in gladiator academies, hoping to achieve glory in the arena.[38]

Gladiators were the sports heroes of the classical world. Their portraits were seen on public walls, children played with clay gladiator action figures, and the most popular warriors endorsed commercial products.[39]

It all sounds very familiar. Except that the ancient Roman nickname for these sports celebrities was *hordearii*: barley men.[40] Real men did not eat meat.

Funny how it can take human beings thousands of years to circle back to wisdom that we always had.

When I watch Timothy Shieff leap with grace and assurance across the gap between tall urban rooftops, or see Lara Heimann press into a handstand before slowly folding her legs, upside down, into a full lotus, I am filled with awe at the potential of the human body. I think of Rich Roll, at the age of 44, doing five Ironmans in under a week, and his buddy Jason Lester, who did them with one functional arm. All plant-fueled, optimum performance athletes.

Every great athlete is a testament to the human capacity for transformation. Remember that nearly every cell in our bodies is regenerated, every six to eight months, using the building blocks of the food we eat.

Our bodies have an instinctive intelligence. They want to heal. They want to be strong and free of pain. You can grow a stronger body. You can grow a younger body.

What are you truly capable of?

CHAPTER 18
THINGS SPIRAL AROUND

In 1946, R.J. Reynolds Tobacco Company launched a major ad campaign with the centerpiece slogan, "More doctors smoke Camels than any other cigarettes."[1] Print and TV spots featured capable, kindly doctors in white coats puffing on their Camels. In the early 1940s, Reynolds created a "Medical Relations Division"—which was in fact part of the company's advertising firm—that directly recruited the help of physicians and researchers to support the faux health claims made in Camel ads.[2]

It wasn't hard to do. During the American Medical Association convention in 1947, doctors in the hundreds lined up for free cigarettes.[3]

The country's physicians were a crucial component of cigarette marketing tactics for decades. The tobacco industry placed ads in medical journals and bulletins beginning in the 1930s, solidifying relationships with doctors and their professional organizations.

Smoking had not yet entered the sphere of public health, and the cigarette companies wanted to keep it that way. Many people believed that the dangers of smoking were dependent on the individual. That myth was very useful to the tobacco industry. As long as the public was convinced that some people could smoke without damaging their health, while unlucky others—for whatever reason—would suffer ill effects, then anti-smoking measures would remain on a private level.[4]

But despite powerful marketing forces, science began to fracture the façade. The first major study to link smoking and lung cancer was published in 1950.[5] It was the first falling rock in an avalanche of scientific literature warning against tobacco use.[6]

Fourteen years later, in 1964, the US Surgeon General released the first federal report, based on over 7,000 medical studies,[7] cautioning the American public of the significant connection between smoking, lung cancer, and heart disease.[8]

In 1965, the year after the Surgeon General's warning, 42.4 percent of adults in the US smoked.[9] That number has fallen to 14.9 percent in 2015.[10] More people quit smoking in 2015 than in any other single year reaching back to 1993.[11]

And those Camel-loving doctors? Their smoking rate plummeted to 3.3 percent.[12]

In the 1960s, public awareness of the connection between cigarettes and fatal, preventable disease precipitated a crisis for the tobacco industry.

The country was on to them. Something had to be done.

In 1969, Brown and Williamson Tobacco Corporation circulated a now famous internal document:

Doubt is our product since it is the best means of competing with the 'body of fact' that exists in the mind of the general public. It is also the means of establishing a controversy.[13]

And the tobacco industry has continued to manufacture doubt, even in the face of irrefutable scientific evidence and social stigma. Perhaps more significantly, it has provided a blueprint for other industries wishing to drip uncertainty into the ears of the public, on issues such as global warming, acid rain, the hole in the ozone layer, DDT, and, of course, the health risks of eating animal products.

"If there's enough controversy, people throw up their hands," Dr. Greger said. "'I'm just going to eat whatever I like.' That's what the food industry wants. The strategy is to confuse the public."

"The animal agriculture industries, like the tobacco industry, know exactly what they're doing," Dr. Barnard said. "They know meat and eggs contain saturated fat that affects your blood cholesterol; they know dairy doesn't build strong bones. But they fund research to say, 'Maybe these products aren't so bad,' and enormous ad campaigns. If you can't promote the fact that beef is going to damage your heart health or contribute to cancer, what can you say? 'Well, it's got a good sizzle.' And when the bottom falls out of their North American market, they go overseas."

The aggressive passage of Cheeseburger Bills and Ag-Gag laws certainly suggests that the food industries know their products are risky.

Former US Surgeon General, C. Everett Koop, wrote in the foreword to *The Cigarette Papers*:

> *During my years as surgeon general and since, I have often wondered how many people died as a result of the fact that the medical and public health professions were misled by the tobacco industry...I frequently spoke of the sleazy behavior of the tobacco industry in its attempts to discredit legitimate science as part of its overall effort to create controversy and doubt... But, although the tobacco companies possess enormous clout with Congress and almost inexhaustible funds for advertising, promotion, and propaganda, the public knows about the deleterious effects of smoking, and most*

smokers would like to quit—a difficult task because they are addicted.[14]

Widespread knowledge is the crucial piece of the puzzle.

"My patients tell me, 'You say milk fat is bad for me, but these studies say milk fat is good for me. I don't know what to believe, so I'm eating the cheese,'" Dr. Davis said. "If the food industries can get my colleagues to speak against myself and other doctors who are advocating a health-promoting, plant-based diet, and make me look extreme, then they've neutralized my message. And that's the goal."

("Being vegan is extreme?" Dr. Greger exclaimed. "How about being bisected in half, having your chest cracked open, surgeons taking veins from your legs, rewiring your plumbing and trying to literally bypass the problem metaphorically and literally?")

Another goal is to hook consumers while they're young.

"Some people remember the Joe Camel ads that targeted kids," David Robinson Simon said to us. "Camel came under a lot of fire for that, but now the dairy industry, for example, spends about $50 million each year promoting milk in schools."[15]

I can hear the dairy industry furiously protesting that unlike cigarettes, milk provides a host of nutritional benefits—strong bones! Strong teeth! Hydration! What they forget to mention are the many, often serious, health risks that children are sipping up from those cartons of cow's milk. And the same benefits can be found in soymilk, almond milk, cashew and soy cheese, or soy and almond yogurt—without the health consequences.

In 1965, a year after the Surgeon General's warning, Congress required warning labels to be put on cigarettes.[16]

I thought back to the day I heard that the WHO had declared red meat a carcinogen, launching me on this journey. Even then, I wondered why the Surgeon General hasn't gone after meat.

"I think it's a matter of time," Dr. Barnard said. "It took time to show that tobacco was linked to lung cancer, but eventually we could say, 'Tobacco industry, fight all you want. We've got enough evidence now.' We're now at the point where we have enough evidence against eating animal products. There's no question that people who avoid animal products are healthier in many ways than those who eat them. It's a matter of time before the government tackles this more seriously. We're already seeing that movement. Every five years, the dietary guidelines inch closer to a plant-based diet. In 2011, the meat group was thrown out of My Plate. They've now got a protein group, which could be beans or tofu. There's a dairy group, but to their credit, soymilk is included. It's not perfect, but we're moving along."

Dr. Klaper loved the idea of warning labels. "The science is solid, and just as a cigarette package says, 'This has been shown to increase your chance of lung cancer,' packages of meat, dairy, and eggs should clearly state, 'These products have been shown to increase your risk of heart attacks, strokes, high blood pressure, diabetes, erectile dysfunction, autoimmune diseases, cancers of various types, and rheumatoid arthritis, among other conditions.' I'd also push for an analysis of contents: pesticides, heavy metals, antibiotics, bovine hormones, etc. etc. People should know what they're buying."

Progress occurs in waves—scientific, political, cultural, and individual waves. When a contested fact is finally absorbed into public consciousness and acted upon, a revolution happens. What was heresy becomes self-evident. The world is not flat. The earth revolves around the sun. Global warming is driven by human activity. Smoking kills. Animal protein kills.

"Think of all those years in which it was considered rude if you told a guest not to smoke in your house," said Dr. Goldhamer. "We put up with that crap for a long time before it became acceptable to say no."

Nobody wants a smoker in their house, because of a little thing called secondhand smoke. You're breathing in the toxic byproducts of their bad habit. But someone else eating a burger doesn't affect you...does it?

"Diet is not a personal choice," said Dr. McMacken. "I understand how people think it is, but in reality, we are all not only funding the food industry, but also the health care industry. We are funding people to be on medications, to get procedures, heart bypasses, and cancer treatments through our escalating health care costs. Our individual food choices affect our nation, our planet, billions of animals, and they affect us as a human species."

"Right now, we spend more on healthcare than any other country in the world,"[17] Dr. Davis said. "We're getting bigger and bigger, and sicker and sicker. That affects everybody. There's a serious problem with people who say, 'You do what you want, and I do what I want. Leave me alone with my decisions.' A healthy person might be eating their vegetables and legumes, living disease-free, but a significant chunk of their tax dollars are going towards the unhealthy people, and that's only going to get worse. I do a lot of weight-loss surgery. I love my job because my patients change their lives, but these surgeries are expensive, and the taxpayers are paying for it. I do a lot of Medicare, so that's directly paid for by the government. The more surgeries we do, the more it's going to cost the insurance companies, and the more they're going to increase premiums.

"It's wrong to blame the overweight patient. What we need to address is the food system and the politics. My tax dollars fund the agribusinesses that are producing the food that's making us sick. That kills me. Not only are your tax dollars paying for sick people, they're paying for the food that makes them sick."

Call it secondhand eating.

Of every US federal income tax dollar in 2015, 28.7 cents went to healthcare. That's the biggest single chunk of the dollar, larger now even than the military (25.4 cents). Compare that to 3.6 cents for education, and 1.6 cents on the environment.[18] Talk about priorities.

And yet for all that healthcare spending, the US has the lowest life expectancy among 12 high-income nations, and some of the worst health outcomes.[19]

"We have got to reduce the demand on the healthcare system," said Dr. Mills, "because the way we are delivering healthcare right now is just too damned expensive. The average bypass operation is $70,000 to $200,000 or more.[20] Multiply that by millions, you're breaking the bank."

Our healthcare costs are bankrupting the country.

Kevin Murphy and Robert Topel, economists from the University of Chicago and the National Bureau of Economic Research, estimate that reducing the country's mortality from heart disease or cancer by a mere *1 percent* is currently worth nearly $500 billion.[21] Reducing all causes of mortality by only 10 percent would be worth $18.5 *trillion*.[22] Remember, chronic diseases are responsible for 70 percent of deaths.[23] If those deaths were prevented by lifestyle changes, the country would save a stupefying *$129.5 trillion dollars.*

What could we do with that money? The American Society for Civil Engineers (ASCE) releases a Report Card for the country's infrastructure every four years, and the 2013 Report Card was a D+, showing "a significant backlog of overdue maintenance." Cs and Ds were smacked on our country's drinking water, schools, roads, energy, transit, levees, dams, wastewater, hazardous waste, public parks, and bridges. ASCE estimates that we need $3.6 trillion to repair our country's collapsing infrastructure.[24] If we took that out of the $129.5 trillion, that would leave $125 trillion to maybe send every child to college, wipe out hunger and homelessness, fit our nation with renewable energy technology, and fund business-evolution programs for farmers who sell animals or feed crops. Congress did the same thing in 2004, using $10 billion to fund the Tobacco Transition Payment Program to shift tobacco farmers to different crops.[25]

But the medical system, as we've seen, is currently built on sickness, not health.

"It's extremely tempting for medicine to continue doing these procedures for the income," Dr. Esselstyn said. "What would really turn the system in the right direction is if we paid physicians for making people healthy. If a patient has a first, second, or third stent, somebody ought to be penalized for not treating the causation of the illness. Dr. Kim Williams, president of the American College of Cardiology, made it clear that our motivation as cardiologists ought to be to put ourselves out of business. That is medical leadership with integrity."

In some industries, sickness pays the bills, and in others, death is a financially savvy outcome.

"We presented our [TrueNorth] program to a large labor union interested in making it a covered medical benefit," Dr. Goldhamer told us. "There was an actuary [who compiles statistics to calculate risks and premiums] at the meeting. He said, 'Dr. Goldhamer, if we do this program for our members, won't it make them live longer, thereby increasing our retirement costs?' I was startled that people actually think that way. Then one of the union members stood up and said to the actuary, 'Listen, little man! Remember who you work for! You work for us! Why don't you calculate how much money we're going to save if I come over there and break your neck!'"

I laughed. It's not really funny. Well, just a little.

"They voted unanimously to make our program a fully covered benefit," Dr. Goldhamer continued, "and we carried out a study showing that yes, in fact it's cheaper to make people healthy than treating heart attacks in the hospital, or allowing diabetes to lead to a foot amputation."

"It's in the best interest of self-insured employers to have healthy employees, because the employer is paying for the healthcare," said Dr. Esselstyn. "Suppose you, as an employer, never had to worry about your employees having heart disease, bypass operations, stents, or the drugs that accompany them, and none of your employees were diabetic, hypertensive, or obese?"

Plant-based solutions aren't—yet—profitable to the medical and pharmaceutical industries. But they could be an incalculable boon to the insurance industry. That's why Kaiser Permanente, one of the country's largest non-profit health plans,[26] began advocating in 2013 for its 17,000 doctors[27] to actively encourage their patients to avoid eating animal products. Kaiser published a booklet called "The Plant-Based Diet," steering their 10.6 million members[28] to resources like PCRM and Dr. Greger's NutritionFacts.org.[29]

And in a "Nutritional Update for Physicians: Plant-Based Diets," which references Drs. Esselstyn, Barnard, Ornish, McDougall, and Campbell, as well as the Adventist Health and EPIC studies, the *Permanente Journal* writes,

> *Healthy eating may be best achieved with a plant-based diet, which we define as a regimen that encourages whole, plant-based foods and discourages meats, dairy products, and eggs as well as all refined and processed foods... Physicians should consider recommending a plant-based diet **to all their patients**, especially those with high blood pressure, diabetes, cardiovascular disease, or obesity... Despite the strong body of evidence favoring plant-based diets, **including studies showing a willingness of the general public to embrace them**, many physicians are not stressing the importance of plant-based diets as a first-line treatment for chronic illness... The purpose of this article is to help physicians understand the potential benefits of a plant-based diet, **to the end of working together to create a societal shift toward plant-based nutrition**... Too often, physicians ignore the potential benefits of good nutrition and quickly prescribe medications instead of giving patients a chance to correct their disease through healthy eating and active living...The future of health care will involve an evolution toward a paradigm where the prevention and treatment of disease is centered, not on a pill or surgical procedure, but on another serving of fruits and vegetables* (emphasis added).[30]

BOOM. From an insurance industry giant. It is all. About. Money.

"The transformation is happening," Dr. Kim Williams said. "Look at the variety of meat, cheese, and dairy substitutes in the stores, the egg replacers. Look at the increasing numbers of vegetarian and vegan restaurants. There must be a market for them, and the market is growing."

The Los Angeles Times reported in 2015 that *47 percent* of Americans are willing to be vegetarian or vegan part of the time.[31] The little hippie movement is growing up.

In fact, the vegan food market is one of the fastest growing segments of the food industry today, appealing not only to vegans, but also to vegetarians, "flexitarians," and "reducetarians"—meat eaters consciously cutting back on animal consumption, usually because of health.[32] The Global Food and Drink Trends 2016 report, published by a world leader in market analysis, stated, "Veggie burgers and non-dairy milks...appeal to the everyday consumer, foreshadowing a profoundly changed marketplace in which what was formerly 'alternative' could take over the mainstream."[33]

"What food manufacturers want is your money," said Dr. Goldhamer. "If you control your money, you control some power. Spend your money only on the things you support. Even big box stores now carry organic products. Is it because they care about the environment, health, or moral justice? No. It's because they want your money. So tell them what you want with your money, and perhaps we will see things change."

What was formerly 'alternative' could take over the mainstream...

Fortunately, the story of the tobacco industry doesn't only provide a prototype for confusing your customers. It also offers strategies to rein in a monstrous, national health crisis.

"Each pack of cigarettes results in about ten dollars of externalized costs, mostly for health care, according to the CDC," said David Robinson Simon. "Because of that, state and federal governments decided in the last several decades to heavily tax cigarettes, both to reduce consumption and to increase revenues to help pay those costs.

"As a result, tobacco consumption is down by over 50 percent in this country.[34] If a sizeable tax is imposed on meat and dairy, consumption will drop, tax revenues will go up, and those dollars could fund programs like organic farming, transition programs for animal farmers, and better consumer education.

"I think it's inevitable that we will tax meat and dairy in this country," Simon continued. "It took a long time for cigarette taxes to be imposed because the tobacco industry is so strong, but when we know clinically that certain products cause illness, we will find the political will to tax them and reduce their consumption."

Simon also advocates eliminating subsidies and restructuring the USDA.

"Eliminating the $38 billion in animal agriculture subsidies every year would also help raise prices and lower consumption. And instead of the USDA and the Department of Health and Human Services producing the dietary guidelines, why not let DHHS issue the guidelines itself? This would remove USDA's dangerous conflict of interest."

Cigarette companies knew that high taxes were their Achilles' heel. Tobacco giant Phillip Morris, in internal documents, plainly revealed that fear:

Of all the concerns, there is one—taxation—that alarms us the most. While marketing restrictions and public and passive smoking [restrictions] do depress volume, in our experience taxation depresses it much more severely[35]...the 1982-83 round of price increases caused two million adults to quit smoking and prevented 600,000 teenagers from starting to smoke...We don't need to have that happen again.[36]

At least they're honest among themselves.

***

"People don't know what they should eat, but they do know that what they're eating is wrong, and that's important," said Dr. Davis. "There's been a drop in beef and dairy consumption. I see more and more scientific literature about plant-based diets, growing numbers of doctors are coming out in support of it, and I really think that 15 years from now, we'll be in disbelief that we ever ate all this meat.

"I don't tell my patients to go vegan. To me, vegan is a philosophy, and it's not my job to bring ethics into the room with a patient. I didn't get here by being vegan. I got here through health. I practice evidence-based medicine, and the evidence is way on my side."

What does Dr. Davis' evidence-based meal plan look like?

"I suggest oatmeal and berries for breakfast, with ground flax seeds, agave syrup, and shaved almonds. Lunch is a big salad with beans, nuts, and seeds. Snack on an apple or some almonds. Dinner can be a bean-vegetable-grain type meal. My patients come back to me amazed. 'I've never felt this good in my life.' Just the smiles are worth it."

"You can't live on kale," Dr. McDougall said sternly. "You'll starve to death. A lot of people try that, and after a few days of living on vegetables, they say, 'I can't do this.' Of course you can't. Nobody can. You have to include whole grains, legumes, bread, pasta, potatoes, sweet potatoes, bean burritos, rice. Now, you can do it."

If you're on medications for chronic conditions, it's important that you work with your doctor when transitioning to a plant-based diet.

"The only 'negative' side effect of eating this way is that you may come off your medication faster than you anticipated—your blood pressure drugs, your insulin dose—so stay in contact with your doctor," Dr. McMacken said. "And of course, not all doctors are aware of the benefits—she or he may tell you you need to eat more protein, which reflects a global lack of nutrition training in the medical community. So prepare yourself with credible information. Educate yourself. There will be a day in which a lot of doctors start to realize, 'I myself should probably not be eating this hamburger or steak.'

"Personally," she mused, "as a physician who, like most of us, went to medical school to try to heal people, to me, this is true healing. This is the most reward I have ever felt in my medical practice. I never felt this kind of reward when I doled out countless prescriptions and drugs."

"People keep eating healthy because they feel healthy," said Dr. Greger. "Nothing tastes as good as health feels. All the pleasures of life can feel better when you're not blasting your dopamine system every day with high caloric density animal foods and hyper-processed foods. When you get your dopamine system back to a normal sensitivity, everything feels better. A sunrise. Food. Sex. Laughter. Exercise.

"Try it as an experiment," he went on. "That's what I tell my patients. You can do anything for a few weeks. They're like, okay doc, I'll give you 3 weeks.

"And then they're hooked on health. Not only are all their lab numbers great, but they *feel* better. Once they get a taste of that, they think, maybe I'll try this a little longer. Years later, they're still living healthy and feeling great. They've reversed their disease. I hardly see them anymore.

"Give it a try. People can wrap their heads around giving it a try."

For people taking their first plant-based steps, I thought it would be inspiring to hear the personal stories of the doctors we've gotten to know. So I asked them.

"I brought cattle to slaughter when I was a kid," said Dr. Barnard, leaning back in his chair. "Somehow you compartmentalize. I brought them off the truck. They were scared. You hang them up by their leg and slit their throats. It takes a while to wake up to it. I don't know why it took me so long.

"I've been vegan since 1984. I'm still alive. Before I went to medical school, I worked as an autopsy assistant in a hospital morgue. One day a guy died of a massive heart attack. The pathologist took the ribs off the chest and showed me all the atherosclerotic disease in the body. His scissors went crunch, crunch, crunch, through the coronary arteries. The main arteries to the brain were nearly closed off by plaque. He wrote up his findings and left the room. I replaced the section of ribs that had been removed, sewed up the skin, cleaned up, and put the body back in the cooler. Then I went to the cafeteria for lunch. I lifted the lid off my plate, and an overturned chicken breast with ribs looking exactly like the chest I'd just closed looked up at me. I couldn't eat it, because it was like a dead body. Then I realized—it *is* a dead body."

It's hard to build something living from something dead.

"I've been vegan since 2003," Dr. Kim Williams told us. "The day I saw my LDL (bad) cholesterol was extremely high, I went vegan and never looked back. My LDL levels went from 170 to 90 in six weeks by changing my diet. But many people take long years to change, and I'm sympathetic about that."

"My whole life before 35, I swear I never ate a vegetable, except for a slice of tomato on a burger," Dr. Davis laughed. "I failed the life insurance policy test. I had a fatty liver, even though I don't drink. My cholesterol was through the roof, and I was hypertensive. A doctor friend said, 'No big deal, that's how it is, here are a few pills.' I took them, but I knew where it would lead. When I began feeling sicker, I started studying plant-based diets. I began pesco-vegetarian, but as I told you, my mercury was sky high. I cut the fish, my cholesterol levels were coming down, and I felt so good, I thought, 'What if I went vegan?' That's when I really started feeling fantastic.

The better I felt, the more I wanted to move. I see this in my patients all the time. I started challenging myself. Maybe a 5k, maybe a 10k. Then triathlons. What about an Ironman? 'There's no way I can do an Ironman'—and then I did it. I am stronger and faster every year, and I blame that on a plant-based diet."

Dr. Davis also told us about the transformation of some of his patients.

"One of my patients was too obese for weight-loss surgery. She lost over 200 pounds on a plant-based diet. There's another man I know, morbidly obese, and he tried a plant-based diet. He's now faster than me in marathons. These stories are everywhere, and they're growing in number. This is almost like a new medical field, in which you can cure disease."

Dr. Mills told us another incredible story.

"I had one patient who, when I started seeing her, had been living with terrible diabetes for 17 years. She was on insulin twice a day, plus pills. Her blood sugars were running the 300 range. In the morning she'd have to sit on the side of her bed for 15 minutes before her vision would clear and her legs would stop cramping, and she could summon up the energy to go about her daily life, such as it was."

He paused. He was fighting back tears.

"I'm sorry. It's hard for me to talk about her without becoming emotional. She became vegan, and within three months she was off all her diabetes medications. She was off 2 out of 3 of her blood pressure meds. Over the next six months she lost 65 pounds and was walking a mile a day. She went back to work. All because she changed her diet. Something like that is an authentic, bona fide miracle, but it is a miracle accessible to anybody if they're willing to change."

***

Michael Abdalla, Jane Chapman, and Amy Resnic, all of whom we met earlier as they struggled with diabetes, severe osteoarthritis, and an impending heart attack, decided to work with the TrueNorth Center in an attempt to regain their health, using water and juice fasting, as well as a whole foods, plant-based diet. In many ways, they felt they had nothing to lose.

Keegan and I took a trip to TrueNorth to see how they were doing.

The first person we saw was Jane Chapman. I didn't recognize her at first. Instead of an old lady hunched over a walker, I saw a vibrant woman strolling on her own with ease and lightness.

"Whoa, what are you doing?!" I couldn't believe this was the same woman I had met a few months ago.

Jane beamed. "Yeah, look at this!" She spread her arms out and did a little twirl.

"You're not using your walker?"

"Don't need that anymore. I've been here for fifty days. Cleaning out the body has been a life-changer."

Jane told us about her process at TrueNorth.

"I came here with a bucket of 28 meds and supplements that I'd been ordered to take. My doctor here at TrueNorth put together a check sheet for how to taper off the medications. There were many I was able to cut out right away. And I didn't feel any different! I thought, 'What was I doing, taking all that stuff?' It used to be my pre-breakfast to take a handful of pills and then again at night.

"After being at TrueNorth for 2 weeks and changing my diet, I was off all my medicines. I don't anticipate needing them again. I could tell, even from the first 2 weeks of eating a whole foods, plant-based diet, that the inflammation was draining out of my body. I wasn't as achy. I could move better. So far I've lost 38.8 pounds since I got here, and maybe another 20 before I go."

After getting off her medications, the doctors at TrueNorth started Jane on a water fast, which was then followed by a carefully monitored re-introduction of juice, steamed vegetables, and eventually different foods.

"Did you ever think you'd be walking around without a walker in less than two months?" I asked.

"Never in a million years. Traditional medicine certainly did not indicate that this was in my future. A lot of healing occurred very rapidly just by doing the right things for my body."

"When you go home, will you be able to stick to a plant-based diet?"

"I believe I will, yes. I will have to embrace some changes, but considering the alternatives, it's worth it. I feel like at least 20 years have been shaved off. I'm back in my 40s. Now when I visit my grandchildren, I can get on the floor and play with them. I won't be stuck just spinning the dial. My daughter turned me on to TrueNorth. She and her family eat this way and are amazingly healthy. I want that. This is a dream come true. There is going to be more life."

Michael Abdalla came to True North Health Center and hasn't eaten meat for six months.

"You look great!" I said. "How are you feeling?"

"I feel like a million dollars after taxes!" he laughed. "I have cut out all meat. I haven't had meat since February 14. I remember that because that's when I fell in love with myself. My pills have been cut in half. My insulin has been cut in half. Can I have an Amen! When I first told my endocrinologist I was trying a vegan diet, he said, 'No, this won't work. You've got to have protein.' Even doctors don't understand that protein is in everything you eat. But six months later, I saw him recently, and he said, 'Go for it!' Because he saw what a difference it made. I've lost 29 pounds. Now I'm going for the moon—I'm going to get off all animal products."

Just like Jane, the thought of having more time with his grandchildren is enormous for Michael.

"If I'd known grandchildren were this special, I'd have had them before I had kids," he joked. "I have five grandchildren; they're drop dead gorgeous. If I talk too much about it I'll cry, but that's where you want to be. You want to be here with your family. That is everything. You want to help them grow up. My ugly face is going to be around to see them graduate high school and college. I'm going to be here. I'm a hardheaded stubborn Lebanese, and I'm going to be here whatever it takes. Can I get an Amen, brother?"

"Amen!"

The last time we talked with Amy Resnic, she was on track for a heart attack within 30 days. She was exhausted all the time and unable to breathe properly. But when we saw her again, she was positively glowing. She had been at the Center for two weeks, on a juice fast and a plant-based diet.

She greeted us with a big smile.

"In only two weeks, I don't have to take any more asthma medication. My breathing is normal. Don't have to take any heart medication. My pulse is normal. No pain medication. And I'm completely off all my anxiety medication. In only two weeks. It's crazy!"

"How do you feel?" I asked her.

"I feel exhilarated. And I have tools for health now—a plant-based diet free of salt, oil, and sugar. I was suffering for so long and there was such an easy answer. I lost 29 pounds in two weeks. I'm walking one to three miles a day. I'm healing from the inside.

"I came here as a last ditch effort to get my life back. At first I thought, it's a little wacky—juice fasting and being vegan. But it works—not eating egg salad is a small price to pay. I don't have to be on medication. I have energy. I feel good physically, emotionally, spiritually. I'm happy. *I'm happy.* I didn't realize how bad things had gotten. You don't realize until you're out of it.

"I don't want to end up like my parents, not being able to move in their old age, dependent on all these medications. My life has changed. It is so easy and so doable to be healthy. I feel so blessed. I'm hoping I can be a role model for others and not be pushy about it, because everyone's going to do it in their own time. But thank God—my time is now."

Her voice shook and she stopped, fighting back a sob. I had no words. This woman had her life back. I stepped forward to give her a hug.

She beamed at me through her tears. "Thanks."

Dr. Ruby Lathon, a young African-American woman who is a holistic nutrition consultant and thyroid cancer survivor, told us her story in Washington, D.C.

"My background is in industrial and systems engineering, which was my career path for a long time until I got thyroid cancer and everything changed. I wanted to try alternative medicine rather than having my thyroid removed, which meant I'd be on medication forever—I didn't want that. I started researching, turning my research acumen as an engineer to myself. I read how a plant-based diet can heal the body and has worked for so many people. I immediately switched to a completely whole food, plant-based diet, and after about 14 months, the cancer was completely gone. My thyroid had shrunk to a normal size.

"A lot of people discouraged me from going the natural route, including all the medical doctors I knew. I decided at the end of the year if the cancer was not gone, then I would reconsider surgery, but I was going to do everything within my power to avoid that, to let my body heal itself. My cancer was slow-growing and diagnosed early, so of course that was an advantage for me. But the effect of meat and dairy on most people is a compromised immune system, and it's extremely hard to prevent or reverse very aggressive things like cancers, heart disease, and kidney failure while maintaining a diet that includes meat and dairy.

"After three months," Lathon recalled, "the nodule was still there; there was no change. I was expecting it to at least shrink, so I was a little discouraged, but I wasn't going to quit. I had accepted that this diet wasn't just a temporary plan to get rid of the cancer, but that this was a better way of living for myself. At the one year point, I asked the doctor to do a biopsy to test the nodule, because sometimes although the nodule remains, it becomes benign. And that's what happened with me."

"Really?"

"Yes, and then several months later, the actual nodule disappeared."

"Oh, wow."

"That was a wonderful day. I wish I could do cartwheels, because I would have cartwheeled out of the doctor's office. My doctor's reaction was very odd though. He said, 'Yeah, there's no cancer there, but I still recommend surgery.'"

"Huh."

"I became a nutrition and health consultant because I want to show people that they can also heal their bodies from cancer naturally. There is nothing unique about my body that allowed that to happen. The key is boosting your immune system and allowing the body to heal, and a huge part of that is the diet.

"The tide is changing. This information can't stay hidden forever. It's the secret that isn't a secret. There might be resistance to it, but you really cannot get past the facts and the stories like mine and the people I work with."

Lathon paused.

"My grandmother had diabetes," she said slowly, barely controlling her emotion. "And—I didn't know what I know now—about healing the body. If I did, I feel she could have lived at least a few years longer. It's in her honor that I do what I do. Because I can save someone else's grandmother, aunt, uncle, father…"

***

Sometimes I hear people ask, "Will being vegan make me live forever?" As though immortality were the true measure of health.

But there is the length of your life to consider, and then there is the quality of your life.

"You're not going to live forever no matter what you do," Dr. Barnard said. "But if you continue to eat the standard American diet, you could be overweight by age 30, with high blood pressure and developing diabetes. Your life is in a state of decline year after year. Finally, your candle is snuffed out when you're 65 or 75. That's not the life you want. You want to eat foods that keep you maximally healthy all life long. And when the end comes, it's quick. For me, who knows, maybe I'll die at age 120 in the Formula One race in Monaco, in a flaming inferno as my car hits the wall." He laughed. "But the bottom line is, while we're alive, let's *be alive*."

I looked back at the world's Blue Zones, containing the most long-lived cultures on the planet, with more people reaching the age of 100—and healthy—than anywhere else. Ellsworth Wareham, one of the Loma Linda Adventist vegans, turned 101 in 2015. He retired at age 96. As a heart surgeon. In retirement, he still drives and walks without a cane. He has no problems with his joints or his balance.[37]

Even if you were only to live to the age of 80, what a gift it would be to have a healthy last decade of life. People dread old age, anticipating crippled time in nursing homes and wheelchairs, lost in dementia, chronic illnesses, going in and out of the hospital like a revolving door. But what if we could prevent the chronic diseases that destroy the quality of life in our last ten to twenty years, and compress it all to the very end?

While we're alive, let's be alive.

It is within our power. Dying from old age may be a myth. Forty-two thousand autopsies of people who lived past 100 showed that in every single case, disease was the cause of death.[38] Not one died from old age. Old age is not a disease. A disease is a condition that prevents our bodies and minds from functioning normally. Normal function means health.

And the human body strives for health. It knows how to do it if we let it. There is a tremendous healing force within each one of us.

"One of the most amazing things I learned in medical school is that within ten to fifteen years of quitting smoking, your lung cancer risk approaches that of a life-long non-smoker," said Dr. Greger. "Isn't that amazing? Every morning of our smoking life, that healing process had started until, wham, the first cigarette of the day. Re-damaging our lungs with every puff, just as we re-damage our arteries with every bite. The miracle cure is to stop re-injuring ourselves three times a day, and let our bodies bring us back towards health."

"When I was in medical school, I thought diseases were one-way streets," said Dr. Barnard. "I thought diabetes couldn't get better. For heart attacks, it was surgery or nothing. Alzheimer's—nothing we could do. But now, to discover that we have an answer, and the answer is as close as the food on our plate—that is miraculous. Sick people come in here and I've got something to change their lives.

"I only wish I could turn back the clock and give that answer to my dad and my grandpa, and so many others who have paid with their lives for this lack of knowledge."

I thought of my own dad, my own grandpa.

"There's this sense that everything's okay in moderation," said Dr. McMacken. "But we haven't seen that moderation works. I challenge anyone to show me that eating meat and eggs in moderation will actually arrest and reverse any disease. There's a chance you might be able to stay stable, but most of us in clinical practice see patients getting worse. We see people getting on more and more medications. If the best we can hope for is staying stable, well, that's not really a great goal. On the other hand, we know for certain that you can turn things around and feel a lot better, and most people can come off medications, when they eat foods that don't interfere with their body's natural ability to heal itself."

"We are on the cusp of what can truly be a seismic revolution in health," said Dr. Esselstyn. "It's never going to occur because of another pill or operation. That revolution will occur when we in the healing profession have the grit and the determination to share the nutritional literacy that will empower the public to absolutely destroy this common, chronic, killing disease. When somebody orders pizza with cheese or a steak, it will be the same as smoking today. Look how long it took us, but it happened; nobody would even dream about smoking in your house now. It will be the same with food."

"This evolution is going to happen despite the major health organizations, despite the government, despite the lobbying groups," Dr. Klaper said. "It's going to be the public who leads on this one. The only way we will change the heads of our state is when we change the state of our heads. Americans are slowly changing the state of their heads as the truth gets out, but government is going to be the last to act. They will do that only when the public demands it."

"It's up to each of us to make our own decisions as to what to eat and how to live, but we should make those choices consciously," Dr. Greger said. "We have to be educated about the predictable consequences of our actions. As long as people understand the benefits and risks, they can make up their minds for themselves and their families.

"People can't be blamed for eating unhealthy if they didn't know it was unhealthy. What did they get taught in school? Have three servings of dairy a day. That's what their teachers taught them because that's what the dairy council sent the teachers. The answer is to educate people so they know that the power is in their hands to prevent, treat, and reverse chronic disease. Personal responsibility comes from knowledge."

***

I began this journey worried about my own health. But my understanding of health has expanded to include my family, friends, community, country, and the planet we live on. Just as the current food, medical, and pharmaceutical industries are woven together, there is another convergence emerging, and this one is for the good.

All injustices, and fights against injustice, are linked together. We become stronger when we can finally see those links.

"As I get older, I see a lot of value in building strong communities around collective liberation," Jake Conroy said to Keegan and I. "It's not just about the animals, the environment, or human health. It's going to take all three. When you see how things intersect, that is when real change will start to happen. When there's injustice in the world, speak up about it. Do it because it's the right thing to do.

"The power of the individual is giant. I don't think it can be overstated. Writing a letter, making a movie, writing a book, or engaging in civil disobedience or nonviolent direct action—those are very real tools in bringing about justice. I've seen movements of tens of thousands of people who have done amazing things. I've also seen one or two people who do just as equally amazing things."

The power of the individual means that you—yes, you, reading this book right now—can directly take back control from the corporations who feed on your sickness, the sickness of your loved ones, or the sickness you will develop from their products. You can do this every single time you make a decision in the grocery store, a restaurant, or your kitchen.

"I don't want my gains to be at the detriment of the planet or billions of animals," Tim Shieff told us as we walked out of the Parkour gym into the sunshine. "If a plant-based diet made me weaker, I would still do it. And yet, I'm not weaker. I'm stronger. That's the beauty of it. When you make choices for the greater good of others, it comes around. It benefits me. It benefits us all."

I thought of George McGovern, struggling to present the truth to a society that wasn't ready to hear it. Since I first learned about the McGovern Report, he's become a hero of mine. The animal agriculture industries mercilessly snuffed out—for the moment—his attempt to tell the truth, just as other powerful political forces snuffed out his attempts to bring justice to a war-ravaged nation.

McGovern lived until he was 90. He celebrated his 88th birthday by skydiving. I guess he took his own dietary advice. He considered his 1972 acceptance address for the Democratic Presidential nomination[39] the best speech of his life:[40]

> *And this is the time to stand for those things that are close to the American spirit. We are not content with things as they are. We reject the view of those who say, "America — love it or leave it." We reply, "Let us change it so we may love it the more." And this is the time.*

The Democratic National Convention was in complete chaos that year, and McGovern couldn't give his speech until 3am. Most TV viewers had gone to bed.[41] This was way before YouTube or even widely available VCRs. It was another era. Very, very few Americans ever heard his great speech.

McGovern lost the presidency, of course, to Richard Nixon. And the country took a very different path than it might have.

But things spiral around. We stand now at another threshold in history.

There is a health revolution brewing in the country. A groundswell of awareness is surfacing, and people are feeling the change before they can articulate it. We know there is something terribly broken about the industrial food, medical, and pharmaceutical systems, but most people don't know what it is. It's no wonder, because, as we've discovered, there is an intricate political and corporate apparatus in place to keep us from finding out.

How soon will this become public knowledge? More and more people are joining the movement. How soon will it be important enough for us to take action?

As René Miller walked us back up the burning asphalt road from her family's graveyard, past the boxes of putrefying corpses, she told us, "I'm taking a risk by talking to you, because I feel I can make a difference. If nobody don't stand with you, you stand by yourself.

There's a risk that something could happen to me, but I don't think like that."

"What do you think like?" I asked her.

She smiled her radiant, beautiful smile, and turned to me. "I think I'm going to be all right. I'm doing it for my family. It's not all about me. I'm doing it for the whole community, because we all are related. Everybody way down this block know René. Some of them looks at me funny, but I hold my head up, because I believe in this. Where there's a will, there is a way. And *I believe that*. Maybe I can't figure it out, but somebody can. *You* might can figure it out. *You* go tell people. Somebody going to make a difference."

We are not content with things as they are.

Let us change our lives so we may love them the more.

Things spiral around.

And this is the time.

ACKNOWLEDGEMENTS

Deep thanks to Lara Heimann, my ahimsa teacher; Keegan and Kip for telling the truth and changing the lives of millions of people—including myself and my family—with their revolutionary films; the lovely Lisa Bankoff of ICM who believed in this book; Dr. Michael Greger to whom we owe an enormous debt; Jenny Cabrera, Margaret Wright, Amelia Pang, and Sophie Schnitzlein without whom this book could not have been written; Mom, Dad, and Eugene for my deepest roots, and as always, forever and ever, world without end, Marina, Konrad, and my darling Chris. They are the reason why.

—E.W.

We would like to thank, first and foremost, Eunice Wong, for without her incredible talent, her dedication to truth, and her tireless work for justice on all levels, this book would not have been possible, as well as all the courageous physicians, scientists, healthcare professionals, lawyers, economists, and public health advocates who are exposing the truth and fighting back against the corporate and government hammerlock on our nation's health.

—K.A. & K.K.

Notes

Part One
Prologue

1. Lumley, Thomas. "What's a Group 1 carcinogen?" Stats Chat website. July 1, 2013. Accessed May 2016. http://www.statschat.org.nz/2013/07/01/whats-a-group-1-carcinogen/
2. "IARC Monographs Evaluate Consumption of Red Meat and Processed Meat." World Health Organization website. Accessed May 2016. https://www.iarc.fr/en/media-centre/pr/2015/pdfs/pr240_E.pdf
3. "Cancer Increasing Among Meat Eaters." The New York Times archive website. September 24, 1907. Accessed May 2016. http://query.nytimes.com/mem/archive-free/pdf?res=9502E1D81331E733A25757C2A96F9C946697D6CF
4. "Q&A on the Carcinogenicity of the Consumption of Red Meat and Processed Meat." World Health Organization website. October 2015. Accessed May 2016. http://www.who.int/features/qa/cancer-red-meat/en/
5. "Five Meats By the Slice: See How Little 50 Grams Actually Is." CBC News website. October 26, 2015. Accessed May 2016. http://www.cbc.ca/news/canada/saskatoon/five-meats-by-the-slice-see-how-little-50-grams-actually-is-1.3289822
6. Bradbury, K.E. and T.J. Key. "The Association of Red and Processed Meat, and Dietary Fibre with Colorectal Cancer in UK Biobank." Cambridge University Press website. September 2015. Accessed May 2016. https://www.cambridge.org/core/journals/proceedings-of-the-nutrition-society/article/the-association-of-red-and-processed-meat-and-dietary-fibre-with-colorectal-cancer-in-uk-biobank/7AA4A287A8F36AB35971D06CBE7A645A
7. Shopping List: Basic Ingredients for a Healthy Kitchen. American Cancer Society website. Accessed May 2016. https://www.cancer.org/healthy/eat-healthy-get-active/eat-healthy/shopping-list-basic-ingredients-for-a-healthy-kitchen.html
8. Quick Entrees: Healthy in a Hurry. American Cancer Society website. Accessed May 2016. https://www.cancer.org/healthy/eat-healthy-get-active/eat-healthy/quick-entrees.html
9. Innovations in Home Cooking. American Cancer Society website. Accessed May 2016. Accessed May 2016. https://www.cancer.org/healthy/eat-healthy-get-active/eat-healthy/innovations-in-home-cooking.html

Chapter One: Genetics

1. "Study is the First to Show Higher Dietary Acid Load Increases Risk of Diabetes." EurekAlert! website. November 11, 2013. Accessed May 2016. https://www.eurekalert.org/pub_releases/2013-11/d-sit110813.php InterAct Consortium, Bendinelli B, Palli D, Masala G, Sharp SJ, Schulze MB, et al; Association between

dietary meat consumption and incident type 2 diabetes: the EPIC-InterAct study. Diabetologia. 2013;56(1):47-59. doi: 10.1007/s00125-012-2718-7. Feskens EJ, Sluik D, van Woudenbergh GJ. Meat consumption, diabetes, and its complications. Current Diabetes Reports. 2013;13(2):298-306. doi: 10.1007/s11892-013-0365-0. Vlassara H, Cai W, Crandall J, Goldberg T, Oberstein R, Dardaine V, et al; Inflammatory mediators are induced by dietary glycotoxins, a major risk factor for diabetic angiopathy. Proceedings of the National Academy of Sciences of the United States of America. 2002;99(24):15596-601. Neal Barnard, Susan Levin, and Caroline Trapp. Meat Consumption as a Risk Factor for Type 2 Diabetes. Nutrients. 2014; 6(2): 897–910. doi: 10.3390/nu6020897.

2.   "Diabetes Meal Plans and a Healthy Diet." American Diabetes Association website. Accessed May 2016. http://www.diabetes.org/food-and-fitness/food/planning-meals/diabetes-meal-plans-and-a-healthy-diet.html?loc=ff-slabnav

3.   "Recipes For a Healthy Living." Diabetes.org. Accessed May 2016. http://www.diabetes.org/mfa-recipes/recipes/recipes-archive.html. "One-Day Meal Plan." Diabetes.org. Accessed May 2016. http://www.diabetes.org/mfa-recipes/meal-plans/

4.   Neal D Barnard, Joshua Cohen, David JA Jenkins, Gabrielle Turner-McGrievy, Lise Gloede, Amber Green, et al; A low-fat vegan diet and a conventional diabetes diet in the treatment of type 2 diabetes: a randomized, controlled, 74-wk clinical trial. American Journal of Clinical Nutrition. 2009; 89(5): 1588S–1596S. doi: 10.3945/ajcn.2009.26736H.

5.   The *American Journal of Clinical Nutrition* is the most highly rated, peer-reviewed journal in the Institute of Scientific Information's nutrition and dietetics category. The Institute of Scientific Information, now part of the Intellectual Property and Science business of Thomson Reuters, maintains a list of over 14,000 journals. http://ajcn.nutrition.org/site/misc/about.xhtml http://isindexing.com/isi/journals.php

6.   "Genes and Human Disease." World Health Organization website. Accessed May 2016. http://www.who.int/genomics/public/geneticdiseases/en/index2.html

7.   "Leading Causes of Death." Centers for Disease Control and Prevention website. Accessed May 2016. http://www.cdc.gov/nchs/fastats/leading-causes-of-death.htm

8.   Boji Huang, Beatriz L Rodriguez, Cecil M. Burchfiel, Po-Huang Chyou, J. David Curb, and Katsuhiko Yano. Acculturation and Prevalence of Diabetes among Japanese-American Men in Hawaii. American Journal of Epidemiology. 1996; 144:674-81

9.   Physicians Committee For Responsible Medicine website. Accessed May 2016. http://www.pcrm.org/about/about/about-pcrm

10.   Saleh, Nivien."Proteinaholic Says Meat, Not Sugar, Causes Diabetes." SweetOnion.net. October 9, 2015. Accessed May 2016. http://sweetonion.net/garth-davis-proteinaholic-diabetes/

11.   "Garth Davis." Vegan Bodybuilding & Fitness website. Accessed May 2016. http://www.veganbodybuilding.com/?page=bio_davis

12.   Talmadge, Eric. "Ancient Okinawans Share Secrets of Long Life." Los Angeles Times website. November 18, 2001. Accessed May 2016. http://articles.latimes.com/2001/nov/18/news/mn-5410

13. "Best Hospitals for Cardiology & Heart Surgery." U.S. News & World Report website. Accessed May 2016. http://health.usnews.com/best-hospitals/rankings/cardiology-and-heart-surgery

14. U.S. Burden of Disease Collaborators, "The State of U.S. Health, 1990-2010: Burden of Diseases, Injuries, and Risk Factors," Journal of the American Medical Association 310 n. 6 (2013): 591-608.

15. J. Michael McGinnis, "Actual Causes of Death, 1990-2010," Workshop on Determinants of Premature Mortality, Sept. 18, 2013, National Research Council, Washington, DC.

16. Willett W.C. Balancing Life-Style and Genomics Research for Disease Prevention. *Science.* 2002; 296(5568):695-8.

17. Preetha Anand, Ajaikumar B. Kunnumakara, Chitra Sundaram, Kuzhuvelil B. Harikumar, Sheeja T. Tharakan, Oiki S. Lai, Bokyung Sung, and Bharat B. Aggarwal. Cancer is a Preventable Disease that Requires Major Lifestyle Changes. Pharmaceutical Research. 2008; 25(9): 2097–2116.

18. Chan, Amanda. "The 10 Deadliest Cancers and Why There's No Cure." Live Science website. September 10, 2010. Accessed May 2016. http://www.livescience.com/11041-10-deadliest-cancers-cure.html

19. Messina, Mark and Virginia Messina. *The Dietitian's Guide to Vegetarian Diets.* Port Townshend, Washington: Aspen Publishers. 1996. Pg. 39.

20. "Overview - Preventing Chronic Diseases: A Vital Investment." World Health Organization website. Accessed May 2016. http://www.who.int/chp/chronic_disease_report/part1/en/index11.html

21. Park, Alice. "Nearly Half of US Deaths Can Be Prevented With Lifestyle Changes." TIME website. May 1, 2014. Accessed May 2016. http://time.com/84514/nearly-half-of-us-deaths-can-be-prevented-with-lifestyle-changes/

22. Department of Health and Human Services; Department of Agriculture, The Relationship Between Dietary Cholesterol and Blood Cholesterol and Human Health and Nutrition, a report to the Congress pursuant to the Food Security Act of 1985 P.L. 99-198, Subtitle B, Section 1453. (Washington, D.C., 1987).

23. Burkitt, DP. Epidemiology of cancer of the colon and rectum. Diseases of the Colon & Rectum. 1993;36(11):1071-82.

24. Lipski E. Traditional non-Western diets. Nutrition in Clinical Practice. 2010;25(6):585-93. doi: 10.1177/0884533610385821.

CHAPTER TWO: MEDICAL SCHOOLS

1. Mikkelson, David. "The Doctor of the Future." Snopes.com. Accessed May 2016. http://www.snopes.com/quotes/futuredoctor.asp

2. Ward BW, Schiller JS, Goodman RA. Multiple Chronic Conditions Among US Adults: A 2012 Update. Prev Chronic Dis. 2014;11:130389. doi: http://dx.doi.org/10.5888/pcd11.130389

3. Gerteis J, Izrael D, Deitz D, LeRoy L, Ricciardi R, Miller T, Basu J. Multiple Chronic Conditions Chartbook. AHRQ Publications No, Q14-0038. Rockville, MD: Agency for Healthcare Research and Quality; 2014.

4.   Go AS, Mozaffarian D, Roger VL, Benjamin EJ, Berry JD, Blaha MJ, et al; American Heart Association Statistics Committee and Stroke Statistics Subcommittee. Heart disease and stroke statistics--2014 update: a report from the American Heart Association. Circulation. 2014;129(3):e28-292.

5.   "Cancer Prevalence and Cost of Care Projections." National Cancer Institute website. Accessed May 2016. http://costprojections.cancer.gov/

6.   "The Cost of Diabetes." American Diabetes Association website. Accessed May 2016. http://www.diabetes.org/advocacy/news-events/cost-of-diabetes.html

7.   Finkelstein EA, Trogdon JG, Cohen JW, Dietz W. Annual medical spending attributable to obesity: payer- and service-specific estimates. *Health Aff.* 2009;28(5):w822-31.

8.   "Clinic & Services." TrueNorth Health Center website. Accessed May 2016. http://www.healthpromoting.com/clinic-services

9.   "Michelle McMacken, MD." Forks Over Knives website. Accessed May 2016. http://www.forksoverknives.com/contributors/michelle-mcmacken/

10.   Adams KM, Kohlmeier M, and Zeisel SH. Nutrition education in U.S. medical schools: latest update of a national survey. Academic Medicine. 2010;85(9):1537-42. doi: 10.1097/ACM.0b013e3181eab71b.

11.   Committee on Nutrition in Medical Education, Food and Nutrition Board, Commission on Life Sciences, National Research Council. Nutrition Education In U.S. Medical Schools. Washington, D.C.: The National Academies Press, 1985.

12.   Kelly M Adams, Karen C Lindell, Martin Kohlmeier, and Steven H Zeisel. Status of nutrition education in medical schools. The American Journal of Clinical Nutrition. 2006; 83(4): 941S–944S.

13.   "Average Required Week of Instruction and Contact Hours: Average Weeks of Instruction." Association of American Medical Colleges website. Accessed May 2016. https://www.aamc.org/initiatives/cir/406474/03b.html.

14.   "ACGME Program Requirements for Graduate Medical Education in Cardiovascular Disease (Internal Medicine)." Accreditation Council for Graduate Medical Education website. Accessed May 2016. https://www.acgme.org/Portals/0/PFAssets/ProgramRequirements/141_cardiovascular_disease_int_med_2016.pdf

15.   "ACGME Program Requirements for Graduate Medical Education in Internal Medicine." Accreditation Council for Graduate Medical Education website. Accessed May 2016. http://www.acgme.org/portals/0/pfassets/programrequirements/140_internal_medicine_2016.pdf

16.   "Senate Committee on Business, Professions and Economic Development Hearing on Bill No: SB 380." California Legislative Information website. April 25, 2011. Accessed May 2016. http://www.leginfo.ca.gov/pub/11-12/bill/sen/sb_0351-0400/sb_380_cfa_20110421_125358_sen_comm.html

17.   Vegan Streams. "Disease for Profit or Health Care? Dr. McDougall: Senate Bill (SB) 380". Filmed [April 2011]. Youtube video. Posted [May 2011]. https://www.youtube.com/watch?v=mmlEKOGp5rY

18.   "An act to add Section 2190.7 to the Business and Professions Code, relating to medicine." California Legislative Information website. February 15, 2011. Accessed May 2016. ftp://www.leginfo.ca.gov/pub/11-12/bill/sen/sb_0351-0400/sb_380_bill_20110215_introduced.html

19. "Senate Committee on Business, Professions and Economic Development Hearing on Bill No: SB 380." California Legislative Information website.

20. "Medical Associations Oppose Bill to Mandate Nutrition Training." NutritionFacts.org. November 14, 2011. Accessed May 2016. http://nutritionfacts.org/video/medical-associations-oppose-bill-to-mandate-nutrition-training/

21. "Current State Physician CME Requirements."My CME Site. Accessed May 2016. http://mycmesite.com/phys-reqs.cfm

22. "Chronic Disease Prevention and Health Promotion." Centers for Disease Control and Prevention website. Accessed May 2016. http://www.cdc.gov/chronicdisease/index.htm

23. "Mentoring Future Leaders 2015." SheShares.net. Accessed May 2016. http://www.sheshares.net/mentorship-program/2015-mentorship-class/

24. "Medical Associations Oppose Bill to Mandate Nutrition Training." NutritionFacts.org.

25. "Mark Wyland Republican (Elected 2006), Senate District 38." MapLight website. Accessed May 2016. http://maplight.org/california/legislator/1359-mark-wyland

26. "An Amendment of BILL NUMBER: SB 380." California Legislative Information website. February 15, 2011. Accessed May 2016. http://www.leginfo.ca.gov/pub/11-12/bill/sen/sb_0351-0400/sb_380_bill_20110427_amended_sen_v96.html

27. "State CME Requirements." Medscape website. Accessed May 2016. http://www.medscape.org/public/staterequirements

28. Ibid.

CHAPTER THREE: DIABETES

1. Taylor, Jessica. "All Your Questions About Seventh-Day Adventism And Ben Carson Answered." NPR website. October 27, 2015. Accessed May 2016. http://www.npr.org/sections/itsallpolitics/2015/10/27/452314794/all-your-questions-about-seventh-day-adventism-and-ben-carson-answered

2. "The Most and Least Racially Diverse U.S. Religious Groups." Pew Research Center website. July 27, 2015. Accessed May 2016. http://www.pewresearch.org/fact-tank/2015/07/27/the-most-and-least-racially-diverse-u-s-religious-groups/

3. "Living a Healthy Life." Seventh-Day Adventist Church website. Accessed May 2016. https://www.adventist.org/en/vitality/health/

4. "Loma Linda Exploration Backgrounds." Blue Zones website. Accessed May 2016. https://www.bluezones.com/2014/03/loma-linda-exploration-backgrounds/

5. "Explorations." Blue Zones website. Accessed May 2016. https://www.bluezones.com/about-blue-zones/explorations/

6. "Appendix C Adventist Health Study." Loma Linda University website. Accessed May 2016. http://www.llu.edu/info/legacy/appendixc/

7. "Loma Linda University. About Adventist Health Study-2." Loma Linda University website. Accessed May 2016. http://publichealth.llu.edu/adventist-health-studies/about

8. "Adventist Lifestyle in the Media." Loma Linda University website. Accessed May 2016. http://publichealth.llu.edu/adventist-health-studies/videos-and-media-reports

9. Serena Tonstad, Terry Butler, Ru Yan, and Gary E. Fraser. Type of Vegetarian Diet, Body Weight, and Prevalence of Type 2 Diabetes. Diabetes Care. 2009; 32(5): 791-796. Rizzo NS, Sabaté J, Jaceldo-Siegl K, Fraser GE.Vegetarian dietary patterns are associated with a lower risk of metabolic syndrome: the adventist health study 2. Diabetes Care. 2011;34(5):1225-7. doi: 10.2337/dc10-1221. Snowdon DA. Animal product consumption and mortality because of all causes combined, coronary heart disease, stroke, diabetes, and cancer in Seventh-day Adventists. The American Journal of Clinical Nutrition. 1988;48(3 Suppl):739-48. Vang A, Singh PN, Lee JW, Haddad EH, Brinegar CH. Meats, processed meats, obesity, weight gain and occurrence of diabetes among adults: findings from Adventist Health Studies. Annals of Nutrition & Metabolism. 2008;52(2):96-104. doi: 10.1159/000121365.

10. Vang A, Singh PN, Lee JW, Haddad EH, Brinegar CH. Meats, processed meats, obesity, weight gain and occurrence of diabetes among adults: findings from Adventist Health Studies. Annals of Nutrition & Metabolism. 2008;52(2):96-104. doi: 10.1159/000121365.

11. "European Prospective Investigation into Cancer and Nutrition (EPIC)." National Cancer Institute website. Accessed May 2016. https://epi.grants.cancer.gov/Consortia/members/epic.html

12. "EPIC Study." World Health Organization website. Accessed May 2016. http://epic.iarc.fr/

13. Consortium, I. (2013). Association between dietary meat consumption and incident type 2 diabetes: The EPIC-InterAct study. Diabetologia. 56(1), 47-59. doi:10.1007/s00125-012-2718-7. Consortium, I. (2014). Adherence to predefined dietary patterns and incident type 2 diabetes in European populations: EPIC-InterAct Study. Diabetologia. 57(2), 321-333. doi: 10.1007/s00125-013-3092-9.

14. Ahmadi-Abhari, S., Luben, R.N., Powell, N., Bhaniani, A., Chowdhury, R., Wareham, N.J., et al; Dietary intake of carbohydrates and risk of type 2 diabetes: the European Prospective Investigation into Cancer-Norfolk study. British Journal of Nutrition, 2014;111(2), 342-352. Doi:10.1017/S0007114513002298.

15. Fung TT, Schulze M, Manson JE, Willett WC and Hu FB. Dietary patterns, meat intake, and the risk of type 2 diabetes in women. Arch Intern Med. 2004;164(20), 2235-2240. Pan A., Sun Q., Berstein AM, Schulze MB, Manson JE, Willett WC, Hu FB. Red meat consumption and risk of type 2 diabetes: 3 cohorts of US adults and an updated meta-analysis. American Journal of Clinical Nutrition. 2011;94(4), 1088-1096. Leh SH, Sun Q, Willett WC, Eliassen AH, Wu K, Pan A, et al; Associations between red meat intake and biomarkers of inflammation and glucose metabolism in women. American Journal of Clinical Nutrition. 2014;99(2), 352-360. Van Dam RM, Willett WC, Rimm EB, Stampfer MJ, Hu FB. Dietary fat and meat intake in relation to risk of type 2 diabetes in men. Diabetes Care. 2002;25(3), 417-424.

16. "Mexico vs. Arizona Pima Indians." Indian Country Today Media Network. December 1, 2010. Accessed May 2016. http://indiancountrytodaymedianetwork.com/article/mexico-vs.-arizona-pima-indians-3258

17. Leslie Schulz, Peter H. Bennett, Eric Ravussin, Judith R. Kidd, Kenneth K. Kidd, Julian Esparza, et al; Effects of Traditional and Western Environments on Prevalence of Type 2 Diabetes in Pima Indians in Mexico and the U.S. Diabetes Care. 2006; 29(8): 1866-1871.

18. "AACE/ACE COMPREHENSIVE TYPE 2 DIABETES MANAGEMENT ALGORITHM 2016."The American Association of Clinical Endocrinologists website. Page 9. Accessed May 2016. https://www.aace.com/publications/algorithm

19. Lars Rydén, Peter J. Grant, Stefan D. Anker, Christian Berne, Francesco Cosentino, Nicolas Danchin, et al; ESC Guidelines on diabetes, pre-diabetes, and cardiovascular diseases developed in collaboration with the EASD. European Heart Journal. 2013; doi: http://dx.doi.org/10.1093/eurheartj/eht108

20. American Diabetes Association Standards of Medical Care in Diabetes—2016. Journal of Clinical and Applied Research and Education. 2016.

21. Ibid. Pg. S36.

22. "AICR HealthTalk." American Institute for Cancer Research. Accessed May 2016. http://www.aicr.org/press/health-features/health-talk/2014/jun14/Processed-Meats-Diabetes-Risk.html?referrer=https://www.google.com/

23. Jukka Montonen, Paul Knekt, Ritva Järvinen, Arpo Aromaa, and Antti Reunanen. Whole-grain and fiber intake and the incidence of type 2 diabetes. American Journal of Clinical Nutrition. 2003; vol. 77 no. 3 622-629.

24. Rosqvist F, Iggman D, Kullberg H, Jonathan Cedernaeas J, Johansson HE, Larsson A, et al; Overfeeding polyunsaturated and saturated fat causes distinct effects on liver and visceral fat accumulation in humans. Diabetes. 2014; doi:10.2337/db13-1622. Nolan CJ, Larter CZ. Lipotoxicity: why do saturated fatty acids cause and monounsaturates protect against it? Journal of Gastroenterology and Hepatology. 2009;24(5):703-6. Evans WJ. Oxygen-carrying proteins in meat and risk of diabetes mellitus. Journal of the American Medical Association of Internal Medicine. 2013;173(14):1335-6. Egnatchik RA, Leamy AK, Jacobson DA, Shiota M, Young JD. ER calcium release promotes mitochondrial dystunction and hepatic cell lipotoxicity in response to palmitate overload. Molecular Metabolism. 2014;3(5):544-53.

25. Estella D, da Penha Oller do Nascimento CM, Oyama LM, Ribeiro EB, Damaso AR, de Piano A. Lipotoxicity: effects of dietary saturated and transfatty acids. Mediators of Inflammation. 2013; 2013:137579.

26. "What Mitochondria Do." The Wellcome Trust Centre for Mitochondrial Research website. Accessed May 2016. http://www.newcastle-mitochondria.com/patient-and-public-home-page/what-mitochondria-do/

27. Nolan CJ and CZ Larter. Lipotoxicity: why do saturated fatty acids cause and monounsaturates protect against it? Journal of Gastroenterology and Hepatology. 2009;24(5):703-6

28. Ibid.

29. Goff LM, Bell JD, So PW, Dornhorst A, and GS Frost.Veganism and its relationship with insulin resistance and intramyocellular lipid. European Journal of Clinical Nutrition. 2005;59(2):291-8

30. G Perseghin, P Scifo, F De Cobelli, E Pagliato, A Battezzati, C Arcelloni, A Vanzulli, G Testolin, G Pozza, and A Del Maschio and L Luzi. Intramyocellular triglyceride content is a determinant of in vivo insulin resistance in humans: a 1H-13C nuclear magnetic resonance spectroscopy assessment in offspring of type 2 diabetic parents. American Diabetes Association. 1999; 48(8): 1600-1606.

31. Goff. "Veganism and its relationship with insulin resistance and intramyocellular lipid."

32. "Number of Americans with Diabetes Projected to Double or Triple by 2050." Centers for Disease Control and Prevention website. Accessed May 2016. https://www.cdc.gov/media/pressrel/2010/r101022.html

33. "Diabetes (diabetes mellitus)." Medical News Today website. Accessed May 2016. http://www.medicalnewstoday.com/articles/282929.php?page=2#diabetes

34. "Diseases and Conditions Diabetes." Mayo Clinic website. Accessed May 2016. http://www.mayoclinic.org/diseases-conditions/diabetes/basics/complications/con-20033091

35. "Capillary." About.com. Accessed May 2016. http://biology.about.com/od/anatomy/ss/capillary.htm.

36. Mayo Clinic. Diseases and Conditions Diabetes.

37. Haddrill, Marilyn. "Diabetic Retinopathy." All About Vision website Accessed May 2016. http://www.allaboutvision.com/conditions/diabetic.htm

38. "More than 29 million Americans have diabetes; 1 in 4 doesn't know." Centers for Disease Control and Prevention website. Accessed May 2016. http://www.cdc.gov/features/diabetesfactsheet/

39. "New Cases of Diagnosed Diabetes on the Rise." Centers for Disease Control and Prevention website. Accessed May 2016. https://www.cdc.gov/media/pressrel/2008/r081030.htm

40. "Diabetes and African Americans." U.S. Department of Health and Human Services Office of Minority Health website. Accessed May 2016. http://minorityhealth.hhs.gov/omh/browse.aspx?lvl=4&lvlID=18

41. "African Americans Have Five Times Higher Amputation Rate." Northwestern University website. May 13, 2008. Accessed May 2016. http://www.northwestern.edu/newscenter/stories/2008/05/feinglass.html

42. U.S. Department of Health and Human Services Office of Minority Health. Diabetes and African Americans.

43. "Diabetes Disparities Among Racial and Ethnic Minorities." Agency for Healthcare Research and Quality Archive website. Accessed May 2016. https://archive.ahrq.gov/research/findings/factsheets/diabetes/diabdisp/diabdisp.html

44. Centers for Disease Control and Prevention website. "Number of Americans with Diabetes Projected to Double or Triple by 2050."

45. Centers for Disease Control and Prevention website. "More than 29 million Americans have diabetes; 1 in 4 doesn't know."

46. "Metformin Side Effects. Diabetes.co.uk. Accessed May 2016. http://www.diabetes.co.uk/diabetes-medication/metformin-side-effects.html

47. "Metformin and Fatal Lactic Acidosis." New Zealand Medicines and Medical Devices Safety Authority website. http://www.medsafe.govt.nz/profs/PUarticles/5.htm

48. "Popular Diabetes Treatment Could Trigger Pancreatitis, Pancreatic Cancer, Study Suggests." Science Daily website. Accessed May 2016. https://www.sciencedaily.com/releases/2009/04/090430161238.htm

49.   "Medication Guide TRULICITY (Trū-li-si-tee) (dulaglutide) injection, for subcutaneous use." Eli Lilly and Company website. Accessed May 2016. http://pi.lilly.com/us/trulicity-mg.pdf

50.   Effects of Intensive Glucose Lowering in Type 2 Diabetes. New England Journal of Medicine. 2008; 358:2545-2559. doi: 10.1056/NEJMoa0802743.

51.   Ferdman, Roberto A. "Why diets don't actually work, according to a researcher who has studied them for decades." Washington Post website. May 4, 2015. Accessed May 2016. https://www.washingtonpost.com/news/wonk/wp/2015/05/04/why-diets-dont-actually-work-according-to-a-researcher-who-has-studied-them-for-decades/?utm_term=.ee70aa2b9460

52.   American Society for Nutrition website. Accessed May 2016. http://www.nutrition.org/

53.   Neal D. Barnard, Joshua Cohen, David J.A. Jenkins, Gabrielle Turner-McGrievy, Lise Gloede, Brent Jaster, et al; A Low-Fat Vegan Diet Improves Glycemic Control and Cardiovascular Risk Factors in a Randomized Clinical Trial in Individuals With Type 2 Diabetes. Diabetes Care. 2006; 29(8): 1777-1783

54.   Ibid.

55.   Mollard RC, Luhovyy BL, Panahi S, Nunez M, Hanley A and Anderson GH. Regular consumption of pulses for 8 weeks reduces metabolic syndrome risk factors in overweight and obese adults. British Journal of Nutrition. 2012;108 Suppl 1:S111-22. Kahleova H, Hrachovinova T, Hill M, et al. Vegetarian diet in type 2 diabetes—improvement in quality of life, mood and eating behavior. Diabetic Medicine. 2013;30(1):127-9. Nicholson AS, Sklar M, Barnard ND, Gore S, Sullivan R, Browning S. Toward improved management of NIDDM: A randomized, controlled, pilot intervention using a lowfat, vegetarian diet. Preventive Medicine. 1999;29(2), 87-91. Bloomer RJ, Kabir, MM, Canale RE, Trepanowski JF, Marshall KE, Farney TM, Hammond KG. Effect of a 21 day Daniel Fast on metabolic and cardiovascular disease risk factors in men and women. Lipids in Health and Disease. 2010;9, 94. Trapp CB, Barnard ND. Usefulness of vegetarian and vegan diets for treating type 2 diabetes. Current Diabetes Reports. 2010;10(2):152-8.

56.   Singhal P, Kaushik G, Mathur P. Antidiabetic potential of commonly consumed legumes: a review. Critical Reviews in Food Science and Nutrition. 2014;54(5):655-72. doi: 10.1080/10408398.2011.604141. Song S, Paik HY, Song Y. High intake of whole grains and beans pattern is inversely associated with insulin resistance in healthy Korean adult population. Diabetes Research and Clinical Practice. 2012;98(3):e28-31. doi: 10.1016/j.diabres.2012.09.038. Thompson SV1, Winham DM, Hutchins AM. Bean and rice meals reduce postprandial glycemic response in adults with type 2 diabetes: a cross-over study. Nutrition Journal. 2012;11:23. doi: 10.1186/1475-2891-11-23. Sievenpiper JL, Kendall CW, Esfahani A, Wong JM, Carleton AJ, Jiang HY, et al; Effect of non-oil-seed pulses on glycaemic control: a systematic review and meta-analysis of randomised controlled experimental trials in people with and without diabetes. Diabetologia. 2009;52(8):1479-95. doi: 10.1007/s00125-009-1395-7. Helmstädter A. Beans and diabetes: Phaseolus vulgaris preparations as antihyperglycemic agents. Journal of Medicinal Food. 2010;13(2):251-4. doi: 10.1089/jmf.2009.0002.

57.   Anderson JW, Ward K. High-carbohydrate, high-fiber diets for insulin-treated men with diabetes mellitus. The American Journal of Clinical Nutrition. 1979;32(11):2312-21.

58.   Neal D. Barnard. A Low-Fat Vegan Diet Improves Glycemic Control and Cardiovascular Risk Factors in a Randomized Clinical Trial in Individuals With Type 2 Diabetes. Accessed May 2016. http://care.diabetesjournals.org/content/29/8/1777

CHAPTER FOUR: CHICKEN

1.   "Per Capita Consumption of Poultry and Livestock, 1965 to Estimated 2016, in Pounds." National Chicken Council website. Accessed May 2016. http://www.nationalchickencouncil.org/about-the-industry/statistics/per-capita-consumption-of-poultry-and-livestock-1965-to-estimated-2012-in-pounds/

2.   "The Golden Age of Poultry." Priceonomics website. Accessed May 2016. https://priceonomics.com/the-golden-age-of-poultry/

3.   Sugimura T, Wakabayashi K, Nakagama H, Nagao M. Heterocyclic amines: Mutagens/carcinogens produced during cooking of meat and fish. Cancer Science. 2004;95(4):290-9.

4.   Sullivan KM, Erickson MA, Sandusky CB, Barnard ND. Detection of PhIP in grilled chicken entrées at popular chain restaurants throughout California. Nutrition and Cancer. 2008; 60:592-602.

5.   Zheng W, Lee SA. Well-done meat intake, heterocyclic amine exposure, and cancer risk. Nutrition and Cancer. 2009; 61(4):437-46.

6.   Steck SE, Gaudet MM, Eng SM, et al; Cooked meat and risk of breast cancer—lifetime versus recent dietary intake. Epidemiology. 2007;18(3):373-82.

7.   Foer, Janathan Safran. *Eating Animals*. New York: Back Bay Books. 2009. Pg.107.

8.   Richman EL, Stampfer MJ, Paciorek A, Broering JM, Carroll PR, Chan JM. Intakes of meat, fish, poultry, and eggs and risk of prostate cancer progression. American Journal of Clinical Nutrition. 2010;91(3):712-21. doi: 10.3945/ajcn.2009.28474.

9.   Singh PN, Fraser GE. Dietary risk factors for colon cancer in a low-risk population. American Journal of Epidemiology. 1998; 148(8):761-74.

10.   "Prognosis." Hirshberg Foundation for Pancreatic Cancer Research website. Accessed May 2016. http://pancreatic.org/pancreatic-cancer/about-the-pancreas/prognosis/

11.   Rohrmann S, Linseisen J, Nothlings U, et al; Meat and fish consumption and risk of pancreatic cancer: results from the European Prospective Investigation into Cancer and Nutrition. International Journal of Cancer. 2013; 132(3):617-24.

12.   "European Prospective Investigation into Cancer and Nutrition (EPIC)." National Cancer Institute website. Accessed May 2016. https://epi.grants.cancer.gov/Consortia/members/epic.html

13.   Lynch SM, Vrieling A, Lubin JH, et al; Cigarette smoking and pancreatic cancer: a pooled analysis from the pancreatic cancer cohort consortium. American Journal of Epidemiology. 2009;170(4):403-13.

14. Johnson ES, Zhou Y, Yau LC, et al; Mortality from malignant diseases-update of the Baltimore union poultry cohort. Cancer Causes Control. 2010; 21(2):215-21.

15. Rohrmann S, Linseisen J, Jakobsen MU, et al; Consumption of meat and dairy and l ymphoma risk in the European Prospective Investigation into Cancer and Nutrition. *International Journal of Cancer.* 2011;128(3): 623-34.

16. U.S. Department of Agriculture Agricultural Research Service. National Nutrient Database for Standard Reference Release 27. Basic Report: 05358, Chicken, broiler, rotisserie, BBQ, breast meat and skin. http://ndb.nal.usda.gov/ndb/foods/show/1058.

17. Pohl H, Welch HG. The role of overdiagnosis and reclassification in the marked increase of esophageal adenocarcinoma incidence. Journal of National Cancer Institute. 2005; 97(2):142-6.

18. De Ceglie A, Fisher DA, Filiberti R, Blanchi S, Conio M. Barrett's esophagus, esophageal and esophagogastric junction adenocarcinomas: the role of diet. Clinics and Research in Hepatology and Gastroenterology. 2011; 35(1): 7-16.

19. Navarro Silvera SA, Mayne ST, Risch H, et al; Food group intake and risk of subtypes of esophageal and gastric cancer. International Journal of Cancer. 2008;123(4): 852-60.

20. Parasa S, Sharma P. Complications of gastro-oesophageal reflux disease. Best Pract Res Clin Gastroenterol. 2013;27(3):433-42. Best Practice & Research Clinical Gastroenterology.

21. Vergnaud AC, Norat T, Romaguera D, et al; Meat consumption and prospective weight change in particpants of the EPIC-PANACEA study. American Journal of Clinical Nutrition. 2010;92(2):398-407.

22. Popper, Pamela. *Food Over Medicine.* Dallas: BenBella Books. 2013. Pg.75.

23. Greger, Michael. *How Not to Die.* New York: Flatiron Books. 2015. Pg.116.

24. "29 Ways to Love Lean Beef." Healthy Eating for Healthy Living website. Accessed May 2016. http://www.healthyeatingforhealthyliving.com/leaders-guide/beef/29-lean-cuts-chart.pdf

25. "Eat More Chicken, Fish and Beans." American Heart Association website. Accessed May 2016. http://www.heart.org/HEARTORG/HealthyLiving/HealthyEating/Nutrition/Eat-More-Chicken-Fish-and-Beans_UCM_320278_Article.jsp#

26. Barnard, Neal. *The Power of Your Plate.* Summertown, Tennessee: Book Publishing Company. 1995. Pg.18.

27. "Study shows pork lower in fat and leaner than ever before." University of Wisconsin-Madison website. Accessed May 2016. http://news.wisc.edu/study-shows-pork-lower-in-fat-and-leaner-than-ever-before/

28. Krans, Brian. "Cholesterol Control: Chicken vs. Beef." Healthline website. http://www.healthline.com/health/high-cholesterol/chicken-vs-beef#2

29. "Sodium and Your Health." American Heart Association website. Accessed May 2016. https://sodiumbreakup.heart.org/sodium_and_your_health

30. Stephen S Lim, Theo Vos, Abraham D Flaxman, Goodarz Danaei, Kenji Shibuya, Heather Adair-Rohani, et al; A comparative risk assessment of burden of disease and injury attributable to 67 risk factors and risk factor clusters in 21 regions, 1990–2010: a systematic analysis for the Global Burden of Disease Study 2010. The Lancet. 2012; p2224–2260. doi: http://dx.doi.org/10.1016/S0140-6736(12)61766-8.

31. Drewnowski, Adam and Colin D. Rehm. Sodium Intakes of US Children and Adults from Foods and Beverages by Location of Origin and by Specific Food Source. Nutrients. 2013;5(6): 1840–1855. doi: 10.3390/nu5061840.

32. *Buying this chicken?* Consumer Reports. June 2008; 7.

33. Cook, Michelle. "How Much Salt is in Your McDonald's Meal?" Care2 website. http://www.care2.com/greenliving/1353754.html

34. Bergeron CR, Prussing C, Boerlin P, et al; Chicken as reservoir for extraintestinal pathogenic Escherichia coli in humans, Canada. Journal of Emerging Infectious Diseases. 2012;18(3):415-21.

35. "Table 4: Food Sources of Arachidonic Acid." National Cancer Institute website. Accessed May 2016. https://epi.grants.cancer.gov/diet/foodsources/fatty_acids/table4.html

36. Vaz JS, Kac G, Nardi AE, Hibbeln JR. Omega-6 fatty acids and greater likelihood of suicide risk and major depression in early pregnancy. Journal of Affective Disorders 2014;152-154:76-82.

37. Semba RD, Nicklett EJ, Ferrucci L. Does accumulation of advanced glycation end products contribute to the aging phenotype? Journals of Gerontology Series A: Biological Sciences and Medical Sciences. 2010;65(9):963-75.

38. Uribarri J, Woodruff S, Goodman S, et al; Advanced glycation end products in foods and a practical guide to their reduction in the diet. Journal of the American Dietetic Association. 2010;110(6):911-6.e12.

39. Uribarri J, Cai W, Sandu O, Peppa M, Goldberg T, Vlassara H. Diet-derived advanced glycation end products are major contributors to the body's AGE pool and induce inflammation in healthy subjects. Annals of the New York Academy of Sciences. 2005;1043:461-6.

40. "NARMS 2011 retail meat annual report." U.S. Food and Drug Administration website. Accessed May 2016. http://www.fda.gov/downloads/AnimalVeterinary/SafetyHealth/AntimicrobialResistance/NationalAntimicrobialResistanceMonitoringSystem/UCM334834.pdf.

41. "Causes and Symptoms of Salmonellosis." Minnesota Department of Health website. Accessed May 2016. http://www.health.state.mn.us/divs/idepc/diseases/salmonellosis/basics.html

42. "Gentrification and Public Health. Playing Chicken with America's Health. Injury Control Through Collaboration." The Mailman School of Public Health Columbia University website. Accessed May 2016. https://www.mailman.columbia.edu/sites/default/files/legacy/2x2_fall15_final_web.pdf

43. Michael Batz, Sandra Hoffman, J. Glenn Morris Jr. Ranking the Disease Burden of 14 Pathogens in Food Sources in the United States Using Attribution Data from Outbreak Investigations and Expert Elicitation. Journal of Food Protection. 2012; 1278-1291. doi: 10.4315/0362-028X.JFP-11-418.

44. "Gentrification and Public Health. Playing Chicken with America's Health. Injury Control Through Collaboration." The Mailman School of Public Health Columbia University website.

45. Cogan TA, Bloomfield SF, Humphrey TJ. The effectiveness of hygiene procedures for prevention of cross-contamination from chicken carcases in the domestic kitchen. Letters in Applied Microbiology.1999;29(5):354-8.

46. Rusin P, Orosz-Coughlin P, Gerba C. Reduction of faecal coliform, coliform and heterotrophic plate count bacteria in the household kitchen and bathroom by disinfection with hypochlorite cleaners. Journal of Applied Microbiology. 1998;85(5):819-28.

47. Greger. *How Not to Die.* Pg. 95.

48. Hoffman S, Batz MB, Morris Jr JG. Annual cost of illness and quality-adjusted life year losses in the United States due to 14 foodborne pathogens. Journal of Food Protection. 2012;75(7):1292-302.

CHAPTER FIVE: FLESH FOOD

1. Popper. *Food Over Medicine.* Pg.75.

2. "NIH-AARP Diet and Health Study." National Cancer Institute website. Accessed May 2016. https://epi.grants.cancer.gov/Consortia/members/nihaarp.html

3. Sinha R, Cross AJ, Graubard BI, Leitzmann MF, Schatzkin A. Meat intake and mortality: a prospective study of over half a million people. Archives of Internal Medicine. 2009;169(6):562-71.

4. Pan A, Sun Q, Bernstein AM, et al; Red meat consumption and mortality: Results from 2 prospective cohort studies. Archives of Internal Medicine. 2012;172(7):555-63.

5. "Overweight and Obesity Statistics." National Institute of Diabetes and Digestive and Kidney Diseases website. Accessed May 2016. https://www.niddk.nih.gov/health-information/health-statistics/Pages/overweight-obesity-statistics.aspx

6. Coletta DK, Mandarino LJ. Mitochondrial dysfunction and insulin resistance from the outside in: extracellular matrix, the cytoskeleton, and mitochondria. American Journal of Physiology - Endocrinology and Metabolism. 2011;301(5), E749-E755. doi: 10.1152/ajpendo.00363.2011.

7. Christine Gorman, Alice Park and Kristina Dell. "Cellular Inflammation: The Secret Killer." Inflammation Research Foundation website. Accessed May 2016. http://www.inflammationresearchfoundation.org/inflammation-science/inflammation-details/time-cellular-inflammation-article/

8. Vogel RA, Corretti MC, Plotnick GD. Effect of a single high-fat meal on endothelial function in healthy subjects. American Journal of Cardiology. 1997;79(3):350-4.

9. Erridge C. The capacity of foodstuffs to induce innate immune activation of human monocytes in vitro is dependent on food content of stimulants of Toll-like receptors 2 and 4. British Journal of Nutrition. 2011; 105(1):15-23.

10. Greger, Michael. "Bowel Wars: Hydrogen Sulfide vs. Butyrate." Nutrition Facts. http://nutritionfacts.org/video/bowel-wars-hydrogen-sulfide-vs-butyrate/

11. "Anemia." New York Times website. Accessed May 2016. http://www.nytimes.com/health/guides/disease/anemia/risk-factors.html

12. "Micronutrient deficiencies." World Health Organization website. Accessed May 2016. http://www.who.int/nutrition/topics/ida/en/

13. Mangels, Reed. "Iron in the Vegan Diet." Vegetarians Resource Group website. Accessed May 2016. http://www.vrg.org/nutrition/iron.php

14. Davis, Brenda and Vesanto Melina. *Becoming Vegan: Comprehensive Edition.* Summertown, Tennessee: Book Publishing Company. 2014. Pg.186.

15. Cook JD. Adaptation in iron metabolism. American Journal of Clinical Nutrition. 1990;51(2):301-8.

16. Hurrell R, Egli I. Iron bioavailability and dietary reference values. American Journal of Clinical Nutrition. 2010;91(5):1461S-7S.

17. Anu Rahal, Amit Kumar, Vivek Singh, Brijesh Yadav, Ruchi Tiwari, Sandip Chakraborty, et al; Oxidative Stress, Prooxidants, and Antioxidants: The Interplay. BioMed Research International. 2014; Article ID 761264, 19 pages. doi: http://dx.doi.org/10.1155/2014/761264.

18. Yang W, Li B, Dong X, Zhang XQ, Zeng Y, Zhou JL, et al; Is heme iron intake associated with risk of coronary heart disease? A meta-analysis of prospective studies. European Journal of Nutrition. 2014;53(2):395-400. doi: 10.1007/s00394-013-0535-5. Hunnicutt J, He K, Xun P. Dietary iron intake and body iron stores are associated with risk of coronary heart disease in a meta-analysis of prospective cohort studies. Journal of Nutrition. 2014;144(3):359-66. doi: 10.3945/jn.113.185124.

19. Joanna Kaluza, Alicja Wolk, Susanna C. Larsson. Heme Iron Intake and Risk of Stroke, A Prospective Study of Men. Journal of the American Heart Association. 2013;44:334-339.

20. Bao W, Rong Y, Rong S, Liu L. Dietary iron intake, body iron stores, and the risk of type 2 diabetes: a systematic review and meta-analysis. BMC Medicine. 2012;10:119. doi: 10.1186/1741-7015-10-119.

21. Dixon, SJ, Stockwell BR. The role of iron and reactive oxygen species in cell death. Nature Chemical Biology. 2014;10(1):9-17.

22. Fonseca-Nunes A, Jakszyn P, Agudo A. Iron and cancer risk--a systematic review and meta-analysis of the epidemiological evidence. Cancer Epidemiology, Biomarkers & Prevention. 2014;23(1):12-3. doi: 10.1158/1055-9965.EPI-13-0733. Lam TK, Rotunno M, Ryan BM, Pesatori AC, Bertazzi PA, Spitz M, et al; Heme-related gene expression signatures of meat intakes in lung cancer tissues. Molecular Carcinogenesis. 2014;53(7):548-56. doi: 10.1002/mc.22006.

23. Carlsen MH, Halvorsen BL, Holte K, et al; The total antioxidant content of more than 3100 foods, beverages, spices, herbs and supplements used worldwide. Nutrition Journal. 2010 Jan 22, 9:3.

24. Mangels, Reed. "Iron in the Vegan Diet."

25. Ruscigno, Matt. "What Every Vegetarian Needs to Know About Iron." No Meat Athlete website. Accessed May 2016. http://www.nomeatathlete.com/iron-for-vegetarians/

26. Mangels, Reed. "Iron in the Vegan Diet."

27. Ruscigno, Matt. "What Every Vegetarian Needs to Know About Iron."

28. "Iron Deficiency Anemia: Nutritional Considerations." NutritionMD website. Accessed May 2016. http://www.nutritionmd.org/health_care_providers/hematology/ironanemia_nutrition.html

29. David LA, Maurice CF, Carmody RN, Gootenberg DB, Button JE, Wolfe BE, et al; Diet rapidly and reproducibly alters the human gut microbiome. Nature. 2014;505(7484):559-63. doi: 10.1038/nature12820.

30.   Appleby PN, Davey, GK, Key, TJ. Hypertension and blood pressure among meat eaters, fish eaters, vegetarians and vegans in EPIC-Oxford. Public Health Nutrition. 2002;5(5), 645-654. doi:10.1079/PHN2002332. ApplebyPN, Key TJ, Thorogood M, Burr ML and Mann J. Mortality in British Vegetarians. Public Health Nutrition. 2002;5(1), 29-36. doi: 10.1079/PHN2001248. Appleby PN, Thorogood M, Mann, JI, Key TJ. The Oxford Vegetarian Study: an overview. American Journal of Clinical Nutrition. 1999;70(3 Suppl0, 525S-531S. Appleby, PN, Thorogood M, McPherson K, Mann J. Associations between plasma lipid concentrations and dietary, lifestyle and physical factors in the Oxford Vegetarian Study. Journal of Human Nutrition and Dietetics.1995;8(5), 305-314.

31.   "Adventist Health Studies." Loma Linda University website. Accessed May 2016. http://publichealth.llu.edu/adventist-health-studies

32.   Nassauer, Sarah. "When the Box Says 'Protein,' Shoppers Say 'I'll Take It.'" Wall Street Journal website. Accessed May 2016. http://www.wsj.com/articles/SB10001 424127887324789504578384351639102798

33.   "Dietary Reference Intakes (DRIs): Acceptable Macronutrient Distribution Ranges." The National Academies Press website. Accessed May 2016. http://web.archive.org/web/20111112025848/http://www.nap.edu/openbook. php?record_id=10490&page=1325 "Protein Intake For Optimal Muscle Maintenance." American College of Sports Medicine website. Accessed May 2016. https://www.acsm.org/docs/default-source/brochures/protein-intake-for-optimal-muscle-maintenance.pdf. "Dietary Guidelines for Americans." GB Healthwatch website. Accessed May 2016. https://www.gbhealthwatch.com/Diet-Dietary-Guidelines-Americans.php

34.   "Protein Intake For Optimal Muscle Maintenance." American College of Sports Medicine website.

35.   "Table 1. Nutrient Intakes from Food: Mean Amounts Consumed per Individual1, by Gender and Age, in the United States, 2009-2010." United States Department of Agriculture website. Accessed May 2016. https://www.ars.usda.gov/ARSUserFiles/80400530/pdf/0910/Table_1_NIN_GEN_09.pdf

36.   "Increasing Fiber Intake." UCSF Medical Center website. Accessed May 2016. https://www.ucsfhealth.org/education/increasing_fiber_intake/

37.   Krashinsky, Susan. "Maple Leaf puts new face on processed meat with 'Protein Builds' campaign." Globe and Mail website. Accessed May 2016. http://www.theglobeandmail.com/report-on-business/industry-news/marketing/maple-leaf-puts-new-face-on-processed-meat-with-protein-builds-campaign/article27586562/

38.   Davis. *Becoming Vegan: Comprehensive Edition.* Pg. 97-103.

39.   Messina M. Soybean isoflavone exposure does not have feminizing effects on men: a critical examination of the clinical evidence. Fertility and Sterility. 2010;93(7):2095-104. doi: 10.1016/j.fertnstert.2010.03.002.

40.   Nechuta SJ, Caan BJ, Chen WY, et al; "Soy food intake after diagnosis of breast cancer and survival: an in-depth analysis of combined evidence from cohort studies of US and Chinese women." American Journal of Clinical Nutrition. 2012; 96:123-132.

41.   Shu XO, Zheng Y, Cai H, et al; "Soy food intake and breast cancer survival." Journal of American Medical Association. 2009; 302:2437-2443.

42.   Wu AH, Yu MC, Tseng CC, Pike MC. "Epidemiology of soy exposures and breast cancer risk." British Journal of Cancer. 2008;98:9-14.

43.   McCullough, Marji. "The Bottom Line on Soy and Breast Cancer Risk." American Cancer Society website. Accessed May 2016. http://blogs.cancer.org/expertvoices/2012/08/02/the-bottom-line-on-soy-and-breast-cancer-risk/

44.   "Marjorie McCullough, ScD Strategic Director, Nutritional Epidemiology." American Cancer Society website. Accessed May 2016. http://www.cancer.org/research/acsresearchers/marjorie-mccullough-scd

45.   McCullough. "The Bottom Line on Soy and Breast Cancer Risk."

46.   Hamilton-Reeves JM, Vazquez G, Duval SJ, Phipps WR, Kurzer MS, Messina MJ. Clinical studies show no effects of soy protein or isoflavones on reproductive hormones in men: results of a meta-analysis. Fertility and Sterility. 2010;94:997-1007.

47.   Yan L, Spitznagel EL. Soy consumption and prostate cancer risk in men: a revisit of a meta-analysis. American Journal of Clinical Nutrition. 2009;89:1155-1163.

48.   Greger, Michael. "How Much Soy Is Too Much?" NutritionFacts.org. Accessed May 2016. http://nutritionfacts.org/video/how-much-soy-is-too-much/

49.   "Top 10 Herbivores You Probably Want To Avoid." Listverse website. Accessed May 2016. http://listverse.com/2010/01/10/top-10-herbivores-you-probably-want-to-avoid/

50.   "These 10 Animals Are the Strongest Mammals on Earth." UdderlyPettable website. Accessed May 2016. http://udderlypettable.com/these-10-animals-are-the-strongest-mammals-on-earth/?fb_comment_id=834681149885639_10087522 12478531

51.   Novick, Jeff. "The Myth Of Complementing Proteins." Jeff Novick website. Accessed May 2016. http://www.jeffnovick.com/RD/Articles/Entries/2012/3/28_The_Myth_Of_Complimenting_Proteins.html

CHAPTER SIX: CANCER

1.   Eveleth, Rose. "There are 37.2 Trillion Cells in Your Body." Smithsonian website. Accessed May 2016. http://www.smithsonianmag.com/smart-news/there-are-372-trillion-cells-in-your-body-4941473/

2.   Campbell, T. Colin and Thomas M. Campbell II. *The China Study*. Dallas: BenBella Books. 2006. Pg. 48-49.

3.   Nielsen M, Thomsen JL, Primdahl S, Dyreborg U, Andersen JA. Breast cancer and atypia among young and middle-aged women: a study of 110 medicolegal autopsies. British Journal of Cancer. 1987;56(6):814-9.

4.   Campbell. *The China Study*. Pg.50.

5.   Popper. *Food Over Medicine*. Pg.75.

6.   Greger. *How Not to Die*. Pg.62.

7.   "Our History." American Institute for Cancer Research website. Accessed May 2016. http://www.aicr.org/about/about_history.html

8.   "Recommendations for Cancer Prevention." American Institute for Cancer Research website. Accessed May 2016. http://www.aicr.org/reduce-your-cancer-risk/recommendations-for-cancer-prevention/

9.   "Cancer prevention." World Health Organization website. Accessed May 2016. http://www.who.int/cancer/prevention/en/

10.   "Survey: Overwhelming Majority of Americans Are Not Living Cancer-Protective Lives - But Think They Are." American Institute for Cancer Research website. Accessed May 2016. http://www.aicr.org/press/press-releases/2016/Overwhelming_Majority_of_Americans_Not_Living_Cancer_Protective_Lives.html

11.   Wang H, Khor TO, Shu L, Su ZY, Fuentes F, Lee JH, Kong AN. Plants vs. cancer: a review on natural phytochemicals in preventing and treating cancers and their druggability. Anti-Cancer Agents in Medicinal Chemistry. 2012;12(10):1281-305. Steinmetz KA, Potter JD. Vegetables, fruit, and cancer. I. Epidemiology. Cancer Causes Control. 1991;2(5):325-57. Steinmetz KA, Potter JD.Vegetables, fruit, and cancer. II. Mechanisms. Cancer Causes Control.1991;2(6):427-42. Chu YF, Sun J, Wu X, Liu RH. Antioxidant and antiproliferative activities of common vegetables. Journal of Agricultural and Food Chemistry. 2002;50(23):6910-6. Lord-Dufour S, et al; Antiproliferative and antioxidant activities of common vegetables: a comparative study. Food Chemistry. 2009;112:374-380. Annema N, Heyworth JS, McNaughton SA, Iacopetta B, Fritschi L. Fruit and vegetable consumption and the risk of proximal colon, distal colon, and rectal cancers in a case-control study in Western Australia. Journal of the American Dietetic Association. 2011;111(10):1479-90. doi: 10.1016/j.jada.2011.07.008.

12.   Vucenik I, Shamsuddin AM. Protection against cancer by dietary IP6 and inositol. Nutrition and Cancer. 2006;55(2):109-25.

13.   Vucenik I, Shamsuddin AM. Cancer inhibition by inositol hexaphosphate (IP6) and inositol: from laboratory to clinic. Journal of Nutrition. 2003;133(11-Suppl-1):3778S—84S.

14.   Vucenik I, Shamsuddin AM. Protection against cancer by dietary IP6 and inositol. Nutrition and Cancer. 2006;55(2):109-25.

15.   World Cancer Research Fund/American Institute for Cancer Research. Food, Nutrition, Physical Activity, and the Prevention of Cancer: a Global Perspective. Washington, D.C.:AICR, 2007.

16.   Moshfegh A, Goldman J, Cleveland I. What We Eat in America. NHANES 2001-2002: Usual Nutrient Intakes from Food Compared to Dietary Reference Intakes. Washington, D.C.: US Department of Agriculture Agricultural Research Service; 2005.

17.   Li Q, Holford TR, Zhang Y, et al; Dietary fiber intake and risk of breast cancer by menopausal and estrogen receptor status. European Journal of Nutrition. 2013;52(1):217-23.

18.   Coleman HG, Murray LJ, Hicks B, et al. Dietary fiber and the risk of precancerous lesions and cancer of the esophagus: a systematic review and meta-analysis. Nutrition Reviews. 2013;71(7):474-82.

19.   Fuchs CS, Giovannucci EL, Colditz GA, et al; Dietary fiber and the risk of colorectal cancer and adenoma in women. New England Journal of Medicine.

1999;340:169-176. Avivi-Green C, Polak-Charcon S, Madar Z, et al; Apoptosis cascade proteins are regulated in vivo by high intracolonic butyrate concentration: correlation with colon cancer inhibition. Oncology Research. 2000;12:83-95.

20. World Cancer Research Fund/American Institute for Cancer Research. Food Nutrition, Physical Activity, and the Prevention of Cancer: a Global Perspective. Washington, D.C., AICR, 2007.

21. Boivin D, Lamy S, Lord-Dufour S, et al; Antiproliferative and antioxidant activities of common vegetables: a comparative study. Food Chemistry. 2009;112:374-380.

22. Ibid.

23. Ibid.

24. Santiago Ropero, Manel Esteller. The role of histone deacetylases (HDACs) in human cancer. Molecular Oncology. 2007;19–25. doi: http://dx.doi.org/10.1016/j.molonc.2007.01.001.

25. Dashwood RH, Ho E. Dietary histone deacetylase inhibitors: from cells to mice to man. Seminars in Cancer Biology. 2007;17(5):363-9. doi: 10.1016/j.semcancer.2007.04.001.

26. Cornblatt BS, Ye L, Dinkova-Kostova AT, et al; Preclinical and clinical evaluation of sulforaphane for chemoprevention in the breast. Carcinogenesis. 2007;28(7):1485-90.

27. Benaron DA, Cheong WF, Stevenson DK. Tissue Optics. Science.1997;276(5321):2002-2003.

28. Jubert C, Mata J, Bench G, et al; Effects of chlorophyll and chlorophyllin on low-dose aflatoxin B(1) pharmacokinetics in human volunteers. Cancer Prevention Research. 2009;2(12):1015-22.

29. Annema N, Heyworth JS, McNaughton SA, Iacopetta B, Fritschi L. Fruit and vegetable consumption and the risk of proximal colon, distal colon, and rectal cancers in a case-control study in Western Australia. Journal of the American Dietetic Association. 2011;111(10):1479-90. doi: 10.1016/j.jada.2011.07.008.

30. Boivin D, Lamy S, Lord-Dufour S, et al; Antiproliferative and antioxidant activities of common vegetables: a comparative study. Food Chemistry. 2009;112:374-380.

31. Ornish D, Weidner G, Fair WR, et al; Intensive lifestyle changes may affect the progression of prostate cancer. Journal of Urology. 2005;174(3):1065-9; discussion 1069-70.

32. Barnard RJ, Gonzalez JH, Liva ME, Ngo TH. Effects of a low-fat, high-fiber diet and exercise program on breast cancer risk factors in vivo and tumor cell growth and apoptosis in vitro. Nutrition and Cancer. 2006;55(1):28-34. doi: 10.1207/s15327914nc5501_4.

CHAPTER SEVEN: MILK

1. Waters, Kalyn. "Factors Affecting Birth Weight." iGrow website. March 25, 2013. Accessed May 2016. http://igrow.org/livestock/beef/factors-affecting-birth-weight/

2. "How much do cows weigh?" Dairy Moos blog. August 18, 2013. Accessed May 2016. http://www.dairymoos.com/how-much-do-cows-weight/

3. "Why are Calves Separated from their Mothers at Such a Young Age?" This is Dairy Farming website. Accessed May 2016. http://www.thisisdairyfarming.com/discover/dairy-farming-facts/why-are-calves-separated-from-their-mothers-at-such-a-young-age/. "4.0 After the Calf is Born." Food and Agriculture Organization of the United Nations website. Accessed May 2016. http://www.fao.org/ag/agp/AGPC/doc/Publicat/PUB6/P604.htm.

4. "Today's Veal." Veal Farm website. Accessed May 2016. http://www.vealfarm.com/veal-farming/

5. "Cattle Raised for Dairy and Meat Production." Farm Sanctuary website. Accessed May 2016. https://www.farmsanctuary.org/learn/factory-farming/dairy/#

6. "4.0 After the Calf is Born." Food and Agriculture Organization of the United Nations website. Accessed May 2016. http://www.fao.org/ag/agp/AGPC/doc/Publicat/PUB6/P604.htm

7. Kurlansky, Mark. "Inside the Milk Machine: How Modern Dairy Works." Modern Farmer website. March 17, 2014. Accessed May 2016. http://modernfarmer.com/2014/03/real-talk-milk/

8. Colb, Sherry F. *Mind if I Order the Cheeseburger?* New York: Lantern Books. 2013. Pg. 41-43.

9. Ireland, Corydon. "Hormones in milk can be dangerous." Harvard Gazette website. December 7, 2006. Accessed May 2016. http://news.harvard.edu/gazette/story/2006/12/hormones-in-milk-can-be-dangerous/

10. Maruyama K, Oshima T, Ohyama K. Exposure to exogenous estrogen through intake of commercial milk produced from pregnant cows. Pediatrics International. 2010;52(1):33-8. doi: 10.1111/j.1442-200X.2009.02890.x.

11. Kroenke CH, Kwan ML, Sweeney C, Castillo A, Caan BJ. High- and low-fat dairy intake, recurrence, and mortality after breast cancer diagnosis. The Journal of the National Cancer Institute. 2013;105(9):616-23. doi: 10.1093/jnci/djt027.

12. Ganmaa D, Cui X, Feskanich D, Hankinson SE, Willett WC. Milk, dairy intake and risk of endometrial cancer: a 26-year follow-up. International Journal of Cancer. 2012;130(11):2664-71. doi: 10.1002/ijc.26265.

13. Maruyama K1, Oshima T, Ohyama K. Exposure to exogenous estrogen through intake of commercial milk produced from pregnant cows. Pediatrics International. 2010;52(1):33-8. doi: 10.1111/j.1442-200X.2009.02890.x.

14. Popper. *Food Over Medicine.* Pg. 77.

15. Ireland, Corydon. "Hormones in milk can be dangerous." Harvard Gazette website. December 7, 2006. Accessed May 2016. http://news.harvard.edu/gazette/story/2006/12/hormones-in-milk-can-be-dangerous/

16. Kroenke CH, Kwan ML, Sweeney C, Castillo A, Caan BJ. High- and low-fat dairy intake, recurrence, and mortality after breast cancer diagnosis. Journal of the National Cancer Institute. 2013;105(9):616-23. doi: 10.1093/jnci/djt027. Outwater JL, Nicholson A, Barnard N. Dairy products and breast cancer: the IGF-I, estrogen, and bGH hypothesis. Medical Hypotheses. 1997;48(6):453-61.

17. Ganmaa D, Cui X, Feskanich D. Milk, dairy intake and risk of endometrial cancer: a 26-year follow-up.

18. Kurahashi N, Inoue M, Iwasaki M, et al; Dairy product, saturated fatty acid, and calcium intake and prostate cancer in a prospective cohort of Japanese men.

Cancer Epidemiol Biomarkers Prevent. 2008;17(4):930-37. Rohrmann S1, Platz EA, Kavanaugh CJ, et al; Meat and dairy consumption and subsequent risk of prostate cancer in a US cohort study. Cancer Causes & Control. 2007;18(1):41-50.

19. Davies TW, Palmer CR, Ruja E, Lipscombe JM. Adolescent milk, dairy product and fruit consumption and testicular cancer. British Journal of Cancer. 1996;74(4):657-60.

20. Larsson SC, Bergkvist L, Wolk A. Milk and lactose intakes and ovarian cancer risk in the Swedish Mammography Cohort. American Journal of Clinical Nutrition. 2004;80:1353–1357.

21. Keszei AP, Shoutin LJ, Goldbohm RA, et al; Dairy intake and the risk of bladder cancer in the Netherlands Cohort Study on Diet and Cancer. American Journal of Epidemiology. 2010; 171(4):436-46. doi: 10.1093/aje/kwp399.

22. van der Pols JC, Bain C, Gunnell D, et al; Childhood dairy intake and adult cancer risk: 65-y follow-up of the Boyd Orr cohort. American Journal of Clinical Nutrition. 2007;86(6):1722-9.

23. Karpf, Anne. "Dairy monsters." The Guardian website. December 12, 2003. Accessed May 2016. https://www.theguardian.com/lifeandstyle/2003/dec/13/foodanddrink.weekend.

24. Campbell. *The China Study.*

25. Brody, Jane. "Huge Study Of Diet Indicts Fat And Meat." New York Times website. May 8, 1990. Accessed May 2016. http://www.nytimes.com/1990/05/08/science/huge-study-of-diet-indicts-fat-and-meat.html?pagewanted=all

26. Voskuil DW, Vieling A, Van't Veer LJ, Kampman E, Rookus MA. The insulin-like growth factor system in cancer prevention: potential of dietary intervention strategies. Cancer Epidemiology, Biomarkers & Prevention. 2005;14(1):195-203. Cohen P. Serum insulin-like growth factor 1 levels and prostate cancer risk— interpreting the evidence. Journal of the National Cancer Institute. 1998(90):876-79. Chan JM, Stampfer MJ, Giovannucci E, et al; Plasma insulin-like growth factor-1 and prostate risk: a prospective study. Science. 1998(279):563-65.

27. Hicks, Cherrill. "Give up dairy products to beat cancer." Telegraph website. June 2, 2014. Accessed May 2016. http://www.telegraph.co.uk/foodanddrink/healthyeating/10868428/Give-up-dairy-products-to-beat-cancer.html

28. Ganmaa D, Li XM, Wang J, Qin LQ, et al; Incidence and mortality of testicular and prostatic cancers in relation to world dietary practices. International Journal of Cancer. 2002;98(2):262-7.

29. Chan JM, Stampfer MJ, Ma J, et al; Dairy products, calcium, and prostate cancer risk in the Physicians' Health Study. American Journal of Clinical Nutrition. 2001;74(4):549-54.

30. "All About the Dairy Group." United States Department of Agriculture website. Accessed May 2016. https://www.choosemyplate.gov/dairy

31. "Suggested Servings from Each Food Group." American Heart Association website. Accessed May 2016. http://www.heart.org/HEARTORG/HealthyLiving/HealthyEating/HealthyDietGoals/Suggested-Servings-from-Each-Food-Group_UCM_318186_Article.jsp#.WEc5vuErLHd

32. Bosetti C, Tzonou A, Lagiou P, et al; Fraction of prostate cancer attributed to diet in Athens, Greece. European Journal of Cancer Prevention. 2000;9(2):119-23.

Tseng M, Breslow RA, Graubard BI, Ziegler RG. Dairy, calcium and vitamin D intakes an dprostate cancer risk in the National Health and Nutrition Examination Epidemiologic Follow-up Study cohort. American Journal of Clinical Nutrition. 2005;(81)1147-54. Park S, Murphy S, Wilkens L, Stram D, et al; Calcium, vitamin D, and dairy product intake and prostate cancer risk: the Multiethnic Cohort Study. American Journal of Epidemiology. 2007;166(11) 1259-69. Qin LQ, Xu JY, Wang PY, Kaneko T, Hoshi K, Sato A. Milk consumption is a risk factor for prostsate cancer: meta-analysis of case-control studies. Nutrition and Cancer. 2004;48(1):22-7. Qin LQ, Xu JY, Wang PY, Tong J, Hoshi K. Milk consumption is a risk factor for prostate cancer in Western countries: evidence from cohort studies. Asia Pacific Journal of Clinical Nutrition. 2007;16(3):467-76. Aune D, Navarro Rosenblatt DA, Chan DS, et al; Dairy products, calcium, and prostate cancer risk: a systematic review and meta-analysis of cohort studies. American Journal of Clinical Nutrition. 2015;101(1):87-117.

33. "Key statistics for prostate cancer." American Cancer Society website. Accessed May 2016. http://www.cancer.org/cancer/prostatecancer/detailedguide/prostate-cancer-key-statistics

34. Tate PL, Bibb R, Larcom LL. Milk stimulates growth of prostate cancer cells in culture. Nutrition and Cancer. 2011;63(8):1361-6.

35. Maruyama K, Oshima T, Ohyama K. Exposure to exogenous estrogen through intake of commercial milk produced from pregnant cows. Pediatrics International. 2010;52(1):33-8. doi: 10.1111/j.1442-200X.2009.02890.x.

36. Afeiche M, Williams PL, Mendiola J, et al; Dairy food intake in relation to semen quality and reproductive hormone levels among physically active young men. Human Reproduction. 2013;(8):2265-75. doi: 10.1093/humrep/det133.

37. Kroenke CH, Kwan ML, Sweeney C, et al; High- and low-fat dairy intake, recurrence, and mortality after breast cancer diagnosis. Journal of the National Cancer Institute. 2013;105(9):616-23. doi: 10.1093/jnci/djt027. Outwater JL, Nicholson A, Barnard N. Dairy products and breast cancer: the IGF-I, estrogen, and bGH hypothesis. Medical Hypotheses. 1997;48(6):453-61.

38. Ganmaa D, Cui X, Feskanich D. Milk, dairy intake and risk of endometrial cancer: a 26-year follow-up.

39. Kushi LH, Mink PJ, Folsom AR, et al; Prospective study of diet and ovarian cancer. American Journal of Epidemiology. 1999;149(1):21-31.

40. Larsson SC, Bergkvist L, Wolk A. Milk and lactose intakes and ovarian cancer risk in the Swedish Mammography Cohort. American Journal of Clinical Nutrition. 2004;80:1353–1357.

41. "Survival rates for ovarian cancer, by stage." American Cancer Society website. Accessed May 2016. http://www.cancer.org/cancer/ovariancancer/detailedguide/ovarian-cancer-survival-rates

42. Borges, Michael. "Strontium for bone health." Dr. Ronald Hoffman website. October 4, 2013. Accessed May 2016. http://drhoffman.com/article/strontium-for-bone-health-2/

43. "Dioxins & Furans: The Most Toxic Chemicals Known to Science." EJnet.org: Web Resources for Environmental Justice Activists. Accessed May 2016. http://www.ejnet.org/dioxin/

44. "Eating. Drinking. Touching. Breathing. Nursing. Conceiving." Agent Orange Record website. Accessed May 2016. http://www.agentorangerecord.com/impact_on_vietnam/health/

45. "Chlorine Gone Wild." Agent Orange Record website. Accessed May 2016. http://www.agentorangerecord.com/information/what_is_dioxin/

46. "Dioxins & Furans: The Most Toxic Chemicals Known to Science." EJnet.org: Web Resources for Environmental Justice Activists.

47. Soneda S, Fukami M, Fujimoto M, et al; Association of micropenis with Pro185Ala polymorphism of the gene for aryl hydrocarbon receptor repressor involved in dioxin signaling. Endocrine Journal. 2005;52(1):83-8. Dold, Catherine. "Hormone Hell." Discover Magazine website. September 1, 1996. Accessed May 2016. http://discovermagazine.com/1996/sep/hormonehell865. "Hormone Facts." Sex Love and Hormones website. Accessed May 2016. http://www.sexloveandhormones.com/facts.htm

48. Cashin-Garbutt, April. "What is a Micropenis?" News Medical Life Sciences website. Accessed May 2016. http://www.news-medical.net/health/What-is-Micropenis.aspx

49. "Dioxins & Furans: The Most Toxic Chemicals Known to Science." EJnet.org: Web Resources for Environmental Justice Activists.

50. "Dioxins and their effects on human health." World Health Organization website. Accessed May 2016. http://www.who.int/mediacentre/factsheets/fs225/en/

51. Ibid.

52. Kanthasamy AG, Kitazawa M, Kanthasamy A, Anantharam V. Dieldrin-induced neurotoxicity: relevance to Parkinson's disease pathogenesis. Neurotoxicology. 2005;26(4):701-19. "Polychlorinated Biphenyls (PCBs)." Illinois Department of Public Health website. Accessed May 2016. http://www.idph.state.il.us/envhealth/factsheets/polychlorinatedbiphenyls.htm

53. Richardson JR, Shalat SL, Buckley B, et al; Elevated serum pesticide levels and risk of Parkinson disease. Archives of Neurology and Psychiatry. 2009;66(7):870-5. Corrigan FM, Wienburg CL, Shore RF, Daniel SE, Mann D. Organochlorine insecticides in substantia nigra in Parkinson's disease. Journal of Toxicology Environmental Health, Part A. 2000;59(4):229-34. Hatcher-Martin JM, Gearing M, Steenland K, Level AI, Miller GW, Pennell KD. Association between polychlorinated biphenyls and Parkinson's disease neuropathology. Neurotoxicology. 2012;33(5):1298-304.

54. "What is Parkinson's Disease?" Parkinson's Disease Foundation website. Accessed May 2016. http://www.pdf.org/about_pd

55. Jiang W, Ju C, Jiang H, Zhang D. Dairy foods intake and risk of Parkinson's disease: a close-response meta-analysis of prospective cohort studies. European Journal of Epidemiology. 2014;29(9):613-9.

56. Park M, Ross GW, Petrovitch H, et al; Consumption of milk and calcium in midlife and the future risk of Parkinson disease. Neurology. 2005;64(6):1047-51.

57. Ulamek-Koziol M, Bogucka-Kocka A, Kocki J, Pluta R. Good and bad sides of diet in Parkinson's disease. Nutrition. 2013;29(2):474-5.

58. Kurlansky, Mark. "Inside the Milk Machine: How Modern Dairy Works."

59. "Mastitis in Diary Cows." Agriculture and Horticulture Development Board website. Accessed May 2016. https://dairy.ahdb.org.uk/technical-information/animal-health-welfare/mastitis/#.WEdAbeErLHe

60. "Mastits Control." Food and Agriculture Organization of the United Nations website. Accessed May 2016. http://www.fao.org/docrep/004/t0218e/T0218E04.htm

61. "Dairy 2007 Part II: Changes in the U.S. Dairy Cattle Industry, 1991–2007." U.S. Department of Agriculture's Animal and Plant Health Inspection Service website. Accessed May 2016. https://www.aphis.usda.gov/animal_health/nahms/dairy/downloads/dairy07/Dairy07_dr_PartII_rev.pdf

62. "Questions about milk quality: What is the difference between clinical and subclinical mastitis." Progressive Dairy Man website. Accessed may 2016. http://www.progressivedairy.com/topics/herd-health/questions-about-milk-quality-what-is-the-difference-between-clinical-and-subclinical-mastitis

63. "Mastitis and Somatic Cells." Milk Facts website. Accessed May 2016. http://milkfacts.info/Milk%20Microbiology/Mastitis%20and%20SCC.htm

64. "Mastitis in Cattle." Merck Veterinary Manual website. Accessed May 2016. http://www.merckvetmanual.com/mvm/reproductive_system/mastitis_in_large_animals/mastitis_in_cattle.html

65. "Questions about milk quality: What is the difference between clinical and subclinical mastitis." Progressive Dairy Man website.

66. Marcus, Erik. *Vegan: The New Ethics of Eating.* Ithaca: McBooks Press. 2001. Pg.127.

67. "Questions about milk quality: What is the difference between clinical and subclinical mastitis." Progressive Dairy Man website.

68. "Somatic Cell Count—Milk Quality Indicator." Agriculture and Horticulture Development Board website. Accessed May 2016. https://dairy.ahdb.org.uk/technical-information/animal-health-welfare/mastitis/symptoms-of-mastitis/somatic-cell-count-milk-quality-indicator/#.WEdDxOErLHd

69. Nordqvist, Christian. "Pus - What Is Pus?" Medical News Today website. August 4, 2015. Accessed May 2016. http://www.medicalnewstoday.com/articles/249182.php

70. "UV Milk Quality" University of Wisconsin–Madison website. Accessed May 2016. http://milkquality.wisc.edu/

71. "2010 Bulk Tank SCC Data." National Mastitis Council website. Accessed May 2016. http://nmconline.org/articles/USDA_SCC_2010.htm

72. Torres, Bob and Jenna Torres. *Vegan Freak.* Oakland: PM Press. 2010. Pg.27.

73. "Cheese Is Number-One Source of Artery-Clogging Fat in American Diet." Center for Science in the Public Interest website. February 6, 2001. Accessed May 2016. https://cspinet.org/new/cheese.html

74. Fuhrman, Joel. *Eat to Live.* New York: Little, Brown, and Company. 2011. Pg.182.

75. Torres. *Vegan Freak.* Pg.28.

76. Becker, RA. "For a Healthy Heart, You May Have to Eat More Cheese." PBS website. April 2015. Accessed May 2016. http://www.pbs.org/wgbh/nova/next/body/for-a-healthy-heart-you-may-have-to-eat-more-cheese/.

77. Phillip, Abby. "Study: Milk may not be very good for bones or the body." Washington Post website. October 31, 2014. Accessed May 2016.

https://www.washingtonpost.com/news/to-your-health/wp/2014/10/31/study-milk-may-not-be-very-good-for-bones-or-the-body/

78.   Fuhrman. *Eat to Live*. Pg.99.

79.   Ibid. Pg.98.

80.   Lohan, Tara. "Got Milk? A Disturbing Look at the Dairy Industry." AlterNet website. January 25, 2010. Accessed May 2016. http://www.alternet.org/story/145378/got_milk_a_disturbing_look_at_the_dairy_industry

81.   Pacific Vegan. "Colleen Patrick-Goudreau: Debunking the Myths of Veganism." Filmed [April 2013]. Youtube video. Posted [April 2013]. https://www.youtube.com/watch?v=od_cqvr-ueY

82.   Fuhrman. *Eat to Live*. Pg.145.

83.   "What is Osteoporosis and What Causes It?" National Osteoporosis Foundation website. Accessed May 2016. https://www.nof.org/patients/what-is-osteoporosis/

84.   "What Is Osteoporosis? Fast Facts: An Easy-to-Read Series of Publications for the Public." National Institute of Health website. Accessed May 2016. https://www.niams.nih.gov/health_info/bone/osteoporosis/osteoporosis_ff.asp

85.   Campbell. *The China Study*. Pg. 205.

86.   Frassetto LA, Todd KM, Morris C, Jr., et al; Worldwide incidence of hip fracture in elderly women: relation to consumption of animal and vegetable foods. Journal of Gerontology. 2000; 55: M585-M592.

87.   Campbell. *The China Study*. Pg. 204.

88.   Frassetto LA. Worldwide incidence of hip fracture in elderly women: relation to consumption of animal and vegetable foods.

89.   Feskanich D, Willett WC, Colditz GA. Calcium, vitamin D, milk consumption, and hip fractures: a prospective study among postmenopausal women. American Journal of Clinical Nutrition. 2003;77:504–511.

90.   Sonneville KR, Gordon CM, Kocher MS, Pierce LM, Ramappa A, Field AE. Vitamin D, calcium, and dairy intakes and stress fractures among female adolescents. The Archives of Pediatrics & Adolescent Medicine. 2012;166:595-600. Lanou AJ, Berkow SE, Barnard ND. Calcium, dairy products, and bone health in children and young adults: a reevaluation of the evidence. Pediatrics. 2005;115:736–743.

CHAPTER EIGHT: EGGS

1.   Heather J. Baer, Robert J. Glynn, Frank B. Hu, et al; Risk Factors for Mortality in the Nurses' Health Study: A Competing Risks Analysis. American Journal of Epidemiology. 2011; 173 (3): 319-329. doi: 10.1093/aje/kwq368.

2.   J. David Spence, David J.A. Jenkins, Jean Davignon. "Egg yolk consumption and carotid plaque." Atherosclerosis. 2012; 469–473. doi: http://dx.doi.org/10.1016/j.atherosclerosis.2012.07.032.

3.   Winter, Michael. "Cigarette firms must run ads saying they lied." USA Today website. November 27, 2012. Accessed May 2016. http://www.usatoday.com/story/news/nation/2012/11/27/judge-orders-tobacco-ads-declaring-deception/1730211/ "Tobacco Explained." World Health Organization website. Accessed May 2016.

http://www.who.int/tobacco/media/en/TobaccoExplained.pdf Suzaynn F Schick and Stanton A Glantz. Old ways, new means: tobacco industry funding of academic and private sector scientists since the Master Settlement Agreement. Tobacco Control. 2007; 16(3): 157–164. doi: 10.1136/tc.2006.017186

4. "National Commission on Egg Nutrition v. Federal Trade Commission." June 17, 1977. http://openjurist.org/570/f2d/157/national-commission-on-egg-nutrition-v-federal-trade-commission "Letters to the Editor." Dr. McDougall's Health & Medical Center website. Accessed May 2016. https://www.drmcdougall.com/misc/2016nl/jan/cholesterolstamler.pdf

5. "National Commission on Egg Nutrition v. Federal Trade Commission." June 17, 1977.

6. "Eggland's Best Cholesterol Claims Called Deceptive." Federal Trade Commission website. March 13, 1996. Accessed May 2016. https://www.ftc.gov/news-events/press-releases/1996/03/egglands-best-cholesterol-claims-called-deceptive Walsh, Sharon. "Eggland's Best Settles FTC False Advertising Charges." Washington Post website. March 14, 1996. Accessed May 2016. https://www.washingtonpost.com/archive/business/1996/03/14/egglands-best-settles-ftc-false-advertising-charges/049c9156-8472-4a21-832a-dd17aa99d65d/?utm_term=.4dd41e6954a9

7. Greger, Michael. "Who Says Eggs Aren't Healthy or Safe?" NutritionFacts.org. February 17, 2014. Accessed May 2016. http://nutritionfacts.org/video/who-says-eggs-arent-healthy-or-safe/

8. Ibid.

9. "American Egg Board 2009 Annual Report." American Egg Board website. Accessed May 2016. http://www.aeb.org/images/website/documents/about-aeb/annual-report/annual-report_2008.pdf

10. "An Egg a Day is More Than Ok!" American Egg Board website. 2008. Accessed May 2016. http://www.aeb.org/images/website/documents/retailers/eggstra-newsletter/Eggstra-Fall-2008.pdf

11. Ibid.

12. Matthew Boyle and Paul Jarvis. "Unilever Spreads Split Boosts Chance of Exit as Shares Gain." Bloomberg website. December 4, 2014. Accessed May 2016. https://www.bloomberg.com/news/articles/2014-12-04/unilever-plans-to-split-spreads-business-into-standalone-unit

13. Bercovici, Jeff. "Avian Flu Is the Best Thing That Ever Happened to This Startup." Inc website. Accessed May 2016. http://www.inc.com/jeff-bercovici/hampton-creek-avian-flu.html

14. Kaplan, Sarah. "How little 'Just Mayo' took on Big Egg and won." Washington Post website. December 18, 2015. Accessed May 2016. https://www.washingtonpost.com/news/morning-mix/wp/2015/12/18/how-little-just-mayo-took-on-big-egg-and-won/

15. Sam Thielman and Dominic Rushe. "Government-backed egg lobby tried to crack food startup, emails show." The Guardian website. September 2, 2015. Accessed May 2016. https://www.theguardian.com/us-news/2015/sep/02/usda-american-egg-board-hampton-creek-just-mayo

16. Thielman, Sam. "Experts scramble to defend and denounce US dietary guidelines on eggs." The Guardian website. January 9, 2016. Accessed

May 2016. https://www.theguardian.com/lifeandstyle/2016/jan/09/eggs-new-us-dietary-guidelines-cholesterol

17. Luc Djoussé and J Michael Gaziano. Egg consumption in relation to cardiovascular disease and mortality: the Physicians' Health Study. American Journal of Clinical Nutrition. 2008; vol. 87 no. 4 964-969.

18. Katz, David L., Joseph Gnanaraj, Judith A. Treu, et al; Effects of egg ingestion on endothelial function in adults with coronary artery disease: A randomized, controlled, crossover trial. American Heart Journal. 2015; Volume 169, Issue 1, 162–169. doi: http://dx.doi.org/10.1016/j.ahj.2014.10.001

19. "American Egg Board 2009 Annual Report." American Egg Board website. Accessed May 2016. http://www.aeb.org/images/website/documents/about-aeb/annual-report/annual-report_2008.pdf

20. Dubois C, Armand M, Mekki N, et al; Effects of increasing amounts of dietary cholesterol on postprandial lipemia and lipoproteins in human subjects. Journal of Lipid Research. 1994;35(11):1993-2007.

21. Frank M. Sacks, Lynn Miller, Michael Sutherland. Ingestion of egg raises plasma low density lipoproteins in free-living subjects. The Lancet.1984; Volume 323, No. 8378, 647–649.

22. J. David Spence, David J.A. Jenkins, Jean Davignon. Egg yolk consumption, smoking and carotid plaque: Reply to letters to the Editor by Sean Lucan and T Dylan Olver et al. Atherosclerosis. 2013; 227, Issue 1, 189–191. doi: http://dx.doi.org/10.1016/j.atherosclerosis.2012.10.075.

23. C J Fielding, R J Havel, K M Todd. Effects of dietary cholesterol and fat saturation on plasma lipoproteins in an ethnically diverse population of healthy young men. Journal of Clinical Investigation. 1995; 95(2): 611–618. doi: 10.1172/JCI117705.

24. "Making Sense of Food." Nutrition MD website. Accessed May 2016. http://www.nutritionmd.org/nutrition_tips/nutrition_tips_understand_foods/cholesterol_lowering.html

25. "Top Food Sources of Cholesterol Among U.S. Population, 2005-06 NHANES." National Institute of Health website. Accessed May 2016. https://epi.grants.cancer.gov/diet/foodsources/cholesterol/table1.html

26. Greger, Michael. How the Egg Board Designs Misleading Studies. NutritionFacts.org. September 12, 2014. Accessed May 2016. http://nutritionfacts.org/video/how-the-egg-board-designs-misleading-studies/

27. "About the U.S. Egg Industry." American Egg Board website. Accessed May 2016. http://www.aeb.org/farmers-and-marketers/industry-overview

28. "GLOBAL POULTRY TRENDS - Egg Consumption Continues to Grow in Americas." The Poultry Site. March 2015. Accessed May 2016. http://www.thepoultrysite.com/articles/3395/global-poultry-trends-egg-consumption-continues-to-grow-in-americas/

29. Djousse L, Gaziano JM. Egg consumption in relation to cardiovascular disease and mortality: the Physicians' Health Study. American Journal of Clinical Nutrition. 2008;87:964-969. Qureshi AI, Suri FK, Ahmed S, et al. Regular egg consumption does not increase the risk of stroke and cardiovascular diseases. Medical Science Monitor. 2007;13:CR1-8. Hu FB, Stampfer MJ, Rimm EB, et al. A prospective study

of egg consumption and risk of cardiovascular disease in men and women. Journal of the American Medical Association.1999;281:1387-1394.

30. A. Trichopoulou, T. Psaltopoulou, P. Orfanos. Diet and physical activity in relation to overall mortality amongst adult diabetics in a general population cohort. 2006; 583–591. doi: 10.1111/j.1365-2796.2006.01638.x

31. "Facts and Statistics." Zero Cancer website. Accessed May 2016. https://zerocancer.org/learn/about-prostate-cancer/facts-statistics/

32. Erin L Richman, Meir J Stampfer, Alan Paciorek. Intakes of meat, fish, poultry, and eggs and risk of prostate cancer progression. American Journal of Clinical Nutrition. 2010; 91 no. 3 712-721. doi: 10.3945/ajcn.2009.28474.

33. Mattias Johansson, Bethany Van Guelpen, Stein Emil Vollset, et al; One-Carbon Metabolism and Prostate Cancer Risk: Prospective Investigation of Seven Circulating B Vitamins and Metabolites. Cancer Epidemiology, Biomarkers & Prevention. 2009; Volume 18, Issue 5. doi: 10.1158/1055-9965.EPI-08-1193.

34. Erin L Richman, Stacey A Kenfield, Meir J Stampfer. Choline intake and risk of lethal prostate cancer: incidence and survival. American Journal of Clinical Nutrition. 2012; vol. 96 no. 4 855-863. doi: 10.3945/ajcn.112.039784.

35. Erin L. Richman, Stacey A. Kenfield, Meir J. Stampfer, et al; Egg, Red Meat, and Poultry Intake and Risk of Lethal Prostate Cancer in the Prostate-Specific Antigen-Era: Incidence and Survival. Cancer Prevention Research. 2011; Volume 4, Issue 12. doi: 10.1158/1940-6207.

36. Tang WH, Wang Z, Levison BS, et al; Intestinal microbial metabolism of phosphatidylcholine and cardiovascular risk. New England Journal of Medicine. 2013;368(17):1575-84.

37. Koeth RA, Wang Z, Levison BS et al; Intestinal microbiota metabolism of L-carnitine, a nutrient in red meat, promotes atherosclerosis. Nature Medicine. 2013;19:576-85.

38. Tang WH, Wang Z, Levison BS, et al; Intestinal microbial metabolism of phosphatidylcholine and cardiovascular risk. New England Journal of Medicine. 2013;368(17):1575-84. doi: 10.1056/NEJMoa1109400.

39. Ibid.

40. Hayward DG, Nortrup D, Gardner A, Clower M. Elevated TCDD in chicken eggs and farm-raised catfish fed a diet with ball clay from a Southern United States mine. Environmental Research. 1999;81(3):248-56.

41. Aune D, De Stefani E, Ronco AL, et al; Egg consumption and the risk of cancer: a multisite case-control study in Uruguay. Asian Pacific Journal of Cancer Prevention. 2009;10(5):869-76.

42. Hoogenboom LA, Kan CA, Zeilmaker MJ. Carry-over of dioxins and PCBs from feed and soil to eggs at low contamination levels-- influence of mycotoxin binders on the carry-over from feed to eggs. Food Additives and Contaminants. 2006;23(5):518-27. doi: 10.1080/02652030500512037.

43. "Salmonella Technical Information." Centers for Disease Control and Prevention website. Accessed May 2016. http://www.cdc.gov/salmonella/general/technical.html

44.   "Salmonella is a Sneaky Germ: Seven Tips for Safer Eating." Centers for Disease Control and Prevention website. Accessed May 2016. http://www.cdc.gov/features/vitalsigns/foodsafety/

45.   "Transmission of Salmonella Bacteria." About Salmonella website. Accessed May 2016. http://www.about-salmonella.com/salmonella_transmission/#.WEdbzuErLeS

46.   Brown, David. "Egg-loving salmonella bacteria have been sickening people for decades." Washington Post website. September 14, 2010. Accessed May 2016. http://www.washingtonpost.com/wp-dyn/content/article/2010/09/13/AR2010091303594.html

47.   "Transmission of Salmonella Bacteria." About Salmonella website. Accessed May 2016. http://www.about-salmonella.com/salmonella_transmission/#.WEdbzuErLeS

48.   Brown, David. "Egg-loving salmonella bacteria have been sickening people for decades." Washington Post website.

49.   "Largest Egg Recall in US History Brings Renewed Attention to Dangers of Industrial Farming." Democracy Now! website. August 2010. Accessed May 2016. https://www.democracynow.org/2010/8/24/largest_egg_recall_in_us_history

50.   Brown, David. "Egg-loving salmonella bacteria have been sickening people for decades." Washington Post website.

51.   "Symptoms of Salmonella Infection." About Salmonella website. Accessed May 2016. http://www.about-salmonella.com/salmonella_symptoms_risks/#.WEdcuOErLeR

52.   "Largest Egg Recall in History Exposes Cracks in Egg Oversight." Center for Science in the Public Interest website. August 19, 2010. Accessed May 2016. https://cspinet.org/new/201008191.html

53.   T.J. Humphrey, M. Greenwood, R.J. Gilbert, et al; The survival of salmonellas in shell eggs cooked under simulated domestic conditions. Epidemiology and Infection. 1989;103, 35-45.

54.   A. L. Davis, P. A. Curtis, D. E. Conner, S. R. McKee, et al; Validation of Cooking Methods Using Shell Eggs Inoculated with Salmonella Serotypes Enteritidis and Heidelberg. Poultry Science. 2008; 87 (8): 1637-1642. doi: 10.3382/ps.2007-00419.

Chapter Nine: Fish

1.   "Omega-3 Fatty Acids: An Essential Contribution." Harvard T.H. Chan School of Public Health website. Accessed May 2016. https://www.hsph.harvard.edu/nutritionsource/omega-3-fats/

2.   Bakalar, Nicholas. "Fish as Brain Food." New York Times website. August 20, 2014. Accessed May 2016. http://well.blogs.nytimes.com/2014/08/20/fish-as-brain-food/?_r=1

3.   Fuhrman. *Eat to Live*. Pg.170.

4.   "Mercury and Health." World Health Organization website. Accessed May 2016. http://www.who.int/mediacentre/factsheets/fs361/en/. Cruz, Gilbert. "Minamata Disease." TIME website. May 3, 2010. Accessed May 2016. http://content.time.com/time/specials/packages/article/0,28804,1986457_1986501_1986450,00.html

5. "Mercury poisoning from fish." Consumer Reports website. August 2014. Accessed May 2016. http://www.consumerreports.org/cro/magazine/2014/10/sick-from-sushi/index.htm Guida, Tony. "Study finds unsafe mercury levels in 84 percent of all fish." CBS website. January 13, 2013. Accessed May 2016. http://www.cbsnews.com/news/study-finds-unsafe-mercury-levels-in-84-percent-of-all-fish/

6. "What are PCBs?" Navy Medicine website. Accessed May 2016. http://www.med.navy.mil/sites/nmcphc/Documents/environmental-programs/risk-communication/posters/PCBSML.pdf

7. "Polychlorinated Biphenyls (PCBs)." Illinois Department of Environmental Health website. Accessed May 2016. http://www.idph.state.il.us/envhealth/factsheets/polychlorinatedbiphenyls.htm

8. "What Are The Human Health Effects Of PCBs?" Clear Water website. Accessed May 2016. http://www.clearwater.org/news/pcbhealth.html

9. Ibid.

10. Black JJ, Bauman PC. Carcinogens and cancers in freshwater fishes. Environmental Health Perspectives. 1991;90:27-33.

11. "PUBLIC HEALTH IMPLICATIONS OF EXPOSURE TO POLYCHLORINATED BIPHENYLS (PCBs)." United States Environmental Protection Agency website. Accessed May 2016. https://www.epa.gov/sites/production/files/2015-01/documents/pcb99.pdf

12. Corliss, J. Pesticide Metabolite Linked to Breast Cancer. Journal of the National Cancer Institute. 1993; 85 (8): 602. doi: 10.1093/jnci/85.8.602.

13. "PCBS IN FARMED SALMON." Environmental Working Group website. July 31, 2003. Accessed May 2016. http://www.ewg.org/research/pcbs-farmed-salmon

14. Ibid.

15. Ibid.

16. Rohland, Tracy. "Essential Fatty Acids from Plant Foods." Down to Earth website. Accessed May 2016. https://www.downtoearth.org/health/nutrition/essential-fatty-acids-plant-foods

17. J. David Spence, David J.A. Jenkins, Jean Davignon. Egg yolk consumption, smoking and carotid plaque: Reply to letters to the Editor by Sean Lucan and T Dylan Olver et al. Atherosclerosis. 2013; 227, Issue 1, 189–191. doi: http://dx.doi.org/10.1016/j.atherosclerosis.2012.10.075. Y G Doyle, A Furey, and J Flowers. Sick individuals and sick populations: 20 years later. Journal of Epidemiology & Community Health. 2006; 60(5): 396–398. doi: 10.1136/jech.2005.042770.

18. "Eating Fish for Heart Health." American Heart Association website. Accessed May 2016. http://www.heart.org/HEARTORG/HealthyLiving/HealthyEating/Nutrition/Eating-Fish-for-Heart-Health_UCM_440433_Article.jsp#.WEdinOErLeR

19. "What You Can Do to Prevent Atherosclerosis." University of Rochester Medical Center website. Accessed May 2016. https://www.urmc.rochester.edu/encyclopedia/content.aspx?ContentTypeID=1&ContentID=1583

20. Libby, Peter. "The interface of atherosclerosis and thrombosis: basic mechanisms." Vascular Medicine. 1998; vol. 3 no. 3 225-229. doi: 10.1177/1358836X9800300309.

21. "What is a Heart Attack?" National Institute of Health website. Accessed May 2016. https://www.nhlbi.nih.gov/health/health-topics/topics/heartattack

22. "Ischemic Strokes (Clots)." American Heart Association website. Accessed May 2016. http://www.strokeassociation.org/STROKEORG/AboutStroke/TypesofStroke/IschemicClots/Ischemic-Strokes-Clots_UCM_310939_Article.jsp# Fuhrman. *Eat to Live*. Pg.168.

23. Fuhrman. *Eat to Live*. Pg.168.

24. Ibid. Pg.169.

25. Wouter D. van Dijk, Yvonne Heijdra, Jacques W.M. Lenders, et al; Cigarette smoke retention and bronchodilation in patients with COPD. A controlled randomized trial. 2013; Volume 107, Issue 1, Pages 112–119. doi: http://dx.doi.org/10.1016/j.rmed.2012.09.019.

26. Guida, Tony. "Study finds unsafe mercury levels in 84 percent of all fish." CBS website. January 13, 2013. Accessed May 2016. http://www.cbsnews.com/news/study-finds-unsafe-mercury-levels-in-84-percent-of-all-fish/

27. Mozaffarian D, Rimm EB. Fish intake, contaminants, and human health: evaluating the risks and the benefits. Journal of the American Medical Association. 2006 Oct; 296(5):1885-99. Salonen JT, Seppanen K, NyyssonenK, et al; Intake of mercury from fish, lipid peroxidation, and the risk of myocardial infarction and coronary, cardiovascular, and any death in eastern Finnish men. Circulation. 1995; 91:645-55.

28. O'Connor, Anahad. "Fish Oil Claims Not Supported by Research." New York Times website. March 30, 2015. Accessed May 2016. http://well.blogs.nytimes.com/2015/03/30/fish-oil-claims-not-supported-by-research/

29. "Billion Dollar Omega-3 Fish Oil Market Forecasted to Continue to Grow - Company Receives FDA Approval for High Potency Omega-3 Recovery Supplements." PR Newswire website. March 16, 2015. Accessed May 2016. http://www.prnewswire.com/news-releases/billion-dollar-omega-3-fish-oil-market-forecasted-to-continue-to-grow---company-receives-fda-approval-for-high-potency-omega-3-recovery-supplements-296421951.html

30. O'Connor, Anahad. "Fish Oil Claims Not Supported by Research." New York Times website.

31. Ibid.

32. Andrew Grey and Mark Bolland. Clinical Trial Evidence and Use of Fish Oil Supplements. Journal of the American Medical Association Internal Medicine. 2014; 2014;174(3):460-462. doi:10.1001/jamainternmed.2013.12765.

33. Ibid.

34. Whoriskey, Peter. "Fish oil pills: A $1.2 billion industry built, so far, on empty promises." Washington Post website. July 8, 2015. Accessed May 2016. https://www.washingtonpost.com/business/economy/claims-that-fish-oil-boosts-health-linger-despite-science-saying-the-opposite/2015/07/08/db7567d2-1848-11e5-bd7f-4611a60dd8e5_story.html?utm_term=.ce92a7b30222

35. Rizos EC, Ntzani EE, Bika E, et al; Association between omega-3 fatty acid supplementation and risk of major cardiovascular disease events: a systematic review and meta-analysis. Journal of the American Medical Association. 2012;308(10):1024-33. doi: 10.1001/2012.jama.11374. Lee Hooper, Roger A Harrison, Carolyn D Summerbell, et al; Omega 3 fatty acids for prevention and treatment of cardiovascular disease. Cochrane Library. 2004; doi: 10.1002/14651858.CD003177.pub2.

36.   O'Connor, Anahad. "Fish Oil Claims Not Supported by Research." New York Times website.

37.   Whoriskey, Peter. "Fish oil pills: A $1.2 billion industry built, so far, on empty promises." Washington Post website.

38.   "Wild Atlantic Salmon Calorie Counter." Fat Secret website. Accessed May 2016. https://www.fatsecret.com/calories-nutrition/usda/wild-atlantic-salmon?portionid =37199&portionamount=4.000/

39.   Insull W Jr, Lang PD, His BP, Yoshimura S. Studies of arteriosclerosis in Japanese and American men. I. Comparison of fatty acid composition of adipose tissue. Journal of Clinical Investigation.1969; 48(7):1313-27.

40.   Zhang M, Picard-Deland E, Marette A. Fish and marine omega-3 polyunsatured Fatty Acid consumption and incidence of type 2 diabetes: a systematic review and meta-analysis. International Journal of Endocrinology. 2013; 501015. doi: 10.1155/2013/501015. Lee C, Liese A, Wagenknecht L, et al; Fish consumption, insulin sensitivity and beta-cell function in the Insulin Resistance Atherosclerosis Study (IRAS). Nutrition, Metabolism and Cardiovascular Diseases. 2013;23(9):829-35. doi: 10.1016/j.numecd.2012.06.001.

41.   McDougall, John. "Fish is Not Health Food." Earth Save website. Accessed May 2016. http://www.earthsave.org/news/03summer/fish.htm. Davidson MH, Hunninghake D, Maki KC, et al. Comparison of the effects of lean red meat vs lean white meat on serum lipid levels among free-living persons with hypercholesterolemia: a long-term, randomized clinical trial. Archives of Internal Medicine.1999;159(12):1331-38.

42.   "Pollutants in Fish Inhibit Humans' Natural Defense System." Scripps Institution of Oceanography website. Accessed May 2016. https://scripps.ucsd.edu/news/ pollutants-fish-inhibit-humans-natural-defense-system

43.   "Modern VS Traditional Life." Inuit Cultural Online Resource website. Accessed May 2016. http://icor.ottawainuitchildrens.com/node/48

44.   H.O. Bang, J. Dyerberg, et al; PLASMA LIPID AND LIPOPROTEIN PATTERN IN GREENLANDIC WEST-COAST ESKIMOS.

45.   Bohemier, Gerry. "Taking a Closer Look at the Inuit Paradox and Cardiovascular Disease." Natural News. March 21, 2008. Accessed May 2016. http://www. naturalnews.com/022868_disease_diet_fat.html

46.   "Extreme Nutrition: The Diet of Eskimo." Dr. McDougall's Health & Medical Center website. Accessed May 2016. https://www.drmcdougall.com/misc/2015nl/ apr/eskimos.htm

47.   "Investigators Find Something Fishy with the Classical Evidence for Dietary Fish Recommendations." Elsevier website. Accessed May 2016. https://www.elsevier. com/about/press-releases/research-and-journals/investigators-find-something-fishy-with-the-classical-evidence-for-dietary-fish-recommendations

48.   "Popular fish oil study deeply flawed, new research says." CBC News. May 9, 2014. Accessed May 2016. http://www.cbc.ca/news/canada/ottawa/ popular-fish-oil-study-deeply-flawed-new-research-says-1.2637702

49.   George Fodor, Eftyhia Helis, Narges Yazdekhasti, et al; "'Fishing' for the Origins of the 'Eskimos and Heart Disease' Story: Facts or Wishful Thinking?" Canadian Journal of Cardiology. 2014; Volume 30, Issue 8, Pages 864–868.

doi: http://dx.doi.org/10.1016/j.cjca.2014.04.007. Perry, Susan. "Fish oil and the 'Eskimo diet': another medical myth debunked." MinnPost website. August 2014. Accessed May 2016. https://www.minnpost.com/second-opinion/2014/08/fish-oil-and-eskimo-diet-another-medical-myth-debunked

50.   George Fodor, Eftyhia Helis, Narges Yazdekhasti, et al; "'Fishing' for the Origins of the 'Eskimos and Heart Disease' Story: Facts or Wishful Thinking?"

51.   Bjerregaard P. Validity of Greenlandic mortality statistics. Arctic Medical Research. 1986;42:18-24. Perry, Susan. "Fish oil and the 'Eskimo diet': another medical myth debunked." MinnPost website. August 2014. Accessed May 2016. https://www.minnpost.com/second-opinion/2014/08/fish-oil-and-eskimo-diet-another-medical-myth-debunked.

52.   George Fodor, Eftyhia Helis, Narges Yazdekhasti, et al; "'Fishing' for the Origins of the 'Eskimos and Heart Disease' Story: Facts or Wishful Thinking?"

53.   Peter Bjerregaard, Kue Young, Robert A Hegele. Low incidence of cardiovascular disease among the Inuit - What is the evidence? Atherosclerosis. 2003;166(2):351-7. doi: 10.1016/S0021-9150(02)00364-7.

54.   George Fodor, Eftyhia Helis, Narges Yazdekhasti, et al; "'Fishing' for the Origins of the 'Eskimos and Heart Disease' Story: Facts or Wishful Thinking?"

55.   "Aleut Tribe." War Paths 2 Peace Pipes website. Accessed May 2016. https://www.warpaths2peacepipes.com/indian-tribes/aleut-tribe.htm.

56.   Thompson RC, Allam AH, Lombardi GP, et al; Atherosclerosis across 4000 years of human history: the Horus study of four ancient populations. Lancet. 2013 Apr 6;381(9873):1211-22. doi: 10.1016/S0140-6736(13)60598-X.

57.   "Extreme Nutrition: The Diet of Eskimo." Dr. McDougall's Health & Medical Center website.

58.   Robertson W. The effect of high animal protein intake on the risk of calcium stone-formation in the urinary tract. Clinical Science.1979 Sep; 57(3):285-88.

59.   Richard B. Mazess and Warren Mather. Bone mineral content of North Alaskan Eskimos. American Journal of Clinical Nutrition. 1974; vol. 27 no. 9 916-925.

60.   "Toxic Contamination in The Arctic." Blue Voice website. Accessed May 2016. http://www.bluevoice.org/news_toxicarctic.php

Chapter Ten: Blood Vessel Disease

1.   Didion, Joan. *The Year of Magical Thinking*. New York: Alfred A. Knopf. 2005. Pg. 3-11.

2.   Myerburg RJ, Junttila MJ. Sudden cardiac death caused by coronary heart disease. Circulation. 2012; 28;125(8):1043-52.

3.   "Heart Disease and Stroke Statistics." American Heart Association website. Accessed May 2016. https://www.heart.org/idc/groups/ahamah-public/@wcm/@sop/@smd/documents/downloadable/ucm_470704.pdf

4.   "Blood Capillaries." InnerBody website. Accessed May 2016. http://www.innerbody.com/image_lymp01/card66.html

5. Esselstyn Jr., Caldwell. "Abolishing Heart Disease." Center for Nutritional Studies website. Accessed May 2016. http://nutritionstudies.org/abolishing-heart-disease

6. Bremner, John B. *Words on Words: A Dictionary for Writers and Others Who Care About Words.* New York: Columbia University Press. 1980. Pg. 43.

7. "atheroma (n.)." Online Etymology Dictionary website. Accessed May 2016. http://www.etymonline.com/index.php?term=atheroma&allowed_in_frame=0

8. Ibid.

9. "Atherosclerosis." American Heart Association website. Accessed May 2016. http://www.heart.org/HEARTORG/Conditions/Cholesterol/WhyCholesterolMatters/Atherosclerosis_UCM_305564_Article.jsp#.WEhKLuErLeR

10. "Diseases & Conditions." Cleveland Clinic website. Accessed May 2016. http://my.clevelandclinic.org/health/diseases_conditions/hic_Cholesterol/hic_Diseases_Linked_to_High_Cholesterol

11. "What Causes High Blood Cholesterol?" National Institute of Health website. Accessed May 2016. https://www.nhlbi.nih.gov/health/health-topics/topics/hbc/causes

12. "NORTH KARELIA PROJECT." University of Minnesota website. Accessed May 2016. http://www.epi.umn.edu/cvdepi/study-synopsis/north-karelia-project/ "Community-based programmes." World Health Organization website. Accessed May 2016. http://www.who.int/chp/about/integrated_cd/index2.html

13. Joyce Hendley and Rachael Moeller Gorman. "Miracle Up North." Eating Well website. Accessed May 2016. http://www.eatingwell.com/nutrition_health/nutrition_news_information/miracle_up_north

14. Buettner, Dan. "The Finnish Town That Went on a Diet." The Atlantic website. April 7, 2015. Accessed May 2016. http://www.theatlantic.com/health/archive/2015/04/finlands-radical-heart-health-transformation/389766/

15. Joyce Hendley and Rachael Moeller Gorman. "Miracle Up North." Eating Well website.

16. Buettner, Dan. "The Finnish Town That Went on a Diet." The Atlantic website.

17. Joyce Hendley and Rachael Moeller Gorman. "Miracle Up North." Eating Well website.

18. Ibid.

19. "Pekka Puska." World Public Health Nutrition Association website. Accessed May 2016. http://wphna.org/our-members/pekka-puska/.

20. Joyce Hendley and Rachael Moeller Gorman. "Miracle Up North." Eating Well website.

21. Ibid.

22. Ibid.

23. Buettner, Dan. "The Finnish Town That Went on a Diet." The Atlantic website.

24. Ibid.

25. Joyce Hendley and Rachael Moeller Gorman. "Miracle Up North." Eating Well website.

26. Buettner, Dan. "The Finnish Town That Went on a Diet." The Atlantic website.

27. Joyce Hendley and Rachael Moeller Gorman. "Miracle Up North." Eating Well website.

28. Ibid.

29.   "NORTH KARELIA PROJECT." University of Minnesota website.

30.   "Nathan Pritikin, Founder." Pritikin website. Accessed May 2016. https://www. pritikin.com/home-the-basics/about-pritikin/38-nathan-pritikin.html

31.   Dean Ornish, Shirley E. Brown, Larry W. Scherwitz, et al; Can lifestyle changes reverse coronary heart disease? The Lancet. 1990; Vol. 36, No 8708, Pages 129-133.

32.   Levingston, Suzanne. "Dean Ornish talks about cheeseburgers and yoga, and what they mean for heart health." Washington Post website. June 16, 2014. Accessed May 2016. https://www.washingtonpost.com/national/health-science/ dean-ornish-talks-about-cheeseburgers-and-yoga-and-what-they-mean-for- heart-health/2014/06/16/2b619778-e4f8-11e3-8f90-73e071f3d637_story. html?utm_term=.d375ced79cbd

33.   Caldwell B Esselstyn Jr, Gina Gendy, Jonathan Doyle, et al; A way to reverse CAD? Journal of Family Practice. 2014; Vol 63, No.7.

34.   Ibid.

35.   Ibid.

36.   "Pork Tenderloin and Spinach with Parmesan." American Heart Association website. Accessed May 2016. https://recipes.heart.org/Recipes/1019/ Pork-Tenderloin-and-Spinach-with-Parmesan

37.   "Slow-Cooker Steak Stroganoff." American Heart Association website. Accessed May 2016. https://recipes.heart.org/Recipes/1285/Slow-Cooker-Steak-Stroganoff

38.   "The American Heart Association's Diet and Lifestyle Recommendations." American Heart Association website. Accessed May 2016. http://www.heart. org/HEARTORG/HealthyLiving/HealthyEating/Nutrition/The-American-Heart- Associations-Diet-and-Lifestyle-Recommendations_UCM_305855_Article.jsp#. WEhSoeErLeR

39.   "Try These Tips for Heart-Healthy Grocery Shopping." American Heart Association website. Accessed May 2016. http://www.heart.org/HEARTORG/ HealthyLiving/HealthyEating/Nutrition/Try-These-Tips-for-Heart-Healthy- Grocery-Shopping_UCM_001884_Article.jsp#.WEhS3eErLeR

40.   "Vegetarian Diets." American Heart Association website. Accessed May 2016. http://www.heart.org/HEARTORG/HealthyLiving/HealthyEating/Nutrition/ Vegetarian-Diets_UCM_306032_Article.jsp#.WEhTEOErLeR

41.   G.V. Mann, R.D. Shaffer, R.S. Anderson, et al; Cardiovascular disease in the masai. 1964; Pages 289-312. doi:10.1016/S0368-1319(64)80041-7. Campbell, Thomas. "Masai and Inuit High-Protein Diets: A Closer Look." T. Colin Campbell Center for Nutrition Studies website. July 17, 2015. Accessed May 2016. http://nutritionstudies. org/masai-and-inuit-high-protein-diets-a-closer-look/

42.   Campbell, Thomas. "Masai and Inuit High-Protein Diets: A Closer Look." T. Colin Campbell Center for Nutrition Studies website. July 17, 2015. Accessed May 2016. http://nutritionstudies.org/masai-and-inuit-high-protein-diets-a-closer-look/

43.   G.V. Mann, R.D. Shaffer, R.S. Anderson, et al; Cardiovascular disease in the masai. 1964; Pages 289-312. doi:10.1016/S0368-1319(64)80041-7.

44.   "Life expectancy data by country." World Health Organization website. Accessed May 2016. http://apps.who.int/gho/data/node.main.688?lang=en

45.   "LIFE EXPECTANCY ALL RACES MALE." USA Life Expectancy website. Accessed May 2016. http://www.worldlifeexpectancy.com/usa/life-expectancy-male

46.   G.V. Mann, R.D. Shaffer, R.S. Anderson, et al; Cardiovascular disease in the masai. 1964; Pages 289-312. doi:10.1016/S0368-1319(64)80041-7.

47.   Nestel P. A society in transition; developmental and seasonal influences on the nutrition of Maasai women and children. Food and Nutrition Bulletin.1986;8:2-18.

48.   Mbalilaki JA, Masesa Z, Strømme SB, et al; Daily energy expenditure and cardiovascular risk in Masai, rural and urban Bantu Tanzanians. British Journal of Sports Medicine. 2010;44(2):121-6. doi: 10.1136/bjsm.2007.044966.

49.   Nestel P. A society in transition; developmental and seasonal influences on the nutrition of Maasai women and children. Food and Nutrition Bulletin.1986;8:2-18.

50.   Mann, George V., Anne Spoerry, Margarete Gary, et al; ATHEROSCLEROSIS IN THE MASAI. American Journal of Epidemiology. (1972) 95 (1): 26-37.

51.   "2016 ALZHEIMER'S DISEASE FACTS AND FIGURES." Alzheimer's Association website. Accessed May 2016. http://www.alz.org/facts/

52.   M. C. Morris. The role of nutrition in Alzheimer's disease: epidemiological evidence. European Journal of Neurology. 2009; 16(Suppl 1): 1–7. doi: 10.1111/j.1468-1331.2009.02735.x.

CHAPTER ELEVEN: OUR CHILDREN

1.   Strong JP, McGill HC. The pediatric aspect of atherosclerosis. Journal of Atherosclerosis Research. 1969; 9(3);251-265. Newman III WP, Freedman DS, Voors AW, Gard PD, Srinivasan SR, Cresanta JL, Williamson GD, Webber LS, Berenson GS. Relation of serum lipoprotein levels and systolic blood pressure to early atherosclerosis. The Bogalusa Heart Study. New England Journal of Medicine. 1986; 314(3):138-144.

2.   Stary HC, Chandler AB, Glagov S. A definition of initial, fatty streak, and intermediate lesions of atherosclerosis. A report from the Committee on Vascular Lesions of the Council on Arteriosclerosis, American Heart Association. Circulation. 1994;89(5):2462-78.

3.   "Pathogenesis of Atherosclerosis." Boston University School of Public Health website. Accessed May 2016. http://sphweb.bumc.bu.edu/otlt/MPH-Modules/PH/PH709_Heart/PH709_Heart3.html

4.   "Lumen." The Free Dictionary website. Accessed May 2016. http://www.thefreedictionary.com/lumen.

5.   "Lumen (n.)." Online Etymology Dictionary website. Accessed May 2016. http://www.etymonline.com/index.php?term=lumen

6.   William F. Enos, Robert H. Holmes, James Beyer. CORONARY DISEASE AMONG UNITED STATES SOLDIERS KILLED IN ACTION IN KOREA PRELIMINARY REPORT. Journal of the American Medical Association. 1953;152(12):1090-1093. doi:10.1001/jama.1953.03690120006002.

7.   Jack P. Strong. Coronary Atherosclerosis in Soldiers: A Clue to the Natural History of Atherosclerosis in the Young. Journal of the American Medical Association. 1986;256(20):2863-2866. doi:10.1001/jama.1986.03380200101029.

8.   Enos Jr. WF, Beyer JC, Holmes RH. Pathogenesis of coronary disease in American soldiers killed in Korea. Journal of the American Medical Association. 1955;158(11);912-914.

9.   McMahan CA, Gidding SS, Malcom GT. Pathobiological determinants of atherosclerosis in youth risk scores are associated with early and advanced atherosclerosis. Pediatrics. 2006;118(4):1447-55. doi: 10.1542/peds.2006-0970.

10.   Trumbo PR, Shimakawa T. Tolerable upper intake levels for trans fat, saturated fat, and cholesterol. Nutrition Reviews. 2011;69(5):270-8.

11.   Fox MK, Pac S, Devaney B, Jankowski L. Feeding infants and toddlers study: What foods are infants and toddlers eating? Journal of the American Dietetic Association. 2004;104(1 Suppl):s22-s30.

12.   Fuhrman, Joel. *Disease-Proof Your Child: Feeding Kids Right*. New York: St. Martin's Griffin. 2005. Pg. xix.

13.   F E Thompson and B A Dennison. Dietary sources of fats and cholesterol in US children aged 2 through 5 years. American Journal of Public Health. 1994; 84(5): 799–806.

14.   Vogt R, Bennet D, Cassady D, Frost J, Ritz B, Hertz-Picciotto I. Cancer and non-cancer health effects from food contaminant exposures for children and adults in California: a risk assessment. Environmental Health. 2012;11:83.

15.   F E Thompson and B A Dennison. Dietary sources of fats and cholesterol in US children aged 2 through 5 years. American Journal of Public Health. 1994; 84(5): 799–806.

16.   Ogden CL, Carroll MD, Kit BK, Flegal KM. Prevalence of childhood and adult obesity in the United States, 2011-2012. Journal of the American Medical Association. 2014;311(8):806-814.

17.   Ibid.

18.   National Center for Health Statistics. Health, United States, 2011: With Special Features on Socioeconomic Status and Health. Hyattsville, MD; U.S. Department of Health and Human Services; 2012.

19.   Vincent SD, Pangrazi RP, Raustorp LM, et al; Activity levels and body mass index of children in the United States, Sweden, and Australia. Medicine & Science in Sports & Exercise. 2003;35(8);1367-1373.

20.   Chubhippo. "7 year old boy weighs 250 lb." Youtube video. Posted [February 2008]. https://www.youtube.com/watch?v=ZUpZ_2tOA_Q

21.   "Support offered to Polk 7-year-old." BlueRidgeNow Times-News website. March 27, 2007. Accessed May 2016. http://www.blueridgenow.com/news/20070327/support-offered-to-polk-7-year-old

22.   Guo SS, Chumlea WC. Tracking of body mass index in children in relation to overweight in adulthood. American Journal of Clinical Nutrition. 1999;70:S145–148. Freedman DS, Kettel L, Serdula MK, Dietz WH, Srinivasan SR, Berenson GS. The relation of childhood BMI to adult adiposity: the Bogalusa Heart Study. Pediatrics. 2005;115:22–27. Freedman D, Wang J, Thornton JC, et al. Classification of body fatness by body mass index-for-age categories among children. Archives of Pediatric and Adolescent Medicine. 2009;163:801–811. Freedman DS, Khan LK, Dietz WH, Srinivasan SA, Berenson GS. Relationship of

childhood obesity to coronary heart disease risk factors in adulthood: the Bogalusa Heart Study. Pediatrics. 2001;108:712–718.

23. Office of the Surgeon General. The Surgeon General's Vision for a Healthy and Fit Nation.[PDF - 840 KB]. Rockville, MD, U.S. Department of Health and Human Services; 2010.

24. Kushi LH, Byers T, Doyle C, Bandera EV, McCullough M, Gansler T, et al; American Cancer Society guidelines on nutrition and physical activity for cancer prevention: reducing the risk of cancer with healthy food choices and physical activity. CA: A Cancer Journal for Clinicians. 2006;56:254–281.

25. "Obesity In Children And Teens." American Academy of Child Adolescent Psychiatry. April 2016. Accessed May 2016. http://www.aacap.org/AACAP/ Families_and_Youth/Facts_for_Families/FFF-Guide/Obesity-In-Children-And-Teens-079.aspx

26. Hannon TS, Rao G, Arslanian SA. Childhood obesity and type 2 diabetes mellitus. Pediatrics. 2005;116(2):473-480.

27. Must A, Jaques PF, Dallai GE, Baiema CJ, Dietz WH. Long-term morbidity and mortality of overweight adolescents. New England Journal of Medicine.1992;327(19):1350-5.

28. Powell, Alvin. "Obesity? Diabetes? We've been set up." Harvard Gazette. March 7, 2012. Accessed May 2016. http://news.harvard.edu/gazette/story/2012/03/ the-big-setup/

29. Halter, Reese. "Fed Up Spotlights the American Sugar Epidemic." Huffington Post website. May 2014. Accessed May 2016. http://www.huffingtonpost.com/dr-reese-halter/fed-up-spotlights-the-ame_b_5387098.html

30. Grady, Denise. "Obesity-Linked Diabetes in Children Resists Treatment." New York Times website. April 2012. Accessed May 2016. http://www.nytimes. com/2012/04/30/health/research/obesity-and-type-2-diabetes-cases-take-toll-on-children.html?_r=0

31. Hannon TS, Rao G, Arslanian SA. Childhood obesity and type 2 diabetes mellitus. Pediatrics. 2005;116(2):473-480. Ebe D'Adamo and Sonia Caprio. "Type 2 Diabetes in Youth: Epidemiology and Pathophysiology." Diabetes Care. 2011; 34(Supplement 2): S161-S165. doi: http://dx.doi.org/10.2337/dc11-s212.

32. TODAY Study Group, Zeitler P, Hirst K, et al; A clinical trial to maintain glycemic control in youth with type 2 diabetes. New England Journal of Medicine. 2012;366(24):2247-56. doi: 10.1056/NEJMoa1109333.

33. Grady, Denise. "Obesity-Linked Diabetes in Children Resists Treatment." New York Times website.

34. Ibid.

35. Cali AM, Caprio S. Prediabetes and type 2 diabetes in youth: an emerging epidemic disease? Current Opinion in Endocrinology, Diabetes and Obesity. 2008;15(2):123-7.

36. "Type 1 Diabetes." American Diabetes Association. Accessed May 2016. http:// www.diabetes.org/diabetes-basics/type-1/?referrer=https://www.google.com/

37. Ibid.

38. Egro FM. Why is type 1 diabetes increasing? Journal of Molecular Endocrinology. 2013;51(1):R1-13. doi: 10.1530/JME-13-0067.

39. Tedeschi A, Airaghi L. Is affluence a risk factor for bronchial asthma and type 1 diabetes?Pediatric Allergy and Immunology. 2006;17(7):533-7. doi: 10.1111/j.1399-3038.2006.00445.x. 545 Jukka Karjalainen, Julio M. Martin, Mikael Knip, et al; A Bovine Albumin Peptide As a Possible Trigger of Insulin-Dependent Diabetes Mellitus. New England Journal of Medicine. 1992;327(5):302-7. doi: 10.1056/NEJM199207303270502. M Virtanen, T Saukkonen, E Savilahti, et al; Diet, cow's milk protein antibodies and the risk of IDDM in Finnish children. Childhood Diabetes in Finland Study Group. Diabetologia. 1994;37(4):381-7. B E Birgisdottir, J P Hill, D P Harris, et al; Variation in consumption of cow milk proteins and lower incidence of Type 1 diabetes in Iceland vs the other 4 Nordic countries. Diabetes Nutr Metab. 2002 Aug;15(4):240-5.

40. Jukka Karjalainen, Julio M. Martin, Mikael Knip, et al; A Bovine Albumin Peptide As a Possible Trigger of Insulin-Dependent Diabetes Mellitus. New England Journal of Medicine. 1992;327(5):302-7. doi: 10.1056/NEJM199207303270502.

41. Akerblom H, Knip M. Putative environmental factors and Type 1 diabetes. Diabetes/Metabolism Research and Reviews.1998;31-67. Verge C, Howard NJ, Irwig L, et al; Environmental factors in childhood IDDM. Diabetes Care. 1994;1381-9.

42. Parker, Helen. "Diabetic Daniella Meads-Barlow, 17, among rising number of 'dead in bed' victims." News Corp Australia Network. April 2013. Accessed May 2016. http://www.news.com.au/national/incidence-of-diabetes-linked-dead-in-bed-cases-rising/news-story/5e57d9e31c62e163acfd9425e47aa24a

43. Kaplan, Sarah. "While his parents slept, this 7-year-old boy's life was saved by Jedi, his diabetes-sniffing dog." Washington Post website. Accessed May 2016. https://www.washingtonpost.com/news/morning-mix/wp/2016/03/09/while-his-parents-slept-this-7-year-old-boys-life-was-saved-by-jedi-his-diabetes-sniffing-dog/?utm_term=.c4fba3c1cacc

44. Ibid.

45. Kostraba JN, Cruickshanks KJ, Lawler-Heavner J, et al; Early exposure to cow's milk and solid foods in infancy, genetic predisposition, and risk of IDDM. Diabetes. 1992;42(2):288-295.

46. McKenna, Maryn. "Diabetes Mystery: Why Are Type 1 Cases Surging?" Scientific America website. February 2012. Accessed May 2016. https://www.scientificamerican.com/article/a-diabetes-cliffhanger/

47. Parker, Helen. "Diabetic Daniella Meads-Barlow, 17, among rising number of 'dead in bed' victims."

48. "Princeton Public Schools." Niche K-12 School Search website. Accessed May 2016. https://k12.niche.com/d/princeton-public-schools-nj/

49. "2017 Best School Districts in America." Niche K-12 School Search website. Accessed May 2016. https://k12.niche.com/rankings/public-school-districts/best-overall/

50. "Princeton Public Schools." Niche K-12 School Search website.

51. "School Funding." New America website. Accessed May 2016. https://www.newamerica.org/education-policy/policy-explainers/early-ed-prek-12/school-funding/

52. Ravo, Nick. "If You're Thinking of Living In/Princeton; A Diverse Academic-Corporate Citadel." New York Times website. March 20, 1994. Accessed May 2016. http://www.nytimes.com/1994/03/20/realestate/if-you-re-thinking-of-living-in-princeton-a-diverse-academic-corporate-citadel.html?pagewanted=all

53. "Nutri-Serve Food Management." Princeton Public Schools website. Accessed May 2016. http://www.princetonk12.org/Food_Service/

54. Fuhrman. *Disease-Proof Your Children*. Pg. xix-xx, 12.

55. Ibid. Pg. xxiii.

56. Michael R Skilton, Nick Evans, Kaye A Griffiths, et al; Aortic wall thickness in newborns with intrauterine growth restriction. 2005; Volume 365, No. 9469, p1484–1486. doi: http://dx.doi.org/10.1016/S0140-6736(05)66419-7.

57. Napoli C, D'Armiento FB, Mancini FB, Postiglione A, Witztum JL, Palumbo G, Palinski W. Fatty streak formation occurs in human fetal aortas and is greatly enhanced by maternal hypercholesterolemia. Intimal accumulation of low density lipoprotein and its oxidation precede monocyte recruitment into early atherosclerotic lesions. Journal of Clinical Investigation.1997;100(11):2680-90.

58. "Foods to Avoid During Pregnancy." American Pregnancy Association. Accessed May 2016. http://americanpregnancy.org/pregnancy-health/foods-to-avoid-during-pregnancy/

59. Dorea JG, Bezerra VL, Fajon V, Horvat M. Speciation of methyl-and ethyl-mercury in hair of breastfed infants acutely exposed to thimerosal-containing vaccines. Clinica Chimica Acta.2011;412(17-18):1563-6.

60. Clarkson TW. The toxicology of mercury. Critical Reviews in Clinical Laboratory Sciences.1997;34(4):369-403.

61. Oken E, Bellinger DC. Fish consumption, methylmercury and child neurodevelopment. Current Opinion in Pediatrics. 2008;20(2):178-83. Murata K, Dakeishi M, Shimada M, et al; Assessment of intrauterine methylmercury exposure affecting child development: messages from the newborn. The Tohoku Journal of Experimental Medicine. 2007; 213(3):187-202. Jedrychowski W, Perera F, Jankowski J, et al; Fish consumption in pregnancy, cord blood mercury level and cognitive and psychomotor development of infants followed over the first three years of life: Krakow epidemiologic study. Environment International. 2007;339(8):1057-62. Gilbertson M. Male cerebral palsy hospitalization as a potential indicator of neurological effects of methylmercury exposure in Great Lakes communities. Environmental Research. 2004;95(3):375-84. Rylander L, Stromberg U, Hagmar L. Dietary intake of fish contaminated with persistent organochlorine compounds in relation to low birthweight. Scandinavian Journal of Work, Environment & Health. 1996;2(4):260-66. Does methylmercury have a role in causing developmental disabilities in children? Environmental Health Perspectives. 2000;108(suppl.3):S413-20.

62. Jedrychowski W, Perera FP, Tang D, et al; Impact of barbecued meat consumed in pregnancy on birth outcomes accounting for personal prenatal exposure to airborne polycyclic aromatic hydrocarbons: birth cohort study in Poland. Nutrition. 2012;28(4):372-7.

63. Brekke HK, Ludvigsson J. Daily vegetable intake during pregnancy negatively associated to islet autoimmunity in the offspring—The ABIS study. Pediatric Diabetes. 2009; doi: 10.1111/j.1399-5448.2009.00563.x.

64. Woodruff TJ, Zota AR, Schwartz JM. Environmental chemicals in pregnant women in the United States: NHANES 2003-2004. Environmental Health Perspectives. 2011;119(6):878-85.

65. Glynn A, Larsdotter M, Aune M, Darnerud PO, Bjerselius R, Bergman A. Changes in serum concentrations of polychlorinated biphenyls (PCBs), hydroxylated PCB metabolites and pentachlorophenol during pregnancy. Chemosphere. 2011;83(2):144-51.

66. Soechitram SD, Athanasiadou M, Hovander L, Bergman A, Sauer PJ. Fetal exposure to PCBs and their hydroxylated metabolites in a Dutch cohort. Environmental Health Perspectives. 2004;112(11):1208-12.

67. Mariscal-Arcas M, Lopez-Martinez C, Granada A, Olea N, Lorenzo-Tovar ML, Olea-Serrano F. Organochlorine pesticides in umbilical cord blood serum of women form Southern Spain and adherence to the Mediterranean diet. Food Chemical Toxicology. 2010;48(5):1311-5.

68. "Dioxins and their effects on human health." World Health Organization. Accessed May 2016. http://www.who.int/mediacentre/factsheets/fs225/en/

69. "Breastfeeding: Human Milk Versus Animal Milk." Nutrition MD website. Accessed May 2016. http://www.nutritionmd.org/nutrition_tips/nutrition_tips_infant_nutrition/breastfeeding_milks.html

70. Sabaté, J, Lindsted KD, Harris RD, Sanchez A. Attained height of lacto-ovo vegetarian children and adolescents. European Journal of Clinical Nutrition. 1991;45(1):51-8.

71. Dwyer JT, Miller LG, Arduino NL, Andrew EM, Dietz Jr WH, Reed JC, Reed Jr HB. Mental age and I.Q. of predominantly vegetarian children. Journal of the American Dietetic Association.76(2):142-7, 1980.

72. Gale CR, Deary IJ, Schoon I, Batty GD. IQ in childhood and vegetarianism in adulthood: 1970 British cohort study. British Medical Journal. 2007;334(7587):245.

73. Willett WC. Balancing life-style and genomics research for disease prevention. Science. 2002; 296(5568):695-8.

PART TWO

CHAPTER TWELVE: POST-ANTIBIOTIC ERA

1. "World Health Day 2011." World Health Organization website. Accessed May 2016. http://www.who.int/mediacentre/news/statements/2011/whd_20110407/en/

2. Chan, Margaret. "Antimicrobial resistance in the European Union and the world." World Health Organization website. March 2012. Accessed June 2016. http://www.who.int/dg/speeches/2012/amr_20120314/en/

3. Chan, Margaret. "WHO Director-General addresses G7 health ministers meeting on antimicrobial resistance." World Health Organization website.

October 2015 Accessed June 2016. http://www.who.int/dg/speeches/2015/g7-antimicrobial-resistance/en/

4. Chan, Margaret. "WHO Director-General addresses ministerial conference on antimicrobial resistance." World Health Organization website. February 2016. Accessed June 2016. http://www.who.int/dg/speeches/2016/antimicrobial-resistance-conference/en/

5. Ibid.

6. Chan, Margaret. "WHO Director-General addresses G7 health ministers meeting on antimicrobial resistance." World Health Organization website.

7. Chan, Margaret. "WHO Director-General addresses ministerial conference on antimicrobial resistance." World Health Organization website.

8. McKenna, Maryn. "Apocalypse Pig: The Last Antibiotic Begins to Fail." National Geographic website. November 2015. Accessed June 2016. http://phenomena.nationalgeographic.com/2015/11/21/mcr-gene-colistin/

9. "Gram-negative Bacteria Infections in Healthcare Settings." Centers for Disease Control and Prevention website. Accessed June 2016. http://www.cdc.gov/hai/organisms/gram-negative-bacteria.html

10. Beaubien, Jason. "E. Coli Bacteria Can Transfer Antibiotic Resistance To Other Bacteria." NPR website. November 2015. Accessed June 2016. http://www.npr.org/sections/goatsandsoda/2015/11/20/456689272/e-coli-bacteria-can-transfer-antibiotic-resistance-to-other-bacteria

11. "Kidney-Damaging Drug Seen Attacking Spread of Superbugs." Bloomberg website. June 2012. Accessed June 2016. http://www.bloomberg.com/news/articles/2012-06-10/kidney-damaging-drug-seen-attacking-spread-of-superbugs-health

12. Stromberg, Joseph. "Factory Farms May Be Ground-Zero For Drug Resistant Staph Bacteria." Smithsonian website. July 2013. Accessed June 2016. http://www.smithsonianmag.com/science-nature/factory-farms-may-be-ground-zero-for-drug-resistant-staph-bacteria-6055013/?no-ist

13. "Factory Farming and Food Safety." Food & Water Watch website. Accessed June 2016. https://www.foodandwaterwatch.org/problems/factory-farming-food-safety

14. Yi-Yun Liu, Yang Wang, Timothy R Walsh, et al; Emergence of plasmid-mediated colistin resistance mechanism MCR-1 in animals and human beings in China: a microbiological and molecular biological study. The Lancet. 2016; p161–168. doi: http://dx.doi.org/10.1016/S1473-3099(15)00424-7.

15. McKenna, Maryn. "Apocalypse Pig: The Last Antibiotic Begins to Fail."

16. McKenna, Maryn. "More Countries Are Seeing a Last-Ditch Antibiotic Failing." National Geographic website. December 2015. Accessed June 2016. http://phenomena.nationalgeographic.com/2015/12/15/colistin-r-3/

17. Ibid.

18. Beaubien, Jason. "E. Coli Bacteria Can Transfer Antibiotic Resistance To Other Bacteria."

19. McKenna, Maryn. "Resistance to a Last-Ditch Antibiotic: Invisible Spread." National Geographic website. December 2015. Accessed June 2016. http://phenomena.nationalgeographic.com/2015/12/18/colistin-r-4/

20. Tavernise, Sabrina and Denise Grady. "An Infection Raises the Specter of Superbugs Resistant to All Antibiotics." New York Times website. May 26, 2016. Accessed June 2016. http://www.nytimes.com/2016/05/27/health/infection-raises-specter-of-superbugs-resistant-to-all-antibiotics.html

21. Yi-Yun Liu, Yang Wang, Timothy R Walsh, et al; Emergence of plasmid-mediated colistin resistance mechanism MCR-1 in animals and human beings in China: a microbiological and molecular biological study.

22. Estabrook, Barry. *Pig Tales: An Omnivore's Quest for Sustainable Meat.*W.W.Norton & Company: New York. 2015. 163-165.

23. "Statistics United States 2005 Data." MRSA Survivors Network. Accessed June 2016. http://www.mrsasurvivors.org/statistics. "HIV in the United States: At A Glance." Centers for Disease Control and Prevention website. Accessed June 2016. http://www.cdc.gov/hiv/statistics/overview/ataglance.html

24. Estabrook. *Pig Tales*. 163-165.

25. "Undercover Exposé: Animals Locked in Cramped Cages, Piglets Fed to their Mothers at Kentucky Pig Factory." Humane Society of the United States website. February 2014. Accessed June 2016. http://www.humanesociety.org/news/press_releases/2014/02/Iron_Maiden_022014.html

26. "New Animal Drugs and New Animal Drug Combination Products Administered in or on Medicated Feed or Drinking Water of Food Producing Animals: Recommendations for Drug Sponsors for Voluntarily Aligning Product Use Conditions with GFI #209." U.S. Food and Drug Administration website. Accessed June 2016. http://www.fda.gov/downloads/AnimalVeterinary/GuidanceComplianceEnforcement/GuidanceforIndustry/UCM299624.pdf

27. "FDA's Strategy on Antimicrobial Resistance - Questions and Answers." U.S. Food and Drug Administration website. Accessed June 2016. http://www.fda.gov/AnimalVeterinary/GuidanceComplianceEnforcement/GuidanceforIndustry/ucm216939.htm

28. Ibid.

29. Estabrook. *Pig Tales*. P.165.

30. Ibid. P.167-168.

31. Karst, Kurt. "Nonprofit Groups Sue FDA Over Subtherapeutic Uses of Penicillin and Tetracyclines in Animal Feed, Seek Approval Withdrawals and Citizen Petition Response." FDA Law Blog website. May 26, 2011. Accessed June 2016. http://www.fdalawblog.net/fda_law_blog_hyman_phelps/2011/05/nonprofit-groups-sue-fda-over-subtherapeutic-uses-of-penicillin-and-tetracyclines-in-animal-feed-see.html

32. Mellon, Margaret. "Judge Rules FDA Must Act to Protect Americans from Overuse of Antibiotics in Livestock." Union of Concerned Scientists website. March 23, 2012. Accessed June 2016. http://www.ucsusa.org/news/press_release/FDA-must-curb-antibiotic-overuse-in-livestock-1380.html#.WEiF-uErLeR

33. "Superbug Suit: Court Slams FDA on Antibiotics in Animal Feed...Again." Natural Resources Defense Council website. June 5, 2012. Accessed June 2016. https://www.nrdc.org/media/2012/120605

34. "2014 SUMMARY REPORT On Antimicrobials Sold or Distributed for Use in Food-Producing Animals." U.S. Food and Drug Administration website.

Accessed June 2016. http://www.fda.gov/downloads/ForIndustry/UserFees/AnimalDrugUserFeeActADUFA/UCM476258.pdf

35. "Global cooperation in countering emerging animal and zoonotic diseases." World Organisation for Animal Health website. Accessed June 2016. http://www.oie.int/fileadmin/Home/fr/Our_scientific_expertise/docs/pdf/Globalcooperation_oie1.pdf

36. Ibid.

37. "HISTORY OF THE DOMESTICATION OF ANIMALS." History World website. Accessed June 2016. http://www.historyworld.net/wrldhis/PlainTextHistories.asp?historyid=ab57

38. Greger, Michael. "The Human/Animal Interface: Emergence and Resurgence of Zoonotic Infectious Diseases." Critical Reviews in Microbiology. 2007;33:243–299. doi: 10.1080/10408410701647594.

39. "List of zoonotic diseases." Public Health England website. Accessed June 2016. https://www.gov.uk/government/publications/list-of-zoonotic-diseases/list-of-zoonotic-diseases

40. "Zoonoses and the Human-Animal-Ecosystems Interface." World Health Organization website. Accessed June 2016. http://www.who.int/zoonoses/en/

41. Patton, Lindsay. "The Human Victims of Factory Farming." One Green Planet website. February 13, 2015. Accessed June 2016. http://www.onegreenplanet.org/environment/the-human-victims-of-factory-farming/

42. "FDA to Withdraw Approval for Arsenic-Based Drug Used in Poultry." Food Safety News website. April 2015. Accessed June 2016. http://www.foodsafetynews.com/2015/04/fda-to-withdraw-approval-for-arsenic-based-drug-used-in-poultry/#.WEiJd-ErLeR

43. "RACTOPAMINE FACTSHEET Lean Meat = Mean Meat." Center For Food Safety website. February 2013. Accessed June 2016. http://www.centerforfoodsafety.org/files/ractopamine_factsheet_02211.pdf

44. "Statement of FDA Mission." U.S. Food and Drug Administration website. Accessed June 2016. http://www.fda.gov/downloads/aboutfda/reportsmanualsforms/reports/budgetreports/ucm298331.pdf

45. "What is FOIA?" Freedom of Information Act website. Accessed June 2016. https://www.foia.gov/

46. "Burden of Foodborne Illness: Findings." Centers for Disease Control and Prevention website. Accessed June 2016. http://www.cdc.gov/foodborneburden/2011-foodborne-estimates.html

47. "Antibiotic Resistance Threats in the United States, 2013." Centers for Disease Control and Prevention website. Accessed June 2016. http://www.cdc.gov/drugresistance/threat-report-2013/

48. Imhoff, Daniel, ed. CAFO. San Rafael: Earth Aware, 2010. Pg. 160.

49. Eisnitz, Gail. Slaughterhouse. Amherst, NY: Prometheus Books. 2007. Pg. 163.

50. "Factory Farming Chickens." Farm Sanctuary website. Accessed June 2016. https://www.farmsanctuary.org/learn/factory-farming/chickens/

51. Roth, Anna. "What You Need to Know About the Corporate Shift to Cage-Free Eggs." Civil Eats website. January 2016. Accessed June 2016. http://civileats.com/2016/01/28/what-you-need-to-know-about-the-corporate-shift-to-cage-free-eggs/

52. Friedrich, Bruce. "The Cruelest of All Factory Farm Products: Eggs From Caged Hens." Huffington Post website. January 2013. Accessed June 2016. http://www.huffingtonpost.com/bruce-friedrich/eggs-from-caged-hens_b_2458525.html

53. Solotaroff, Paul. "Animal Cruelty Is the Price We Pay for Cheap Meat." Rolling Stone website. December 2013. Accessed June 2016. http://www.rollingstone.com/feature/belly-beast-meat-factory-farms-animal-activists

54. Tuttle, Will. *The World Peace Diet: Eating for Spiritual Health and Social Harmony.* New York: Lantern Books. 2005. Pg. 125.

55. Solotaroff, Paul. "Animal Cruelty Is the Price We Pay for Cheap Meat." Rolling Stone website. December 2013. Accessed June 2016. http://www.rollingstone.com/feature/belly-beast-meat-factory-farms-animal-activists

56. Roth, Anna."What You Need to Know About the Corporate Shift to Cage-Free Eggs."

57. Hladky, Gregory. "Proposed Bill Would Ban Tiny Cages For Egg-Laying Chickens." Hartford Courant website. November 2014. Accessed June 2016. http://www.courant.com/politics/hc-chicken-battery-cage-battle-20141116-story.html

58. "A Closer Look at Animals on Factory Farms." American Society for the Prevention of Cruelty to Animals website. Accessed June 2015. http://www.aspca.org/animal-cruelty/farm-animal-welfare/animals-factory-farms#gestation

59. Marcus. *Vegan: The New Ethics of Eating.* Pg. 116.

60. Philpott, Tom. "You Won't Believe What Pork Producers Do to Pregnant Pigs." Mother Jones website. August 2013. Accessed June 2016. http://www.motherjones.com/environment/2013/06/pregnant-sows-gestation-crates-abuse

61. "A Closer Look at Animals on Factory Farms." American Society for the Prevention of Cruelty to Animals website.

62. Marcus. *Vegan: The New Ethics of Eating.* P. 136.

63. "FACT SHEET: Feedlot Finishing Cattle." National Cattlemen's Beef Association website. Accessed June 2016. http://www.beefusa.org/uDocs/Feedlot%20finishing%20fact%20sheet%20FINAL_4%2026%2006.pdf

64. Marcus. *Vegan: The New Ethics of Eating.* Pg. 135.

65. Lyman, Howard. *Mad Cowboy.* New York: Touchstone.1998. Pg. 12.

66. "Big Chicken: Pollution and Industrial Poultry Production in America." The Pew Charitable Trusts website. 2011. Accessed June 2016. http://www.pewtrusts.org/~/media/legacy/uploadedfiles/peg/publications/report/pegbigchickenjuly2011pdf.pdf

67. Jacobson, Brad. "They're Feeding WHAT to Cows?" OnEarth website. December 12, 2013. Accessed June 2016. http://archive.onearth.org/articles/2013/12/you-wont-believe-the-crap-literally-that-factory-farms-feed-to-cattle

68. "Are humans endangered if cattle dine on chicken manure?" CNN website. August 23, 1997. Accessed June 2016. http://www.cnn.com/US/9708/23/chicken.manure/

69. Lyman. *Mad Cowboy.* Pg. 13.

70. "Former Chief Inspector for the USDA, Dr. Friedlander joins as Advisory Board Member in SAVING AMERICA'S HORSES, the movie." Saving America's Horses website. Sept 27, 2012. Accessed June 2016. http://savingamericashorses.blogspot.com/2012/09/former-chief-inspector-for-usda-dr.html

71. "National Conference to End Factory Farming 2011 Speakers." Farm Sanctuary website. Accessed June 2016. http://conference.farmsanctuary.org/speakers.php#lf

72. "Former Chief Inspector for the USDA, Dr. Friedlander joins as Advisory Board Member in SAVING AMERICA'S HORSES, the movie." Saving America's Horses website. Sept 27, 2012. Accessed June 2016. http://savingamericashorses.blogspot.com/2012/09/former-chief-inspector-for-usda-dr.html

73. Finelli, Mary. "Mad Cow: The Man Who Knew Too Much." EnviroLink website. January 2004. Accessed June 2016. http://lists.envirolink.org/pipermail/ar-news/Week-of-Mon-20031229/014785.html

74. Pachirat, Timothy. *Every Twelve Seconds: Industrialized Slaughter and the Politics of Sight*. New Haven: Yale University Press. 2011. Pg. 187-8.

75. Ibid. Pg. 192-195.

76. Ibid. Pg. 186-7.

77. Ibid. Pg. 145.

Chapter Thirteen: A Civil Rights Issue

1. Factory Farm Map website. Accessed June 2016. http://www.factoryfarmmap.org/

2. "North Carolina Facts." Factory Farm Map website. Accessed June 2016. http://www.factoryfarmmap.org/states/nc/

3. "Swine Facts." North Carolina Riverkeepers & Waterkeeper Alliance website. Accessed June 2016. http://www.riverlaw.us/realhogfacts.html

4. Sturgis, Sue. "Environmentalists urge emergency declaration over mass pig deaths in North Carolina (video)." Facing South website. February 28, 2014. Accessed June 2016. https://www.facingsouth.org/2014/02/environmentalists-urge-emergency-declaration-over-.html

5. Estabrook. *Pig Tales*. Pg. 122.

6. Bienkowski, Brian. "North Carolina Factory Farms Contaminating Local Waterways." TruthOut website. March 2015. Accessed June 2016. http://www.truth-out.org/news/item/29488-north-carolina-factory-farms-contaminating-local-waterways

7. Sturgis, Sue. "Environmentalists urge emergency declaration over mass pig deaths in North Carolina (video)."

8. "The 2006 Masters of the Pork Industry." National Hog Farmer website. May 15, 2006. June 2016. http://www.nationalhogfarmer.com/mag/farming_masters

9. Estabrook. *Pig Tales*. Pg. 119.

10. Ibid. Pg. 120.

11. Bienkowski, Brian. "North Carolina Factory Farms Contaminating Local Waterways."

12. "Wendell Murphy: Timeline." UNC TV website. Accessed June 2016. http://www.unctv.org/content/biocon/wendellmurphy/timeline

13. "North Carolina Facts." Factory Farm Map website.

14. Estabrook. *Pig Tales*. Pg. 122.

15. "Industrial Hog Operations in North Carolina Disproportionately Impact African-Americans, Hispanics and American Indians." North Carolina Policy Watch website. Accessed June 2016. http://www.ncpolicywatch.com/wp-content/uploads/2014/09/UNC-Report.pdf

16. "Warsaw Demographics Profile." Area Vibes website. Accessed June 2016. http://www.areavibes.com/warsaw-nc/demographics/

17. "Exhibit 5 Declaration of Professor Steven B. Wing, Ph.D." Buffalo River Watershed Alliance website. Accessed June 2016. http://buffaloriveralliance.org/Resources/Documents/Ex.%205%20-%20Wing%20declaration%20FINAL%20w%20Exhibits%20-%20reduced%20size.pdf

18. Tietz, Jeff. "Boss Hog: The Dark Side of America's Top Pork Producer." Rolling Stone website. December 14, 2006. Accessed June 2016. http://www.rollingstone.com/culture/news/boss-hog-the-dark-side-of-americas-top-pork-producer-20061214

19. Holleman, Marybeth. "After 25 years, Exxon Valdez oil spill hasn't ended." CNN website. March 25, 2014. Accessed June 2016. http://www.cnn.com/2014/03/23/opinion/holleman-exxon-valdez-anniversary/

20. Kilborn, Peter. "Hurricane Reveals Flaws in Farm Law as Animal Waste Threatens N. Carolina Water." New York Times website. October 17, 1999. Accessed June 2016. http://www.nytimes.com/1999/10/17/us/hurricane-reveals-flaws-in-farm-law-as-animal-waste-threatens-n-carolina-water.html?pagewanted=all

21. Smothers, Ronald. "Spill Puts a Spotlight On a Powerful Industry." New York Times website. June 30, 1995. Accessed June 2016. http://www.nytimes.com/1995/06/30/us/spill-puts-a-spotlight-on-a-powerful-industry.html

22. "Huge Spill of Hog Waste Fuels an Old Debate in North Carolina." New York Times website. June 25, 1995. Accessed June 2016. http://www.nytimes.com/1995/06/25/us/huge-spill-of-hog-waste-fuels-an-old-debate-in-north-carolina.html

23. Tietz, Jeff. "Boss Hog: The Dark Side of America's Top Pork Producer."

24. Marks, Robbin. "CESSPOOLS OF SHAME: How Factory Farm Lagoons and Sprayfields Threaten Environmental and Public Health." Natural Resources Defense Council and the Clean Water Network. 2001; Pg. 46.

25. Ibid. Pg. 49.

26. Ibid. Pg. 48.

27. Horsman, Jennifer, & Jaime Flowers. *Please Don't Eat the Animals.* Sanger, CA: Quill Driver Books. 2006. Pg. 47. "Addressing the True Impacts of Concentrated Animal Feeding Operations." Socially Responsible Agricultural Project website. Accessed June 2016. http://www.sraproject.org/wp-content/uploads/2007/12/addressingthetrueimpactsofcafos.pdf

28. Tietz, Jeff. "Boss Hog: The Dark Side of America's Top Pork Producer."

29. Kuo, Lily. "The world eats cheap bacon at the expense of North Carolina's rural poor." Quartz website. July 14, 2015. Accessed June 2016. http://qz.com/433750/the-world-eats-cheap-bacon-at-the-expense-of-north-carolinas-rural-poor/

30. "Lactose Intolerance." National Institute of Diabetes and Digestive and Kidney Diseases website. Accessed June 2016. https://www.niddk.nih.gov/health-information/health-topics/digestive-diseases/lactose-intolerance/Pages/facts.aspx

31. Lang, Susan. "Lactose intolerance seems linked to ancestral struggles with harsh climate and cattle diseases, Cornell study finds." Cornell Chronicle website. June 1, 2005. Accessed June 2016. http://www.news.cornell.edu/stories/2005/06/lactose-intolerance-linked-ancestral-struggles-climate-diseases

32. Daniel L. Swagerty, Jr., Anne D. Walling, and Robert M. Klein. Lactose Intolerance. American Family Physician. 2002;65(9):1845-1851.

33. Lang, Susan. "Lactose intolerance seems linked to ancestral struggles with harsh climate and cattle diseases, Cornell study finds."

34. "Lactose Intolerance." Genetics Home Reference website. Accessed June 2016. https://ghr.nlm.nih.gov/condition/lactose-intolerance

35. Lang, Susan. "Lactose intolerance seems linked to ancestral struggles with harsh climate and cattle diseases, Cornell study finds."

36. National Dairy Council. "Lactose Intolerance Rates May Be Significantly Lower Than Previously Believed." Science Daily website. November 6, 2009. Accessed June 2016. https://www.sciencedaily.com/releases/2009/11/091105102718.htm

37. "My Plate." United States Department of Agriculture website. Accessed June 2016. https://www.choosemyplate.gov/MyPlate

38. "Racism, Food, and Health." John Robbins website. April 18, 2010. Accessed June 2016. http://johnrobbins.info/blog/racism-food-and-health/

39. Witt, Doris. *Black Hunger: Soul Food and America*. Minneapolis: University of Minneapolis Press. 2004. Pg. 133-134.

40. Ibid.

41. Harper, A. Breeze, ed. *Sistah Vegan: Black Female Vegans Speak on Food, Identity, Health, and Society*. New York: Lantern Books. 2010. Pg. 37.

42. hooks, bell and Cornel West. *Breaking Bread: Insurgent Black Intellectual Life*. Boston: South End Press. 1991. Pg. 98.

43. Goldhamer, Alan and Douglas Lisle. *The Pleasure Trap: Mastering the Hidden Force that Undermines Health and Happiness*. Summertown, Tennessee: Healthy Living Publications. 2003. Pg. 42.

44. Ibid. Pg. 90.

45. Ibid. Pg. 47.

46. Iozzo P, Guiducci L, Guzzardi MA, Pagotto U. Brain PET imaging in obesity and food addiction: current evidence and hypothesis. Obesity Facts. 2012;5(2):155-64.

47. "Understanding Addiction." HelpGuide.org. Accessed June 2016. http://www.helpguide.org/harvard/how-addiction-hijacks-the-brain.htm

48. "The Neurobiology of Drug Addiction." National Institute on Drug Abuse website. Accessed June 2016. https://www.drugabuse.gov/publications/teaching-packets/neurobiology-drug-addiction/section-iii-action-heroin-morphine/6-definition-tolerance

49. "Neuroadaptation to Drugs and Alcohol." Alcohol Rehab website. Accessed June 2016. http://alcoholrehab.com/addiction-articles/neuroadaptation-to-drugs-and-alcohol/

50. Goldhamer. *The Pleasure Trap*. Pg. 89.

51. Ibid. Pg. 88.

52. "What Is Marbling in Meat?" about.com. Accessed June 2016. http://culinaryarts.about.com/od/glossary/g/marbling.htm

53. Lagerquist, Ron. "Cows Milk Compared to Human Milk." Freedom You website. Accessed June 2016. http://www.freedomyou.com/cows_milk_compared_to_human_milk_freedomyou.aspx

54. Lim SS, Vos T, Flaxman AD, et al. A comparative risk assessment of burden of disease and injury attributable to 67 risk factors and risk factor clusters in 21 regions, 1990-2010: a systematic analysis for the Global Burden of Disease Study 2010. The Lancet. 2012; 380(9859):2224-60.

55. Ibid.

56. Das P, Samarasekera U. The story of GBD 2010: a "super-human" effort. The Lancet. 2012;380(9859):2067-70.

57. Goldhamer. *The Pleasure Trap.* Pg. 84.

58. "Understanding Addiction." HelpGuide.org. Accessed June 2016. http://www. helpguide.org/harvard/how-addiction-hijacks-the-brain.htm.

CHAPTER FOURTEEN: HENS IN THE FOX DEN

1. Select Committee on Nutrition and Human Needs. "Dietary Goals For the United States." 95ᵗʰ Congress 1ˢᵗ Session. February 1977. Accessed June 2016. http:// zerodisease.com/archive/Dietary_Goals_For_The_United_States.pdf

2. G. McGovern, Statement of Senator George McGovern on the Publication of *Dietary Goals for the United States*, Press Conference, Friday, February 14, 1977, in United States Senate Select Committee on Nutrition and Human Needs, *Dietary Goals for the United States* (Washington, DC: US Government Printing Office, February 1977), 1.

3. Select Committee on Nutrition and Human Needs. "Dietary Goals For the United States."

4. Ibid.

5. Gerald M. Oppenheimer and Daniel Benrubi. McGovern's Senate Select Committee on Nutrition and Human Needs Versus the: Meat Industry on the Diet-Heart Question (1976–1977). American Journal of Public Health. 2014 January; 104(1): 59–69. doi: 10.2105/AJPH.2013.301464.

6. W. Robbins. "Nutrition Study Finds US Lacks a Goal." *New York Times* (1923– current file), June 22, 1974; ProQuest Historical Newspapers: *New York Times* (1851–2008) with index (1851–1993): 21.

7. "Select Committee on Nutrition and Human Needs Agenda for Executive Session," January 29, 1976, George S. McGovern Papers, Box 1002 Folder 1976; Public Policy Papers, Department of Rare Books and Special Collections, Princeton University Library.

8. Gerald M. Oppenheimer and Daniel Benrubi. McGovern's Senate Select Committee on Nutrition and Human Needs Versus the: Meat Industry on the Diet-Heart Question (1976–1977).

9. "The Impact of Selected Attitudes Toward the American Livestock and Meat Industry. Some Observations of the Congressional Climate," February 1976, George S. McGovern Papers, Box 993 Folder Beef; Public Policy Papers, Department of Rare Books and Special Collections, Princeton University Library.

10. Select Committee on Nutrition and Human Needs. "Dietary Goals For the United States."

11. "Dietary Advice for the 1990's: The Political History of the Food Guide Pyramid." Caduceus. 1993; Volume IX, Number 3. http://www.foodpolitics.com/wp-content/ uploads/caduceus_93.pdf

12. Select Committee on Nutrition and Human Needs. "Dietary Goals For the United States."

13. Brody, Jane E. "U.S. Acts to Reshape Diets of Americans." New York Times. February 5, 1980. Accessed June 2016.

14. "Washington- Dietary Guidelines." Food Politics website. Accessed June 2016. http://www.foodpolitics.com/wp-content/uploads/Hegsted.pdf

15. Letter to Senator Charles Percy From David Stroud, February 4, 1977, George S. McGovern Papers, Box 993 Folder Untitled; Public Policy Papers, Department of Rare Books and Special Collections, Princeton University Library.

16. *Meat Board Reports*, March 14, 1977, George S. McGovern Papers, Box 993 Folder Untitled; Public Policy Papers, Department of Rare Books and Special Collections, Princeton University Library.

17. Greger, Michael. "Big Food Wants Final Say Over Health Reports." Care 2 website. May 24, 2013. Accessed June 2016. http://www.care2.com/greenliving/the-mcgovern-report.html

18. Select Committee on the Nutrition and Human Needs United States Senate. "Dietary Goals for the United States: Second Edition." 95th Congress 1st Session. Accessed June 2016. https://naldc.nal.usda.gov/naldc/download.xhtml?id=1759572&content=PDF

19. W. Finney, "American National Cattlemen's Association News Release," February 16, 1977, George S. McGovern Papers, Box 993 Folder Meat; Public Policy Papers, Department of Rare Books and Special Collections, Princeton University Library.

20. Select Committee on the Nutrition and Human Needs United States Senate. "Dietary Goals for the United States: Second Edition."

21. Gerald M. Oppenheimer and Daniel Benrubi. McGovern's Senate Select Committee on Nutrition and Human Needs Versus the: Meat Industry on the Diet-Heart Question (1976–1977).

22. Ibid.

23. J. Mayer and J. Dwyer. "Experts Polled on Diet, Heart Disease." *Los Angeles Times.* August 10, 1978: K6.

24. Hearings Before the Select Committee on Nutrition and Human Needs of the United States Senate, *Diet Related to Killer Diseases, III*, March 24, 1977 (Washington, DC: US Government Printing Office, 1977), Pg. 17-19.

25. "Panel Stands by Its Dietary Goals But Eases a View on Eating Meat." *New York Times.* January 24, 1978. Accessed June 2016.

26. Select Committee on the Nutrition and Human Needs United States Senate. "Dietary Goals for the United States: Second Edition."

27. Ibid.

28. Ibid.

29. Select Committee on Nutrition and Human Needs. "Dietary Goals For the United States."

30. Select Committee on the Nutrition and Human Needs United States Senate. "Dietary Goals for the United States: Second Edition."

31. "Panel Stands by Its Dietary Goals But Eases a View on Eating Meat." *New York Times.*

32. "Feeding, and Heeding, the Poor." New York Times website. February 2, 1977. Accessed June 2016. http://www.nytimes.com/1977/02/02/archives/feeding-and-heeding-the-poor.html

33. McFadden, Robert. "James Abdnor, Former South Dakota Senator, Dies at 89." New York Times website. May 16, 2012. Accessed June 2016. http://www.nytimes.com/2012/05/17/us/james-abdnor-former-south-dakota-senator-dies-at-89.html

34. The Future of the American Cattle Industry. Hearing Before the Subcommittee on Agriculture and Transportation of the Joint Economic Committee. March 31, 1986. Accessed June 2016. http://www.jec.senate.gov/reports/99th%20Congress/The%20Future%20of%20the%20American%20Cattle%20Industry%20(1389).pdf

35. "History of Dietary Guidelines for Americans." U.S. Department of Health and Human Services website. Accessed June 2016. https://health.gov/dietaryguidelines/history.htm

36. "Scientific Report of the 2015 Dietary Guidelines Advisory Committee." Office of Disease Prevention and Health Promotion website. Accessed June 2016. https://health.gov/dietaryguidelines/2015-scientific-report/02-executive-summary.asp

37. "International Life Sciences Institute." Center for Media and Democracy Source Watch website. Accessed June 2016. http://www.sourcewatch.org/index.php/International_Life_Sciences_Institute. "WORLD: WHO Shuts Life Sciences Industry Group Out of Setting Health Standards." Corp Watch website. February 2, 2006. Accessed June 2016. http://www.corpwatch.org/article.php?id=13204

38. Herman, Jeff. "Saving U.S. Dietary Advice from Conflicts of Interest." Food and Drug Law Journal. 2010; Volume 65, No. 2. Pg. 309-316.

39. "American Council on Science and Health." Center for Media and Democracy Source Watch website. Accessed June 2016. http://www.sourcewatch.org/index.php/American_Council_on_Science_and_Health

40. "International Food Information Council." Center for Media and Democracy Source Watch website. Accessed June 2016. http://www.sourcewatch.org/index.php/International_Food_Information_Council

41. "WORLD: WHO Shuts Life Sciences Industry Group Out of Setting Health Standards." Corp Watch website. "International Life Sciences Institute." Center for Media and Democracy Source Watch website.

42. Herman, Jeff. "Saving U.S. Dietary Advice from Conflicts of Interest."

43. "Scientific Report of the 2015 Dietary Guidelines Advisory Committee. Part D. Chapter 2: Dietary Patterns, Foods and Nutrients, and Health Outcomes - Continued." Office of Disease Prevention and Health Promotion website. Accessed June 2016. https://health.gov/dietaryguidelines/2015-scientific-report/07-chapter-2/d2-6.asp

44. "Scientific Report of the 2015 Dietary Guidelines Advisory Committee. Part D. Chapter 5: Food Sustainability and Safety - Continued." Office of Disease Prevention and Health Promotion website. Accessed June 2016. https://health.gov/dietaryguidelines/2015-scientific-report/10-chapter-5/d5-3.asp

45. "The 2015 Dietary Guidelines Advisory Committee releases its courageous report." Food Politics website. February 20, 2015. Accessed June 2016. http://www.foodpolitics.com/2015/02/the-2015-dietary-guidelines-advisory-committee-releases-its-courageous-report/

46. Take a look at almost every one of the major USDA officeholders in 2004 and their industry ties: Secretary Ann Veneman: **lobbying firms specializing in food and agriculture**; Deputy Secretary James Moseley: **owner of hog and feed-grain**

farm; Deputy Under Secretary for Farm and Foreign Agricultural Services Floyd Gaibler: **International Dairy Foods Association and National Cheese Institute/American Butter Institute**; Deputy Under Secretary for Marketing Charles Lambert: **National Cattlemen's Beef Association**; Under Secretary for Marketing Bill Hawks: **owner of pesticide aerial application service**; Director of the Center for Nutrition Policy and Promotion Eric Hentges: **National Pork Board and National Livestock and Meat Board**; Former Deputy Assistant Secretary for Congressional Relations Michael Torrey: **Ice Cream, Milk and Cheese Political Action Committee**. "Politics 101." Center for Science in the Public Interest website. Accessed June 2016. ^{http://www.cspinet.org/nah/09_04/cspinews.pdf} The current USDA Secretary, Tom Vilsack, is a huge supporter of Monsanto, and in 2011 authorized, despite loud opposition, unrestricted commercial farming of genetically modified alfalfa—a crop developed, coincidentally, by Monsanto, and used primarily for feeding dairy cows. Pollack, Andrew. "U.S. Approves Genetically Modified Alfalfa." New York Times website. January 27, 2011. Accessed June 2016. http://www.nytimes.com/2011/01/28/business/28alfalfa.html

47.   "Thune Leads Call for USDA, HHS to Include Lean Red Meat in 2015 Dietary Guidelines." U.S. Senator John Thune website. March 12, 2015. Accessed June 2016. http://www.thune.senate.gov/public/index.cfm/2015/3/thune-leads-call-for-usda-hhs-to-include-lean-red-meat-in-2015-dietary-guidelines

48.   "CSPI report Congressional Catering: How Big Food and Agricultural Special Interests Wield Influence in Congress and Undermine Public Health." Center for Science in the Public Interest website. June 1, 2015. Accessed June 2016. https://cspinet.org/resource/congressional-catering-report

49.   "Chapter 2. Shifts Needed To Align With Healthy Eating Patterns." Office of Disease Prevention and Health Promotion website. Accessed June 2016. https://health.gov/dietaryguidelines/2015/guidelines/chapter-2/a-closer-look-at-current-intakes-and-recommended-shifts/

50.   "Appendix 3. USDA Food Patterns: Healthy U.S.-Style Eating Pattern." Office of Disease Prevention and Health Promotion website. Accessed June 2016. https://health.gov/dietaryguidelines/2015/guidelines/appendix-3/

51.   Scudellari, Megan. "Nutrition experts criticize new federal dietary guidelines." The Boston Globe. January 12, 2016. Accessed June 2016. https://www.bostonglobe.com/lifestyle/food-dining/2016/01/12/nutritionists-criticize-new-federal-dietary-guidelines/bx7b9lU5jAQ7thec97h52L/story.html

52.   Simon, Michele. "Whitewashed: How Industry and Government Promote Dairy Junk Foods." Huffington Post website. August 18, 2014. Accessed June 2016. http://www.huffingtonpost.com/michele-simon/dairy-junk-foods_b_5485922.html

53.   Butler, Kiera. "How the US Government Helps McDonald's Sell Junk Food." Mother Jones website. June 23, 2014. Accessed June 2016. http://www.motherjones.com/environment/2014/06/usda-dairy-checkoff-mcdonalds-taco-bell

54.   "Dairy Checkoff Leader Tells Farmers from Across the Country How They Can Help Grow Sales and Trust." Dairy Management Inc. November 15, 2013. Accessed June 2016. http://hoards.com/article-10927-dairy-checkoff-leader-tells-farmers-from-across-the-country-how-they-can-help-grow-sales-and-trust.html

55. Simon, Michele. "Whitewashed: How Industry and Government Promote Dairy Junk Foods."

56. Orwell, George. Sonia Orwell & Ian Angus, ed. *In Front of Your Nose: 1945-1950*. Boston: Nonpareil Books, David R. Godine. 2000. Pg. 137.

57. Becker, Geoffrey S. Federal Farm Promotion ("Check-Off") Programs. *CRS (Congressional Research Service) Report for Congress*. The Library of Congress. October 20, 2008.

58. "Grain Harvest Sets Record, But Supplies Still Tight." World Watch Institute. Accessed June 2016. http://www.worldwatch.org/node/5539

59. "U.S. and Wisconsin Soybean Facts." Wisconsin Soybean Association. Accessed June 2016. http://www.wisoybean.org/news/soybean_facts.php

60. Becker, Geoffrey S. Federal Farm Promotion ("Check-Off") Programs. *CRS (Congressional Research Service) Report for Congress*.

61. Simon, David Robinson. *Meatonomics*. San Francisco: Conari Press. 2013. Pg. 8.

62. Ibid. Pg. xxii.

63. US Census Bureau, Statistical Abtracts (1940); US Bureau of Labor Statistics, "Average Prices (2011)"; USDA Economic Research Service, "Red Meat and Poultry – Per Capita Availability."

64. Simon. *Meatonomics*. Pg. 76.

65. "Canada GDP 1960-2016." Trading Economics website. Accessed June 2016. http://www.tradingeconomics.com/canada/gdp

66. Paul A. Heidenreich et al., "Forecasting the Future of Cardiovascular Disease in the United States: A Policy Statement from the American Heart Association," *Circulation* 123 (2011) 933–-944; American Cancer Society, "Cancer Facts & Figures 2012"; American Diabetes Association, "Economic Costs of Diabetes in the US in 2007," *Diabetes Care* 31, no. 3 (2008); US Centers for Disease Control and Prevention, "Diabetes – Success and Opportunities for Population-Based Prevention and Control: At a Glance 2010."

67. US Department of Health and Human Services, "2014 Budget."

68. Grey, Clark, Shih and Associates, Limited, "Farming the Mailbox: US Federal and State Subsidies to Agriculture – Study Prepared for Dairy Farmers of Canada" (2010); U. Rashid Sumaila et al., "A Bottom-Up Re-Estimation of Global Fisheries Subsidies," *Journal of Bioeconomics* 12 (2010): 201–225; Physicians Committee for Responsible Medicine (PCRM), "Agriculture and Health Policies in Conflict" (2011); Simon, David Robinson. *Meatonomics*. San Francisco: Conari Press. 2013. Pg. 79-80.

69. F. Bailey Norwood and Jayson L. Lusk, *Compassion by the Pound: The Economics of Farm Animal Welfare* (New York: Oxford University Press, 2011), 344–45.

70. Friedrich, Bruce. "Meatonomics: The Bizarre Economics of the Meat & Dairy Industries." Huffington Post website. November 2013. Accessed June 2016. http://www.huffingtonpost.com/bruce-friedrich/meatonomics-the-bizarre-e_b_3853414.html

71. "IRRIGATED LANDS DEGRADATION: A GLOBAL PERSPECTIVE." Civilizations Future website. Accessed June 2016. http://www.civilizationsfuture.com/bsundquist/ir0.html

72. Simon. *Meatonomics*. Pg. 80.

73. Stewart, James. "Richer Farmers, Bigger Subsidies." New York Times website. July 19, 2013. Accessed June 2016. http://www.nytimes.com/2013/07/20/business/richer-farmers-bigger-subsidies.html?_r=0

74. 2009 US Federal Income Tax Return for National Cattlemen's Beef Association; 2010 US Federal Income Tax Returns for National Pork Council, American Meat Institute, National Meat Association, National Chicken Council, National Turkey Federation, US Poultry and Egg Association, United Egg Association, National Milk Producers Federation, and Western United Dairymen. http://www.guidestar.org

75. Lopez, Rigoberto A. "Campaign Contributions and Agricultural Subsidies," *Economics and Politics* 13, no. 3 (2001): 257-78.

76. "H.R.812 - Commonsense Consumption Act of 2009." 111th Congress (2009-2010). Accessed June 2016. https://www.congress.gov/bill/111th-congress/house-bill/812

77. Wilking CL, Daynard RA. Beyond cheeseburgers: the impact of commonsense consumption acts on future obesity-related lawsuits. Food and Drug Law Journal. 2013;68(3):229-39, i.

78. "'Cheeseburger bill' puts bite on lawsuits." CNN website. October 20, 2005. Accessed June 2016. http://www.cnn.com/2005/POLITICS/10/20/cheeseburger.bill/index.html?_s=PM:POLITICS

79. "United States of ALEC." BillMoyers.com: Moyers & Company website. September 28, 2012. Accessed April 2016. http://billmoyers.com/segment/united-states-of-alec/

80. Collins, Jon. "Minnesota bills traced to controversial corporate group ALEC." Daily Planet website. August 3, 2011. Accessed June 2016. http://www.tcdailyplanet.net/minnesota-bills-traced-controversial-corporate-group-alec/

81. "ALEC Corporations." Center for Media and Democracy Source Watch website. Accessed June 2016. http://www.sourcewatch.org/index.php/ALEC_Corporations. "ALEC Trade Groups." Center for Media and Democracy Source Watch website. Accessed June 2016. http://www.sourcewatch.org/index.php/ALEC_Trade_Groups

82. The Editorial Board. "No More Exposés in North Carolina." New York Times website. February 1, 2016. Accessed June 2016. http://www.nytimes.com/2016/02/01/opinion/no-more-exposes-in-north-carolina.html

83. "U.S. v. SHAC 7." Center for Constitutional Rights website. Accessed June 2016. http://ccrjustice.org/home/what-we-do/our-cases/us-v-shac-7#

84. Ibid.

85. "The Animal Enterprise Terrorism Act (AETA)." Center for Constitutional Rights website. November 19, 2007. Accessed June 2016. http://ccrjustice.org/home/get-involved/tools-resources/fact-sheets-and-faqs/animal-enterprise-terrorism-act-aeta#

86. "Taking Ag-Gag to Court." Animal Legal Defense Fund website. Accessed June 2016. http://aldf.org/cases-campaigns/features/taking-ag-gag-to-court/

87. Armour, Stephanie. "Industrial Terrorism of Undercover Livestock Videos Targeted." Bloomberg website. February 21, 2012. Accessed June 2016.

88. Flynn, Dan. "2013 Legislative Season Ends with 'Ag-Gag' Bills Defeated in 11 States: Food Safety News." Food Safety News. July 30, 2013. Accessed June 2016. http://www.foodsafetynews.

com/2013/07/2013-legislative-season-ends-with-ag-gag-bills-defeated-in-11-states/#.WEngO-ErLeQ

89. Dominguez, Matt. "The Animal Agriculture Industry Fails Again Trying to Silence Whistleblowers." One Green Planet website. November 3, 2014. Accessed June 2016. http://www.onegreenplanet.org/animalsandnature/the-animal-agriculture-industry-fails-again-trying-to-silence-whistleblowers/

90. Galli, Cindy. "Turn Off That Camera! Idaho Gov Signs Tough 'Ag-Gag' Into Law." ABC News website. February 28, 2014. Accessed June 2016. http://abcnews.go.com/Blotter/turn-off-camera-idaho-gov-signs-tough-ag/story?id=22726424

91. Weiss, Rick. "Video Reveals Violations of Laws, Abuse of Cows at Slaughterhouse." Washington Post website. January 30, 2008. Accessed June 2016. http://www.washingtonpost.com/wp-dyn/content/article/2008/01/29/AR2008012903054.html

92. Testimony by Wayne Pacelle, President and CEO—The Humane Society of the United States, House Committee on Oversight and Government Reform, Domestic Policy Subcommittee, Hearing on March 4, 2010, "Continuing Problems in USDA's Enforcement of the Humane Methods of Slaughter Act."

93. "Cow Disease May Have 30 Year Incubation Period." Dr. Mercola's Natural Health News website. March 22, 2001. Accessed June 2016. http://www.mercola.com/beef/incubation.htm

94. Weiss, Rick. "Video Reveals Violations of Laws, Abuse of Cows at Slaughterhouse."

95. "Torture on Tape." The Humane Society of the United States website. January 30, 2008. Accessed June 2016. http://blog.humanesociety.org/wayne/2008/01/calif-cow-abuse.html

96. Weiss, Rick. "Video Reveals Violations of Laws, Abuse of Cows at Slaughterhouse."

97. Martin, Andrew. "Largest Recall of Ground Beef Is Ordered." New York Times website. February 18, 2008. Accessed June 2016. http://www.nytimes.com/2008/02/18/business/18recall.html

98. Gumbel, Andrew. "Sick cattle footage prompts recall of US beef." The Independent website. February 2008. Accessed June 2016. http://www.independent.co.uk/news/world/americas/sick-cattle-footage-prompts-recall-of-us-beef-784042.html

99. "Rampant Animal Cruelty at California Slaughter Plant." The Humane Society of the United States website. January 30, 2008. Accessed June 2016. http://www.humanesociety.org/news/news/2008/01/undercover_investigation_013008.html?credit=blog_post_013008_id5555

100. Wald, Matthew. "Meat Packer Admits Slaughter of Sick Cows." New York Times website. March 2008. Accessed June 2016. http://www.nytimes.com/2008/03/13/business/13meat.html

101. Weiss, Rick. "Video Reveals Violations of Laws, Abuse of Cows at Slaughterhouse."

102. Gumbel, Andrew. "Sick cattle footage prompts recall of US beef."

103. Healey, James and Julie Schmit. "USDA orders largest beef recall: 143.4 million pounds." USA Today website. February 18, 2008. Accessed June 2016. http://usatoday30.usatoday.com/money/industries/food/2008-02-17-slaughterhouse-recall_N.htm

104. Moss, Michael and Andrew Martin. "Food Problems Elude Private Inspectors." New York Times website. March 5, 2009. Accessed June 2016. http://www.nytimes.com/2009/03/06/business/06food.html

105. American Institute of Baking. Food Safety Audit Report. March 27, 2008. Accessed June 2016. http://documents.nytimes.com/food-safety-peanut-inspection#p=41&a=63

106. Weiss, Rick. "Video Reveals Violations of Laws, Abuse of Cows at Slaughterhouse."

107. Flaccus, Gillian. "Packing plant sued over use of 'downer' animals." Seattle Times website. September 25, 2009. Accessed June 2016. http://www.seattletimes.com/nation-world/packing-plant-sued-over-use-of-downer-animals/

CHAPTER FIFTEEN: PHARM TO TABLE TO PHARM

1. Reier, Sharon and International Herald Tribune. "Blockbuster drugs: Take the hype in small doses." New York Times website. March 1, 2003. Accessed June 2016. http://www.nytimes.com/2003/03/01/your-money/blockbuster-drugstake-the-hype-in-small-doses.html

2. Petersen, Melody. *Our Daily Meds*. New York: Farrar, Straus, and Giroux. 2008. Pg. 63.

3. "Medicines Use and Spending Shifts: A Review of the Use of Medicines in the U.S. in 2014." QuintilesIMS website. Accessed June 2016. http://www.imshealth.com/en/thought-leadership/quintilesims-institute/reports/medicines-use-in-the-us-2014

4. "Gross Domestic Product 2015." World Bank website. Accessed June 2016. http://databank.worldbank.org/data/download/GDP.pdf

5. "Federal Education Spending." New America website. Accessed June 2016. http://www.newamerica.org/education-policy/policy-explainers/federal-education-budget/federal-education-budget/

6. Pollack, Andrew. "Cancer Doctors Offer Way to Compare Medicines, Including by Cost." New York Times website. June 22, 2015. Accessed June 2016. http://www.nytimes.com/2015/06/23/business/cancer-doctors-offer-way-to-compare-medicines-including-by-cost.html?_r=0

7. Elkins, Chris. "How Much Cancer Costs." Drug Watch website. October 7, 2015. Accessed June 2016. https://www.drugwatch.com/2015/10/07/cost-of-cancer/

8. Pollack, Andrew. "Cancer Doctors Offer Way to Compare Medicines, Including by Cost."

9. Petersen. *Our Daily Meds*. Pg.147.

10. Ibid. Pg.147-148.

11. Light, Donald. "New Prescription Drugs: A Major Health Risk With Few Offsetting Advantages." Edmond J. Safra Center for Ethics at Harvard website. June 27, 2014. Accessed June 2016. http://ethics.harvard.edu/blog/new-prescription-drugs-major-health-risk-few-offsetting-advantages

12. Petersen. *Our Daily Meds*. Pg.47.

13. Personalized Medicine: The Road Ahead. The Wharton Healthcare Leadership Exchange. February 2008. Accessed June 2016. http://whcbc.org/conf2010/whle2006.pdf

14. Parisi, A. A comparison of Angioplasty with Medical Treatment of Single Vessel Coronary Artery Disease. New England Journal of Medicine. 1992;326:10. Graboys T. Results of a Second-Opinion Trial among Patients Recommended for Coronary

Angioplasty. Journal of the American Medical Association. 1992;268:2537. Graboys T. Second-Opinion Trial in Patients Recommended for Coronary Angiography. Journal of the American Medical Association. 1993; 269:1504. McGivney S. Angioplasty vs. Medical Therapy for Single-Vessel Coronary Artery Disease. New England Journal of Medicine. 1992;326:1632.

15.   Park, Alice. "A Cardiac Conundrum." Harvard Magazine website. March-April 2013. Accessed June 2016. http://harvardmagazine.com/2013/03/a-cardiac-conundrum

16.   S. Carpenter. "Cognitive problems after heart bypass linked to long-term decline." Monitor on Psychology. 2001;Vol 32, No. 5. Xiumei Sun, Joseph Lindsay, Lee H. Monsein, et al; Silent Brain Injury After Cardiac Surgery: A Review. Journal of the American College of Cardiology. 2012; Volume 60, Issue 9. doi: 10.1016/j.jacc.2012.02.079. Matthews, Robert. "Heart bypass patients left with brain damage." The Telegraph website. October 8, 2000. Accessed June 2016. http://www.telegraph.co.uk/news/worldnews/1369435/Heart-bypass-patients-left-with-brain-damage.html. "Bill Clinton's Madness: A Consequence of Heart-Bypass Surgery Brain Damage." Dr. McDougall's Health & Medical Center website. Accessed June 2016. https://www.drmcdougall.com/health/education/health-science/featured-articles/articles/bill-clintons-madness/. Hill J. Neuropathological Manifestations of Cardiac Surger. Annals of Thoracic Surgery 7. 1969;409. Editorial, Brain Damage after Open-Heart Surgery. Lancet 1.1982;1161. Henriksen L. Evidence Suggestive of Diffuse Brain Damage Following Cardiac Operations. Lancet 1.1984;816. Editorial, Brain Damage and Open Heart Surgery. Lancet 2.1989;364. Murkin J. Anesthesia, the Brain, and Cardiopulmonary Bypass. Annals of Thoracic Surgery. 1993;56:1461. McDougall, John. *The McDougall Program for a Healthy Heart*. New York: Dutton.1996. Pg. 206-7.

17.   Park, Alice. "A Cardiac Conundrum."

18.   McDougall. *The McDougall Program*. Pg. 210.

19.   Light, Donald. "New Prescription Drugs: A Major Health Risk With Few Offsetting Advantages."

20.   Ibid.

21.   Anderson, Richard. "Pharmaceutical industry gets high on fat profits." BBC News website. November 6, 2014. Accessed June 2016. http://www.bbc.com/news/business-28212223

22.   Swanson, Ana. "Big pharmaceutical companies are spending far more on marketing than research." Washington Post website. February 11, 2015. Accessed June 2016. https://www.washingtonpost.com/news/wonk/wp/2015/02/11/big-pharmaceutical-companies-are-spending-far-more-on-marketing-than-research/?utm_term=.d26c14708da2

23.   "Selling Side Effects: Big Pharma's Marketing Machine." Drug Watch website. Accessed June 2016. https://www.drugwatch.com/featured/big-pharma-marketing/

24.   Petersen. *Our Daily Meds*. Pg. 67.

25.   "Selling Side Effects: Big Pharma's Marketing Machine."

26.   Engelberg, Joseph, Christopher A. Parsons, and Nathan Tefft. "Financial Conflicts of Interest in Medicine." Rady School of Management, University of California San Diego. January 2014. Accessed June 2016. http://rady.ucsd.edu/faculty/directory/engelberg/pub/portfolios/DOCTORS.pdf

27. Petersen. *Our Daily Meds*. Pg.185.

28. Ibid.

29. Davis. *Proteinaholic*. Pg. 151-152.

30. Siri-Tarino PW, Sun Q, Hu FB, Krauss RM. Meta-analysis of prospective cohort studies evaluating the association of saturated fat with cardiovascular disease. American Journal of Clinical Nutrition. 2010; 91(3), 535-546.doi:10.3945/ajcn.2009.27725.

31. Davis. *Proteinaholic*. Pg. 164-5.

32. Chowdhury R, Warnakula S, Kunutsor S, DiAngelantonio E, et al; Association of dietary, circulating, and supplement fatty acids with coronary risk: a systematic review and meta-analysis. Annals of Internal Medicine.2014;160(6), 398-406. doi:10.7326/M13-1788.

33. Patty W. Siri-Tarino, Qi Sun, Frank B. Hu, et al; Saturated Fatty Acids and Risk of Coronary Heart Disease: Modulation by Replacement Nutrients. Current Atherosclerosis Reports. 2010; 12(6): 384–390. doi: 10.1007/s11883-010-0131-6.

34. Patty W Siri-Tarino, Qi Sun, Frank B Hu, et al; Meta-analysis of prospective cohort studies evaluating the association of saturated fat with cardiovascular disease.

35. Burton, Bob. "Something Fishy." Center for Media and Democracy's PR Watch website. October 2, 2007. Accessed June 2016. http://www.prwatch.org/node/6401/print

36. "Our Brands." Unilever website. Accessed June 2016. https://www.unilever.com/brands/

37. Davis, Garth. *Proteinaholic*. Pg. 166. Corti MC, Guralnik JM, Salive ME Harris T, Ferrucci L, Glynn RJ, Havlik RJ. Clarifying the direct relation between total cholesterol levels and death from coronary heart disease in older persons. Annals of Internal Medicine. 1997;126(10), 753-760.

38. Davis. *Proteinaholic*. Pg.166.

39. "Scientific Report of the 2015 Dietary Guidelines Advisory Committee. Part D. Chapter 1: Food and Nutrient Intakes, and Health: Current Status and Trends." Office of Disease Prevention and Health Promotion website. Accessed June 2016. https://health.gov/dietaryguidelines/2015-scientific-report/06-chapter-1/d1-2.asp.

40. "The Physicians Committee Sues USDA and DHHS, Exposing Industry Corruption in Dietary Guidelines Decision on Cholesterol." Physicians Committee for Responsible Medicine website. Accessed June 2016. https://www.pcrm.org/media/news/physicians-committee-sues-usda-and-dhhs

41. Ibid.

42. Ibid.

43. "CHAPTER 1 Key Elements of Healthy Eating Patterns." Office of Disease Prevention and Health Promotion website. Accessed June 2016. https://health.gov/dietaryguidelines/2015/guidelines/chapter-1/a-closer-look-inside-healthy-eating-patterns/

44. "Benefits of Chewing." Wrigley website. Accessed June 2016. http://www.wrigley.com/global/benefits-of-chewing.aspx

45. "Fat Under Fire: New findings or shaky science?" Center for Science in the Public Interest website. May 1, 2014. Accessed June 2016. https://cspinet.org/resource/fat-under-fire

CHAPTER SIXTEEN: EXPLODING MYTHS

1. Santora, Marc. "In Diabetes Fight, Raising Cash and Keeping Trust." New York Times website. November 25, 2006. Accessed June 2016. http://www.nytimes.com/2006/11/25/health/25ada.html

2. "Our Corporate Supporters." American Diabetes Association website. Accessed June 2016. http://www.diabetes.org/about-us/corporate-support/our-corporate-supporters.html

3. "Percentage of product class sales of Walgreens in the United States from 2013 to 2016." The Statistics Portal website. Accessed June 2016. https://www.statista.com/statistics/269555/percentage-of-product-class-sales-of-walgreens-in-the-us-since-2005/

4. "Momentum Builds: American Diabetes Association Annual Report 2012." American Diabetes Association website. Accessed June 2016. http://main.diabetes.org/dorg/PDFs/Financial/2012-american-diabetes-association-annual-report.pdf

5. Santora, Marc. "In Diabetes Fight, Raising Cash and Keeping Trust."

6. "Our Corporate Supporters." American Diabetes Association website.

7. "American Heart Association." Center for Science in the Public Interest website. Accessed June 2016. http://www.cspinet.org/integrity/nonprofits/american_heart_association.html

8. "Life is Why: 2013-14 Annual Report." American Heart Association website. Accessed June 2016. https://www.heart.org/idc/groups/heart-public/@wcm/@cmc/documents/downloadable/ucm_469976.pdf

9. "American Heart Association Annual Report 2011-2012." American Heart Association website. Accessed June 2016. https://www.heart.org/idc/groups/heart-public/@wcm/@adt/documents/downloadable/ucm_449081.pdf

10. "American Heart Association." Center for Science in the Public Interest website.

11. "National Supporters and Sponsors." American Heart Association website. Accessed June 2016. http://www.heart.org/HEARTORG/HealthyLiving/National-Supporters-and-Sponsors_UCM_436493_Article.jsp#.WEn26-ErLHd

12. Mitchell, Stacy. "Eaters, beware: Walmart is taking over our food system." Grist website. December 30, 2011. Accessed June 2016. http://grist.org/food/2011-12-30-eaters-beware-walmart-is-taking-over-our-food-system/

13. Hutchison, Courtney. "Fried Chicken for the Cure?" ABC News website. April 24, 2010. Accessed June 2016. http://abcnews.go.com/Health/Wellness/kfc-fights-breast-cancer-fried-chicken/story?id=10458830

14. "Factbox: Key facts about French yoghurt group Yoplait." Reuters website. November 2010. Accessed June 2016. http://www.reuters.com/article/us-yoplait-factbox-idUSTRE6AP2BA20101126

15. "Partners With Passion." Susan G. Komen website. Accessed June 2016. http://ww5.komen.org/Meet_Our_Partners/

16. Butler, Kiera. "I Went to the Nutritionists' Annual Confab. It Was Catered by McDonald's." Mother Jones website. May 12, 2014. Accessed June 2016. http://www.motherjones.com/environment/2014/05/my-trip-mcdonalds-sponsored-nutritionist-convention

17. Brownell KD, Warner KE. The perils of ignoring history: Big Tobacco played dirty and millions died. How similar is Big Food? The Milbank Quarterly. 2009;87(1):259-94. doi: 10.1111/j.1468-0009.2009.00555.x.

18. Bradford, Alina. "What Is the Paleo Diet?" Live Science website. January 13, 2016. Accessed June 2016. http://www.livescience.com/53368-paleo-diet.html.

19. Davis. *Proteinaholic*. Pg. 97.

20. Kolbert, Elizabeth. "Stone Soup: How the Paleolithic life style got trendy." New Yorker Magazine. July 28, 2014. http://www.newyorker.com/magazine/2014/07/28/stone-soup

21. Joulwan, Melissa, and Kellyann Petrucci. "PALEO DIET: FOODS TO AVOID." Dummies website. Accessed June 2016. http://www.dummies.com/food-drink/special-diets/paleo-diet/paleo-diet-foods-to-avoid/

22. Ibid.

23. "PALEO DIET 101." Paleo Leap website. Accessed June 2016. http://paleoleap.com/paleo-101/.

24. Davis. *Proteinaholic*. Pg. 98.

25. Amanda G. Henry Peter S. Ungar Benjamin H, et al; The diet of *Australopithecus sediba*. Nature. 2012; 487, 90–93. doi:10.1038/nature11185.

26. Davis. *Proteinaholic*. Pg. 98.

27. "[Journals]: PALEO DIET: Big Brains Needed Carbs - The importance of dietary carbohydrate in human evolution." University of Chicago Press website. Accessed June 2016. http://press.uchicago.edu/pressReleases/2015/August/150806_qrb_hardy_et_al_paleo_diet.html

28. Popper. *Food Over Medicine*. Pg. 76.

29. Davis. *Proteinaholic*. Pg. 98.

30. "Top 5 Worst Celebrity Diets to Avoid in 2015." The Association of UK Dietitians website. December 2014. Accessed June 2016. https://www.bda.uk.com/news/view?id=39

31. Davis. *Proteinaholic*. Pg. 100.

32. Pobiner, Briana. "Meat-Eating Among the Earliest Humans." American Scientist website. May-June 2016. Accessed June 2016. http://www.americanscientist.org/issues/pub/2016/3/meat-eating-among-the-earliest-humans

33. Mills, Milton. "The Comparative Anatomy of Eating." Animals Deserve Absolute Protection Today and Tomorrow website. Accessed June 2016. http://www.adaptt.org/Mills%20The%20Comparative%20Anatomy%20of%20Eating1.pdf

34. Parker-Pope, Tara. "The Human Body Is Built for Distance." New York Times website. October 26, 2009. Accessed June 2016. http://www.nytimes.com/2009/10/27/health/27well.html

35. Meat Month website. Accessed June 2016. http://www.meatmonth.co.uk/

36. "Ten Physical Differences Between Carnivores (Meat Eaters) and Herbivores (Plant Eaters). Is the Human Body Designed to Eat Animal Products?" Winnipeg Assembly of Yahweh website. Accessed June 2016. http://www.waoy.org/26.html

37. "What is Battery Acid?" about.com Accessed June 2016. http://chemistry.about.com/od/chemicalcomposition/f/What-Is-Battery-Acid.htm

38. "Understanding Body pH Balance." Even Better Health website. Accessed June 2016. http://www.evenbetterhealth.com/Body_pH_Balance.php

39. "Pets and Onions." Pet Insurance website. Accessed June 2016. https://phz8. petinsurance.com/healthzone/pet-health/pet-toxins/pets-and-onions

40. Andrews, Ryan. "All About Sodium." Precision Nutrition website. Accessed June 2016. http://www.precisionnutrition.com/all-about-sodium

41. Moore, Paul E. *The Hidden Power of Smell*. New York: Springer. 2015. Pg.191. Havlicek J, Lenochova P. The effect of meat consumption on body odor attractiveness. Chemical Senses. 2006;31(8):747-52. doi: 10.1093/chemse/bjl017

42. "Smell may play a big role in selecting your potential mate." News Medical Life Sciences website. Accessed June 2016. http://www.news-medical.net/news/2005/05/09/9900.aspx

43. Mills, Milton. "The Anatomy of a Vegan." All Creatures website. July 2012. Accessed June 2016. http://www.all-creatures.org/health/veganpalooza2012-mills. html

44. Nazaryan, Alexander. "You're 100 Percent Wrong About Steak Tartare." Newsweek website. January 23, 2016. Accessed June 2016. http://www.newsweek. com/2016/02/05/youre-100-percent-wrong-about-steak-tartare-418803.html

45. "Nurse in critical condition, six others sick, after eating beef tartare." CTV News Montreal website. January 15, 2014. Accessed June 2016. http://montreal. ctvnews.ca/nurse-in-critical-condition-six-others-sick-after-eating-beef-tartare-1.1640352 Aubrey, Allison. "Raw Beef Kibbeh Blamed In Salmonella Outbreak. Is Steak Tartare Next?." NPR website. January 29, 2013. Accessed June 2016. http://www.npr.org/sections/thesalt/2013/01/28/170483873/raw-beef-kibbeh-blamed-in-salmonella-outbreak-is-steak-tartare-next

46. Dean, Sam. "15 Raw Meat Dishes from Around the World." Bon Appétit website. May 20, 2013. Accessed June 2016. http://www.bonappetit.com/trends/article/15-raw-meat-dishes-from-around-the-world

47. "Study Says Eyes Evolved for X-Ray Vision." Rensselaer Polytechnic Institute website. Accessed June 2016. https://news.rpi.edu/luwakkey/2486

48. Goldman, Jason. "Evolution: Why Do Your Eyes Face Forward?" BBC website. October 28, 2014. Accessed June 2016. http://www.bbc.com/future/story/20141013-why-do-your-eyes-face-forwards

49. "Study Says Eyes Evolved for X-Ray Vision." Rensselaer Polytechnic Institute website. Accessed June 2016. https://news.rpi.edu/luwakkey/2486

50. "Plant Based on A Budget." Toni Okamoto website. Accessed June 2016. http://www.toniokamoto.com/#/plantbasedonabudget/

51. "Supplemental Nutrition Assistance Program (SNAP)." USDA's Food and Nutrition Service website. Accessed June 2016. http://www.fns.usda.gov/snap/eligibility

52. Freston, Kathy. "8 Ways to Eat Vegan (You Don't Have to Be Rich to Eat Healthy)" Alternet website. March 28, 2011. Accessed June 2016. http://www.alternet.org/story/150404/8_cheap_ways_to_eat_vegan_%28you_don't_have_to_be_rich_to_eat_healthy%29

CHAPTER SEVENTEEN: VEGAN ATHLETES

1. "Par." Reverso Dictionary website. Accessed June 2016. http://dictionary.reverso.net/french-english/par

2. "Courir.' Reverso Dictionary website. Accessed June 2016. http://dictionary.reverso.net/french-english/courir

3. "What is Parkour?" World Freerunning Parkour Federation website. Accessed June 2016. http://www.wfpf.com/parkour/

4. "Vegetarian Times Study Shows 7.3 Million Americans Are Vegetarians. Additional 22.8 Million Follow a Vegetarian-Inclined Diet." Vegetarian Times website. Accessed June 2016. http://www.vegetariantimes.com/article/vegetarianism-in-america

5. "Israelis Go Vegan." Vegetarian Times website. Accessed June 2016. https://vegetariannewsandviews.org/2014/12/09/israelis-go-vegan/

6. Dean, Tommy. "China's Vegan Population is Largest in the World." Veg News website. January 13, 2014. Accessed June 2016. http://vegnews.com/articles/page.do?pageId=6392&catId=8

7. Kirkova, Deni. "12 vegan athletes smashing it on a meat-free diet." metro.co.uk. Aug 26, 2015. Accessed June 2016. http://maetro.co.uk/2015/08/26/13-vegan-athletes-smashing-it-on-a-meat-free-diet-5349835/#ixzz4SIb9P634. Great Vegan Athletes website. Accessed June 2016. http://www.greatveganathletes.com/. Della Costa, Chloe. "10 Male Athletes You Didn't Know Were Vegan." Health & Fitness Cheat Sheet website. February 16, 2016. Accessed June 2016. http://www.cheatsheet.com/health-fitness/10-male-athletes-you-didnt-know-were-vegan.html/?a=viewall. Curreri, Frank. Ultimate Fighting Championship website. April 5, 2012. Accessed June 2016. http://www.ufc.com/news/Mac-Danzig-Diet-The-Truth-About-Vegan?id=. "Charlotte Willis lists her top ten vegan athletes, along with why they're so awe-inspiring." The Vegan Society website. October 2, 2015. Accessed June 2016. https://www.vegansociety.com/whats-new/blog/ten-best-plant-powered-athletes. Fox, Kit. "Scott Jurek Celebrates a New Appalachian Trail Thru-Hike Speed Record." Runner's World website. July 13, 2015. Accessed June 2016. http://www.runnersworld.com/trail-racing/scott-jurek-celebrates-a-new-appalachian-trail-thru-hike-speed-record. "Williams Sisters." Duck Stars website. Accessed June 2016. http://www.ducksters.com/sports/williams_sisters.php. Bilow, Rochelle. "This Man Ran the Entire Appalachian Trail in 46 Days. Here's What He Ate Along the Way." Bon Appétit website. August 17, 2015. Accessed June 2016. http://www.bonappetit.com/people/article/scott-jurek-ultrarunner-diet. Desaulniers, Élise. "You Can Be a Vegan AND a High-Performing Athlete." Huffington Post website. June 16, 2014. Accessed June 2016. http://www.huffingtonpost.ca/elise-desaulniers/athletes-and-vegan_b_5500373.html.

8. Webb, Densie. "Athletes and Protein Intake." Today's Dietitian website. June 2014. Accessed June 2016. http://www.todaysdietitian.com/newarchives/060114p22.shtml

9. Brazier, Brendan. *Thrive: The Vegan Nutrition Guide to Optimal Performance in Sports and Life*. Philadelphia: Da Capo Press. 2008. Pg. 3.

10. Ibid. Pg. 3-5.

11. Ibid. Pg. 34-39.

12. Connealy, Leigh. "Cure Acidosis and Inflammation, Root Causes of Disease." Newport Natural Health. August 28, 2014. Accessed June 2016. https://www.newportnaturalhealth.com/2014/08/cure-acidosis-and-inflammation-root-causes-of-disease/

13. Brazier. *Thrive*. Pg. 47-48.

14. Ibid. Pg. 49-51.

15. Ibid. Pg. 17.

16. Ibid. Pg. 27.

17. Davis. *Becoming Vegan: Comprehensive Edition*. Pg. 214.

18. Ibid.

19. McBride, Judy. "B12 Deficiency May Be More Widespread Than Thought." United States Department of Agriculture Agricultural Research Service website. August 2, 2000. Accessed June 2016. https://www.ars.usda.gov/news-events/news/research-news/2000/b12-deficiency-may-be-more-widespread-than-thought/

20. Davis. *Becoming Vegan: Comprehensive Edition*. Pg. 217.

21. Watanabe F. Vitamin B12 sources and bioavailability. Experimental Biology and Medicine. 2007;232(10):1266-74. doi: 10.3181/0703-MR-67. Levine AS, Doscherholmen A. Vitamin B12 bioavailability from egg yolk and egg white: relationship to binding proteins. American Journal of Clinical Nutrition. 1983;38(3):436-9. Herbert V. Vitamin B-12: plant sources, requirements, and assay. American Journal of Clinical Nutrition. 1988;48(3 Suppl):852-8. Greger, Michael. "Safest Source of B12." NutritionFacts.org. February 6, 2012. Accessed June 2016. http://nutritionfacts.org/video/safest-source-of-b12/

22. Holick MF, Chen TC. Vitamin D deficiency: a worldwide problem with health consequences. American Journal of Clinical Nutrition. 2008;87(4):1080S-6S.

23. "Top 10 Foods Highest in Vitamin D." HealthAliciousNess.com. Accessed June 2016. https://www.healthaliciousness.com/articles/high-vitamin-D-foods.php

24. Johnson, Ana. "Vitamin D Supplements: Does the Source Matter?" Smartypants Vitamins website. Accessed June 2016. https://smartypantsvitamins.com/vitamin-d-supplements-does-the-source-matter/

25. Davis. *Becoming Vegan: Comprehensive Edition*. Pg. 227.

26. Ibid. Pg. 242.

27. Ibid. Pg. 415.

28. Ibid. Pg. 416.

29. Sandra Lösch, Negahnaz Moghaddam, Karl Grossschmidt, et al; "Stable Isotope and Trace Element Studies on Gladiators and Contemporary Romans from Ephesus (Turkey, 2nd and 3rd Ct. AD) - Implications for Differences in Diet." Plos One. 2014. doi: http://dx.doi.org/10.1371/journal.pone.0110489.

30. Kupper, Monika and Huw Jones. "Gladiators' graveyard discovered." BBC News website. May 2, 2007. Accessed June 2016. http://news.bbc.co.uk/2/hi/science/nature/6614479.stm

31. Sandra Lösch, Negahnaz Moghaddam, Karl Grossschmidt, et al; "Stable Isotope and Trace Element Studies on Gladiators and Contemporary Romans from Ephesus (Turkey, 2nd and 3rd Ct. AD) - Implications for Differences in Diet."

32. Coughlan, Sean. "Gladiators were 'mostly vegetarian.'" BBC News website. October 22, 2014. Accessed June 2016. http://www.bbc.com/news/education-29723384

33. Dean, Ward. "Strontium: Breakthrough Against Osteoporosis." World Health website. May 5, 2004. Accessed June 2016. http://www.worldhealth.net/news/strontium_breakthrough_against_osteoporo/

34. Sandra Lösch, Negahnaz Moghaddam, Karl Grossschmidt, et al; "Stable Isotope and Trace Element Studies on Gladiators and Contemporary Romans from Ephesus (Turkey, 2nd and 3rd Ct. AD) - Implications for Differences in Diet."

35. Ibid.

36. "Barley as Food." Botanical-Online website. Accessed June 2016. http://www.botanical-online.com/english/barleyfoods.htm

37. Sandra Lösch, Negahnaz Moghaddam, Karl Grossschmidt, et al; "Stable Isotope and Trace Element Studies on Gladiators and Contemporary Romans from Ephesus (Turkey, 2nd and 3rd Ct. AD) - Implications for Differences in Diet."

38. Andrews, Evan. "10 Things You May Not Know About Roman Gladiators." History website. March 4, 2014. Accessed June 2016. http://www.history.com/news/history-lists/10-things-you-may-not-know-about-roman-gladiators

39. Ibid.

40. Hadley, Kathryn. "Gladiators Were Vegetarians." History Today website. September 9, 2009. Accessed June 2016. http://www.historytoday.com/blog/news-blog/kathryn-hadley/gladiators-were-vegetarians

CHAPTER EIGHTEEN: THINGS SPIRAL AROUND

1. Gardner, Martha N. and Allan M. Brandt. "The Doctors' Choice Is America's Choice": The Physician in US Cigarette Advertisements, 1930-1953. American Journal of Public Health. 2006; 96(2): 222-232. doi:10.2105/AJPH.2005.066654.

2. Ibid.

3. DeVoto B. "Doctors Along the Boardwalk." *Harper's Magazine* (1947); reprinted in DeVoto, *The Easy Chair* (Boston: Houghton Mifflin Company, 1955) Pg. 91.

4. Gardner, Martha N. and Allan M. Brandt. "'The Doctors' Choice Is America's Choice": The Physician in US Cigarette Advertisements, 1930-1953.

5. Saxon, Wolfgang. "Ernst Wynder, 77, a Cancer Researcher, Dies." New York Times website. July 16, 1999. Accessed June 2016. http://www.nytimes.com/1999/07/16/us/ernst-wynder-77-a-cancer-researcher-dies.html.

6. Ernest L. Wynder and Evarts A. Graham. "Tobacco Smoking as a Possible Etiologic Factor in Bronchiogenic Carcinoma. A Study of Six Hundred and Eighty-Four Proved Cases." Journal of the American Medical Association.1985; Vol 253, No. 20. Richard Doll and A. Bradford Hill. Smoking and Carcinoma of the Lung. British Medical Journal. 1950; 2(4682): 739–748. "History of the Surgeon General's Reports on Smoking and Health." Centers for Disease Control and Prevention website. Accessed June 2016. http://www.cdc.gov/tobacco/data_statistics/sgr/history/

7.   "Tobacco." The Surgeon General of the United States website. Accessed June 2016. https://www.surgeongeneral.gov/priorities/tobacco/

8.   "Trends in Current Cigarette Smoking Among High School Students and Adults, United States, 1965–2014." Centers for Disease Control and Prevention website. Accessed June 2016. http://www.cdc.gov/tobacco/data_statistics/tables/trends/cig_smoking/

9.   Goldschmidt, Debra. "Smoking rate continues to decline among U.S. adults." CNN website. November 19, 2015. Accessed June 2016. http://www.cnn.com/2015/11/17/health/smoking-rate-decline/

10.   Feller, Stephen. "CDC: More people quit smoking in 2015 than in decades." UPI News website. May 24, 2016. Accessed June 2016. http://www.upi.com/Health_News/2016/05/24/CDC-More-people-quit-smoking-in-2015-than-in-decades/8841464091361/?spt=hts&or=1

11.   Nelson DE, Giovino GA, Emont S. Trends in cigarette smoking among US physicians and nurses. Journal of the American Medical Association. 1994;271(16):1273-5.

12.   "Smoking and Health Proposal." Brown & Williamson Records; Minnesota Litigation Documents. 1969. University of California San Francisco website. https://www.industrydocumentslibrary.ucsf.edu/tobacco/docs/#id=psdw0147.

13.   Munafò, Marcus. "'Doubt is Our Product': It's vital that scientists engage with the public and the media to ensure that their research is accurately represented." The London School of Economics and Political Science website. August 12, 2013. Accessed June 2016. http://blogs.lse.ac.uk/politicsandpolicy/doubt-is-our-product/ The full document is on Truth Tobacco Industry Documents: https://www.industrydocumentslibrary.ucsf.edu/tobacco/docs/#id=psdw0147 Accessed June 2016.

14.   Glantz, Stanton, John Slade, Lisa A. Bero, Peter Hanauer, Deborah E. Barnes, eds. *The Cigarette Papers*. Oakland: University of California Press. 1998. Pg. xiv.

15.   Butler, Kiera. "The Surprising Reason Why School Cafeterias Sell Chocolate Milk." Mother Jones website. November 18, 2015. Accessed June 2016. http://www.motherjones.com/environment/2015/10/milk-companies-market-schools-fast-food

16.   "Smoking & Tobacco Use. Highlights: Warning Labels." Centers for Disease Control and Prevention website. Accessed June 2016. http://www.cdc.gov/tobacco/data_statistics/sgr/2000/highlights/labels/

17.   "US Spends More on Health Care Than Other High-Income Nations But Has Lower Life Expectancy, Worse Health." The Commonwealth Fund website. October 8, 2015. Accessed June 2016. http://www.commonwealthfund.org/publications/press-releases/2015/oct/us-spends-more-on-health-care-than-other-nations

18.   Sahadi, Jeanne. "What your 2015 income tax dollars paid for." CNN News website. April 18, 2016. Accessed June 2016. http://money.cnn.com/2016/04/18/pf/taxes/how-are-tax-dollars-spent/

19.   "US Spends More on Health Care Than Other High-Income Nations But Has Lower Life Expectancy, Worse Health." The Commonwealth Fund website.

20.   "How Much Does Heart Surgery Cost?" Cost Helper website. Accessed June 2016. http://health.costhelper.com/heart-surgery.html

21.   Kevin M. Murphy and Robert H. Topel. "The Value of Health and Longevity." University of Chicago and National Bureau of Economic Research. Pg. 902.

22. Ibid. Pg. 898.

23. "Chronic Disease Prevention and Health Promotion." Centers for Disease Control and Prevention website. Accessed June 2016. http://www.cdc.gov/chronicdisease/index.htm

24. America's Infrastructure 2013 Report Card website. http://www.infrastructurereportcard.org/

25. Simon. *Meatonomics*. Pg.177.

26. "Fast Facts." Kaiser Permanente website. Accessed June 2016. https://share.kaiserpermanente.org/article/fast-facts-about-kaiser-permanente/

27. Abelson, Reed. "The Face of Future Health Care." New York Times website. March 20, 2013. Accessed June 2016. http://www.nytimes.com/2013/03/21/business/kaiser-permanente-is-seen-as-face-of-future-health-care.html?_r=0

28. "Fast Facts." Kaiser Permanente website.

29. "The Plant-Based Diet." Kaiser Permanente website. Accessed June 2016. https://share.kaiserpermanente.org/wp-content/uploads/2015/10/The-Plant-Based-Diet-booklet.pdf

30. Phillip J Tuso, Mohamed H Ismail, Benjamin P Ha, et al; Nutritional Update for Physicians: Plant-Based Diets. The Permanente Journal. 2013; 17(2):61-66 doi: https://doi.org/10.7812/TPP/12-085.

31. MacVean, Mary. "Cutting down on meat for health: More people are trying it." Los Angeles Times website. January 23, 2015. Accessed June 2016. http://www.latimes.com/science/sciencenow/la-sci-sn-vegan-health-20150121-story.html#ifrndnloc

32. Crawford, Elizabeth. "Vegan is Going Mainstream, Trend Data Suggests." Food Navigator website. March 2015. Accessed June 2016. http://www.foodnavigator-usa.com/Markets/Vegan-is-going-mainstream-trend-data-suggests.

33. "GLOBAL FOOD AND DRINK TRENDS 2017." Mintel website. Accessed June 2016. http://www.mintel.com/global-food-and-drink-trends. "Plant-Based Food Named a Top Trend for 2016." Latest Vegan News website. December 31, 2015. Accessed June 2016. http://latestvegannews.com/plant-based-food-named-top-trend-2016/#

34. "RAISING CIGARETTE TAXES REDUCES SMOKING, ESPECIALLY AMONG KIDS (AND THE CIGARETTE COMPANIES KNOW IT)." Campaign For Tobacco-Free Kids website. Accessed June 2016.

35. Philip Morris document, "General Comments on Smoking and Health," Appendix I in The Perspective of PM International on Smoking and Health Initiatives, March 29, 1985, Bates No. 2023268329/8348.

36. Philip Morris Executive Jon Zoler, "Handling An Excise Tax Increase," September 3, 1987, Bates No. 2022216179/6180.

37. Kirkova, Deni. "101-year-old heart surgeon reveals vegan diet is secret to his longevity." metro.co.uk. October 15, 2015. Accessed June 2016. http://metro.co.uk/2015/10/15/101-year-old-heart-surgeon-reveals-vegan-diet-is-secret-to-his-longevity-5439590/#ixzz4SJCPm8An

38. Monte T, Pritikin I. *Pritikin: The Man Who Healed America's Heart*. Emmaus, PA: Rodale Press. 1988.

39. efan2011. "McGovern's 1972 Democratic Convention Acceptance Speech." Filmed [1972]. Posted [May 2011]. https://www.youtube.com/watch?v=orx63ix1y-o. "Address Accepting the Presidential Nomination at the Democratic National

Convention in Miami Beach, Florida." University of California Santa Barbara website. Accessed June 2016. http://www.presidency.ucsb.edu/ws/?pid=25967

40.   Rosenbaum, David. "George McGovern Dies at 90, a Liberal Trounced but Never Silenced." New York Times website. October 21, 2012. Accessed June 2016. http://www.nytimes.com/2012/10/22/us/politics/george-mcgovern-a-democratic-presidential-nominee-and-liberal-stalwart-dies-at-90.html

41.   Ibid.

Selected Bibliography and Films

Andersen, Kip, Keegan Kuhn, and Eunice Wong. *The Sustainability Secret*. San Rafael: Earth Aware Editions. 2015.

Barnard, Neal D. *The Power of Your Plate*. Summertown, Tennessee: Book Publishing Company. 1995.

Campbell, Thomas. *The Campbell Plan*. New York: Rodale. 2015.

Campbell, T. Colin and Thomas Campbell. *The China Study*. Dallas: BenBella Books. 2006.

Colb, Sherry F. *Mind if I Order the Cheeseburger? And Other Questions People Ask Vegans*. New York: Lantern Books. 2013.

Cowspiracy: The Sustainability Secret. A.U.M. Films. Directed by Kip Andersen and Keegan Kuhn. 2014.

Davis, Brenda and Vesanto Melina. *Becoming Vegan: Comprehensive Edition*. Summertown, Tennessee: Book Publishing Company. 2014.

Davis, Garth. *Proteinaholic: How our Obsession with Meat is Killing Us and What We Can Do About It*. New York: Harper One. 2015.

Eisnitz, Gail A. *Slaughterhouse*. Amherst, New York: Prometheus Books. 2007.

Estabrook, Barry. *Pig Tales: An Omnivore's Quest for Sustainable Meat*. New York: Norton. 2015.

Forks Over Knives. Monica Beach Media. Directed by Lee Fulkerson. 2011.

Fuhrman, Joel. *Disease-Proof Your Child: Feeding Kids Right*. New York: St. Martin's Griffin. 2005.

-----------------. *Eat to Live*. New York: Little Brown and Company. 2011.

Goldhamer, Alan, and Douglas J. Lisle. *The Pleasure Trap*. Summertown, Tennessee: Healthy Living Publications. 2003.

Greger, Michael. *How Not to Die*. New York: Flatiron Books. 2015.

Harper, A. Breeze, *ed. Sistah Vegan: Black Female Vegans Speak on Food, Identity, Health, and Society*. Brooklyn, Lantern Books. 2010.

Lyman, Howard F. *Mad Cowboy: Plain Truth from the Cattle Rancher Who Won't Eat Meat*. New York: Touchstone. 1998.

Mangels, Reed. *The Everything Vegan Pregnancy Book*. Avon, Massachusetts: Adams Media. 2011.

Marcus, Erik. *Vegan: The New Ethics of Eating*. Ithaca, New York: McBooks Press. 2001.

McDougall, John A. and Mary McDougall. *The Starch Solution*. New York: Rodale. 2012.

Messina, Virginia. *Vegan for Her: The Woman's Guide to Being Healthy and Fit on a Plant-Based Diet*. Boston: Da Capo Press. 2013.

Pachirat, Timothy. *Every Twelve Seconds: Industrialized Slaughter and the Politics of Sight*. New Haven: Yale University Press. 2011.

Peaceable Kingdom: The Journey Home. Tribe of Heart, Ltd. Directed by Jenny Stein. 2012.

Petersen, Melody. *Our Daily Meds*. New York: Sarah Crichton Books. 2008.

Popper, Pamela. *Food Over Medicine*. Dallas: BenBella Books. 2013.

Robbins, John. *The Food Revolution*. San Francisco: Conari Press. 2001.

Simon, David Robinson. *Meatonomics*. San Francisco: Conari Press. 2013.

Simply Raw: Reversing Diabetes in 30 Days. Directed by Aiyana Elliott. 2009.

Torres, Bob and Jenna Torres. *Vegan Freak: Being Vegan in a Non-Vegan World*. Oakland: PM Press. 2010.

Tuttle, Will. *The World Peace Diet*. New York: Lantern Books. 2005.

What The Health, A.U.M. Films. Directed by Kip Andersen and Keegan Kuhn. 2017.

Zaraska, Marta. *Meathooked: The History and Science of our 2.5-Million-Year Obsession with Meat*. New York: Basic Books. 2016.

INDEX

398

Made in the USA
San Bernardino, CA
08 June 2018